# TOFFEE SOCCER

## EVERTON AND NORTH AMERICA

# TOFFEE SOCCER

## EVERTON AND NORTH AMERICA

David France
Rob Sawyer
Darren Griffiths

First published as a limited edition of 1,878 copies in 2021 by

deCoubertin Books, 49 Jamaica St, Baltic Quarter, Liverpool, L1 0AH


ISBN: 978-1-9162784-7-9

A CIP catalogue record for this book is available from the British Library.


Caricatures by Peter King.
Caricatures copyright © David France (Dr Everton's Toffeemen), 2021.


Design and typesetting by Leslie Priestley.


Printed and bound by Gutenberg Press.

# CONTENTS

# DEDICATION

*Toffee Soccer – Everton and North America* is dedicated to the men who shared their North American experiences as players, coaches and tourists with the senior author some 20 years ago and are no longer with us. Their deep and unwavering devotion to Everton Football Club demanded the completion of the book.

Gordon Watson (1914-2001)
Brian Labone (1940-2006)
Alan Ball (1945-2007)
Wally Fielding (1919-2008)
Brian Harris (1935-2008
Alex Parker (1935-2010)
Tommy Jones (1930-2010)
Gary Ablett (1965-2012)
Alex Young (1937-2017)

The three co-authors of *Toffee Soccer – Everton and North America* support Everton in the Community (UK Registered Charity No 10993660), the official charity of Everton Football Club. EitC is committed to helping create a better way of life for our local community and addressing key social issues that are prevalent on the streets of Merseyside such as mental health, employability, dementia, education, disability, poverty and homelessness.

# INTRODUCTION
# COME ON YOU NORTH AMERICAN BLUES!

I am thrilled to be able to introduce this book. I have always been aware of the strong relationship between our great football club and North America – but it has been fascinating to learn the remarkable depth of those roots.

We are proud to have been home to some of the finest players ever to grace the US men's national team – Tim Howard, Landon Donovan, Brian McBride, Joe-Max Moore and Preki. Each of those great players has helped to enhance the popularity of Everton across the USA and Canada. Of course, this book reflects on their impact – and their enduring love-affair with our great club. But it also uncovers many stories of the pioneers, players and characters that didn't quite have the same impact on either side of the Atlantic. Characters who, nonetheless, have contributed to the rich links between our club and North America.

There is so much to learn and marvel at in this book. It reminds me that learning new things about Everton is like painting the Brooklyn Bridge – it never stops. My good friend Dr David France, his co-authors and the contributors to this remarkable volume of work have carried out their research diligently and have accurately captured the longevity and intimacy of the relationship between Everton and North America. And, in doing so, have chronicled a riveting chapter in the rich history of our club.

I have no doubt this book will be of great interest to those who follow the Blues all over the world and am sure it will generate new Evertonians as we cement our position as 'America's Team'. Thank you to David, himself a legendary Evertonian, Rob, Darren and everyone who has contributed to this publication. Of course, that includes the characters and personalities who have played their part in shaping our great history and our unique links with both the USA and Canada.

**Professor Denise Barrett-Baxendale, MBE**
Chief Executive Officer
Everton Football Club

Tim Howard

# FOREWORD
# FOREVER IN MY HEART

My football journey has taken me from the relative obscurity of the North Jersey Imperials, via the New York/New Jersey MetroStars and Manchester United to the greatest of all clubs – The People's Club.

Back in 2006, shortly after I had joined Everton on loan, David Moyes warned me: 'Once you walk onto that pitch, you'll fall in love.' He was right. From the first appearance against Watford in August 2006 to my last against Norwich City almost ten years later, I have been in love with all things Everton and felt privileged to play over 400 games for the club.

I'm thankful to my teammates, coaches, managers and everybody at Finch Farm – and for a while Bellefield – for their commitment and support, and, of course, to the fans who bring such incredible passion to every game. They make Everton what it is.

At Goodison, the intimidating noise and unique passion from 40,000 Evertonians can make a difference. Games under the lights – when all four sides of the stadium are rocking – are extra special, but for me, there was nothing as emotional as the chants of 'U-S-A! U-S-A!' I felt so honoured and humbled to receive such tremendous support.

Having appeared 121 times for my country, I was well aware of the other transatlantic contributions made by my USMNT teammates during the Premier League era, but I have been impressed to learn of Everton's role in the development of US soccer, the impact of so many Evertonians in the North American Soccer League (NASL) as well as Major League soccer (MLS). Further confirmation that there is something very North American about our club!

Recently I was appointed the club's international ambassador to the USA. It's a tremendous honour. Everton has become a part of my soul. My fellow Evertonians will forever be in my heart.

**Tim Howard**
Everton international ambassador in the USA

William Powell Jnr

# PROLOGUE
# THE FIRST DOCTOR EVERTON?

This book was researched, written and published by Evertonians for Evertonians – be they young or bald, optimistic or bitter, newbie or know-it-all, irrespective of accent or proximity to Goodison. Spoiler alert. It confirms Tim Howard's observations that there is something very North American about Merseyside's senior club, which in my eyes is not a bad thing.

Back in 2008, I was tagged by the *Daily Telegraph* as 'Doctor Everton'. Almost immediately, I sought to identify the first person to be blessed with that title. The obvious candidate was Dr James Baxter, one of the founding fathers of Merseyside football who provided unsecured and interest-free loans to expedite the construction of Goodison Park in 1892. While it was well documented that Dr Baxter was the club's medical adviser as well as a key member of the management committee/board of directors from 1889 until his death in 1928, I suspected that there had been an earlier Doctor Everton.

My search led me to the member's card for the 1887/88 season secured in The Everton Collection. Issued to John Douglas, the captain of the second string, this rarity detailed the club's colours as blue and white halves and its headquarters as the Sandon Hotel on Oakfield Road. Its design was similar to those I had been fortunate to snag for previous seasons at Stanley Park, Priory Road and Walton Breck Road (Anfield) during the reign of club president John Houlding between 1881-1892. There was one noticeable difference. The earlier items listed patrons, essentially the good and the great of the city of Liverpool, who had been recruited to add prestige to the embryonic football club, such as the local Conservative MPs, the co-founder of the Cunard Shipping Line, the vice chairman of the Chamber of Commerce, the city coroner and members of the local brewing aristocracy. For the 1887/88 season, these patrons had been replaced by a plethora of 17 vice presidents – mostly Houlding's pals. They included brewer and landowner John Orrell, William Barclay, John Ramsey, Edwin Berry, an assortment of lawyers, bankers, accountants, Freemasons, members of the Orange Order plus a certain Dr Powell. These men would help him run Everton Football Club in a professional manner and later establish Liverpool Football Club.

Intrigued, I set about researching the background of the good doctor – possibly the first North American to be associated with the club. Born in New Bedford, Massachusetts in 1834, William Powell Jnr was raised in New York City where he worked at a pharmacy. At age 16, he accompanied his African American father, his Native American mother and six siblings on the arduous voyage to Liverpool, and settled in Everton village where his family ran a boarding house. Nine years on, his father – a staunch abolitionist – wrote: 'I came to this country a poor despised outcast – an outlawed American negro – driven from my native country for no colour of crime but for the crime of colour.'

Seemingly, life in Liverpool was more welcoming to William Powell Snr and his eldest son was able to study medicine in Dublin and London. While it remains unclear if he received a medical degree, Dr Powell secured employment at St Anne's District Hospital near his home and Southern Hospital in Toxteth before re-crossing the Atlantic Ocean to join the Union forces in the American Civil War, which raged between 1861-1865. There, Dr Powell was contracted to serve as an assistant surgeon at the Contraband Hospital for fugitive slaves and black soldiers in 1863. Later that year, he was placed in charge of the Washington DC facility. His leadership, however, was troubled by claims of reckless drinking and lasted just 12 months. Research confirms that he rejoined his family after a spell as a private physician in California. Also it is known that Dr Powell retired due to ill-health in 1891 and applied for a military pension. After his claim was denied because he had served a as a contract surgeon and not a commissioned military officer, Dr Powell spent 24 frustrating years petitioning the US government without success.

Cue the caution flag. The sequence and timing of events during his stay in the Golden State remain unclear and, in my eyes, insufficient dots have been connected to complete his amazing story. One theory is that he returned to Everton village, set up a private practice and, as an important member of the community, was engaged as Everton Football Club's doctor by John Houlding. Despite accessing copious genealogy databases, at this time there is inadequate evidence for me to be entirely convinced that Dr William Powell Jnr can be crowned the first Doctor Everton.

From my own 44 years living in North America, I have concluded that professional soccer on this side of the North Atlantic, like the story of Dr Powell, remains a work in progress. Once every four years, the afterglow of the World Cup converts North American sports fans into soccer viewers. However, domestically it remains the 'next big thing' and trails in popularity behind American football, baseball and basketball. For example, when chatting to my neighbours in Arizona – who mostly support Manchester City or Manchester United or both – I have become increasingly aware of their ignorance of Everton's pioneering role in the development of the beautiful game in both the countries of my birth and residence.

Hence this tome. It was conceived some 20-odd years ago after I had acquired a diligently assembled scrapbook, now in The Everton Collection, containing North American newspaper cuttings detailing the club's 1956 tour. Around that time, the establishment of Gwladys Street's Hall of Fame, organization of its cacophonous celebrations and registration of the Former-Players' Foundation provided me with unprecedented opportunities to rub shoulders with many of the men who toured North America in 1956 and 1961, or played in the original North American Soccer League (NASL) between 1968-1984. Though enlightening, their recollections simmered on the back-burner until the Covid-19 pandemic lockdowns in 2020. With the assistance of Rob Sawyer and Darren Griffiths – two eloquent wordsmiths, lifelong

Evertonians and dear friends – the resulting collaboration profiles 160 or so individuals who have contributed to our beloved club's special relationship with North America. It includes the results of recent interviews with players both men and women, coaches, trialists and youths. These insights have been amplified by respectful caricatures drawn and objective pen-pictures.

In addition, we contacted a cross-section of North America-based fans to ascertain why they follow the Toffees. Our survey revealed that many of them without Merseyside roots were unaware that the club's transatlantic contributions are deep and multifaceted, or that they commenced when pioneers with convenient maritime links introduced soccer to North America while the locals were still playing cowboys and Indians. Decades later, these early migrants were augmented by waves of wrinkled veterans seeking to extend their professional careers, many as short-contract players – others as long-term coaches. Our old boys have represented more than 170 teams in the American Soccer League (ASL), NASL, Major League Soccer (MLS) and indoor leagues. To date, ten of them have been inducted into the US and Canadian Soccer Halls of Fame with more in the pipeline. Then there are the club's 10 tours across the continent, its recruitment of North America's finest talent and provision of advanced training and trials for young prospects in the MLS era. Surely, no European club has contributed to transatlantic soccer as much as Everton and vice versa.

Still, Everton Football Club was not a household name in North America until relatively recently. The change coincided with the signings of the two preferred faces of the US game. Of course, they are Tim Howard – who with 121 caps is the best USA keeper since Sylvester Stallone in *Escape to Victory* and Landon Donovan – who with 157 caps is widely regarded as the best USA-born player in history. Though relatively few other North Americans have graduated to the Premier League, Everton have recruited many of the best, such as Joe-Max Moore, Brian McBride, Tomasz Radzinski and Predrag Radosavljević. At present, the club's name has been associated with 16 North American internationals, who have been awarded more than 700 senior caps between them, and has granted trials to dozens of others, including some who progressed to captain and manage their national teams.

As for the future? Televised coverage of professional soccer, especially the English Premier League, is unavoidable in North America. It is everywhere. Even though it is unlikely that any single European club will dominate the hearts, minds and dollars of enthusiasts, the continent represents a tremendous opportunity for expanding the royal blue fanbase and commercial partnerships. Indeed, the club has made meaningful headway with its fan engagement initiatives and support for the existing supporters' clubs stateside – some of whose members make semi-annual pilgrimages to Goodison and Finch Farm. Having clocked over two million miles supporting Everton from Indiana, Tennessee, California, Texas, British Columbia, Washington State and Arizona, I fear that I may have set them a bad example.

**Dr David France, OBE**

# PART ONE

# EVERTON AND NORTH AMERICA

Herbert Edwards

# 1.1
# NORTH AMERICAN SOCCER

First, a bit of history. Football was codified with the creation of a rule book and organising body, the Football Association, in London in 1863. The game spread quickly through the British Isles with the creation of federations in Scotland (1873), Wales (1876) and Ireland (1880). The rising soccer-mania culminated in the creation of the Football League in 1888. Everton Football Club entered the mix as St Domingo Football Club in 1878 and was a founder member of this new competition and championed many innovations throughout its illustrious history.

Everywhere the British went, they took the new game of association football (soccer) with them. After thousands of immigrants from the British Isles had moved to the USA to work in the local mills, shipyards and mines, the Newark-based American Football Association was established in 1884 to standardise rules for the teams competing in northern New Jersey and southern New York areas. Elsewhere in the USA, interest in the sport was centred around the textile town of Fall River, Massachusetts where the Bristol County League was organised in 1886 and St Louis, Missouri where, after local churches had introduced soccer into their recreational programmes, the St Louis League was established that same year.

Not surprisingly, Evertonians were involved from the kick-off – although sometimes in a slightly tardy manner. In September 1893, *The Sun*, a New York City-based newspaper, reported on the game between New York and the Longfellows of Brooklyn: 'Association football had an innings yesterday afternoon at the Polo Grounds. If the impression which the game made upon the small crowd can be taken as a criterion, it is almost certain that the venture will not be much of a success. The method of play seemed to be a procession of kicks. No clever tricks or scientific points were attempted. The game was a half-hour delayed by the non-appearance of McKay, the New York goalkeeper who arrived yesterday on the SS Umbria from Liverpool. He is a sturdy fellow and guards the posts like a man who knows his business. McKay has told this newspaper that he had played with the Bootle and

Everton clubs.' Oddly, scrutiny of the available soccer databases for both Merseyside clubs shows no mention of McKay.

The following year saw the advent of the American League of Professional Foot Ball (ALPFB). It was established by baseball club owners to fill their dormant stadiums and generate revenue during the winter months. This attracted the services of Herbert Edwards, a robust defender at the Boston Beaneaters who had turned out for Everton Reserves four years earlier.

The Southport-born defender had played for Everton Ramblers, Clubmoor and Birkdale before making two outings for Everton in the 1889/90 season – as part of a 'scratch' team in a friendly in Glasgow against Battlefield and then for the second string against Aintree Church. Edwards crossed the Mersey to join Tranmere Rovers before traversing the Atlantic to Boston. As a pro footballer, he is known to have made his US debut against the Brooklyn Bridegrooms in the ALPFB in early October 1894. The 26-year-old left-back helped Boston to a fine start of four wins in their five league games before the ALPFB folded due to low crowds and financial ills.

The development of North American soccer was so rapid that in 1888, the year the Football League was founded, an 18-man squad – all but one of whom were born in Canada – toured the British Isles. Drawn from the Western Football Association of Ontario and known simply as the Canadians, they played 23 games during their two month-long stay. In England, their opponents included four of the founding members of the Football League, namely Aston Villa, Blackburn Rovers, Notts County and West Bromwich Albion – but not Everton. That omission was remedied in 1891 when the tourists returned to participate in an even more congested schedule of 58 fixtures during a four-month period. Arguably, the highlight of their second visit was the fixture involving the reigning Football League champions – Everton. Although still labelled the Canadians, the 1891 squad was a Canada-USA hybrid and included representatives of clubs in the Western Football Association and others based in New England. The national mix was evenly balanced with 10 players from Canadian clubs (Berlin Rangers, Osgoode Hall, Ottawa, Toronto, Toronto Scottish and Toronto Varsity) and nine players from American clubs (Fall River Rovers, Fall River Olympic and Pawtucket).

The arrangements for the match with Everton started 10 months prior to their arrival with the tourists guaranteed £35 plus 50% of the gross receipts over £70. However, they could not have picked a worse time. Their hosts were in turmoil. At a meeting of 300 members, president John Houlding clashed with George Mahon over forming a limited liability company and buying the present ground and adjacent site, England star Johnny Holt had demanded a refresher bonus of £75 in addition to his wages of £3 per week and Scotland maverick Dan Doyle, who was registered with Everton, was playing as an 'amateur' for Celtic and running a pub in Glasgow at £5 per week. Finally, the league had imposed a levy on its clubs to pay for the goal-nets patented by John Brodie to be used in all matches from November 1891.

Although Preston North End had been crowned champions in both 1889 and 1890, Everton were the first club to receive the iconic Football League trophy. Determined to retain it, they started the 1891/92 season unconvincingly. A 4-0 mauling at West Bromwich Albion was followed by a 5-3 triumph over Darwen at a raucous Anfield. Two days later, the club rested most of its first team defence including captain Andrew Hannah, terrace favourite Dan Doyle and Dan Kirkwood, but retained its swashbuckling forward line for the visit of the Canadians. As for their opponents, they were playing their ninth competitive game in 23 days.

## Game 1
### 14 September 1891: EVERTON 3 CANADIANS 1

The Merseyside press claimed that Everton ran out comfortable winners in an entertaining encounter in front of 5,000 – 7,000 fans (about half of the typical gate for a first team game at the Walton Breck Road ground in Anfield). In summary, inside-right Patrick Gordon opened the scoring after eight minutes and Fred Geary bagged a brace before inside-left Ernie Senkler responded for the visitors. However, other newspapers were less convinced about the dominance of the hosts.

**Everton:** *Jardine; Collins, McLean; Campbell, Holt, Kelso; Latta, Gordon, Geary, Chadwick, Milward.*

**Canadians:** *Alexander Garrett (Toronto); EJ Gregory (Fall River Rovers), John Forbes (on loan from Blackburn Rovers); JC Warbrick (Toronto Varsity), Henry Waring (Fall River Rovers), Franz Thibodo (Berlin Rangers); James Whittaker (Fall River Olympic), Alex Jeffrey (Pawtucket), Joseph Buckley (Fall River Rovers), Ernie Senkler (Osgoode Hall), Neil Munro (Pawtucket).*

In the days before radio, television and internet coverage, newspapers offered the only detailed accounts of the action. The *Liverpool Mercury* provided an immediate post-match report from Anfield, albeit in Victorian language: 'The Canadians received a hearty welcome from the 7,000 spectators who had assembled around the ropes. Winning the toss, Johnny Holt took the breeze in his favour and Joe Buckley, commencing hostilities, was robbed by Edgar Chadwick, who parted to Fred Geary. The Everton centre-forward only missed scoring by a few inches. After Alf Milward had been smartly dispossessed by Ernie Senkler, Patrick Gordon regained the ball and sent it forward to Alex Latta, who crossed to his left wing, from where Milward beat goalkeeper Alex Garrett with a lofty shot. The Canadians were not slow in making headway towards the home goal, where a couple of corners were awarded without success. With these let offs, Everton attacked in full force, causing great anxiety to Garrett. A grand shot by Wattie Campbell landed right into his hands.'

'Left-winger Alf Milward amused the crowd as he bumped into the "new country" custodian. However, the latter by novel tactics had the best of the argument. With the ball in his hands, he deliberately touched the former's arm and claimed a foul, which had to be granted by referee Mr Lythgoe – the secretary Liverpool District Football Association. From the free-kick, some tricky play took place in midfield and Geary forced his way through the opposition

# CANADIANS v. EVERTON,

## MONDAY, SEPTEMBER 14, 1891.

### KICK OFF AT 6.15 P.M.

ranks and, with no-one in front of him but the custodian, banged in the second goal. With Everton having decidedly the best of matters, centre-forward Fred Geary was soon able to tack on a third.

'The Canadian forwards were playing a fast-and-loose game but were kept at bay by the Everton halves. Ernie Senkler and Neil Munro, however, managed to beat Don McLean. Their sprint resulting in the former sending in a real beauty out of David Jardine's reach. Resuming after the interval, the visitors – with the wind behind them – were quickly on the attack. John Collins, stemming them off. Then Jardine was called upon to fist out a trio of shots. The Anfielders were next seen to advantage as their forwards combined beautifully. Shot after shot was tried at goalkeeper Garrett, but all to no effect. The game was now much of a give-and-take nature and Jim Whittaker ran away from the Everton backs, sending a low shot right at Jardine.'

Days later, the *Liverpool Mercury* was less long-winded: 'The visit of the Canadians to Anfield on Monday was not a rousing event, either in attractiveness or play; but it was useful from a practice point of view for the Everton men, who won comfortably by 3 goals to 1.'

Interest in the fixture between England's top team and the Canadian upstarts stretched beyond the boundaries of Merseyside. The *Birmingham Daily Post* provided a far more concise report of the proceedings: 'About four thousand persons witnessed the game. The visitors made a good impression with their smart play, but they were unable to get near Jardine. After Gordon scored for Everton, the visitors pressed and secured a couple of corners, neither of which was turned to advantage. Everton then had hard line in not scoring, Chadwick hitting the crossbar. But shortly afterwards, Geary scored again from a pass by Gordon. The centre-forward added a third, whilst Senkler scored for the Canadians amidst loud applause. Half-time: 3-1. The visitors played well with the wind and were several times near scoring. Their shooting, however, was faulty.'

'The Loiterer' writing in the *Athletic News* suggested that the score-line flattered the hosts: 'The Yankees turned up at Anfield on Monday last, and were beaten by three goals to one. The game was a fairly good one, and the result hardly represents the play, which was as much in favour of the Canadians as Everton. Garrett proved a good goalkeeper and was up to his "fly" tricks. Forbes frequently beat Latta. Buckley, who plays full-back, was in centre, and has a rare turn of speed, once leaving the opposing backs "standing still". The Everton men were not at their best. Holt, who played with the league team for the first time, being out of condition.'

The *Liverpool Daily Post* offered another detailed account: 'The Colonials who on Saturday were defeated by Ireland by 5 goals to 2, crossed the channel yesterday and engaged Everton on the Anfield ground. Holt put in a first appearance this season and his play showed him to be much want of practice. However, the back division worked the better for his inclusion. Forbes of Blackburn assisted the Canadians, who although they played a good 'staying' game, were completely over matched. The professionals being much too tricky for them. For some time, the play was very even and fast. Then following a short attack on Garrett, Gordon scrimmaged the ball through the posts. A minute had elapsed from the restart when Gordon rushed away and gave possession to Latta, whose shot struck the upright. A couple of unproductive corners ensued before the leather was once more in front of the visiting goal. Geary narrowly missing. A fine passing movement between the centre-forward and his right-wing nearly resulted in a second point. Gregory stepped in and sent the ball over the halfway line. After Gordon and Latta put on a fine show of football, Geary scored a second point with Garrett making little or no effort to stop the ball.

'Coming again, Geary shot into the goalkeeper's hands and, on being charged, Garrett fell on the ball and several Evertonians tried to kick it out of his hands. Geary was soon in evidence again and scored a third via a splendid shot. The play now revisited more in the exhibition mode. The Everton forwards dodging round and round the Canadians until Geary spoiled the fun by taking a shot which went over. A minute or so later, Senkler got past Holt and skipped over McLean's leg but slipped with the goal at his mercy. A similar move was attempted a few minutes later when Senkler at last beat Jardine, which gave immense satisfaction to the crowd.

'The Canadians left-wing putting in some good work, and once or twice had extremely hard luck. They almost defeated Jardine with a long shot, the home custodian nearly "fingering" it through his own posts. The boisterous wind interfered with the play on both sides with the ball going over an adjoining house top. Next, Buckley completely outpaced Collins and McLean, but his tame shot was put into Jardine's hands. Towards the finish, the visitors had as much of the play as their hosts, though probably this was due to the latter being two men short, as Millward and Collins both retired. Nothing was scored in the second-half and Everton won a dull game.'

Irrespective of the perhaps unflattering score-line, the tourists moved onto fulfil their next fixture. Some 48 hours later, they defeated non-League Lincoln City by 2-1. It was a rare victory. The Canadians won only 14 of their 60 games with a goals tally of 105-162, which included a 9-0 spanking by Wolverhampton Wanderers. Despite the fact that many of the visitors were lawyers, doctors and journalists, the 1891 tour was seen by some as a way for the Canadian players to introduce themselves to British clubs with the object of being recruited at high wages. In point of fact, only team captain Walter Bowman stayed in England after the rest of the team returned to North America. He signed with Accrington and later played for Ardwick. As for their hosts, Everton failed to retain the Football League title. In the club's final season at the Walton Breck Road ground in Anfield, it finished fifth – 14 points behind champions Sunderland.

# 1.2
# TRANSATLANTIC MIGRANTS

Contrary to popular belief, late-19th century British migrants did not introduce soccer to North America. In one form or another, it was being played already. Indeed, some wags claim that the Settlers had halted the bloody hostilities of the American Indian Wars to contest a friendly match against the Native American All-Stars – selected from the indigenous Iroquois, Shawnee and Cherokee tribes – one Thanksgiving Day.

In truth, the top universities had been playing different versions of the game for several decades. Harvard University adopted the 16-a-side Boston Game which in turn led to the formation of the Oneida Football Club in 1862 – arguably the first organised football club in the USA, and definitely the first to wear red silk handkerchiefs in the manner of pirates around their heads. Unfortunately for association football, the universities were unwilling to agree on a uniform set of rules. So around 1875, rugby football replaced soccer as the official intercollegiate game and even Princeton University, the bastion of power in soccer, abandoned the kicking game. As a result, no college soccer was played between 1877-1902.

As in the old country, where the initial influence of the English public schools was diluted and overshadowed by the involvement of industrial workers in Lancashire and the Midlands in the final years of the century, dominance of the North American game was transferred to the clubs formed by soccer-playing immigrants. They brought with them organizational skills, standard rules and, most of all, a genuine love of the game.

As for the first club of Merseyside? Everton's roots not only penetrate the bedrock of English football but the club was one of the game's original globetrotters. Stimulated by a successful tour of Bohemia in 1905, where its players exhibited their superior skills in Budapest, Prague and Vienna, the club set sail for South America in 1909 to fulfil fixtures in Buenos Aires and Montevideo. Its impact was so strong that teams in Argentina, Chile and Uruguay were created or renamed to bear the tourists' name. Everton Vina Del Mar are the most famous antecedents and currently play in Chile's Primera Division. Strangely, Everton did not venture to North America until 1956 some six decades after Messrs McKay and Edwards. Possibly the anticipated attendances and quality of the local opponents made such tours unattractive.

Prior to several organizations embracing its name in South America, an Everton Football Club surfaced in New York in December 1907. The *New York Times* reported: 'The sailors from the steamship Arabic were no match for Everton Football Club and lost by 2-0.' The game at Van Cortlandt Park in the Bronx involved two 35-minute halves. Little is known about the participants except that the SS Arabic was a transatlantic liner, built by Harland and Wolff in Belfast, that entered service for the White Star Line in 1903. With accommodations for 1,400 passengers, she spent 12-years on the Liverpool-New York and the Liverpool-Boston services before being torpedoed near Kinsale, Ireland by German submarine U-24 in August 1915, killing 44 passengers and crew.

It should be noted that after the departure of the 1891 Canadians, similarly inspired North Americans visited the club's new home to play baseball. Since the late-19th century games Between professional US teams have been staged at Goodison. The Boston Red Stockings (now the Atlanta Braves), Philadelphia Athletics (now the Oakland Athletics) and Chicago White Stockings (now the Chicago Cubs) promoted the sport in the United Kingdom. Their efforts resulted in the formation of several baseball clubs in Derby by Sir Francis Ley (who all played at The Baseball Ground) and York. In fact, when the National League of Baseball of Great Britain was set up and sponsored by Albert Goodwill Spalding – the founder of the famous US sporting goods brand – the top English baseball sides included three members of the embryonic Football League, namely Preston North End, Aston Villa and Stoke. Decades later, to support the expansion of the international market for the American sport, Everton hosted several exhibition games featuring famous US clubs throughout the 1920s – most notably in October 1924 when the Chicago White Sox of the American League defeated the New York Giants, who had won the National League for the fourth consecutive season in an enthralling slugfest by 16-11.

In contrast to Merseyside's senior club not venturing to play on North American grass, royal blue missionaries continued to cross the Atlantic during the early part of the 20th century. The torchbearers to the USA included Dod Brewster at Brooklyn Athletic and Teddy Glover at the New York Giants, whereas those to Canada included former-England ace Sam Chedgzoy and former-Scotland veteran George Wilson. Other comings and goings involved Tom Bennett, Stan Fazackerley and Billy Easton who, for one reason or another, had returned from North America to join Everton.

Off the pitch, several more prominent stars had moved to the land of opportunity to work, retire and spread the word about Everton. These included Charles Lindsay – Everton's first specialist goalkeeper who played for the club between 1893-1895. With business interests in the USA, he moved to Passaic, New Jersey in 1909. Then there is James Adams – the Scotland international defender who had won the Scottish Cup with Heart of Midlothian before turning out for Everton between 1894-1896. His place in football history was secured by his action in deliberately handling the ball to prevent a goal, and the resulting introduction of the penalty kick rule (now known as Law 14).

Also, Peter Meechan – the Scotland international full-back had won the English League with Sunderland in 1895 and the Scottish title with Celtic in 1896 before playing in the FA Cup final for Everton 1897 and then for Southampton in 1900. His Everton career spanned 1896-1898. Meechan moved to Nova Scotia in 1905 but, after failing to find employment as a football coach, followed his former occupation as a miner until he suffered a terrible industrial injury. And Ted Hughes – Everton's first Wales international, the half-back played for the club between 1898–1899 before capturing the FA Cup with the Southern League's Tottenham Hotspur. And finally, Hugh Bolton – the Scottish inside-right who was a key member of the first Everton team to claim the FA Cup in 1906.

North America was such a favoured resting place for old footballers that the *Vancouver Sun* newspaper boasted that the British Columbia city alone was home to 21 of them from the old county in 1934. Most were Scotsmen, many of whom had played for Heart of Midlothian, but four had represented Everton. Soccer expert Charlie Foster overviewed their careers. 'George Wilson who played for Cowdenbeath, Heart of Midlothian, Everton, Belfast Distillery, Newcastle United, Raith Rovers and East Fife was capped three times by Scotland, was a member of the Hearts team that won the Scottish Cup in 1906 and the Newcastle eleven that won the English Cup in 1910.'

'David Wilson, brother of Geordie, was another member of that Hearts cup-winning side who played for Gainsborough Trinity, Cowdenbeath, Everton and Portsmouth. Dave Cummings was a member of the old Heart of Midlothian and Hibernian teams and one of the trailblazers to cross the border when he joined Everton. Also, Geordie McKay played centre-forward with Port Glasgow Athletic and St Johnstone in Scotland and Everton in England.'

Again, searches through the most comprehensive data bases show no mention of Cummings. As for the legacy of the Canadians, it was some six decades after their visit before two Canadian-born players – Gogie Stewart and Bob Bissett – finally signed for Everton.

## MEMORIES OF THE TRANSATLANTIC MIGRANTS

### Sam Chedgzoy, the *Liverpool Echo* and the cunning corner-kick

*The winger illuminated Goodison on either side of the First World War. After mentoring a young Dixie Dean, he left his family for North America where he played until age 49. In 2020, Gary Chedgzoy reminisced about his great-grandfather …*

'Sam died nine years after my birth, but I never met him as he left for North America in 1926. I'm aware that he enjoyed a rewarding career there, first in New Bedford, Massachusetts and then in Canada where he played and coached Montreal Carsteel. As one of the country's top clubs, it won the National League in 1936 and 1939. Sam didn't hang up his boots until he was nearly 50. His recipe for such longevity? Restraint at the (dining) table, smoking sparingly and eschewing spirituous liquors entirely.

'Our family history is a more complex than most and Syd must have been sad that his father was no longer around to see him wear the blue and white at Goodison or make his debut for Burnley. Sam, who was reunited with his sisters Lily and Edith in the 1950s after 38 years apart, lived out his days in Saint-Eustache near Montreal and died at 77. A posthumous inductee into the Canadian Soccer Hall of Fame, he left a wonderful legacy. Dixie Dean played in the first team with Sam and in the second team with my grandfather Syd. Of course, Sam is infamous for engineering a change in the laws of association football when Ernest Edwards, the sports editor at the *Liverpool Echo*, asked him to help expose a flaw in the reworded corner-kick rule.'

Research shows that Edwards and Chedgzoy chose the Everton home game against Arsenal on 15 November 1924. The local journalist insisted that the winger put their plan into action during the opening 20 minutes so that his report on the incident could make his publication deadline. Therefore, when the opportunity arose, Chedgzoy placed the ball for a corner-kick and dribbled it into the goalmouth where he shot for goal, much to the bewilderment of everyone. Contrary to some accounts, his shot hit the side-netting. Admonished by the referee, the winger quoted the new law back and pointed out that what he had done was perfectly legitimate. Consequently, the Football Association called an emergency meeting to change the law and ensure that the corner taker could only strike the ball once.

### Teddy Glover, the *Liverpool Echo* and bigger bucks

*In mid-1928, some two years after leaving Everton for Southport in the Third Division (North), the Bootle-born defender defected to the USA and joined the New York Generals. His niece Jay Armstrong recalls …*

'I never knew much about Uncle Ted except that he played soccer. That was until I dug through some family photos and found one of him and my Aunt Grace. She was the sister of James Armstrong, the manager of the New York Giants soccer team, who was heavily involved with the 1936 Olympic Games. Also, there was this cutting from the *Liverpool Echo* dated 30 July 1928 in which Ernest Edwards wrote: "Three players accompanied Mr George Moorhouse, manager of the New York Giants, on the White Star liner Celtic, which left Liverpool for New York on Saturday. They are David McMullan, the Irish international half-back of Liverpool; Teddy Glover, who has played for Everton, Southport, New Brighton and Wigan Borough; and Chris Harrington, formerly with Liverpool, Luton Town, and Millwall. All have signed agreements to play for the New York Giants next season. America is still prepared to pay large sums for first-class footballers. It is stated that a bid has been made for Dixie Dean, the Everton and England centre-forward. Dean, however, preferred to remain in England, and the overtures were not successful."'

## Gogie and his technicolour dream coats

*Canadian Gordon 'Gogie' Stewart was a top-class sportsman who joined Everton in 1953. Three years on, the Vancouver journalist Austin Delany reported …*

'When Gogie met his old Everton teammates during their North America tour there was much back-slapping. Peter Farrell said that they were sorry when he returned home because Gogie would have made the first team. Also the Everton captain revealed that the Canadian had created quite a stir in Liverpool by wearing the snazzy coats he had acquired from playing lacrosse, baseball and boxing in his homeland. Any other guy wearing a striped Indian blanket for a coat partly covering a sky-blue and pink sweater would have been arrested for creating a disturbance.'

More recently Brad Stewart talked about his father: 'He was the son of a Scot who enrolled with the North-West Mounted Police. "Gogie" was a nickname that stuck with him – we don't know where it came from. He was an amazing athlete with a God-given talent for any sport – boxing, ice hockey, basketball, lacrosse and soccer. Mainly an outside-left in soccer, lots of British teams wanted him but, in 1953, he chose Everton. My Dad went out there alone. I have a photograph of him being met by trainer Harry Cooke. Then my mother joined him with Gogie Jnr, who was just a baby, and the club sorted them out a place to stay. They looked after them well. But trying to make inroads in English football was a challenge. Some felt that Dad was trying to take their jobs away from them. We still have the letter offering to extend his Everton contract, but Mum was getting homesick.

'My parents had five children. I was the second oldest and was followed by Ross, Kirk and Jim. He coached all of us and, when we played in the back yard, never let us win! On the wall at home I have his jumper with the EFC badge on and photographs from his time there – we think that he looked a bit like Wayne Rooney! I'm very proud that my father was a pioneer who opened the doors for other North American footballers to go to Europe.

'As a grassroots development officer for the Prince George Youth Soccer Association (PGYSA), I attended a youth coaching conference along with Paul Harris and Tosh Farrell, the Everton academy coaches and educated them about Gogie. We kept in touch and my association affiliated with them. They would send a coach over twice a year to train our kids.'

*Caricatures and pen-pictures of the transatlantic migrants involved in the early years of the game in the USA and Canada are presented in alphabetical order. They start with Tom Bennett who was born in the Walton district of Liverpool in 1891 …*

# Tom Bennett

**played for**

Montreal Royal Rovers,
Charlestown,
Everton (trial),
South Liverpool,
Leeds City (guest),
Liverpool,
Bury,
Northwich Victoria,
Wigan Borough,
Halifax Town,
Rochdale

Born in the shadows of Goodison Park, his family emigrated to St John's, New Brunswick when he was a child. After some success with the Montreal Royal Rovers, the 21-year-old forward returned to Merseyside. Despite netting an inspiring hat-trick for the Reserves against Marine in November 1913, he was spurned by Everton. Picked up by South Liverpool in the Lancashire Combination, he scored 48 times in 36 matches prior to First World War. While employed as a plumber at the Harland and Wolff shipyards, he joined Liverpool and proceeded to nab 77 goals in his 70 wartime fixtures. Battling with tuberculosis, Bennett made only one post-war outing and died from the infectious disease in 1923 at age 31.

Everton trialist: 1913/14

# Bob Bissett

**played for**

Westminster Royals,
Vancouver City,
North Shore United,
Everton (trial),
Westminster Royals,
North Shore Carling's,
Vancouver Canadians,
Burnaby Villa

Born in Vancouver BC, the 20-year-old pal of Gogie Stewart made one appearance for the Reserves in 1953. With manager Cliff Britton seeking a back-up for Harry Leyland, the promising goalkeeper was granted an immediate trial. After arriving in London on the Wednesday, his whirlwind schedule involved an overnight train to Liverpool, an extensive trial on Thursday morning, registration as an amateur on Friday and a Central League game against Sheffield United on Saturday afternoon. Though lacking inches, the agile keeper had been selected for the Canadian All-Stars but failed to measure up to the standard required at Everton. He returned to Vancouver and won the 1955 Canada Soccer Championship with the Westminster Royals. During his 1963/64 season with the Vancouver Canadians, Bissett recorded 10 clean-sheets and was voted the Pacific Coast League's MVP.

Everton trialist: 1953/54

# Dod Brewster

**played for**
Mugiemoss,
Aberdeen,
Ayr United (guest),
Falkirk (guest),
Everton,
Wolverhampton Wanderers,
Lovell's Athletic,
Wallasey Athletic,
Brooklands Athletic,
Brooklyn Wanderers,
Inverness Caledonian

**coached at**
Brooklyn Wanderers,
Inverness Caledonian

A product of Logie Buchan, north of Aberdeen, the strapping centre-half was lured to Goodison from his hometown club in 1920 for £2,400, of which he received £500. Like most footballers of his era, the 29-year-old had lost his best years to the battlefields of France where he had fought with the Royal Engineers and was awarded the Military Medal for gallantry under enemy fire in 1918. Despite being club captain and selected for Scotland against England, Brewster struggled at Everton as the team flirted with the drop and it came as no surprise when he was sold to Wolverhampton for £1,500 in 1922. Afterwards he played in the Western League and the Cheshire County League before moving to New York to play for both Brooklands Athletic and Brooklyn Wanderers in 1924.

| Everton 1919/20-1921/22 | | |
| --- | --- | --- |
| | games | goals |
| League | 64 | 4 |
| Total | 68 | 5 |

# Sam Chedgzoy

**played for**

Burnell's Ironworks, Everton,
West Ham United (guest),
Everton,
New Bedford Whalers,
Montreal Carsteel

**coached at**

Grenadier Guards (Canada),
Montreal Carsteel

The Ellesmere Port-born winger swerved down the touchline to immortality at Goodison. Initially, he hit the headlines during the glorious 1914/15 season when his pin-point crosses set up many key goals for centre-forward Bobby Parker. Shortly afterwards, his playing career was disrupted by First World War, during which he served in the 2nd Battalion of the Scots Guards. Then in 1926, he made the national news again by engineering a change to the new corner-kick rule. Promptly, the England star bolted to North America to join the New Bedford Whalers in the American Soccer League and then the Montreal Carsteel in the Canadian National Soccer League – his last first team outing there was at age 49. Posthumously, Sam Chedgzoy was voted into the Canada Soccer Hall of Fame in 2005.

| Everton 1910/11–1925/26 | | |
| --- | --- | --- |
| | games | goals |
| League | 279 | 32 |
| Total | 300 | 35 |

# Billy Easton

**played for**

Blyth Spartans,

Rotherham County,

Montreal Maroons,

Everton,

Swansea Town,

Port Vale,

Aldershot,

Workington

During their 1927/28 title-winning campaign Everton sought to replace the injured Bobby Irvine – the foil for Dixie Dean – and signed the 24-year-old inside-right. The Newcastle-upon-Tyne native had just returned from Quebec, where he had laboured in the shipyards and played for the Montreal Maroons – an off-shoot of the NHL team – in the Canadian National Soccer League and the International Soccer League. Easton was lured to North America from Blyth Spartans, his previous English club in the North Eastern League, in a £400 double swoop which included winger Tom Wilkinson. The following season, he played 12 times as back-up for newly-signed Jimmy Dunn as the Merseyside club flirted with the dreaded drop before moving onto Second Division Swansea Town for £850.

| Everton 1927/28-1929/30 | | |
| --- | --- | --- |
| | games | goals |
| League | 15 | 3 |
| Total | 15 | 3 |

# Stan Fazackerley

**played for**

Lane Ends United,
Preston North End,
Charlestown,
Accrington Stanley,
Hull City,
Sheffield United,
Preston North End (guest),
Blackpool (guest),
Chelsea (guest),
Everton,
Wolverhampton Wanderers,
Kidderminster Harriers,
Derby County

Unable to break into the first team at Deepdale, the 20-year-old forward sailed to Massachusetts. After signing with Charlestown for the 1911/12 season, he scored 20 goals in 12 matches before returning to England to join Accrington Stanley and then Second Division Hull City. Hailed for his ability to shoot powerfully with minimal back-lift, Fazackerley found the net 11 times in a post-season clash with Trondheim. Next, the inside-right moved to Sheffield United and became part of its 1915 FA Cup-winning side. After the end of First World War, he was sold to Everton for a club record fee of £4,000 with permission from the club to train only three times per week in Liverpool. Two years later, he was transferred to Wolverhampton Wanderers for £1,750 and helped them grab the 1924 Third Division (North) title.

| Everton 1920/21-1922/23 | | |
| --- | --- | --- |
| | games | goals |
| League | 51 | 21 |
| Total | 57 | 21 |

# Teddy Glover

**played for**

Stanley (Liverpool),
South Liverpool,
New Brighton,
Everton,
Southport,
Wigan Borough,
New York Giants,
Accrington Stanley,
Leeds United,
Harrogate,
New York Soccer Club (loan),
New York Giants,
New York Americans,
Brookhattan,
Pfaelzer,
Brooklyn

**coached at**

University of Southern
Colorado ThunderWolves

Picked up from New Brighton for about £1,000, the Bootle-born full-back failed to break into the Everton first team and swiftly moved onto Southport and Wigan Borough in the recently formed Third Division (North) before signing for the original New York Giants of the Eastern Soccer League in 1928. Over time, the exponent of 'elementary hoofball' helped the New York Giants (formerly named the New York Nationals) to seize the American Soccer League title. Next at age 32, Glover joined Brookhattan and helped the New York City-based club become the most revered side in North America. Even as late as the early-1990s, he was still involved in soccer – serving as a coach at the University of Southern Colorado. In 1951, Teddy Glover was the very first Evertonian to be inducted into the National Soccer Hall of Fame.

| Everton 1924/25-1925/26 | games | goals |
| --- | --- | --- |
| League | 0 | 0 |
| Total | 0 | 0 |

# Gordon Stewart

**played for**

North Shore United,
Vancouver St Andrew's,
Vancouver City,
Westminster Royals,
Everton,
Westminster Royals,
Nanaimo City,
Vancouver Continentals,
Westminster Royals,
North Shore Carling's,
Vancouver Columbus,
Vancouver Firefighters

Born in British Columbia, the inside-forward joined Second Division Everton in mid-1953. Applauded for his superior athleticism, fiery commitment and clever playmaking, the 24-year-old Canadian was a revelation in the Central League side. Many observers claimed that 'Gogie' possessed the knack of knowing where his teammates were and what they planned to do next. Unfortunately, he failed to make the first team and returned home after 12 months to help pick up Canadian titles in soccer with Vancouver City and Westminster Royals, and in lacrosse with Vancouver Burrards and Nanaimo Timbermen. The one-time Golden Gloves boxing champion received a two-year ban from the BC Soccer Commission after breaking an opponent's jaw in 1965. Nonetheless, Gordon Stewart became a member of the Canada Soccer Hall of Fame in 2004.

| Everton 1953/54 | | |
| --- | --- | --- |
| | games | goals |
| League | 0 | 0 |
| Total | 0 | 0 |

# David Wilson

**played for**

Lochgelly Rangers,
Buckhaven United,
Gainsborough Trinity,
Cowdenbeath,
East Fife,
Heart of Midlothian,
Gainsborough Trinity (loan),
Everton,
Portsmouth,
Vancouver St Andrew's

The Wilson brothers were near inseparable. They had played at Cowdenbeath and then teamed up again at Heart of Midlothian. Admired for his dribbling skills, David was part of the side that won the Scottish Cup in 1906. He was lured to Goodison amid allegations that the club only wanted his brother George, who refused to sign for Everton without him. The 25-year-old inside-left made a mere handful of outings and, in the aftermath of several quarrels with the Goodison hierarchy, bolted to Portsmouth despite his younger brother's transfer there being nixed by a registration dispute. Following the news of the untimely deaths of two other brothers, David struggled to settle in Hampshire and quit the professional game in 1908. Together, the Wilson brothers emigrated to Vancouver, British Columbia.

| Everton 1906/07 | games | goals |
|---|---|---|
| League | 5 | 0 |
| Total | 5 | 0 |

# George Wilson

**played for**

Thomson Rovers,
Cowdenbeath,
Heart of Midlothian,
Everton,
Distillery,
Newcastle United,
Raith Rovers,
East Fife,
Albion Rovers,
Vancouver St Andrew's

**coached at**

Raith Rovers,
Vancouver St Andrew's

Having notched the winner in the 1906 Scottish Cup final, the 23-year-old Scotland star was acquired in a £725 deal which included his brother David. The stocky left-winger became a Goodison favourite as Everton pursued the league and cup double in 1907. But, after being replaced by amateur Harold Hardman before the FA Cup final, he vowed never to play for Everton again. After the club lost to The Wednesday at the Crystal Palace by 2-1 and finished a disappointing third place in the league table, Wilson had a stint in exile at Distillery before joining champions Newcastle United for a record fee of £1,600. He propelled the Magpies to the 1909 League title and victory in the 1910 FA Cup. The winger ended his pro career in Scotland before heading to British Columbia and playing beside his brother at Vancouver St Andrew's.

|  | Everton 1906/07 games | goals |
|---|---|---|
| League | 28 | 3 |
| Total | 34 | 4 |

# PART TWO

# EVERTON IN CANADA
# AND THE USA

*Program and Official*
*Line-ups*

TEN CENTS

SPORT CLUB PORTUGUESE HEADQUARTERS - 51-55 PROSPECT ST., NEWARK, N. J.

## INTERNATIONAL FOOTBALL "SOCCER" GAMES

"UNDER THE LIGHTS"

### FRIDAY, MAY 18 - AT 8:30 P. M.

## EVERTON OF ENGLAND

VS.

## Newark Portuguese-Elizabeth Falcons Select

AT

# NEWARK SCHOOL STADIUM

BLOOMFIELD AND ROSEVILLE AVENUES - NEWARK, N. J.

# 2.1
# VISITS TO CANADA AND THE USA
# IN 1956 AND 1961

North America enjoyed unprecedented economic growth during the post-war boom but, while other spectator sports sky-rocketed in popularity, soccer failed to catch the attention of average Americans – even after the USA national team humbled England at the 1950 World Cup finals in Belo Horizonte, Brazil. Regardless of the entrepreneurial efforts of many investors in soccer franchises, the standard of entertainment was considered underwhelming and attendances, especially in the USA, were disheartening. As a result, the professional game stumbled along from one financial disaster to another.

Despite Rangers and Charlton Athletic making transatlantic journeys before the outbreak of Second World War, the Goodison trailblazers were reluctant to follow their lead and concentrated on summer excursions to Western Europe. Similarly, the club showed little appetite for crossing the pond after the termination of hostilities, even when Liverpool (in 1946 and 1948) and Manchester United (1950 and 1952) had done so.

Therefore when manager Cliff Britton was asked to evaluate the merits of a post-season tour to North America in 1956, he did not expect it would be productive never mind cost him his job. Given the likely duration of six weeks, the directors – without consulting the Everton manager – proposed to appoint Harry Pickering as assistant-manager to look after football matters in England during his absence. After Britton claimed a breach of his contract and quit his job, a sub-committee of directors, consisting of Tom Nuttall, Cyril Balmforth and Fred Micklesfield, took over team selection for the concluding 12 fixtures of the 1955/56 season; while another sub-committee, made up of directors Tom Nuttall and Jack Sharp plus secretary Bill Dickinson, established a budget of £2,965 and tied up the arrangements for the summer tour.

# POST-SEASON TOUR OF 1956

Everton sailed to the USA not knowing what to expect. Directors Ernest Green and Jack Sharp, secretary Bill Dickinson, trainer Charlie Leyfield and 16 players, departed from Liverpool's Lime Street station for Southampton docks on Wednesday 9 May. Thanks to Cunard-White Star and the largest transatlantic liner built at that time, they arrived punctually at their New York headquarters and prepared for their opening fixture at Newark, New Jersey. Jimmy Harris recalled, 'The one week at sea was no problem. There was a large group of British nannies on board who kept us occupied. New York was unbelievable. We had never seen skyscrapers like the Empire State Building. Without fail, when you were looking over the railings at the top, some fun-loving teammate would nudge you in the back and put the shits up you!' Whereas Wally Fielding reflected on his travelling attire, 'I was provided with a smart blazer – which I still have, emblazoned with a magnificent club badge, to be worn during meals onboard the RMS Queen Elizabeth and at all official functions. It made me feel confident and 10ft tall which was important because there was no such thing as player-power in 1956. The directors referred to us by our surnames and received a daily allowance of £3, some 50% more than the players. Someone said it was because they had bigger appetites.'

The arrival of the so-called 'English Booters' was celebrated enthusiastically by the New Jersey newspapers. A typical article proclaimed, 'The Everton FC of the English Soccer League, which opens its American and Canadian 10-game tour on Friday night at Newark School Stadium, will be greeted at City Hall by Newark Mayor Leo Carlin. The reception for the famed English XI will follow a practice session at the Bloomfield Avenue Stadium. The visiting team, which meets the best of the Newark Portuguese and Polish Falcons of Elizabeth under the lights on Friday night, will be honoured at a dinner at the Sports Club Portuguese tonight.'

## Game 2
## 20 May 1956: NEWARK SELECT XI 0 EVERTON 4

The 8.30pm kick-off meant that many of the Everton players were encountering football under basic floodlights for the first time. The lack of both illumination and observers (the attendance was a modest 1,500) at the stadium nicknamed 'The Old Lady of Bloomfield Avenue' did not deter the visitors. Inside-right Don Donovan, aided by Jimmy Harris, kicked off the tour with a goal after only three minutes. Their hosts held their own for the rest of the first-half until Everton's superior fitness and speed allowed them to dominate the rest of the proceedings. Ireland international Donovan netted two more in the 56th and 75th minute to claim a hat-trick. Sandwiched between those strikes, Jimmy Harris caught the Newark defence napping to net from close range. It could have been more – many more. Lou Rotolla, the New Jersey goalkeeper, excelled in the closing 15 minutes saving shot after shot.

**Everton:** *O'Neill; Moore, Tansey; Lello, Jones, P Farrell; B Harris, Donovan, J Harris, Fielding, Eglington.*

Two days on, Everton confirmed that they had found their land-legs by crushing an all-star team drawn from the American Soccer League by 7-0 at Triborough Stadium in New York City. Known officially as Downing Stadium, the venue was a 22,000-capacity, multi-purpose facility located on Randall's Island in the centre of the East River. Again, the official attendance of 4,312 was disheartening.

### Game 3
### 22 May 1956: AMERICAN SOCCER LEAGUE ALL-STARS 0 EVERTON 7

On this occasion, it was the turn of Jimmy Harris to net a hat-trick. The young centre-forward had been the club's leading scorer with a tally of 21 goals in 44 league and cup games during the 1955/56 season and was enjoying a rich vein of form. Other goals were scored by captain Peter Farrell, 20-year-old Alec Farrall, Don Donovan and Brian Harris. The hosts were overwhelmed by Everton's short-passing skills.

Peter Farrell initiated the drubbing with a powerful 20-yard shot past goalkeeper Orlando Jorge. A half-hour on, Jimmy Harris turned a neat pass from Don Donovan into the net (referred to as 'the cords' in local reports). Then shortly before the interval, Alec Farrall hit the post before smashing home the rebound. Centre-forward Harris added goals in the 60th and 66th minutes. His first involved a breathtaking solo run which concluded with his shot sending the keeper the wrong way. These were followed by one from Don Donovan, who scored with a neat header from Tony McNamara's corner. Brian Harris completed the rout with a fierce shot that went in off the outstretched hand of substitute keeper John Moore.

The following day, the *New York Herald Tribune* reported, 'The only serious attack by the All-Stars brought a "no goal" ruling by referee Jim Morrison. Substitute Pascual Pepe booted a 40-yarder at Jimmy O'Neill, who caught it near the goal-line. The impetus of centre-forward Jackie Hynes carried him into the goalie. The referee, ruled that O'Neill but not the ball had been pushed over the goal-line.'

**Everton:** *O'Neill; Moore, Tansey; Birch, Jones, P Farrell; McNamara, Donovan, J Harris, A Farrall, B Harris. Substitute: Woods.*

Certainly, the tourists had made a favourable impression on Orlando Jorge, debatably the best goalkeeper in the American Soccer League. He told the *New Jersey Advocate*, 'Everton are great. Their players are in tremendous condition. They run for 90 minutes. They make short, precise passes and put the ball right on the other guy's toe.' He voiced, 'Jimmy O'Neill is the best goalie and Jimmy Harris is the best all-round player I've ever seen.'

Thereafter, Brian Harris revealed, 'It's a good job that Jimmy O'Neill was a sturdy so-and-so because we didn't have a back-up keeper. Actually, it wasn't too big a problem because I fancied myself as a decent custodian. I think Matt Woods and a few others thought the same about their own cat-like abilities. In truth, we would have played in any position for Everton if required.'

25 Cents

# EVERTON

(England)

vs.

## CHICAGO ALL STARS

International Soccer Game

SUN. JUNE 3rd, 1956

Hanson Park Stadium

Next stop – Western Massachusetts where the *Ludlow Advertiser* lauded Everton's imminent arrival, 'Soccer fans will never get a chance to see a better soccer team than when the Everton of England play at Franklin Park against Lusitanos. It will be one of the USA's better teams against one of the world's best. Everton has a reputation for playing the highest class of soccer, a tradition carried on by the present team. Rarely does it resort to a robust stop-at-nothing type of play.'

**Game 4**
**25 May 1956: LUSITANOS 1 EVERTON 4**

Undeterred by their hosts co-opting Jackie Hynes, the burly Most Valuable Player (MVP) in the American Soccer League and spearhead of the Brooklyn Hakoahs, Everton had too much class for their opponents and won at a canter. The *Ludlow Advertiser* gushed, 'The Everton Soccer Club of Liverpool is as nimble-footed a clan of musclemen as ever appeared on the chewed-up Franklin Park pitch.'

Only a spectacular display by Orlando Jorge kept the score down. After Jimmy Harris had opened the scoring in the 10th minute, Porky Ferreira equalised during the Lusitanos' only meaningful attack of the night. Jorge's goal-kick, which travelled half the length of the field, was picked up by Ferreira. Though Jimmy O'Neill blocked his shot, the goalkeeper could not reach his follow-up effort. Perhaps more surprised than anything, the Ludlow players mobbed the scorer in the centre-circle.

To wipe the smiles off their faces, Alec Farrall set off on a mazy dribble that ended with him beating Jorge. Eric Moore made a similar advance to notch a third. The local newspaper described his effort as 'a clever bit of toe work dribbled through half of the Ludlow team before sending Jorge the wrong way with a low liner.' Brian Harris netted a fourth in the 55th minute but the real hero of the second-half was Jorge. The same reporter noted, 'He was an octopus in the second-half, diving through the dust for a low drive one minute and springing high for a long shot the next.'

**Everton:** *O'Neill; Moore, Tansey; Rea, Woods, P Farrell; McNamara, Fielding, J Harris, A Farrall, B Harris.*

Everton tour party travelled back to New York City for the first of four clashes with Aberdeen, who had captured the Scottish League crown in 1955 and finished runners-up to champions Rangers in 1956. However, a couple of days of torrential rain meant that the fixture planned for 28 May had to be postponed due to the water-logged pitch at Downing Stadium.

As a consequence, the club's next outing took place two days later against Schwaben from Augsburg at a now water-free Downing Stadium. Hardly a household name, the West German outfit had struggled to secure twelfth place in the Oberliga Süd – one of the five regional leagues which formed the top level of post-war football in that country prior to the formation of the Bundesliga in 1963.

## Game 5
## 30 May 1956 SCHWABEN 1 EVERTON 0

Astonishingly, Everton were defeated in a tough and often scrappy match in front of an enthusiastic crowd of 6,782. Outside-right Roland Jungmann netted the only goal 10 minutes from time after a scramble in the Everton goalmouth. The *New York Herald Tribune* noted, 'Jungmann headed the ball into the cage from close up after taking passes from inside-left Hrvoje Matanovic and centre-forward Peter Struzina.'

Earlier, the Merseysiders had missed several chances. The nearest they came to scoring was when Don Donovan raced away only for his effort to be ruled offside. Also, Tommy Eglington had tested goalkeeper Franz Sussman with two sizzling shots and Peter Farrell dribbled half the length of the field only to hit the post. Frustrated by their uninspiring performance, Everton's tempers flared in the second-half. This was highlighted when Tommy Eglington tangled with centre-forward Struzina and then threw punches in the direction of inside-right Ernst Scheirzinger.

**Everton:** *O'Neill; Moore, Tansey; Farrell, Woods, Lello; B Harris, Donovan, J Harris, Fielding, Eglington. Substitute: Birch.*

Everton sought to rebound in Missouri. Their fifth fixture of the tour was against the Catholic Youth Council League All-Stars at the Public Schools Stadium. Prior to kick-off, St Louis coach Bob Guelker speculated, 'I'm sorry that the Germans stung Everton. We had considered them tough enough competitors in their happiest frame of mind. Now, it's a cinch they'll try to regain some prestige by beating us convincingly. Everton is a leading example of an artistic team.' The All-Stars were drawn mainly from St Ambrose, the local amateur champions. Though Everton were favoured to overwhelm them, it had not gone unnoticed that the local soccer fans had recently witnessed St Louis Kutis defeat none other than Schwaben.

## Game 6
## 2 June 1956: CATHOLIC YOUTH COUNCIL LEAGUE ALL-STARS 0 EVERTON 5

There were no further upsets in St Louis. Despite the CYC All-Stars having trained for months in preparation for the match, they were humbled by their superior opponents. Withdrawing into a defensive shell from the outset, the local amateurs held the Merseysiders to a one goal advantage at the interval. Tommy Eglington having netted in the eighth minute when, after fighting his way through a maze of red shirts, he let fly with a screamer which was deflected past goalkeeper Herman Valli. In the second-half, Everton's slick passing overwhelmed their hosts' previously stout defence and right-half Ken Birch's goal in the 60th minute signalled the start of target practice during which Peter Farrell claimed a brace and Tommy Eglington added another.

The *St Louis Globe* concluded: 'The British team moved the ball well and exhibited an almost flawless passing game.' But perhaps the biggest cheer from the crowd of around

3,500 came in the 51st minute. After Everton were awarded a penalty when Gene Cucchi handled the ball, Tony McNamara struck a sizzler that Herman Valli stopped with a spectacular acrobatic save.

**Everton:** *O'Neill; Moore, Tansey; Rea, Donovan, Birch; McNamara, P Farrell, J Harris, A Farrall, Eglington. Substitute: Fielding.*

Visiting the USA was a rude awakening for veteran Wally Fielding: 'Having been born and raised in London and fought overseas with the Army during Second World War, I had come across several Americans and, like many British soldiers, was under the impression that they were brash and loud. Also, I wasn't pleased by Hollywood's claim that John Wayne had defeated Nazi Germany almost single-handedly – even though the actor had avoided any sort of combat in real life. It took about one week for me to change my mind about Yanks. After enjoying the company of our friendly and helpful hosts in New Jersey, New York, New England and Missouri, I concluded that most of them were well-off, many were fervent about everything – especially our new Queen and her family, and like yours truly, were proud of their own homeland.'

The loveable Cockney continued: 'As for professional soccer, our hosts were aware that the USA had embarrassed England by 1-0 in the 1950 World Cup held in Brazil. They didn't rub our noses in it, but everyone wanted to know how their flea-bitten underdogs could have beaten "The Kings of Football". However in St Louis, where half of that USA team had played for the local side, they were bemused that a bunch of teachers, carpenters, postmen and other part-timers could have got the better of Billy Wright, Wilf Mannion, Tom Finney and Stan Mortensen.'

After catching the midnight train at St Louis Union Station, the Everton party travelled through the night to Illinois. They arrived in the Windy City at 7.00am with little time to prepare for the 3.00pm kick-off against the Chicago All-Stars at Hanson Park which was located 12 miles west of the city centre.

### Game 7
### 3 June 1956: CHICAGO ALL-STARS 2 EVERTON 3

For one reason or another, Everton toiled to grind out a narrow victory before 4,800 fans. The outcome could have been much worse. Chicago had taken a 2-0 lead after a half-hour of play through goals by outside-right Joe Gryzik and inside-left Joe Kohlberger before captain Peter Farrell struck twice in the final three minutes of the first-half. Though it didn't appear to be Everton's day when Ken Birch missed a penalty, the visitors persevered and Peter Farrell completed his hat-trick via a powerful 15-yard shot and snatched victory five minutes from the end.

**Everton:** *O'Neill; Tansey, Moore; Birch, Donovan, Rea; McNamara, P Farrell, J Harris, Lello, B Harris. Substitutes: Fielding, Eglington.*

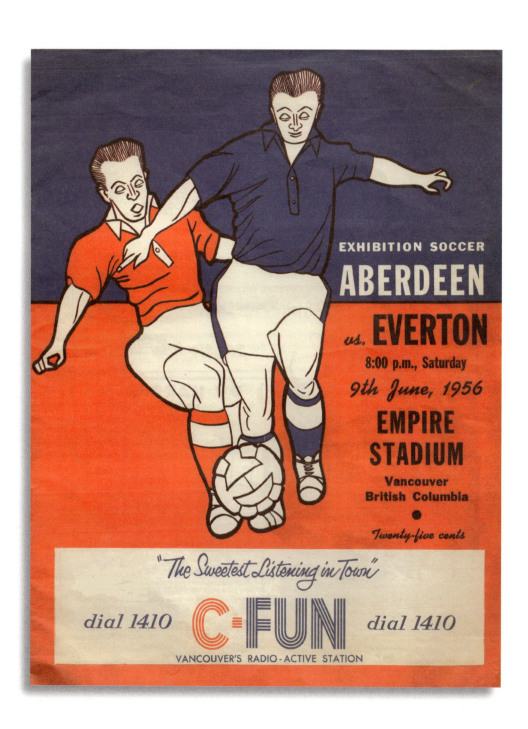

EXHIBITION SOCCER

# ABERDEEN

*vs.* **EVERTON**

8:00 p.m., Saturday

*9th June, 1956*

# EMPIRE STADIUM

Vancouver
British Columbia

•

*Twenty-five cents*

*"The Sweetest Listening in Town"*

dial 1410     **C-FUN**     dial 1410

VANCOUVER'S RADIO-ACTIVE STATION

In his post-match briefing, trainer Charlie Leyfield noted, 'It was nice to play football again. We've had our fill of sides who adopt rough tactics. Centre-halves Tom Jones and Matt Woods are carrying scars from the game against Schwaben, but we hope to have one of them fit for Saturday.'

Next up was Aberdeen, who were on a nine-match tour of Montreal, Ontario, Manitoba, Saskatchewan and British Columbia. Even though the Everton party arrived in Vancouver in good time and good spirits, the nature of the reception did not receive universal approval. Alison Hunt of the *Vancouver Sun* wrote, 'Out by the plane from Seattle, Mayor Hume – sporting a red rose in his buttonhole – was organising the welcoming party. Other officials wore bright smiles. But over the teapot in the airport bar, waitress Dot Jackson and I blushed. "Just look" cried Dot, an Everton fan from back home. "They have sent Highland pipers to welcome a Northern England team." Sure enough, four pipers in Stuart tartans could be seen warming up. "Oh well," said Dot, "I'll have some tea for them. That'll be some comfort". Nevertheless, Kenny Rea questioned me, "So you're all Aberdeen fans in Vancouver, are you?" Apologising hard, I led his teammates away for tea. "Proper tea? No tea bags?" they asked.'

The first match against the Dons took place at the Empire Stadium where Great Britain's Roger Bannister and Australia's John Landy had contested the legendary 'Miracle Mile' in August 1954. Both athletes had broken the four-minute barrier previously that year. Bannister triumphed in a British Empire and Commonwealth record of 3 minutes 58.8 seconds. It was the first time that the impressive venue had been used for a professional soccer game. After the first training session at the stadium, captain Peter Farrell proclaimed, 'Your pitch is the best I've seen outside of Wembley Stadium. Without question, it was the finest we have encountered on our North American tour.'

Winger Tony McNamara concurred, 'The turf is in beautiful shape and should make for grand football on Saturday night.' Somewhat amused by these observations, one local journalist noted, 'If Canadian FA president Jock Hendry has heard these sentiments, he should pass them onto the teams who played at the old Callister Park where the surface was a mixture of two parts clay, one-part clinkers and one-part assorted foreign objects, with an emphasis on broken glass.'

At the conclusion of the training session, Ernest Green held court with the local press, 'If there is one thing we would like to take back, it is the Empire Stadium. It is truly magnificent. The team thinks the ground will lend itself to some good football.' Fellow director Jack Sharp expounded, 'Vancouver protects its pitch during heavy rains with special tarpaulins. I have often felt that some method of pitch-covering with plastic would prevent our grounds being reduced to mud-heaps during the winter.' He suggested that the answer to some of British football's attendance problems could be solved by providing more comfort for the fans in the form of more seats, 'Goodison Park holds 80,000 fans, but only 15,000 of them can be seated. Canadians are amazed that our fans are willing to stand shoulder-to-shoulder in the same spot for two hours.'

## Game 8
## 9 June 1956: ABERDEEN 3 EVERTON 3

The infamous Vancouver rain, which had fallen for four days, continued throughout the 90 minutes, but didn't seem to matter to the players or the crowd of 18,363. It was, without doubt, the finest soccer game that had been played in Vancouver. Though it ended 3-3, even the most ardent Scotsman would agree that Everton were the better team. The Merseysiders controlled the first-half and set the crowd alight with their precise passing. The half-back line of Farrell, Jones and Rea gave the team the edge in breaking up the Scottish attacks and supplying their forwards with a stream of short, crisp passes.

Everton opened the scoring after three minutes when, after a delightful interchange between Brian Harris and Jimmy Harris, Don Donovan blasted the ball past the helpless Fred Martin. From then on, Everton advanced with such finesse and cohesion that the rugged Aberdeen defenders could do little to stop them. Notably, Brian Harris had a field day tormenting left-back David Caldwell. One local reporter noted, 'The kid English displayed the deft touches of a hummingbird.'

Everton's second goal in the 15th minute was a cracker. Moving swiftly down the middle, Brian Harris twice feinted to pass before advancing to score. Some 10 minutes later, the highly touted Graham Leggatt finally escaped the shackles of left-back Jimmy Tansey. He accepted a fine through-pass by centre-forward Paddy Buckley to score. Leading 2-1 at the interval and with their forwards moving with a pattern-like precision, Everton were only prevented from a higher-margin by the goalkeeping of Fred Martin.

Throughout the first-half, Aberdeen's forwards had appeared disinterested. Clearly, manager Davie Shaw had words with them at the interval because they returned to the pitch with flames shooting from their nostrils. Moving with more bite, Jack Hather drifted in from his left and, instead of crossing, feinted goalkeeper Jimmy O'Neill and powered the ball into the net. Incredibly, Hather repeated the trick to put Aberdeen ahead. Right away, Everton launched a storming rally and equalised when Brian Harris sent over a high ball for left-winger Tommy Eglington to equalise.

**Everton:** *O'Neill; Moore, Tansey; Farrell, Jones, Rea; B Harris, Donovan, J Harris, Fielding, Eglington.*

The Canadian sports writers were ecstatic. Previously sceptical, Dick Beddoes of the *Vancouver Sun* confessed, 'Ordinarily, soccer football inspires no divine passion in this Canadian soul. Writing about it, your agent is often all ha-ha with gags. Therefore, this is an apology, a confession of mistakes – a disorderly backtrack. For spirited entertainment, the British pastime is several cuts above hop-scotch or girls' hockey. Certainly, Canadian football can't beat it for speed, pep and action. Canadian football can't even tie it. Played by English professionals, the game contains an impacted passion that makes it a universal amusement, like love.'

Fellow journalist Jimmy Lay reported, 'The soccer was superlative and the fans loved every minute of it. In defiance of the vile weather, they got lots of excitement and lots of goals. English, Scottish, Irish and Canadian, they were loud in their acclaim. If Everton finished 15th in their league, what must the other 14 teams be like?' He proclaimed enthusiastically, 'I've never seen better unity. Their men get into position as though controlled by invisible strings.'

All aboard for Alberta. Both teams travelled the 700 miles to Edmonton for the next match-up at Clarke Stadium which could accommodate 20,000 spectators, albeit in somewhat spartan conditions.

## Game 9
### 13 June 1956: ABERDEEN 1 EVERTON 2

Only 7,021 fans turned up to watch Everton overpower the men from Pittodrie at the home of the Edmonton Eskimos of the Canadian Football League. If the crowd was disappointing, the soccer wasn't. Everton's superior ball skills mesmerised their opponents. Yet inexplicably, they failed to convert their possession into goals. Even though the Red Devils did not venture forward often, their first serious sortie resulted in a goal by Jim Clunie. Paddy Buckley also missed a chance to put Aberdeen 2-0 up in the second-half when he slid the ball just wide of the post. For the rest of the game the Dons were given little choice but to defend. Eventually they cracked and Jimmy Harris scored two late goals to secure the victory.

Although the line-ups were not reported, local commentators observed the superb physical conditioning and courage of the British players, 'Both sides whipped up and down Clarke Stadium more times in one night than the Eskimos will cover throughout the coming season. Three men were heavily shaken up, none went off. In one incident, outside-left Tommy Eglington was tackled extemely heavily and looked due for a long stretcher trip but, by the time they found one, the Everton speedster was back on his feet and tormenting the robust Scottish defenders.'

Like most vacationers to Toronto, the Everton party made a 70-mile detour in order to be amazed and soaked amid the natural splendour of Horseshoe Falls (188ft high and 2,200ft long) at Niagara, but were bedded down by 10.00pm in preparation for the third meeting of the teams. Despite the heavy schedule causing some injuries, the club was able to field its strongest team at Varsity Stadium in Toronto.

## Game 10
### 16 June 1956: ABERDEEN 1 EVERTON 3

Due to the entertaining contests in Vancouver and Edmonton, the third clash between Everton and Aberdeen had caught the attention of the Toronto sports fans, To augment the glamour of the occasion, the 48th Highlanders Pipe Band was engaged to entertain the estimated 15,000 fans prior to kick-off.

ALBERTA FOOTBALL ASSOCIATION

# *Souvenir Program*

## EXHIBITION FOOTBALL GAME

### ABERDEEN
(SCOTTISH 1st DIVISION)
and
### EVERTON
(ENGLISH 1st DIVISION)

WEDNESDAY, JUNE 13th, 1956

CLARKE STADIUM — EDMONTON, ALBERTA

Price 25 Cents

As for the game, Everton gave their foes another soccer lesson throughout the opening 25 minutes. The team's ball control drew rousing applause time and again and their sharp passing had the Scottish side baffled. They took the lead in the seventh minute through an exceptional attack in which Brian Harris outwitted right-back Jimmy Mitchell and passed to Tony McNamara who promptly knocked it back to Jimmy Harris to blast home. Some 25 minutes on, hesitation in the Scottish defence proved costly when Brian Harris completed another fine move involving Tony McNamara and Jimmy Harris by chipping the ball out of Fred Martin's reach. The applause had barely subsided when Alec Farrall left the goalkeeper and left-back Ian MacFarlane on their backs to add another. Aberdeen's only response came in the 58th minute when Paddy Buckley connected with a cross from Harry Yorston to beat Jimmy O'Neill from just inside the penalty area. Ed Waring of the *Globe and Mail* reported, 'Buckley, the centre-forward of Aberdeen, expressed to me the opinion of many of the 15,549 fans. He couldn't understand how Everton finished so far down the First Division last season.'

**Everton:** *O'Neill; Moore, Tansey; Birch, Jones, Lello; McNamara, P Farrell, J Harris, A Farrall, B Harris.*

## Game 11
## 17 June 1956: ABERDEEN 3 EVERTON 6

The Toffees completed its 1956 North American tour by meeting the Dons for the fourth time in eight days in front of a crowd of 7,183 at Downing Stadium on Randall's Island. Once again, they scored during the early exchanges. This time Don Donovan netted in the sixth minute and Brian Harris extended the lead in the 26th minute from a cross by Tommy Eglington. Next, the Irish left-winger outsmarted goalkeeper Fred Martin before tucking the ball into the net.

Though outplayed throughout the first-half, Aberdeen notched three goals within the first 15 minutes after the interval through Harry Yorston and a brace from Bob Wishart. The inside-left's headed equaliser following a goal-mouth scramble sparked Everton into action. Brian Harris made it 4-3 and, then near the end, he completed his hat-trick with another sizzler. Finally, Wally Fielding broke away to nab number six.

**Everton:** *O'Neill; Moore, Tansey; P Farrell, Jones, Rea; B Harris, Donovan, J Harris, Fielding, Eglington.*

Veteran Wally Fielding recalled, 'Because our match with Aberdeen planned for New York City had been postponed in late-May, we had to play them on the afternoon that we were scheduled to return home. Consequently, the lads had to forgo their final night on the town and travel to New York immediately after the Toronto match, play the game against Aberdeen, fly back to Montreal and catch our transatlantic plane – all within 24 hours.' If truth be told, BOAC held up the departure of its signature strato-cruiser service to accommodate the Everton party.

Upon arriving at the US airfield at Burtonwood, secretary Bill Dickinson avoided any reference to the appointment of Ian Buchan, the new head-coach, and focussed on the tour during which Everton had won eight and drawn one of the 10 matches. He affirmed, 'The American standard of football isn't very high. The Chicago side was the best of the bunch.' Chairman Ernest Green concurred and added, 'The trip was successful in every way. Our players received many congratulations on the excellence of their football and sportsmanship.' Director Jack Sharp enlightened the gathered press, 'Soccer tours of North America are long and tiring, but they're a grand thing for players. Every club is eager to make such a trip, and rightly so, because it's something the players would get in no other way.' Even so, the *Liverpool Echo* noted the inexplicable loss to Schwaben: 'Everton had wanted to emulate Liverpool in never being beaten on American soil, but failed in their objective.'

Decades later, Brian Harris agreed whole-heartedly, 'It was fantastic tour. Imagine travelling with your extended family for six weeks? For some people, such long tours build bonds. For others, they cause frictions. We separated into three groups by seniority. The directors and secretary tended to keep to themselves. Tommy Eglington, Peter Farrell, Wally Fielding and Cyril Lello were almost old enough to be our fathers and were more restrained in their pursuits. The rest of us had a smashing time seeing and doing things that we could never have dreamt of. It was a big deal for a lad from Bebbington to celebrate his 21st birthday in Times Square wearing a Stetson cowboy hat.'

Tommy Eglington hinted that the hierarchical differences common at Goodison were still present throughout the North American tour. He divulged, 'Charlie Leyfield handled our important day-to-day activities – such as training and sightseeing. We didn't mix much with Mr Green. To be honest, we didn't like to interact with him because he had an extremely strong personality and spoke to us as if we were his pupils at his Arnot Street School. But looking back, it must have been a challenging itinerary for a 70-odd-year-old. Sadly, he died the following year.'

Tommy Jones, who took over the captaincy in 1957, recalled fondly, 'It was a great adventure in which we travelled by buses, trains, planes and a very big boat. In the mid-1950s, air travel was an uncommon experience for most young men except those who had been in the RAF. Even the most advanced planes were noisy and didn't inspire confidence, especially during bad weather. On occasions the whole plane would shake – for reasons unknown. I remember looking around the cabin and thinking that the directors looked more nervous than us before we ended the tour with a less than smooth landing at Burtonwood.'

The Everton team scored 37 goals and conceded 12 in their ten games. But more important, they proved to be great ambassadors for their club, their city and their country and did more to cement friendship in six weeks than some statesmen accomplish in a lifetime. Tommy Eglington confirmed that Jimmy Harris had been the revelation of the tour: 'He showed everyone that there was much more to his game than his incredible raw pace. That said, Don Donovan and Brian Harris weren't far behind him. Jimmy – an ever-present like Jimmy O'Neill, Eric Moore, Jimmy Tansey and Peter Farrell – scored nine of our 37 goals.'

Not surprisingly, Jimmy Harris has fond memories of his first visit to Canada and the USA, 'To be honest, besides Aberdeen, the standard of opposition wasn't great. So much so that my teammates could have a good night-out and still manage a comfortable win the next day.'

While the 1956 North American tour was a footballing success, the attendances were lower than expected – especially in the USA. Everton's three games in Canada attracted 41,000 fans, the seven games held south of the border totalled 28,000 (only 4,000 per game). By comparison, the average gates of the leading baseball clubs at that time were: Chicago Cubs 9,000, Boston Red Sox 14,600, Brooklyn Dodgers 15,800 and New York Yankees 19,400.

Following a short rest, the players were back at Goodison and grappling with the demanding routines introduced by Ian Buchan, which focussed on circuit training and weightlifting in a new gym constructed under the Gwladys Street Stand. Many of the senior players were horrified by his strenuous regime and some of his other revolutionary ideas. It is part of Everton lore that before the opening first division game of the 1956/57 season, he attempted to play psychological mind games by stopping the team bus and ordering his players to walk the final mile to Elland Road with the match-going fans to convince their opponents that they were about to face a team of super-fit athletes. It failed. Leeds were 5-0 up after 34 minutes.

Worse was to follow. Buchan's team lost six and drew one of its first seven games. To resolve the club's precarious position at the foot of the table, the directors responsible for team selection dropped the entire forward line, including Jimmy Harris and Jimmy Glazzard, who had been signed only 11 days earlier, prior to the game with Burnley in September 1956. Only three months after excelling in North America, the young local centre-forward had become dissatisfied and submitted a transfer request.

Some 40 years on, Wally Fielding summed up the chaos of 1956: 'Many blamed our poor league form on the North American tour. After all, it had caused the resignation of Cliff Britton and the arrival of Ian Buchan. With so much travelling between games, it was too long and too arduous. We had little time to recuperate before being confronted by the demanding training methods introduced by the new head-coach. I'm not a fan of long tours. The season is long enough. We were well and truly knackered before we had kicked a ball. While there were many reasons for our poor form, the harsh reality was that we were a below-average team in need of an overhaul.'

### INTERNATIONAL SOCCER LEAGUE 1961

Five years later Everton ventured across the Atlantic to take part in the International Soccer League as the Football League's representative. The club had changed dramatically during that time due to John Moores' ambition and his cheque-book. Only Tommy Jones and Brian Harris remained in the squad, the rest were some of the finest British footballers that money could buy. The Everton party, composed of directors John Moores, Edward Holland Hughes, Fred Micklesfield, Cyril Balmforth, manager Harry Catterick and trainer Gordon Watson and

# OFFICIAL PROGRAM

## ABERDEEN (SCOTTISH LEAGUE FIRST DIVISION)
## vs.
## EVERTON (ENGLISH LEAGUE FIRST DIVISION)

### Saturday, June 16th, 1956 - Kick-off at 3.00 p.m.

### Varsity Stadium, Toronto

Programs
Donated by
The T. Eaton Co.
Limited.

*Ontario goalie
stops a hard one in
the game between
the All-Stars and
Aberdeen at
this stadium
June 2, 1956*

**15c**

17 players, left for Montreal on 15 May flying via Prestwick in a chartered plane which also carried the teams from Kilmarnock and Bangu. Alex Young planned to meet his teammates in Canada after he had represented Scotland in Czechoslovakia and the British Army in Greece. In point of fact, the club had appealed to John Profumo, the Secretary of State for War, for the Army to grant him additional leave to play for his club in North America. It turned out that Young caught up with his colleagues just 36 hours before the opening match against Montreal Concordia.

'The Golden Vision' recalled, 'At that breakfast, Bobby Collins claimed that I looked unsteady on my feet from the new concept of jet-lag. He was right, but I was shaking from too many take-offs and nail-biting landings. After playing for the British Army against Salonika the previous day, I had caught three different flights to get to Montreal.' He continued: 'I had visited Canada shortly after Hearts had won the Scottish title in 1958 with a goal aggregate of 132-29. Every football fan in Edinburgh knows that statistic. As a 21-year-old, I played a game every other day on that tour and scored goals for fun. We hammered our Canadian opponents (Ontario 6-0, Manitoba 13-2, British Columbia 4-1, Alberta 13-2 and Northern All-Stars 10-0) and met Manchester City in Toronto, New York and Montreal. We certainly saw Canada – which is a massive country. In 1961, I expected to claim fewer goals and use fewer sick bags.'

The 1961 competition involved 16 clubs with the games alternating between stadiums in Montreal and New York throughout the summer. Everton were in the first section along with Montreal Concordia, Kilmarnock, Karlsruhe, Dinamo Bucharest, Bangu, Besiktas and the Americans of New York. The second section of eight clubs would kick off after the completion of the first section and the final between the winners of the two sections would be played in early-August. The tournament gave Everton the chance to make a statement on the international stage. Although Harry Catterick had been against the club's involvement, all the arrangements had been wrapped up before his appointment. In contrast to the manager, Mr Moores was keen. No doubt his enthusiasm was sustained by the guarantee of seven games at $2,500 per game.

It was the first prolonged period that the players had spent with manager Catterick and the arch disciplinarian put a marker down shortly after the arrival in Canada. Roy Vernon told the *Liverpool Echo*, 'After a gruelling flight, we arrived at the Embassy Hotel and went to bed. Rested, we showered and shaved and made our way downstairs for dinner. Punctual, properly dressed, a credit to our club. Quite casually I asked Jimmy Gabriel, "Do you fancy a drink before dinner?" So, we strolled into the hotel bar where skipper Bobby Collins, Alex Parker and George Thomson were sampling the local brew. A harmless aperitif before dinner – but not to Mr Catterick. The next day we were summoned to his room and warned that on this occasion he would overlook our behaviour but the next one of us who got out of line would be on his way home.'

Even after their arrival in Montreal, the club's new management team was perplexed about their involvement in the tournament. Apparently, it had not been sanctioned by FIFA. Alan

Hardaker, the Football League secretary, embraced the club's concerns and wired Sir Stanley Rous, who at the time was concurrently secretary of the Football Association and president of the Fédération Internationale de Football Association (FIFA), 'Everton cabled me. Are they allowed to play or not? Request urgent decision. First match Tuesday.' Rous is understood to have replied that Everton could take part in the competition provided that the US Football Federation, the country's governing body, took full responsibility for the tournament and received the necessary FIFA approval to run it.

Because permission had not been received by the morning of the opening match against Montreal Concordia, an infuriated John Moores telephoned the FIFA secretary general. Dr Helmut Käser conceded, 'The match tonight can go on. It is not Everton's fault that we have not received the rules for the tournament. We do not want to forbid the playing of football anywhere. An event such as the one in North America will do a lot of good for the game, but FIFA is the international body controlling football over the world and we must see the regulations governing competitions before we permit our clubs to play.'

## Game 12
## 24 May 1961: MONTREAL CONCORDIA 0 EVERTON 1

After the brouhaha had died down, Everton won their opening match at the Molson Stadium by 1-0. Alex Young had found his land legs and scored in the 72nd minute. Picking up a glorious through-ball from outside-left Jimmy Fell, the blond centre-forward struck a low shot from 20 yards that deceived and slid under Concordia goalkeeper Tony Macedo, who was on loan from Fulham.

Around 8,000 fans saw Everton outplay their foes throughout the roughly contested game. While the English side concentrated on playing football, the Canadians were guilty of hacking their opponents after the ball had been played. Their behaviour resulted in ugly melees involving men from both sides – two men were sent off and another carried off. Billy Bingham was dismissed midway through the first-half when he had retaliated to a head butt by Concordia's centre-forward Tito Maule. Right-winger Hector Dadderio was stretchered off with a fractured ankle after 65 minutes. Near the end, Concordia full-back Hector Lopez was ordered off after chopping down Jimmy Fell. Because of these stoppages, the game ran over by 13 minutes.

**Everton:** *Dunlop; Parker, Thomson; Gabriel, Labone, Harris; Bingham, Collins, Young, Vernon, Fell.*

Derek Temple, who watched the action from the sidelines, recalled: 'I don't remember much about the games in North America except for the opening one in Montreal which got a bit feisty, especially after a yard-dog with a big Zapata moustache gave Billy Bingham a smack. Not long afterwards the Ulsterman was sent off for retaliating and things turned from feisty to ugly. Mick Meagan and I were sitting on the bench about two yards in front of the spectators. He was getting a bit worried and confessed, "Nat, I don't like the look of this – we could get a knife in our backs." I turned round to see some extremely angry French-Canadians. Whereas Mickey Lill, who was at the other end of the bench, was yelling to his teammates, "Calm down boys – there's no need for that!"'

Reporting for the *Montreal Gazette*, Norman Gillespie quoted the reactions of Jimmy Hill of Fulham, who was on the Concordia promotional staff. 'I have never seen Everton play such a strong tackling game in the Football League. I think they were rankled by Bingham being sent off and were out to give as good as they received.' In the aftermath, Billy Bingham and Hector Lopez were each fined $25 for their part in the fracas. Also, Concordia coach Skender Perolli, who ran onto the field during the fighting, was given a formal warning by the Quebec Soccer Association.

Even though some of his men had been badly bruised during the encounter, Harry Catterick made only one change to his line-up for the second game against Kilmarnock. He included young Frank Wignall at centre-forward and nudged Alex Young to inside-left in place of the injured Roy Vernon. Their Caledonian opponents had enjoyed a good 1960/61 season. They had finished just one point behind champions Rangers in the Scottish League and also runners-up to Rangers in the Scottish League Cup.

### Game 13
### 25 May 1961: KILMARNOCK 1 EVERTON 2

The Merseysiders dominated the game, like they had against Montreal Concordia. Thanks to two goals from Bobby Collins, they defeated Kilmarnock by 2-1. His first came in the 15th minute from a pass by Alex Young. His second arrived in the 22nd minute when he powered in the rebound after Young had hit the post. Kilmarnock tried hard to reduce the arrears but could muster only speculative long-range efforts which were easily dealt with by goalkeeper Albert Dunlop. In the second-half, the Scots pressed harder and centre-forward Andy Kerr scored in the 77th minute.

Stimulated by the goal, Kilmarnock swarmed around the Everton penalty area to such an extent that Dunlop had to dive through a maze of legs to grab the ball on three occasions in the dying minutes. The victory before a crowd of around 4,000 meant that Everton topped their section.

**Everton:** *Dunlop; Parker, Thomson; Gabriel, Labone, Harris; Bingham, Collins, Wignall, Young, Fell.*

The *Montreal Gazette* concluded: 'Everton had a decided edge in the first-half but eased up and Kilmarnock came close to equalising in the dying minutes. Only over anxiousness, poor shooting and bad luck kept them from getting the ball past goalkeeper Albert Dunlop. In contrast to Tuesday evening's game against Montreal Concordia, when Everton were penalised frequently for rough play, there were few stoppages although both teams played robust soccer.'

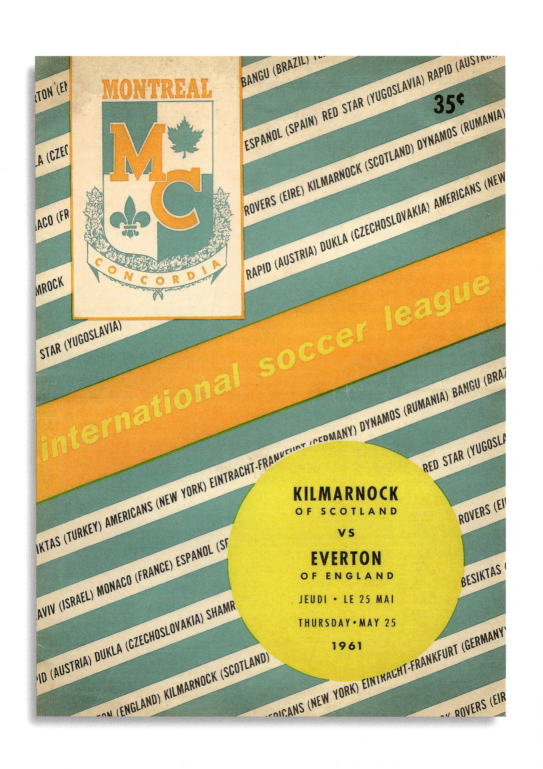

On to the USA where Derek Temple experienced something of a culture shock: 'The Yanks in New York City were a different breed. Because I was recovering from injury and hadn't played, I had to lug the big basket-weave skips containing the kit. At the railway station, Mick Meagan and I were pushing these skips with our suitcases on top when two big porters grabbed our cases and put them on a trolley. We said, "No, we're alright, we'll push them ourselves." But they took them anyway and we pushed the skips. At the end of the long platform, one porter stopped and put his hand out. He said, "It's usual to give a tip." I said, "You're joking, aren't you? I've just pushed the big skip and I told you that I would have taken my own case." He replied, "You Limey something or other." I had not heard the word before but knew that it was not a term of endearment. Then when we got into a taxi at the station, I was amazed to see the driver, a little fella, with his foot on the dashboard – I'd never seen an automatic car before. He took us to our hotel which was a horrible place.'

To the manager's dismay, many of the tour arrangements were a little amateurish. After a tiring 11-hour train journey from Montreal, the Everton party encountered problems at the Empress Hotel, which served as headquarters of the International Soccer League. Discovering that the booked accommodation was third-rate at best, Catterick ordered his men to pack up and leave for the Paramount Hotel near Times Square. Tommy Jones reflected, 'English clubs should think seriously before agreeing to undertake this tour. We are accustomed to arrangements being made to perfection and the planning of this tour left a great deal to be desired.'

Mick Meagan remembers the doss-house: 'After we had seen the filthy rooms. Bobby Collins came down to the lobby with Harry Catterick and said, "The state of this place. Get your bags lads. We are leaving and getting the next flight home!" So, we were taken around to another hotel which was a lovely place with its own share of drama. Shortly after our arrival, we heard a commotion with police sirens coming from a neighbouring building where a fella was threatening to jump from the roof. I heard that there were bookies down below giving odds on whether he'd do it or not. In the end the police talked him down. Worse still, he was slow-clapped by the crowd and called a chicken for not jumping!'

From their new base, the players were expected to travel in their training kit via the New York subway to practise sessions on a baseball pitch at Central Park – where they had to use their tracksuit tops as makeshift goalposts. Under the watchful eye of Gordon Watson, the players underwent intense training sessions and quickly acclimatised to the heat – if not to the humidity – and focused on their fixtures at the Polo Grounds – the domicile of the New York Giants.

After the first session, the squad hired taxis for the two-mile trip. Gordon Watson recalled his frustrations with training in Central Park. 'While the lads were having breakfast, I inflated 10 footballs and stuffed them into a couple of hessian bags, the type with draw-strings. I cut my hand using the bike pump but was able to drag them through the hotel lobby and ask the doorman to hail me a taxi. I remember sitting in the back seat with an odd-shaped duffel on either side of me. At first, the driver didn't speak but kept on glancing at me in his mirror.

He looked at my face. He looked at my hand. He seemed both inquisitive and nervous. As we made our way through the rush-hour traffic towards Central Park, he finally broke down: "Say buddy, what's in them?" I hesitated before responding: "My wife Olive – I've sawn her in half!" He didn't laugh. After all, this was New York City where anything was possible. But after he dropped me off and sped away, I dragged the bags to the park gates and waited for the players to arrive – half expecting to hear the ear-splitting police sirens.

'Back then, we were widely known as "The Merseyside Millionaires". But like most rich men, the club benefactor didn't throw his money about like confetti. I recall that we changed in a public shelter in Central Park. The facilities included secure lockers, rented at 25¢ a time, and hot showers. It was supervised by Hank, a wise-cracking New Yorker. He looked after our kit, provided buckets of cold water, ran occasional errands and helped the lads feel at home in his city. Nothing was too much trouble for him. At the end of our sojourn, I tipped him $10 in appreciation of his services. Mr Moores disapproved and instructed me to recover the gratuity.

'Embarrassingly, I explained my dilemma to Hank. His wrinkled black face grinned at me through his cloud of cigar smoke. In the blink of an eye, he approached Mr Moores and Mr Holland Hughes clutching a rusty container labelled "Tips" and emptied the contents of nickels and dimes at the feet of the Littlewoods tycoon. Training came to a standstill as all of Manhattan watched the Merseyside Multimillionaire kneel down in the grass to count the pieces of silver.'

Footballers often cite waiting and hanging around as mind-numbing. They visit interesting cities but rarely see more than the immediate vicinity of their hotels. The 1961 tour was different as the squad spent eight days in Manhattan without a game. The players enjoyed their free time at nearby Coney Island and the Belmont Park horse track, and their evenings in the bars and restaurants of Greenwich Village. Mick Meagan loved New York: 'Everywhere we went there was fun – horse racing at Belmont Park, boxing at Madison Square Garden. Tommy Jones was the leader of the younger lads, with him having been there before. He took us to places that he'd seen in 1956. They included the Empire State Building – where we walked up the stairs to the top – it took us half a day.'

Tommy Jones added, 'We hadn't been in New York for 24 hours when some of the lads adjusted to their surroundings by getting crew cuts and wearing denim blue jeans as well as jazzy shirts. Worse still, Brian Harris adopted a passable Brooklyn accent – that is one passable to a Merseyside ear. On some days he thought he was a hip-gyrating Elvis Presley. On other days he thought he was a sophisticated Frank Sinatra. Always a joker and a charmer, Brian – nicknamed "Hooky" – made friends everywhere we went.'

Gordon Watson recalled, 'I didn't get much time off. After looking after the players' niggling injuries, I had to organise the washing and repairs to the training and playing kits and plan the training routines for the next day. Yet, I've fond memories of New York. Where else would you see skyscrapers like the Empire State Building, burly cops with guns, neon-lit billboards advertising Nathan's frankfurters, massive Pontiacs and Cadillacs, yellow taxis, kids playing basketball next to their grandfathers playing chess and hordes of well-dressed people ignoring "Don't Walk" signs?

'In my day, footballers took part in other sports. At the end of the season, we played cricket at Bootle and Aigburth – perhaps not to the standards of Jack Sharp or Harry Makepeace who were capped by England at football and cricket. Some of us like Jackie Grant and Stan Bentham played baseball for Everton and Bill Dean played for the Liverpool Caledonians. Of course, the club has some history with the American past-time having hosted the Chicago White Sox and the New York Giants in the 1920s. Also it had the game's biggest advocate in the United Kingdom, namely Mr Moores. Along with former-secretary Theo Kelly and former-director Bill Giddins, he was such an avid fan of baseball that he formed the Liverpool-based National Baseball Association.'

Before the tour, John Moores invited Gordon Watson to accompany him to the iconic Yankee Stadium. Unfortunately, the Yankees were on the road during the time that the Littlewoods tycoon was in New York, so the trainer travelled to 'The House that Ruth Built' in the Bronx with Tommy Jones. He recalled: 'We sat near the top of a triple-decker stand to watch the game against the Kansas City Athletics. No doubt because it was a rainy night, the stadium was only one-third full. The Yankee fans were noisy and went bonkers when their favourites hit homers. It turned out that we had witnessed one of greatest teams in baseball history. Thanks to the slugging of Mickey Mantle, Yogi Berra and Roger Maris – who beat Babe Ruth's record of 61 home runs that year, they went onto dominate the 1961 World Series. But what impressed me about professional baseball was the fielders' ability to throw the ball – so hard, so fast and with such tremendous accuracy. They made it look easy.'

In a similar flash, the fun ended dramatically. When the news broke that Roy Vernon had been expelled, Harry Catterick's opaque statement shed little light: 'Vernon has been sent home as a disciplinary measure. I felt it would be in the boy's best interests and the interests of the team.' With details so scant and murmurings of a curfew being broken, the rumour mill went into overdrive. His biography revealed that he had promised to meet a family friend in Manhattan. Having met for coffee at the hotel, they wandered to the main street to say goodbye and hail her a cab.

He described what happened next: 'It was about 10:50pm – just time to have some supper at the restaurant at the top of the street and get back to the hotel before curfew. It was about 11:20pm when I was greeted by trainer Gordon Watson: "The boss will see you tomorrow."

'I wasn't worried, after all he had seen me in the hotel lounge, so he knew that I hadn't been out on the town. Imagine my dismay when I went up to his room. "Pack your things. You're leaving on the 4:30pm flight. I saw you with a woman in the lounge and then you came in late." The implication was enough. In hindsight, it was just the chance Harry had wanted to impress on everyone that he was the master. Any thoughts that Vernon may have had of going public with his discontent were thwarted as he was driven to the airport with the

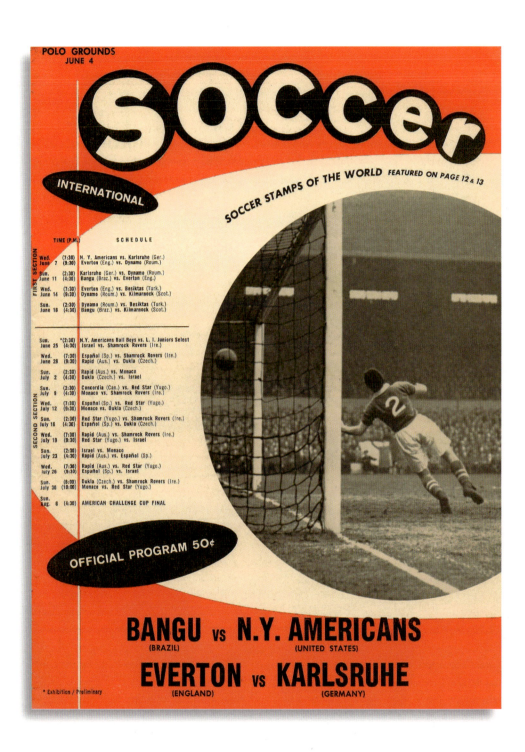

POLO GROUNDS
JUNE 4

# SOCCER

INTERNATIONAL

SOCCER STAMPS OF THE WORLD FEATURED ON PAGE 12 & 13

| TIME (P.M.) | SCHEDULE |
|---|---|

**FIRST SECTION**

| Wed. June 7 | (7:30) (9:30) | N. Y. Americans vs. Karlsruhe (Ger.) Everton (Eng.) vs. Dynamo (Roum.) |
| Sun. June 11 | (2:30) (4:30) | Karlsruhe (Ger.) vs. Dynamo (Roum.) Bangu (Braz.) vs. Everton (Eng.) |
| Wed. June 14 | (7:30) (9:30) | Everton (Eng.) vs. Besiktas (Turk.) Dynamo (Roum.) vs. Kilmarnock (Scot.) |
| Sun. June 18 | (2:30) (4:30) | Dynamo (Roum.) vs. Besiktas (Turk.) Bangu (Braz.) vs. Kilmarnock (Scot.) |

**SECOND SECTION**

| Sun. June 25 | *(2:30) (4:30) | N. Y. Americans Ball Boys vs. L. I. Juniors Select Israel vs. Shamrock Rovers (Ire.) |
| Wed. June 28 | (7:30) (9:30) | Español (Sp.) vs. Shamrock Rovers (Ire.) Rapid (Aus.) vs. Dukla (Czech.) |
| Sun. July 2 | (2:30) (4:30) | Rapid (Aus.) vs. Monaco Dukla (Czech.) vs. Israel |
| Sun. July 9 | (2:30) (4:30) | Concordia (Can.) vs. Red Star (Yugo.) Monaco vs. Shamrock Rovers (Ire.) |
| Wed. July 12 | (7:30) (9:30) | Español (Sp.) vs. Red Star (Yugo.) Monaco vs. Dukla (Czech.) |
| Sun. July 16 | (2:30) (4:30) | Red Star (Yugo.) vs. Shamrock Rovers (Ire.) Español (Sp.) vs. Dukla (Czech.) |
| Wed. July 19 | (7:30) (9:30) | Rapid (Aus.) vs. Shamrock Rovers (Ire.) Red Star (Yugo.) vs. Israel |
| Sun. July 23 | (2:30) (4:30) | Israel vs. Monaco Rapid (Aus.) vs. Español (Sp.) |
| Wed. July 26 | (7:30) (9:30) | Rapid (Aus.) vs. Red Star (Yugo.) Español (Sp.) vs. Israel |
| Sun. July 30 | (8:00) (10:00) | Dukla (Czech.) vs. Shamrock Rovers (Ire.) Monaco vs. Red Star (Yugo.) |
| Sun. Aug. 6 | (4:30) | AMERICAN CHALLENGE CUP FINAL |

OFFICIAL PROGRAM 50¢

* Exhibition / Preliminary

# BANGU vs N.Y. AMERICANS
(BRAZIL)      (UNITED STATES)

# EVERTON vs KARLSRUHE
(ENGLAND)      (GERMANY)

manager, Alex Young, Alex Parker and club director Fred Micklesfield. The latter would fly back with the Welshman – albeit not sat next to him. Harry Catterick's coup de grace was yet to come. On the way to the airport, the manager leaned over and said: 'This incident is closed, but if you speak to the press you will be subjected to further action. If you ask for a transfer it will be refused. If your wife is concerned at the speculation, I will be glad to speak to her when I get home.'

At Manchester's Ringway Airport, the player told journalist Horace Yates in a somewhat terse manner: 'I've absolutely no comment to make.' As speculation – some of it salacious – continued to swirl around, he was quoted by the *Daily Post*: 'Some of the stories I have heard might have been originated by a New York scriptwriter and would have contained just about as much truth. Not until after the tournament will I even consider lifting the veil of secrecy.' Roy Vernon never went public with what happened during the 1961 tour but did cable his teammates, most of whom he had not seen before heading to New York's Idlewild Airport: 'Good luck lads. Hope you win the competition.' Back on Merseyside, the Everton manager concluded: 'As far as I am concerned the matter is closed. There will be no further action.'

After the drama of the unacceptable accommodations and then Vernon's exit, the club got back to business. With no further injury problems except tiredness, the team prepared to play its third game against Eintracht Frankfurt – the European Cup finalists in 1960 and runners-up in the Oberliga Süd in 1961. At the eleventh hour, they were replaced by Karlsruhe – a worthy adversary who had won the Oberliga Süd Championship in 1960 and finished third in 1961.

## Game 14
## 4 June 1961: KARLSRUHE 2 EVERTON 5

In the absence of Roy Vernon, Frank Wignall continued to spearhead the attack as Everton defeated Karlsruhe at the Polo Grounds and kept their unbeaten record. After Alex Young had opened the scoring with a precise header from Billy Bingham's corner in the fourth minute, they never looked back. Even though Karlsruhe equalised through left-winger Reinhold Nedoschil, Young regained the lead in the 17th minute when he smashed the ball into the net after Wignall's shot was partly stopped. Then just before half-time, a long punt by Albert Dunlop led to Frank Wignall netting number three.

In temperatures of around 85F, the Everton forwards continued to look dangerous. Bobby Collins drove in a Jimmy Fell centre for the fourth goal in the 49th minute. Almost directly afterwards, inside-left Reinhold Wischnowsky responded when Albert Dunlop failed to hold Nedoschil's powerful shot. Then some 10 minutes from the end, Jimmy Fell brought the crowd of 14,729 – which included 100 Everton supporters – to their feet when he dribbled through the West German defence and passed for Bingham to net Everton's fifth goal.

**Everton:** *Dunlop; Parker, Thomson; Gabriel, Labone, Harris; Bingham, Young, Wignall, Collins, Fell.*

Buoyed by the emphatic victory, Harry Catterick and his squad looked forward to meeting their next opponents Dinamo Bucharest, who weeks earlier had finished runners-up to Steaua Bucharest in the Romanian League One.

## Game 15
### 7 June 1961: DINAMO BUCHAREST 0 EVERTON 4

Though they won by 4-0 with goals from Bobby Collins, Jimmy Fell and a brace from Billy Bingham, the Everton players suffered a physical battering during the undignified encounter with Dinamo Bucharest in New York. It was little surprise when Collins and his opposing right-half Ivan Dimitra were ordered off just before half-time. Apparently, the diminutive midfield general was trying to separate the warring factions involved in a melee. Renowned for his ability to look after himself and his teammates, he had jumped in between Alex Young and Dimitra. The trouble had begun when the referee awarded a goal by Billy Bingham. The Romanian players pushed the official to the sideline, insisting that he consult the linesman who was getting similar treatment from the Romanian bench. Then for some unknown reason, the referee reversed his decision and disallowed the goal.

Leading 1-0 at the interval thanks to a Bobby Collins goal, Everton controlled the second-half. Outside-right Billy Bingham scored in the 70th minute and the 72nd minute. Near the end, Alex Young's quick free-kick surprised the Bucharest defence and allowed Jimmy Fell to slide the ball home for the fourth.

**Everton:** *Dunlop; Parker, Thomson; Gabriel, Labone, Harris; Bingham, Young, Wignall, Collins, Fell.*

A disgusted Harry Catterick apprised the *Liverpool Echo*, 'The standard of refereeing has to be seen to be believed. We were punched and kicked and Jimmy Fell was stamped on when the ball was at the other end of the pitch. We have five men needing treatment – Wignall (kicked on the knee), Fell (damaged calf muscles when brought down from behind), Young (bruised face), Harris (head-butted) and Parker (deliberately kicked on the thigh). I'll be amazed if we have with 11 fit men for the new season. Are we going to call it a day? We can't, we are under contract. Will this be our last trip to New York for this tourney? That's a leading question which I cannot answer at this time. But you must have a fair idea of what I would say if I could.'

Alex Young later recalled the fisticuffs, 'The Romanians were good footballers with bad manners and even worse attitudes. After a bit of pushing, a Romanian spat at me before thumping the side of my face. I was about to retaliate when Wee Bobby unleashed a barrage of fast and continuous punches. As the pride of Govanhill – one of Scotland's most deprived areas – he left the pitch unbloodied and 10ft tall.'

Right-back Alex Parker provided another version of the conflict, 'Believe me, Alex Young was no pussy cat. He had worked down the coal mines, served in the British Army and excelled in the "take no prisoners' world" of the Scottish First Division. Even so, his approach to pugilism reflected that of the Marquess of Queensberry. Against the Romanians, he adopted the classical stance and pose favoured by John L Sullivan whereas his foes circled him like a pack of rabid hyenas.'

As predicted, Everton struggled to field a healthy side for the next match. Brian Harris recalled: 'Because Tom Jones had strained a muscle in training and Mick Meagan hadn't recovered from an injury picked up playing for Eire against Scotland, the boss wasn't able to rotate his defenders. If anything had happened to me, I think that Gordon Watson would have deputised. The 47-year-old trainer, who had been a teammate of Dixie Dean, Tommy Lawton and Joe Mercer, could ping long balls with more accuracy than me or any other member of the squad.'

Next up were Bangu, the men from Rio de Janeiro who had been runners-up at the 1960 tournament. Alex Parker reflected: 'As expected, the Brazilians were a real handful with their electric pace and unbelievable ball skills. A couple of months earlier, we had played them in a friendly at Goodison. It finished all-square at 2-2 but they won the bout on points. Let's say it was a contest in which the man was kicked more often the ball. There were so many sly fouls and so many South American tantrums.'

### Game 16
### 11 June 1961: BANGU 2 EVERTON 0

In scorching heat with temperatures reaching 94F, which favoured their opponents, Everton slumped to their first defeat in the tournament. Watched by 10,721 spectators at the New York Polo Grounds, Bangu won deservedly with two goals in the first-half. They set the pace in the opening minutes and were denied by the brilliance of goalkeeper Albert Dunlop. The Brazilians finally went ahead when Bato broke through on the left and flicked the ball to inside-left Ademir Da Guia, who scored. Bangu added another after 35 minutes when right-winger Jose Correa netted from point-blank range. In the second-half, Everton tried desperately to reduce the arrears but could not penetrate Bangu's deep-lying defensive plan. Towards the end, the men from Rio de Janeiro frustrated and taunted their exhausted opponents by playing out time with intricate inter-passing.

It was another contentious game and both sides lost men in the second-half. First, Bangu left-back Darcy Defaria was stretchered off with a suspected broken ankle after a collision with Frank Wignall. Then in the 56th minute, Everton outside-right Billy Bingham was sent off by English referee Peter Rhodes following an incident with Bato. Bingham claimed that his Brazilian foe had incited the unpleasant exchange by tugging at his jersey and had no alternative but to thump him. This appeared to be borne out by the award of a free-kick against the Bangu man.

**Everton:** *Dunlop; Parker, Thomson; Gabriel, Labone, Harris; Bingham, Young, Wignall, Collins, Fell.*

POLO GROUNDS
JUNE 7

# SOCCER

INTERNATIONAL

SOCCER STAMPS OF THE WORLD FEATURED ON PAGE 12 & 13

| TIME (P.M.) | | SCHEDULE |
|---|---|---|

FIRST SECTION

| Sun. June 11 | (2:30) (4:30) | Karlsruhe (Ger.) vs. Dynamo (Roum.)<br>Bangu (Braz.) vs. Everton (Eng.) |
| Wed. June 14 | (7:30) (9:30) | Everton (Eng.) vs. Besiktas (Turk.)<br>Dynamo (Roum.) vs. Kilmarnock (Scot.) |
| Sun. June 18 | (2:30) (4:30) | Dynamo (Roum.) vs. Besiktas (Turk.)<br>Bangu (Braz.) vs. Kilmarnock (Scot.) |

SECOND SECTION

| Sun. June 25 | *(2:30) (4:30) | N.Y. Americans Ball Boys vs. L. I. Juniors Select<br>Israel vs. Shamrock Rovers (Ire.) |
| Wed. June 28 | (7:30) (9:30) | Español (Sp.) vs. Shamrock Rovers (Ire.)<br>Rapid (Aus.) vs. Dukla (Czech.) |
| Sun. July 2 | (2:30) (4:30) | Rapid (Aus.) vs. Monaco<br>Dukla (Czech.) vs. Israel |
| Sun. July 9 | (2:30) (4:30) | Concordia (Can.) vs. Red Star (Yugo.)<br>Monaco vs. Shamrock Rovers (Ire.) |
| Wed. July 12 | (7:30) (9:30) | Español (Sp.) vs. Red Star (Yugo.)<br>Monaco vs. Dukla (Czech.) |
| Sun. July 16 | (2:30) (4:30) | Red Star (Yugo.) vs. Shamrock Rovers (Ire.)<br>Español (Sp.) vs. Dukla (Czech.) |
| Wed. July 19 | (7:30) (9:30) | Rapid (Aus.) vs. Shamrock Rovers (Ire.)<br>Red Star (Yugo.) vs. Israel |
| Sun. July 23 | (2:30) (4:30) | Israel vs. Monaco<br>Rapid (Aus.) vs. Español (Sp.) |
| Wed. July 26 | (7:30) (9:30) | Rapid (Aus.) vs. Red Star (Yugo.)<br>Español (Sp.) vs. Israel |
| Sun. July 30 | (2:30) (4:30) | Dukla (Czech.) vs. Shamrock Rovers (Ire.)<br>Monaco vs. Red Star (Yugo.) |
| Sun. Aug. 6 | (4:30) | AMERICAN CHALLENGE CUP FINAL |

OFFICIAL PROGRAM 50¢

DWIGHT D. EISENHOWER
TROPHY
AWARDED FOR SKILL AND SPORTSMANSHIP
DISPLAYED IN
THE INTERNATIONAL SOCCER LEAGUE
SEASON OF 1961

# N.Y. AMERICANS vs KARLSRUHE
### (UNITED STATES)     (GERMANY)

# EVERTON vs DYNAMO
### (ENGLAND)     (ROUMANIA)

Exhibition / Preliminary

Decades later, Tommy Jones reflected on the tournament, 'We played only seven games in five weeks yet had to contest four of them in 11 days. Our forwards, in particular, were exposed to some dangerous challenges and we suffered the stain of having men sent off for retaliating. In addition, we had to contend with some woeful refereeing as well as varying Continental temperaments on the field and off.'

Enter the Turks of Beşiktaş. The Istanbul side had been crowned champions of the Turkish Super League in 1960. More recently, they had finished third behind Fenerbahçe in 1961. Harry Catterick made one change to his line-up. Mickey Lill, who had not played in the first team since undergoing two cartilage operations during the winter, was selected at outside-left in place of injured Jimmy Fell.

## Game 17
## 14 June 1961: BEŞIKTAŞ 0 EVERTON 4

Everton inched closer to winning their section with a 4-0 success against Beşiktaş. Though not as combative as some previous games, several of their opponents were cautioned about their over-robust play. Everton attacked throughout the 90 minutes and Varol Ürkmez, the Turkish goalkeeper, had his work cut out to deter Bingham, Young, Wignall, Collins and Lill. In due course Beşiktaş folded. The 21-year-old centre-forward put Everton ahead. Alex Young got the second goal in the 42nd minute when he smashed in a Wignall pass from close range. Bobby Collins netted another in the 46th minute and then converted a 56th minute penalty.

Tommy Jones recalled: 'The walking wounded not playing, including myself, Mick Meagan, Jimmy Fell and Derek Temple, who picked up an ankle injury in training, made sure that the boys didn't lack refreshments at half-time and at the end of the match. We brought and distributed oranges, lemons and soft drinks. The team played well and if they had been six up at the break, it would not have been an injustice. Frank Wignall played like a man possessed. He chased and harried everyone and everything. To me he looked like a future England centre-forward.'

**Everton:** *Dunlop: Parker, Thomson; Gabriel, Labone, Harris, Bingham, Young, Wignall, Collins, Lill.*

The win gave the Merseysiders a two-point lead over their nearest rivals the Americans of New York, who they would meet in their final fixture. Everton's impressive goal difference of 16-5 meant that they would have to lose by five clear goals not to finish top of the table. Coached by the former Wales international Alf Sherwood, the New York side was primarily an all-star team drawn from New York's German-American Soccer League but included nine British players.

Everton were required to travel to Montreal on 16 June to play their final match; then back to New York to catch their transatlantic flight. Manager Catterick shuffled his forward line.

He reintroduced Jimmy Fell, switched Mickey Lill to the right-wing and Billy Bingham to inside-right in the place of the injured Alex Young.

## Game 18
## 17 June 1961: AMERICANS OF NEW YORK 0 EVERTON 7

Harry Catterick's men clinched their section in style by trouncing the Americans of New York and qualified to meet the winners of the second section in the final in August. It was their sixth win in the seven-match programme. Mickey Lill put Everton ahead in the second minute with a 25-yard shot, after Bingham had paved the way. Frank Wignall, Bobby Collins and Jimmy Fell came close to scoring but their confidence bordered on carelessness as they swarmed over their American opponents. In the second-half, Everton's blitz sank the Americans without trace. After 50 minutes Fell centred, Wignall nodded the ball onto Collins and the diminutive Scot headed in from five yards. Two minutes on, winger Lill accepted a pass from Brian Harris to score from close range. In the 60th minute, every forward took part in a dazzling move which Bingham capped with another goal. Wignall was rampant. He had two goals disallowed for offside and hit the post with two other shots before scoring in the 75th minute. More slick passing produced goals for Collins after 80 minutes and Bingham at the death.

**Everton:** *Dunlop; Parker, Thomson; Gabriel, Labone, B Harris; Lill, Bingham, Wignall, Collins, Fell.*

The fixtures were more competitive than those in 1956. Nonetheless, during the seven games, Everton scored 25 goals. The top marksmen were Collins with 8 goals, Bingham 5, Young 4 and Wignall 3. Thanks to four clean sheets, the defence conceded only five goals.

The five-week tour was a financial success and most of the football was of a high standard. Even so Horace Yates reported in the *Liverpool Daily Post*, 'From the conversations I've had with various members of the party, I've formed the impression that Everton will certainly not volunteer for a trip of this nature in the future. They returned with their playing reputation enhanced – allowed only five goals in seven games – but are faced with possible FA suspensions over the sending-off of Billy Bingham (twice) and Bobby Collins and questions over the future of Roy Vernon, who was sent home for disciplinary reasons.'

In August, Everton returned to New York to contest the two-legged final against Dukla Prague. The only changes to the squad were the inclusion of goalkeeper Willie Mailey and the omission of Derek Temple. Roy Vernon was also back in favour. A less than enthusiastic Harry Catterick noted, 'The humidity is tough and could affect us. We are at full strength but, because they qualified with an unbeaten run, Dukla are fancied to win.' Indeed, the reigning champions of the Czechoslovak First League, a title they would retain for the next three seasons, boasted the nucleus of the national team which would lose to Brazil in the World Cup final the following summer. Their star was in Josef Masopust, who would be awarded the 1962 European Footballer of the Year.

## Game 19
## 2 August 1961: DUKLA PRAGUE 7 EVERTON 2

If the attendance of 12,890 was disappointing, then Everton's listless performance was much worse. They were hammered by Dukla Prague in the first-leg at the Polo Grounds. Harry Catterick's men opened strongly until Alex Young was kicked on the thigh and limped heavily for the rest of the game. The play swung in favour of the Czechoslovakians in the seventh minute when Bobby Collins fluffed a penalty kick awarded for a foul on George Thomson.

Thereafter the royal blue floodgates opened. Almost immediately, inside-left Rudolf Kucera embarrassed Albert Dunlop with a delicate lob. Next, outside-left Josef Jelinek struck from an acute angle. Dukla playing a short passing game, scored again when centre-forward Jaroslav Borovicka beat Dunlop in the air. Worse was to follow. Two goals within a minute by outside-right Jan Brumovsky and inside-right Jaroslav Vacenovsky bought the half-time score to 5-0. All five Dukla forwards had scored during a 30-minute spell.

After the interval, Everton raced into the attack and Billy Bingham laid on a pass for Roy Vernon to score after 49 minutes. Next, the outside-right put Bobby Collins through. Keeper Pavel Kouba could only push the inside-left's shot back to the Alex Young who slammed it into the net. With their tails up, the Merseysiders almost got another but Kouba made a brilliant save from Jimmy Fell. With Everton in control, left-half Josef Masopust scored against the run-of-play and then Rudi Kucera rubbed salt into the royal blue wounds by completing his hat-trick in the last minute.

**Everton:** *Dunlop; Parker, Thomson; Gabriel, Labone, Harris; Bingham, Vernon, Young, Collins, Fell.*

Reluctantly, Brian Labone and Alex Young re-lived the game in 2002. 'The Last of the Corinthians' conceded: 'We fielded our strongest side, but the Czechs ripped us apart. We defended like rank amateurs. Albert Dunlop had a nightmare and George Thomson did his career no favours by being continually out-paced by their skinny outside-right.' 'The Golden Vision' was less critical: 'If only the wee man hadn't wasted the penalty award. He told us that he had made the unforgivable mistake of changing his mind during his run-up. In response, Taffy Vernon claimed that spot-kicks, like male voice choirs, should be the domain of Welshmen.'

Though no-one used Alex Young's injury as an excuse for the 7-2 hammering, Everton were hampered by the lack of local training facilities. It was only after their arrival in Manhattan that they discovered New York City regulations decree that public parks could not be used by professional athletes at the weekend.

Because Everton needed to defeat their more acclimatised opponents by six clear goals in the second-leg, Harry Catterick selected his strongest team except for Frank Wignall who deputised for Young.

POLO GROUNDS
AUGUST 6

# SOCCER

INTERNATIONAL

"THE
AMERICAN CHALLENGE CUP
PRESENTED BY
THE CITY OF NEW YORK
TO THE WINNER OF THE
INTERNATIONAL SOCCER
LEAGUE TOURNAMENT
SPONSORED BY
RUDOLPH SCHAEFER,
PRESIDENT
F & M SCHAEFER
BREWING COMPANY"

OFFICIAL PROGRAM 50¢

AMERICAN CHALLENGE CUP

# DUKLA vs. EVERTON
(CZECHOSLOVAKIA)                    (ENGLAND)

## Inter-Italia vs. Polish Falcons

## Game 20
## 6 August 1961: DUKLA PRAGUE 2 EVERTON 0

Everton fought gallantly in the second-leg of the final in New York. In front of a crowd of around 20,000, they were a tad unfortunate to lose 2-0. The Merseysiders experienced a blow in the fourth minute when Frank Wignall jarred his left ankle. With the novice centre-forward no more than a passenger, the hard-driving Czechs battered away at Albert Dunlop's goal and the acrobatic goalkeeper was forced to make five brilliant saves within the opening 15 minutes. The pressure intensified before the interval when Jaroslav Borovicka had a goal to be disallowed and then missed a penalty kick, Rudi Kucera shot over and Josef Masopust hit the crossbar.

After the intermission, the Merseysiders resumed without Wignall, who had been taken to hospital for X-rays, and surged around the Dukla goal. After absorbing the pressure, their opponents proceeded to grab two breakaway goals within an 11-minute period. First, Jaroslav Vacenovsky outpaced Brian Harris and out-witted man of the match Dunlop with a sharp shot in the 70th minute. Then Jan Brumovsky converted a pass from Josef Vacenovsky.

**Everton:** *Dunlop; Parker, Thomson; Gabriel, Labone, Harris; Bingham, Collins, Wignall, Vernon, Fell.*

Some 40 years later, 'The Golden Vision' recalled: 'I didn't play in the second match but was required to attend the post-mortem performed by Mr Moores and Mr Holland Hughes and suffer their scowls throughout the eight-hour flight to Manchester. Even though the American Challenge Cup trophy looked a bit garish, Mr Moores was dismayed not to have brought it home. Deep down, I think he believed that the British still ruled world football. In actual fact, we were beaten by a much better team. Dukla were a top-class side who took the tournament seriously. In later years, the trophy holder was challenged by that year's champion and, tacky or not, the Czechs retained the trophy again and again.'

In his *Liverpool Echo* autopsy, Leslie Edwards reported, 'Everton will not forget their first, and probably only, involvement in this tournament. The risk to their players is not commensurate with the rewards.' He quoted the excuses and defeatism of director Edward Holland Hughes, 'Dukla were a fine side but I think if Frank Wignall had remained fit, we would have won the second-leg. They had the advantage of being in New York for the second section of the tourney and were therefore better acclimatised. I'm a little disappointed but we did well to reach the final.'

At the board meeting held at Goodison on 23 June, Holland Hughes summarised the tour, 'It was not a happy one, due to it being badly arranged, poor accommodations and lack of training facilities. From a playing point of view, it was quite successful.' After he outlined the reasons for sending home Roy Vernon, the directors agreed that no further disciplinary action should be taken but that offers for the Welshman be quietly sought from other clubs. He also reported that the gross profit from the two trips to North America was in the region of £5,000 and that the $1,000 bonus received for winning the first section should be paid to the players who had played, pro rata.

In later life, Brian Labone loved to recall his North American experiences. 'Manhattan was just like I had imagined from the cinema,' he said. 'Everything was big and modern. The locals were either super friendly or super rude. The former seemed to be beset with learning about the latest Jaguar cars and Triumph motorcycles or worrying about nuclear fallout. My first long tour was a tremendous learning experience. If you discount the games against the Czechs, it was successful in improving fitness, providing a few extra bob and, most important, building team spirit.'

'We had a great bunch of lads. Previously, I had been critical of the Celts enjoying too much of their own company – that is Bobby Collins, Roy Vernon, Alex Young, Billy Bingham, Alex Parker, George Thomson and to a lesser extent Jimmy Gabriel – and not mixing. But that wasn't the case in North America. While we had vocal leaders in Collins, Vernon and Bingham, I was more impressed by our more thoughtful captains Tommy Jones and Alex Parker who went out of their way to include the more withdrawn men. Of course, they couldn't do much with Albert Dunlop.'

'During those six weeks together, we really got to know one another. Also, we all had to contend with the same ailment – blisters from a combination of the rock-hard pitches, woollen socks and soaring temperatures. We were indebted to Gordon Watson and Tommy Jones who would come to our bedrooms to look after our feet. Their favourite patient was Alex Young. I had never seen such ugly feet. I don't know how he could walk, let alone play football.' Alex Young explained: 'Mine had nothing to do with my boots – I had suffered from them since I was a lad at Hearts. Most of my Everton teammates had not seen proper blisters before and were shocked that mine covered such large areas and, when the fluid-filled bubbles burst, massive slices skin would become detached and my soles would turn bright red – almost scarlet. Gordon Watson would treat them with an assortment of ointments and tender loving care. Behind his back, the lads called him "Flo" after Florence Nightingale. But he was an unsung hero. After we had returned home, the conscientious trainer would offer other remedies – some quite bizarre – that he had received from old soldiers, retired policemen and Geordie witch doctors.'

In 2000, Brian Harris reflected on both tours: 'The first was a holiday. I was 21 and the USA was a world of bright lights, thick steaks, cold beers and pretty girls. By and large, we were well-behaved and, to the best of my knowledge, no-one got into trouble. Five years later, the USA had changed. It was even more vibrant with a young President who was far more charismatic than our old Etonian Prime Minister. There was talk on putting a man on the moon. As for the football, Everton mirrored the USA. We were ambitious and there was talk of winning a trophy or two. Our games in 1956 were a walk in the park against part-timers. Those in 1961 were against professionals who wanted to bring us down a peg or two. The boss moaned about the fixture schedule and travel arrangements, but I was thrilled to be in North America playing alongside some top footballers.'

The core of the 1961 tourists went onto win the First Division title in 1963 – the club's first silverware for 24 years. The principal refinements to the line-up were the additions of Gordon West, Dennis Stevens, Johnny Morrissey, Alex Scott and Tony Kay. Many observers thought that Everton could have been crowned one year earlier.

Years later, Alex Parker was still surprised by the lasting impact of the North American drubbings by Dukla. 'The two defeats shook our confidence, and we made a terrible start to the new season – our first under Harry Catterick – by losing four of our opening seven games. We were rooted in the drop zone. For one reason or another, the manager seemed to chop and change his forward line for every game before finding the winning blend. While he attracted a top-class goalkeeper in Gordon West, I have never fully understood the timing of his decision to sell Bobby Collins. After his departure with only a dozen fixtures remaining, we drew five away games – most against teams we should have hammered.'

'I was out injured and vented my frustrations from the stands. It was purgatory watching the title slip from our grasp, one point at a time. Chinese water torture! Hindsight can cloud judgment but, in a below-average First Division season, I believe were the best of the contenders. We finished fourth, spitting distance – that is just five points – behind champions Ipswich Town. No disrespect to Alf Ramsey's side, but with a better start or more consistent away form we could have snatched the title in 1962. As it turned out, we had to wait a year. There again, what if we hadn't had made that humbling second trip the USA?'

Clive Toye, who became one of the driving forces behind the growth of soccer and the NASL in the 1960s and 1970s, recalled the competition: 'I was the chief sportswriter at the *Daily Express* at that time. After interviewing Stanley Matthews, who was playing the Eastern Canada Professional Soccer League with Toronto City, I covered Bill Cox's new competition called The International Soccer League. At that time there were pockets of ethnic soccer, but most Americans didn't know about the game. I watched all the matches involving Everton and Kilmarnock – some of which were feisty. But what I remember most was the upheaval associated with Harry Catterick and his team walking out of their inferior accommodations provided to them in New York City. I found the Everton manager to be very professional.'

After the Dukla debacles, Everton did not visit North America for another 24 years. More specifically, the club did not travel to the USA for 43 years. During that period, it played in excess of 300 pre-season friendlies – with frequent excursions to Western Europe and visits to Australia, Hong Kong, Japan, Malaysia, Mauritius, New Zealand and Thailand.

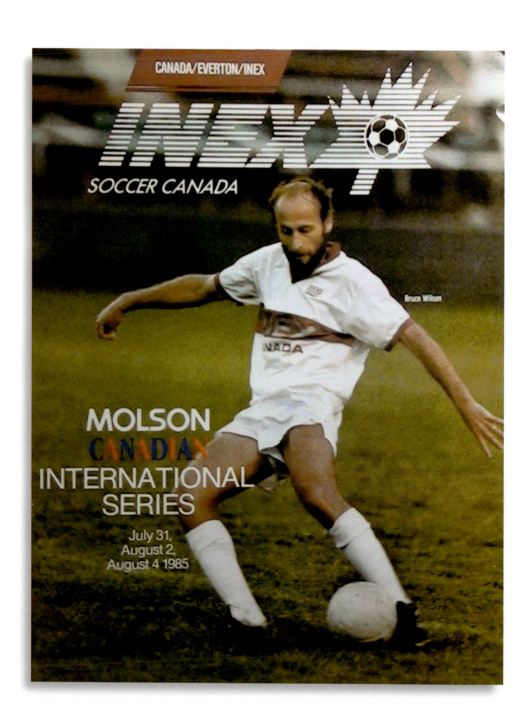

CANADA/EVERTON/INEX

# INEX
## SOCCER CANADA

Bruce Wilson

MOLSON
CANADIAN
INTERNATIONAL
SERIES

July 31,
August 2,
August 4 1985

# 2.2
# VISIT TO CANADA IN 1985

A mixture of over-expansion, economic recession and unabating disputes with the players' union contributed to the death of the North American Soccer League (NASL) whose popularity had boomed in the late-1970s when gates averaged 14,000 per game. Even then, many US experts predicted that the league would struggle to gain further national acceptance because of the lack of home-grown stars. At the time of its inception in 1968, the competing teams fielded only 30 North American players between them. While the contributions of global stars like Pelé, Beckenbauer and Cruyff to the NASL are well documented, many of the imports were mere journeymen in their own countries and failed to capture the imagination of US soccer fans.

In an attempt to build a more sustainable league that would create greater domestic interest, the NASL mandated that each roster accommodate six domestic players. Nevertheless, most 17-man squads were filled with foreign nationals whose fat salaries resulted in every franchise haemorrhaging money. Indeed, the collective deficit of the 24 teams had reached $30 million for the 1980 season alone.

With only nine teams participating in the 1984 season, the NASL suspended its operations when only the Toronto Blizzard and the Minnesota Strikers expressed an interest in playing on. The latter plus the Chicago Sting, New York Cosmos and San Diego Sockers departed to the resurgent Major Indoor Soccer League (MISL) and the Tampa Bay Rowdies joined the American Indoor Soccer Association (AISA). Whereas the Golden Bay Earthquakes headed to the Western Soccer Alliance (WSA) and the Tulsa Roughnecks played independently before folding after a few months.

The NASL's collapse represented a major problem for Canada whose national team sought to qualify for the 1986 World Cup. With no quality North American teams to play, the Toronto

Blizzard was renamed the Inex Canada and, packed with Canadian stars, arranged a series of exhibition games to keep their players fit. One of them was against the reigning Football League champions – Everton.

## MOLSON CANADIAN INTERNATIONAL TOURNAMENT 1985

After the expiration of the NASL, the Toronto Blizzard had planned to continue by arranging exhibition games against Everton, Manchester United, Porto, Red Star Belgrade, Verona and others. But in mid-1985, the club was acquired by Edward Cavalier and rebranded as the Inex Canada Soccer Club after his company, Inex Technologies. The Toronto entrepreneur immediately organised the Molson Tournament to provide the players representing Inex, under the guidance of general-manager Sam Lenarduzzi and player-coach Bruce Wilson, and the other members of the 27-man national squad with competitive outings before the key World Cup qualifying games against Honduras and Costa Rica. Accordingly, the tournament became a key part of the Canadian Soccer Association's drive towards the World Cup finals – labelled 'The March to Mexico' – which until then had failed to capture the attention of the Canadian public.

However, an indication of Canada's general apathy towards soccer was reflected in the limited coverage of the tournament provided by the *Globe and Mail*, the country's national newspaper, the *Toronto Star* and the *Toronto Sun*. Articles were few, far between and strewn with errors. For example, on the morning of Everton clash with Inex, the *Globe and Mail's* Douglas Faulkner began his preview with, 'The Manchester-based soccer team – last season's winner of the English League and European Cup …' To his credit, the author did clarify that a recent decision by FIFA to allow English teams to play in North America and Australia had made it possible for Everton to visit Toronto.

Despite having secured the league title and the European Cup Winners' Cup so convincingly, like all English clubs Everton were expelled from playing in Europe after rioting at the European Cup final led to the deaths of 11-year-old Andrea Casula and 38 other Juventus supporters. As a result, Everton were forced to cancel its pre-season visits to West Germany and Austria. Therefore, when the sanction was relaxed to allow games beyond Europe, the club's board accepted the invitation to play the two games in Canada in order to provide manager Howard Kendall and his coaching staff with opportunities to integrate Gary Lineker, his major summer buy from Leicester City, into his line-up.

Like most lifelong Evertonians, centre-half Derek Mountfield was not quite as understanding. 'We had a great team, probably the best in Europe at the time. The lads had won the league, the European Cup Winners' Cup and narrowly lost the FA Cup but endured a horrible summer. Our plans were in disarray until, at the last minute, we heard that we were going to Toronto. In May we had been celebrating our victory over QPR to win the league and qualification for the European Cup. Then, within no time, we had been banned from the European Cup and were headed to Canada. It seemed so unfair. What had Everton – its players and its well-behaved supporters – done to warrant such punishment?' Even though the tournament had failed to grab the imagination of the Ontario public, Inex's Sam Lenarduzzi predicted somewhat optimistically that 10,000-15,000 spectators would attend the imminent match at Varsity Stadium.

## Game 21
## 1 August 1985: INEX CANADA 1 EVERTON 1

With the £800,000 striker picking up a knock in the pre-season curtain-raiser at Wigan Athletic, Gary Lineker was not selected for the opening fixture and Adrian Heath resumed his highly productive partnership with Graeme Sharp. Although the visitors controlled the game, they only managed a draw 1-1 in front of a derisory crowd of 7,219.

With Sharp shackled by Trevor McCallum, whose prosaic career included the Toronto Blizzard, Edmonton Brickmen and Kitchener Spirit, Adrian Heath confirmed his recovery from an eight-month absence by converting his only chance. Bob Koep of the *Toronto Star* reported: 'Inex Canada held England's top team to a 1-1 tie at Varsity Stadium. Though the Canadians had several chances to score, goaltender Neville Southall made a series of brilliant saves to allow his team to escape with the draw. Striker Adrian Heath put his side up after 72 minutes when he headed a long cross from Kevin Sheedy past keeper Paul Hammond. Inex hit back and almost had the equaliser when John Paskin appeared to have beaten Southall. Somehow, though, the ball stayed out, bouncing along the goal-line. With Everton watching the clock, Inex kept plugging away. A splendid give-and-go between David Byrne and Paskin found Southall guessing and allowed the latter to knock the ball into the goal from eight yards and jar the fans out of their seats with three minutes left.'

From the sidelines, Peter Reid noted: 'It was a tough game in which Neville was required to make a couple of good saves. They were a tough side and were bombing into tackles. Whereas the boss said that we had to get our running in and not do anything daft. Therefore, it was a good training game – a good physical workout.'

While the details of the line-ups and substitutions were not published, the tournament programme confirmed that the Everton squad included Ian Atkins, John Bailey, Paul Bracewell, Alan Harper, Adrian Heath, Gary Lineker, Bobby Mimms, Derek Mountfield, Kevin Ratcliffe, Peter Reid, Kevin Richardson, Graeme Sharp, Kevin Sheedy, Neville Southall, Trevor Steven, Gary Stevens and Pat van den Hauwe. However, it is known that Reid, Lineker and Stevens were injured and did not feature in the game. Howard Kendall clarified: 'We have 15 healthy players on the tour and everybody will play in the tournament.'

There were mere cursory match reports in the Canadian newspapers. Michael Cosgrove of the *Globe and Mail* noted: 'Manager Kendall didn't really want to use it as an alibi, but the grass at Varsity Stadium was too long for his team's tilt with Inex. The long grass, Kendall said, made it difficult for Everton to string passes together and his team had to settle for a 1-1 tie after seemingly having the game under control on the strength of a pretty goal at 72:20 by Adrian Heath. The 1-0 lead lasted until 86:59, when Inex's South African connection, John

Paskin and David Byrne, combined to beat Neville Southall, who had robbed Inex of four goals in the first-half.'

He quoted the Everton manager as saying: 'If we had a better pitch, I think you would see a better game from us.' The *Globe and Mail* journalist added: 'Despite the long grass, Everton did manage to loft together several long passes around the field. But after Heath's goal most were back to Southall when anything remotely resembling a Canadian attack was about to materialise.' In the post-game interview, Kendall was asked if his defenders made too many back-passes to Southall in order to protect the lead. 'If we did, then it was the right thing to do. He's the best in the business. It was an important game for us. It's pre-season and we have to play Manchester United at Wembley, where I hope the grass will be cut.' Bruce Wilson agreed that the grass was long: 'It was the same for both teams. Sure, I would like to see it cut an inch or so shorter, but if we cut it that short, it would burn and the ground would be very hard.'

Weeks later, in the matchday programme for the First Division fixture against West Brom, Howard Kendall continued to complain: 'The grass was long and the pitch uneven, probably because it is used for many other sports. We couldn't put on a show because the players were concentrating on controlling the ball rather than thinking about what they wanted to do with it.' In contrast, striker Graeme Sharp preferred to celebrate Adrian Heath's impressive comeback. 'I was delighted when "Inchy" scored against Inex. It had taken him eight months of hard work to recover from the career-threatening injury he had picked up against Sheffield Wednesday in December 1984. In Toronto, he showed that he was ready for the new season and that he was prepared to play anywhere for Howard Kendall and Everton. With the void created up front by the departure of Andy Gray filled by the recent arrival of Gary Lineker and the injuries to Peter Reid, who missed most of the season, Inchy was required to play a deeper role in midfield as well as appear as a "super-sub" from the bench.'

'But for the rest of the season, he was reduced to crutches and had to watch the action from the bench. It took him 8-months of hard work to recover from the career-threatening injury, but Inchy regained his fitness for the start of the new season. With the void created by the recent departure of Andy Gray filled by the recent arrival of Gary Lineker and the injuries to Peter Reid, who missed most of the season, he was required to play a deeper role in midfield as well as appear from the bench as a "versatile super-sub". Inchy would play anywhere for Howard Kendall and Everton.'

### Game 22
### 4 August 1985: CANADA 0 EVERTON 1

Having drawn with Inex Canada, who had defeated the Canada national side by 3-0, Everton needed a 4-0 victory to win the tournament outright. Even fewer reports were published in Canada or the United Kingdom for the concluding game of the three-team tournament. Troubled by groin and Achilles problems, Peter Reid was not able to train, never mind play against the Canada national side. Gary Lineker returned to the side and scored when he got on the end of a flick from Graeme Sharp and – in typical Lineker fashion – employed his remarkable acceleration to sprint away from the Canadian defenders before slotting the ball home.

Someone with a unique view of Howard Kendall's team in Toronto was Michael McConnell, their bus driver: 'I'm Irish and my boss at the Transport Commission knew that I was into football, so any time a charter bus was required for a soccer team I would drive it. I had chauffeured the Tampa Bay Rowdies, the Fort Lauderdale Strikers and the Washington Diplomats and met the likes of Johan Cruyff, Gerd Müller and Rodney Marsh. When Everton came to town, I would complete my usual morning rush-hour route and then pick up the team to take them to training at Varsity Stadium. I recall that they were staying in the Bond Place Hotel which was central but not one of the best in the city.

'There was no security at the training sessions – people could wander in and out. I remember sitting behind one of the goals as they practiced free-kicks and Howard Kendall shouted: "Don't be sitting behind them effing goals or you'll get hit by a ball." And sure enough one came whizzing past me. The Everton players were a good bunch. The craic was great – I remember the physio, the spitting image of Tom Selleck, laughing as they slagged him off. I got talking to Neville Southall and Peter Reid and ended up with Kevin Ratcliffe's jersey.

'I got to know John Bailey very well – he was down to earth and very funny. He took my name and promised to arrange for complimentary tickets for the first game against Inex. On the night, I went to collect them – but they had nothing in my name at the ticket office – so I bought some instead. When we were having the post-match drinks, I asked him about the tickets. John said, "Yes, I put them in the name of Bus Driver." I suppose it was logical!'

Inex Canada won the tournament and finished its exhibition season with two wins, three losses, three draws, very few fans and untold thousands of dollars in debt. Though it folded, Edward Cavalier's initiative was fruitful as Canada progressed to Mexico, losing 1-0 to France, 2-0 to Hungary and 2-0 to the USSR. It was the only successful World Cup qualification campaign in the country's history.

Inex captain Bruce Wilson, who had declined a move to Everton in 1975, revealed: 'I was disappointed when the NASL folded in 1984. Inex Canada took over for a very short time. Of course, I remember playing for them against Everton in 1985. Even without Gary Lineker, the Merseysiders were a good team. A top team. The reigning English champions. I did play against Lineker when Canada lost narrowly to England, in preparation for the 1986 World Cup. Looking back at the NASL, Canada's good showing in the 1984 Olympics, going all the way to the quarter-finals, and our first ever appearance at the 1986 World Cup were directly related to the league. It gave Canadians as well as Americans the chance to play at a decent level.'

Everton returned home to prepare for the FA Charity Shield encounter with Manchester United, which they won through goals from Trevor Steven and Adrian Heath, then inexplicably lost their opening League game at Leicester – a team that finished next to the drop zone. The Everton manager did not know at the time that the additional points from a win at Filbert Street would have delivered another League title to Goodison as Everton finished two points behind champions Liverpool. That season, the team played 61 senior games in the First Division, FA Cup, League Cup and the Football League Super Cup (known for sponsorship reasons as the ScreenSport Super Cup) but landed only the Charity Shield. As for Gary Lineker? He went onto on to score 40 goals in 57 senior games for his new team in the 1985/86 season, help Everton finish runners-up to Liverpool in both the league and the FA Cup as well as win the 1986 World Cup Golden Boot. Lineker left to make a name for himself with Barcelona, Tottenham Hotspur, England and the BBC.

The final words on the 1986 tour are reserved for John Bailey who almost didn't enter Canada. He recalled, 'My first and last visit to Toronto didn't start well. A polite and chatty customs and immigration officer didn't want to let me in to his country. It was my own fault. When he asked if I'd ever had a criminal conviction, I confessed to having been nicked for drink driving as a teenager. As a result, I was detained at the border for five hours until the boss charmed the staff into releasing me. Howard didn't make a big deal about the inconvenience or the embarrassment that I had caused. But the lads took the mickey out of me and called me "Jailbird" for the next day or so.

'As usual, I was designated the official social scout for the lads. They sent me out early to recce the neighbourhood near our downtown Toronto hotel and find the best watering holes and restaurants. Well one afternoon, I went for a walk along Yonge Street, which must be one of the longest streets in the world, where I discovered that there were plenty of bars, pubs, taverns and clubs to choose from. Anyway, I found this lap-dancing bar and thought I would give it a try. I remember that the place was very dark inside, as you would imagine, and I was enjoying a beer or two when the lights came up and half of the squad walked in! Well, you can imagine the stick I got off them, sitting in there on my own – I was the only male in the adult entertainment establishment – surrounded by Canada's most beautiful scantily clad women. I tried to explain to the lads that I was only casing the joint so I could report back to them. But they weren't having it!'

# 2.3
# VISITS TO THE USA
# IN 2004, 2006, 2007 AND 2008

With the Olympic soccer tournament at the 1984 Games in Los Angeles smashing all attendance records, the USA bid to host the 1994 World Cup finals. It was an enterprising and successful initiative. FIFA was impressed by the size and potential of the US market and the 1994 tournament exceeded all expectations to become the most financially successful in history. By using state-of-the-art National Football League (NFL) venues in California, Florida, Illinois, Massachusetts, Michigan, New Jersey, Texas and Washington DC, the average attendance was 69,000 per game.

Subsequently, the US Soccer Federation fulfilled its promise to FIFA and supported the foundation of a new professional league in North America. The inaugural Major League Soccer (MLS) season took place in 1996 with 10 teams. Although only the Colorado Rapids, Columbus Crew, DC United, Los Angeles Galaxy and New England Revolution have survived, the league has gone from strength to strength and recently expanded to 26 teams. In addition, soccer-specific stadiums have proliferated and average attendances exceed those of the National Hockey League (NHL) and National Basketball Association (NBA). With a regular season that spans from March to October, it is the seventh most popular soccer league in the world. Oddly, Everton did not play against MLS opposition until they faced the Columbus Crew in mid-2006. But first to Space City USA.

## COPA DE TEJAS 2004

Undeterred by friction in the boardroom, the resignation of chief executive Trevor Birch after just six weeks into the job, and mounting speculation about the sale of the club's crown jewel, 18-year-old Wayne Rooney, Everton travelled to the USA to take part in the Copa de Tejas.

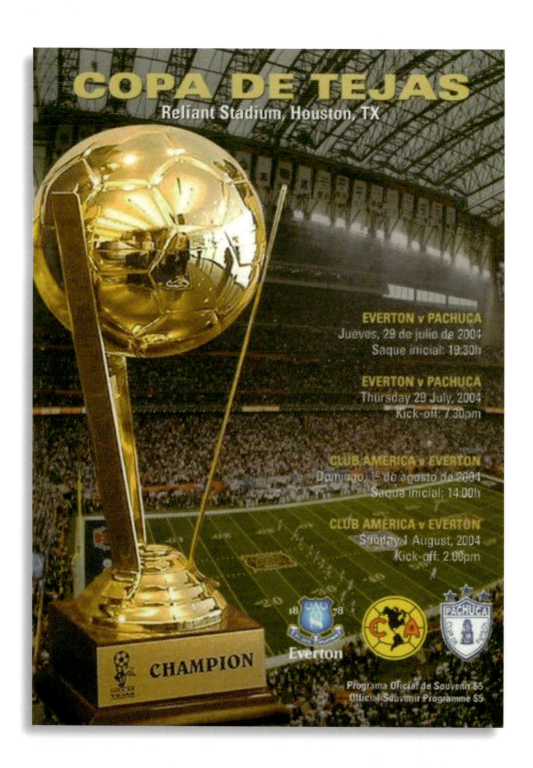

COPA DE TEJAS

Reliant Stadium, Houston, TX

EVERTON v PACHUCA
Jueves, 29 de julio de 2004
Saque inicial: 19:30h

EVERTON v PACHUCA
Thursday 29 July, 2004
Kick-off: 7.30pm

CLUB AMÉRICA v EVERTON
Domingo, 1º de agosto de 2004
Saque inicial: 14:00h

CLUB AMÉRICA v EVERTON
Sunday 1 August, 2004
Kick-off: 2.00pm

Everton

Programa Oficial de Souvenir $5
Official Souvenir Programme $5

CHAMPION

Even though David Moyes had developed a steely resolve among the players at his disposal, his problems were numerical. Wayne Rooney was unavailable, Duncan Ferguson had been denied a USA visa and the previous month had seen the exits of Paul Gerrard, Scot Gemmill, Steve Simonsen, Alex Nyarko, Niclas Alexandersson, David Unsworth, Tomasz Radzinski and Tobias Linderoth. Worse still, after arriving in Texas the threadbare squad was weakened when Steve Watson was admitted into the Houston Medical Center for the removal of an ingrowing toenail.

Both games against the leading Mexican clubs were played under the closed roof at the state-of-the-art Reliant Stadium which had hosted Super Bowl XXXVIII. Opened in 2002, the 72,000-capacity venue had replaced the neighbouring 39-year-old Astrodome. With 37% of the 7 million population of Houston's metropolitan area classified as Hispanic, it was anticipated that the vast majority of the expected 25,000 attendees at the first game would be supporting Pachuca.

## Game 23
### 29 July 2004: PACHUCA 2 EVERTON 5

Respected as Mexico's oldest club, Pachuca had claimed the opening championship of its domestic league in December 2003. By contrast, Everton won only one of their final 10 league games and slumped to 17th place just above the drop-zone at the end of the 2003/04 season. But in the club's first ever game against Mexican opposition, David Moyes and his men forgot about their off-the-field worries and thumped Pachuca by 5-2.

James McFadden, positioned behind centre-forward Kevin Campbell, was the man-of-the-match. That evening, the 21-year-old Scotsman excelled at roaming across the frontline, losing his markers and utilising his skills to infiltrate the box. Everton got off to a flying start when he beat Colombian keeper Miguel Rodriguez from an acute angle in the third minute. Another of McFadden's scintillating runs from the halfway line led to the second when, after charging past two defenders into the penalty area, his blocked shot bounced to Leon Osman whose goal-bound effort was handled by right-back Jesus Angulo. Thomas Gravesen scored from the penalty spot.

The fact that Pachuca had levelled the scores by half-time had more to do with slack English defending than slick Mexican football. Alan Stubbs was caught out both times. In the 23rd minute, he was dispossessed inside his own area by Sergio Piedra who crossed for Juan Cacho to score. Then 20 minutes later, Octavio Martinez nutmegged him before scoring. McFadden's flair peaked after the break. Every time he received the ball it seemed like something exciting would happen. Everton's third goal came in the 57th minute when Campbell headed home an in-swinging cross from Gravesen. Next, Kevin Kilbane headed another from a corner and substitute Nick Chadwick made it 5-2 with six minutes to go.

**Everton:** *Martyn; Hibbert (Clarke 46), Stubbs, Yobo, Naysmith (Bent 70); Osman, Gravesen, Carsley, Kilbane; McFadden, Campbell (Chadwick 79).*

One down, one to play. The decisive score-line meant that Everton needed only to avoid defeat to win the competition. Conscious that their Mexico City-based opponents were one of the most successful and most popular clubs in the country, the Merseysiders expected a boisterous encounter.

## Game 24
## 2 August 2004: CLUB AMERICA 3 EVERTON 1

On the pitch, the sparseness of Everton's touring squad was highlighted by the line-up. With Joseph Yobo, Tony Hibbert and Alessandro Pistone sidelined by minor knocks, David Moyes could name only three outfield substitutes. With the afternoon temperatures exceeding 100F, the Reliant Stadium's retractable roof was again closed as a depleted Everton side succumbed to the wizardry of Club America.

In front of a crowd of 16,434, way below the number anticipated, Everton made a bright start and should have gone ahead after two minutes when Steve Watson's low cross was jabbed over the bar by Marcus Bent from close range. Equally good chances went begging when Bent laid the ball on a plate for Gary Naysmith who miskicked from six yards and then James McFadden scuffed his shot wide. The squandered opportunities proved costly. Club America went ahead in the 19th minute with a goal that owed more to poor defending than attacking skill. A slip by full-back Peter Clarke inside his own area led to Reinaldo Navio beating Alan Stubbs to the loose ball and Francisco Torres firing past goalkeeper Richard Wright. More poor finishing prevented Everton from drawing level six minutes before the break when a low cross found Bent unmarked, but the striker attempted a side-footed shot which almost went out for a throw-in.

The Mexicans showed Bent how it should be done with a well-taken goal in the 56th minute. A neat back-heel by Reinaldo Navia, the Chilean striker, allowed Pavel Pardo to break from midfield and, with the Everton defenders retreating, hit a fierce drive past flat-footed Wright from 25 yards. To their credit, Everton continued to toil and Bent was rewarded two minutes from time when he headed in a Nick Chadwick cross at the far post. But with too many players fatigued from playing two games in three days, there was still time for Club America to score again. Pavel Pardo burst clear, beat the offside-trap and teed up Rodrigo Valenzuela to tap in.

**Everton:** *Wright; Clarke (Chadwick 63), Weir, Stubbs, Naysmith; Watson, Carsley, Osman, Kilbane (Campbell 63); Bent, McFadden.*

In her adopted hometown, Elizabeth France remembers her post-game radio interview with Glenn Davies, the soccer columnist for the *Houston Chronicle* newspaper: 'Realising that I was upset that we had been outplayed by Club America, he went off topic and asked me about the size of crowd. Glenn speculated that the 2,000 or possibly 3,000 Evertonians, many from Merseyside, had out-shouted the Mexicans.' The radio host enquired, "Tell me Elizabeth, is it 2,000 or 3,000?" I responded, "Don't know but we bought a pint for every one of the thirsty buggers last night." He looked shocked and cautioned me, "Mrs France, may I remind you that we are live and salty language is not condoned by KAYD-FM radio." While I wasn't black-listed, I did notice that my microphone was turned off for the Sunday afternoon game against Club America.'

Prior to the 2004 tour, the manager had been an uncompromising taskmaster, mercilessly drilling players to get them in peak physical condition. Many insiders trace the catalyst for the incredible 2004/05 season to Houston. These include David Moyes: 'Houston was terrific, it was a great trip and was the start of many pre-season visits to North America. I've always enjoyed looking around the American football facilities. They are state-of-the-art and make ours look poor in comparison. In Houston, we trained at the Houston Texans facility in the morning and the evening. We were amazed at how good it was. There were cold water sprays at the side of the pitch and also ice baths were available to counter the heat and humidity.

'Away from the training ground, we allowed the players to eat at restaurants outside of the hotel and have some free time. They weren't under as much scrutiny as they would have been back in England. We wanted the players to bond. But when it came to the training, they would work hard – that's the way it was. In subsequent years, we enjoyed some great nights. We would find the best steak restaurant in town, enjoy a few glasses of wine and have a good old singsong. Joseph Yobo would act as MC and everybody had to do a turn. Kitman Jimmy Martin would help the lads out who were in trouble! I also wanted Everton to establish a big following in North America and taking the team over there on six occasions was part of that plan.'

Leon Osman, who had just broken into the first team, confirmed that the Texas tournament set the tone for the 2004/05 season by uniting the squad. 'I remember that I was up at stupid o'clock in the morning for the flight across the Atlantic and that no alcohol was allowed on the plane. The gaffer could be strict and often everything was uptight – no ale and no nights-out. He liked to control what we did … but that was about to change! We landed in Houston at about 4.00pm local time after what had already been a long day. When we arrived at the Western Galleria Hotel, he gathered us together and said, "I know you're tired, but you need to stay up as late as you can. Get yourselves out, have a few drinks and relax. I'll see you tomorrow for breakfast." It was totally out of the blue and someone said: "Let's go before he changes his mind!"

'The hotel was attached to a giant shopping mall that had everything – cinemas, ice-cream parlours, luxury shops, coffee bars, a bowling alley and a Cheesecake Factory restaurant. We were never bored. Like any club, the lads went out in groups and me, Nick Chadwick, Kevin Kilbane, David Weir, James McFadden, Gary Naysmith and Steve Watson went to a sports bar. After last orders, we decided to go onto the ice rink which seemed a good idea at the time. Kevin Kilbane took one step before he flew into the air and landed on his elbow, cutting it quite badly. I thought about that incident when I saw him on the Dancing on Ice television show. He did very well, so his skating skills have come a long way!

'We were still learning about David Moyes. He was so relaxed on that trip and that filtered through to the lads. He pitched it just right. Vividly, I remember one night-out when all of the new players and staff had to stand on a bar stool and belt out a song in front of everyone else. It can be very, very nerve wracking and I've seen some dreadful performances over the years. The lads love to see terror in the eyes of the new singers and are more than a bit annoyed if anyone is quite good! But once we began training it was tough and physically demanding. Faced with six or seven days of intense workouts and two good games, we got our heads down and worked really hard. We all appreciated the freedom that we had been granted and the way we had been treated – and had no intentions of letting down the gaffer. Without question, the seeds of a special season were sown in Houston.'

Kevin Kilbane, the Republic of Ireland stalwart, concurred: 'Moyesy was brilliant in Houston. He appreciated that we needed some fun and gave us a couple of nights out. This bit of freedom helped us bond. Most of the lads still remember it as their best-ever pre-season tour. We came together and respected the manager for his attitude – quite rightly he always expected the maximum from us. We had a great group of characters. One night we went out for a meal and I got roped into singing "Ice, Ice Baby" by rapper Vanilla Ice.'

Back to Elizabeth France who organised a couple of get-togethers for Everton fans: 'We had lived in Houston for 15 years. During that time, my husband kept his season-ticket and would attend many home games. Then a few years after we had relocated to British Columbia, Everton returned the compliment. Better late than never. With the help of Alan Robinson, a young ex-pat living in Houston, the first was a boozy reunion with the fans visiting from the United Kingdom. It was held a downtown sports bar called the Home Plate Bar & Grill located in the shadows of the recently opened Enron Field.

'In the wake of the recent failure of the Kings Dock Stadium proposal, the visiting Blues were impressed by the retractable-roofed stadium, the magnificent entrance which incorporated Houston's abandoned Union Station and the steam train that moved along 300-yards of track when the Astros hit a homer. They were amazed by the Texan can-do attitude and that the stadium had been funded by local taxes levied on rental cars, parking and hotel use. Also, Enron had contributed $100 million, in a 30-year naming rights deal that turned sour.

'I recall that Ian Macdonald, Barry Murray and Paul Wharton of the Independent Blues introduced me to some of their pals. One from Kirkdale had a habit of telling his wife that he was popping to the corner-shop to buy the *Echo* when, in actual fact, he was slinking off to watch Everton – this time, some 5,000 miles from Liverpool. A couple of nights later we hosted a dinner for about 20 fans visiting from the far corners of North America. The Tex-Mex feast was held at the original Ninfa's restaurant on Navigation Boulevard. The fans had travelled from all over the country, many to attend their first Everton match. One guest worked on Wall Street and claimed to have driven the 1,600 miles from New York City to Houston. The other guests treated his tale with some scepticism until they piled outside and watched him side-step a half-dozen excited barrio kids yelling "Cuidar de su coche señor?" and squeeze into a yellow Ferrari Spider convertible boasting an Empire State license plate.'

Although there was no silverware to polish, the manager and his players had been able to build the fitness and sharpness required for the new Premier League season. Back on Merseyside, they focused on the new campaign. The only major additions were Marcus Bent and two Australians, Tim Cahill and Eddie Bosnar. No matter the lack of depth in the first team squad, Everton finished fourth in the Premier League and qualified for Champions League. Best of all, the Blues finished above the Reds in the table. They would not repeat that goal until the 2011/12 and 2012/13 seasons.

Short of fire-power, Everton scored only 45 league goals that season, with 11 from Cahill, six from Osman and Bent, and five from Duncan Ferguson during his six starts and 29 substitute appearances. Many fans were left to speculate what David Moyes' men might have achieved with Wayne Rooney in the side?

## PRE-SEASON TOUR 2006

Two years on, following the path of Everton Ladies who had embarked on a four-game pre-season tour of Canada, David Moyes and his 22-man squad flew to North America to participate in the World Series of Soccer. The tournament was hosted by Major League Soccer to provide its leading clubs with opportunities to compete against top-class international teams. In 2006, the overseas clubs were Club América, Necaxa and Tigres from Mexico, Real Madrid and Barcelona from Spain, Celtic from Scotland plus Everton, who were selected to play against the Columbus Crew.

Having invested in the transfer market, the new men at his disposal included Andrew Johnson, a recent £8.6 million signing from Crystal Palace, Joleon Lescott – a £5 million snip from Wolverhampton Wanderers, South Africa international Delron Buckley – an experienced trialist from Borussia Dortmund and Tim Howard – a season-long loanee from Manchester United. Interviewed by the *Liverpool Echo*, the USA star observed, 'With the signings that the club has brought in and the passion of the fans, we can all hope for good things. I didn't come here under any illusions. There are some really good players and you have got to earn your place.'

Exasperated by unsatisfactory displays against Bury, Preston and Celtic, manager David Moyes demanded an improved performance in Ohio. Peculiarly, his press conference for the friendly against the Columbus Crew was held at the Buffalo Wild Wings Grill. Dominic King of the *Liverpool Echo* reported, 'Safe to say David Moyes will never conduct another briefing within earshot of customers sharing ultimate nachos, hot and tender strips and huge beakers containing ice and soft drinks.'

Well aware that the club's most successful campaign for many years had been achieved after a similar pre-season trip to the USA in 2004, manager Moyes told the gathering at the fast-food restaurant, 'I do not think we will be able to recreate what happened in Houston, where the NFL training facilities were absolutely jaw-dropping, but we are hoping this trip will provide similar results in the long term.'

## Game 25
## 26 July 2006: COLUMBUS CREW 1 EVERTON 1

Everton drew against Columbus Crew in front of 10,259 fans at the Mapfre Stadium. It was another below par performance. Their hosts, inspired by legendary coach Sigi Schmid and his assistant Robert Warzycha, a former Everton player, and buoyed by a fitness advantage from being almost two-thirds through the MLS season, opened at a terrific pace. Therefore, it was no surprise when Sebastian Rozental jinked past Phil Neville and unleashed a powerful effort past Richard Wright in the 13th minute. What was astonishing, however, was the goalkeeper's woeful attempt to stop the shot. Inexplicably for an England international, the ball beat him even though he got both hands to it.

Slowly the tourists grabbed a foothold back in the game and parity was restored within 20 minutes when Kevin Kilbane broke up a Columbus attack to set Delron Buckley free. In turn, the trialist fed Victor Anichebe who crashed a right-footed shot past goalkeeper Bill Gaudette. The 18-year-old striker could have doubled Everton's tally when Leon Osman sent him scampering into an identical position, but this time his drive shaved the woodwork. With wholesale substitutions ruining the flow of the action, the game petered out in the second-half. As Everton tired in the closing 15 minutes, the hosts enjoyed plenty of possession, but substitute goalkeeper Tin Howard never came under threat.

**Everton:** *Wright (Howard 46); Hibbert (Naysmith 86), Lescott, Stubbs (Weir 46), Boyle (Pistone 46); Osman (Arteta 46), Neville, Cahill (Davies 71), Kilbane; Buckley, Anichebe (Beattie 46).*

Next up, Club America who had defeated the Merseysiders in 2004. After Everton had arrived in Dallas, Dominic King reported in the *Liverpool Echo*, 'They don't know how to do anything here other than big. This notion was emphasised last night to Everton's touring party as they clapped eyes on the magnificently monikered Pizza Hut Park. The stadium is not huge in Premiership terms but the vast space surrounding the venue put things into perspective. There are 16 football pitches backing onto the stadium, a gigantic shopping complex and a racetrack nearby.'

On the strength of Mexico's solid performances in the 2006 World Cup, Club America were expected to provide a stern test. Having lost the previous clash by 3-1, Everton sought revenge. Of course, any talk of American tours leads to the Houston question. Why was that 2004 trip – which sparked the club's best league season in 17 years – so beneficial? Defender Joseph Yobo reflected, 'Touring America two years ago helped us a lot. We relaxed and bonded. And because the weather was so harsh, it helped us pick up levels of fitness quickly. We want that again. We would love a repeat of what followed.'

Since arriving in the Lonestar State, the players had been doing double training sessions in the 100F heat an equally challenging humidity and, by and large, were well-prepared for their tussle with the reigning Mexican champions. Irrespective of the scorelines, the tour had succeeded in improving fitness and conditioning.

## Game 26
## 29 July 2006: CLUB AMERICA 1 EVERTON 1

The difference between the way David Moyes' team passed and moved in the sweltering conditions at Pizza Hut Park to their laboured efforts three days earlier was staggering. The display against Club America hinted that the new Premier League campaign would be a fruitful one. Strengthened by the return of Joseph Yobo, James McFadden and Andrew Johnson, Everton lined-up with Lee Carsley sitting in front of the back four. This allowed Mikel Arteta, Simon Davies and Tim Cahill to shine in midfield.

The raucous Hispanic majority in the 18,239-crowd brought out the best in Everton, who took the lead in the fifth minute courtesy of a Mikel Arteta free-kick. That advantage was held until the dying seconds of the match when referee Jair Marufo amazingly tacked on three minutes which allowed Nelson Cuevas the chance to burst forward and drill his shot past substitute Richard Wright from 25 yards. While James McFadden and Andrew Johnson were impressive during the time they were paired together, James Beattie's contributions gave cause for no little concern.

In the eyes of many observers, only erratic officiating by Hilario Grajeda prevented a deserved victory for Everton. Regardless, the game was decided by penalties. Though James Beattie, Mikel Arteta, Alessandro Pistone and Kevin Kilbane all scored from 12 yards, Alan Stubbs' effort clipped the bar. With a 100% record from their first four kicks, Club America edged the verdict by 5-4 when Salvador Cabanas sent keeper Richard Wright the wrong way.

**Everton:** *Howard (Wright 46); Neville, Lescott, Yobo, Naysmith (Pistone 46); Cahill (Kilbane 46), Davies (Stubbs 85), Carsley (Weir 85), Arteta; Johnson (Beattie 46), McFadden (Buckley 46).*

Unbeaten during their brief North American tour, Everton started the 2006/07 Premier League season with a run of four wins and four draws in league and cup games, including a 3-0 success in the Goodison derby. David Moyes' side went onto finish in sixth place with 58 points. Even after the club's huge outlays on strikers, its progress had been impacted by a dearth of goals. Andrew Johnson and James Beattie had failed to form a lethal alliance. The bald one scored 12 goals in his 35 league and cup appearance. Whereas his partner contributed only two goals in his 35 games, 19 of which were as substitute.

Victor Anichebe had burst onto the scene with a debut goal at the end of the 2005/06 campaign – a strike that was overshadowed by the last goal of Duncan Ferguson's career in the same game. It served to alert David Moyes to the 18-year old's potential. The powerful young forward recalled: 'James Vaughan and I were so young at the time that we weren't allowed to go out and socialise with the rest of the lads because we were under-age. They were like our dads! They always made sure we were alright and had stuff to do. I was fortunate that had a few friends in some of the cities we visited so I could meet up with them. I had got to know some of the American players when I played against them in the 2008 Olympics. But it was a lot of fun and a great experience for us both. And, of course, we played against some

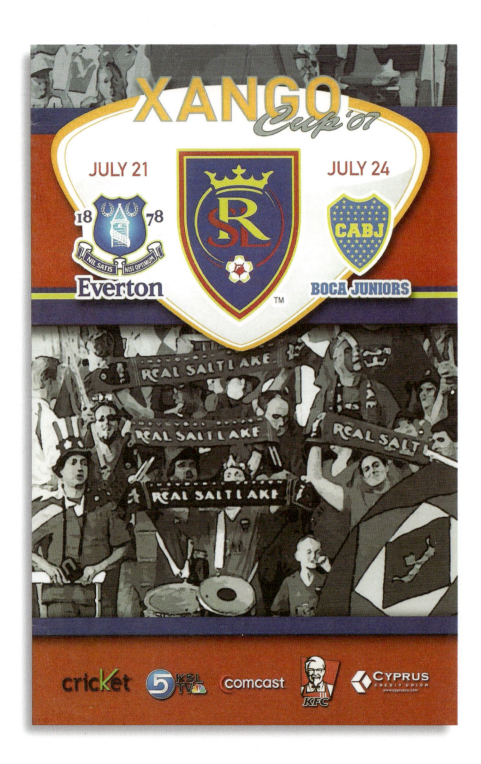

really good American teams. I could tell back then that the MLS was only going to get better and stronger because the teams were so good and so fit.'

**THE XANGA CUP 2007**

With the club embroiled in yet another fierce debate about a new ground move – this time to Kirkby, the Everton squad revisited North America to enhance its pre-season training. Oddly, the Merseysiders played only game during the tour – against Real Salt Lake at the Rice-Eccles Stadium in Salt Lake City. David Checketts, the hosts' owner, claimed proudly, 'Last summer we delivered the world's most recognised team to Utah with Real Madrid. Now in 2007, we combine the heritage of Pioneer Day Weekend with the growing tradition of our own, as we are elated to host one of the world's elite teams in Everton and South America's biggest and brightest star in Boca Juniors.' At 4,600ft above sea level, the 46,000-seater stadium, located on the campus of the University of Utah, was used to razzmatazz, having held the opening and closing ceremonies at the 2002 Winter Olympic Games.

**Game 27**
**21 July 2007: REAL SALT LAKE 2 EVERTON 0**

Pyrotechnics, national anthems and a guard of honour signalled the launch of the Xango Cup competition. Embarrassingly, Everton were lethargic, sloppy in possession and run ragged by their hosts. In front of only 12,221 fans, which barely filled a quarter of the seats, they made their hosts look like Real Madrid rather than Real Salt Lake. From the first minute, the Utah side – who were struggling at the foot of the MLS rankings with one win from 15 fixtures – attacked with purpose and pace. Thankfully, Tim Howard was in top form and made several excellent stops to keep the final score-line respectable.

His performance was out of the top draw. An acrobatic save from Chris Wingert set the tone. The USA ace followed it up by tipping over a crashing shot from Andy Williams. Even so, he flapped at Alecko Eskandarian's centre and Carey Talley powered his header into the net in the 28th minute. The goalkeeper was unable to stop the second when a mistake by Phil Neville allowed Andy Williams to wriggle free and play in Robbie Findley, who raced clear of a static defence to round Howard.

The Merseysiders' cutting edge was blunt. The closest Everton came to scoring was when James Beattie shot straight at keeper Nick Rimando from six yards. Possibly, the way in which their advances were snuffed out provided more long-term worries than the lapses that let in the two goals. Though Mikel Arteta prodded and probed, the Everton midfield struggled for control and Tim Howard had to be at his best to prevent Alecko Eskandarian from making it three when he was one-on-one with the keeper. Only another great reflex stop saved the embarrassment from deepening.

**Everton:** *Howard; Jagielka, Stubbs (Lescott 58), Yobo, Valente (Hibbert 58); Arteta (Anichebe 58), Carsley (Da Silva 58), Neville, Osman; Johnson (Arteta 75), Beattie.*

Because Everton only had four substitutes to call on, David Moyes was grateful that the tournament allowed the use of rolling substitutions. Therefore, he re-introduced Mikel Arteta some 17 minutes after he had made way for Victor Anichebe. After the match, the manager told the *Liverpool Echo*: 'We've got to give Salt Lake credit. It was a good competitive game, a tough game and it challenged us. There are lessons to be learned.' As for the outcome of the Xanga Cup? In the other tie, Real Salt Lake earned a 1-1 draw against Boca Juniors of Argentina and lifted the trophy. The deciding goal was scored by Freddie Adu from the penalty spot.

Cursing their bad luck, Everton flew out to California for the remainder of the tour. Scott McLeod, then a journalist with the *Liverpool Echo,* recalled: 'Over the years, I've been on numerous trips to the USA. During that time, North America's interest and the US media's knowledge of soccer and Everton Football Club had grown exponentially. Back in 2004, it was a case of educating my fellow journalists about the club's history and its big names. Whereas in 2007, the local reporters were well equipped and keen to discuss some of the subtleties of the game.

'There is no doubt that David Beckham had elevated the game's profile stateside. Celebrated as much as a superstar off the pitch than on it during his time with the Los Angeles Galaxy, I remember Phil Neville bumping into his old Manchester United teammate at the Home Depot Center, now known as the Dignity Health Sports Park. I can close my eyes and see members of the Everton squad, including the likes of Mikel Arteta and Nuno Valente, forming an orderly queue to have their photographs taken with him. Only 12 months earlier, the Portugal left-back had marked Beckham out of the game during the 2006 World Cup quarter-final against England in Stuttgart. It was the clash during which Wayne Rooney was sent off and England lost on penalties after Frank Lampard, Steven Gerrard and Jamie Carragher failed to convert their spot-kicks.'

The 2007 tour was organised by Graham Smith, a lifelong Evertonian based in California: 'It was a privilege for my company First Wave Sports International to be involved with Everton. Our first venture had been the 2004 Copa de Tejas tournament in Houston. David Moyes was so delighted with the arrangements that he asked me to schedule five others. But from a personal perspective, the highlight in 2007 was the friendly game arranged against Ventura County Fusion, the local team I was coaching at the time. Predictably, my young players were thrilled to be on the same pitch as so many Premier League stars who, by the way, treated them with tremendous respect before, during and after the match. Collectively, the visiting players were a credit to David Moyes, Alan Irvine, and Everton Football Club. As for the result, Everton won with James Beattie pinching two or perhaps three goals.'

Joleon Lescott, who arrived from Wolverhampton Wanderers in 2006, made his initial impact as a left-back. He did so well that Moyes wanted him to stay there. Indeed, a conversation took place in Los Angeles that could well have changed the course of Everton history: 'I had aspirations of playing for England, but knew that I wouldn't replace Ashley Cole, one of the greatest left-backs of all time. England had some good central-defenders, but I was more confident that I would break through as a centre-half. My first year at Everton had gone well but in mid-June 2007 I called David Moyes and asked where he planned to play me the following season. The boss said that he appreciated the call as it showed I was focused and assured me it would be at centre-half. That was all I wanted to hear.

'During our pre-season in Los Angeles, we played against a local team at the training ground. I think we were losing at half-time when I came off the bench to replace Nuno Valente at left-back. Within 15 minutes I had set up two goals and hit the bar! As we were heading back to our own half after the second goal, Lee Carsley joked: "You know you'll be playing left-back this season now, don't you?" I laughed with him but after the game, on the way to the team coach, the gaffer told me he had a "situation". We all knew the club was linked with Leighton Baines. He said: "If you tell me you want to play left-back, I won't sign him." I just replied: "Sign him because I don't want to play there."'

Leon Osman retains fond memories of the tour: 'Off the pitch, one of the highlights was the initiation ceremony. As in Houston, every new player had to perform a song in front of his teammates and coaching staff. It was great fun. I'll never forget Phil Jagielka's initiation. Captain Phil Neville, who was rooming with him, told us that Jags was really nervous about having to sing in front of the lads. He had been tossing and turning at night thinking about the ordeal. I volunteered to help him – in a mischievous kind of way. One afternoon, as we were reviewing his short-list of favourites, I mentioned the rules – the singer had to stand in the centre – no hiding, sing at full volume – no mumbling, and everyone had to sing a different song. He nodded and picked "Walking in Memphis" by the American folk rock singer-songwriter Marc Cohn. We spent several hours learning the words and finding the right key. He sang it to me a couple of times but must have sung it over and over in his head a hundred times. I assured him: "Don't worry, Jags, you'll be fine. Good or bad, everyone will join in."

'Anyway, the following night at a local bar, the singing started after a couple of drinks. I can't recall who was up first, but he did a really good job. Motivated by the resulting round of applause, I jumped to my feet and sang Jags' song. I couldn't help myself. Everyone sang along except the central-defender who looked mortified. No doubt with references to blue suede shoes, Delta Blues and Graceland still rolling around in his head, he grappled to find a replacement. But credit to him, Jags came up with one and even added some very nifty dance moves which earned him even more respect from his teammates. Since then, I've never been able to listen to Peter Andre's "Mysterious Girl" – without thinking about that night in Houston. All together now … "Oh, oh, oh, oh, oh, oh … Mysterious girl … I wanna get close to you …"'

Having already enlisted Jagielka from Sheffield United in the summer to partner Joleon Lescott, the canny manager prepared for the new season by adding some truly top-class reinforcements including Leighton Baines for £5.6 million from Wigan to partner Tony Hibbert, Yakubu Aiyegbeni for £11.3 million from Middlesbrough, plus Steven Pienaar on loan from Borussia Dortmund, and Thomas Gravesen on loan from Celtic.

Everton began what would turn out to be an eventful season strongly and even headed the table early on. Yet by the time of the Goodison derby in October, David Moyes' men had slipped into mid-table. Predictably, Liverpool triumphed 2-1 with both goals scored by Dirk Kuyt from the spot-kicks – the winner being in injury-time. The Dutchman's contributions were overshadowed by his appalling two-footed kung fu-style lunge at Phil Neville which earned only a yellow card from referee Mark Clattenburg.

Thereafter, the team recovered to spend much of new the season in fourth place until its form faded during the run-in and finished in fifth in the table, with 65 points – more than they had accumulated in the 2004/05 season when they had finished fourth and qualified for the Champions League. Also, the club reached the semi-finals of the League Cup losing to Chelsea and the round of 16 of the UEFA Cup, being eliminated by Fiorentina on penalties after a dramatic fightback.

## PRE-SEASON TOUR 2008

With no new signings, no chief executive after the resignation of Keith Wyness, and little support among the fanbase for the Destination Kirkby project, David Moyes' team sought to escape the mayhem engulfing Goodison. Some claimed that superstition influenced his preferences for pre-season training. And nothing, in his eyes, could beat North America.

Phil Neville told the *Liverpool Echo* that he expected the squad to return in tremendous shape after their nine-day adventure to North America. He reminded the local newspaper, 'The tours to the USA and Canada in the last couple of years have been the key to the success we have enjoyed. We train in top-class facilities and play on perfect pitches against good opposition. Another important aspect, of course, is the team bonding.'

Aware that such trips pull everyone together, the *Liverpool Echo's* Dominic King rested his knife and fork to describe the squad's break in training at the Cheesecake Factory. 'With steaks as thick as telephone directories, pizzas the sise of dustbin lids and signature desserts – there are 30 different types of cheesecake, it should not come as a surprise to learn that the Everton players unanimously decided to hold their pre-season meal in the Chicago branch this week.' He quoted Tim Howard, the popular USA custodian, 'These nights build the camaraderie that catapults you through a season and gets you through the difficult times. Also, the food is simply unbelievable!'

With full-backs Nuno Valente and Tony Hibbert as well as winger Andy van der Meyde absent through injuries and striker Victor Anichebe on Olympic duty for Nigeria, the paper-thin squad included youngsters Jack Rodwell, Jose Baxter, Lucas Jutkiewicz and Dan Gosling. It trained at the University of Illinois complex where intensive double sessions were mandated by the coaching staff in preparation for their clash with the Chicago Fire, a 1998 expansion team lying third in the Eastern Conference of Major League Soccer. Again, the manager could name only four outfield substitutes. Two of them – Leon Osman and Joseph Yobo had not trained for weeks.

## Game 28
## 31 July 2008: CHICAGO FIRE 2 EVERTON 0

Before a crowd of 9,512 at Toyota Park, Everton laboured against their match-fit opponents. If Phil Jagielka set the tone for a poor team performance by heading against his own post in the first minute, then substitute James Vaughan finished the job in the last minute when he was sent off for a reckless tackle on Daniel Woolard.

Even with Steven Pienaar and Jack Rodwell controlling midfield, goalscoring chances were few and far between in the feisty opening period and there was a nagging suspicion that the home side would score on the break. And so it proved when Gonzalo Segares, Justin Mapp and Patrick Nyarko, a cousin of Everton old boy Alex Nyarko, worked a clever opening down the left which allowed for the incoming Chris Rolfe to net in the 42nd minute. In response, the Everton players got rather tetchy especially after a string of questionable decisions against them by the referee.

It was all change for the Chicago Fire after half-time, with every single one of their players being replaced. Against the now diluted opposition, the closest the Merseysiders came to equalising was when Ayegbeni Yakubu had a snapshot tipped wide on the hour. Then in the 70th minute, the Chicago side burst forward in numbers. Peter Lowry's shot was parried by goalkeeper Tim Howard into the path of Tomasz Frankowski who scored unopposed. Joleon Lescott nearly grabbed a consolation goal but his effort was plucked off the line by substitute goalkeeper Nick Noble. Worse was to follow. In the final minutes, two Everton fans were ejected from the pitch after staging an invasion and James Vaughan was dismissed for a rash challenge.

**Everton:** *Howard; Neville, Jagielka, Lescott, Baines; Arteta (Vaughan 63), Rodwell, Gosling, Pienaar (Yobo 84); Yakubu (Jutkiewicz 79), Baxter (Osman 46).*

Following the club's third defeat in five pre-season games, a worried David Moyes noted, 'We are a long way away from where we thought we were going to be. We have to get five or six players in before the season starts.'

Next up were the Colorado Rapids at Dick's Sporting Goods Park, located in Commerce City about 12 miles northeast of downtown Denver. As Everton prepared for their first training sessions at altitude, it was no secret that the Merseyside club did not have enough senior players and its efforts in the transfer markets would have to go into overdrive to strengthen the squad.

Predictably, manager David Moyes had a few irons in the fire and was hopeful that they would come to fruition in time for the opening Premier League fixture against Blackburn Rovers. But with his immediate options limited, the manager made one change to the team beaten in Chicago. Leon Osman started at the expense of Jose Baxter with Ayegbeni Yakubu operating as the lone striker.

## Game 29
## 4 August 2008: COLORADO RAPIDS 1 EVERTON 2

The Merseysiders, undoubtedly smarting from the rocket they received from their manager in the wake of their embarrassment in Illinois, were much livelier and dominated the opening 15 minutes of the game. As an evening breeze took the edge off the baking Denver heat and made conditions more bearable, Mikel Arteta gave the visitors the lead when he struck a 20-yarder past goalkeeper Preston Burpo.

Though his goal provided an injection of confidence, Everton did not have things all their own way and Tim Howard provided a timely reminder of his talents to maintain his team's slim advantage. Former-Manchester United winger Terry Cooke – the forgotten graduate of Old Trafford's famed Class of '92 – clipped in a cross for Conor Casey only for Howard to fling himself horizontally and paw the ball around the post.

Within four minutes of the re-start, the hosts secured parity when the lively Cooke swung in another great ball. This time, Yobo slipped and Casey made no mistake from 10 yards. As the hosts pushed forward Howard needed to be at his best to thwart substitute Herculez Gomez in the 59th minute. Indeed, the goalkeeper made a clutch of fine saves as the Colorado Rapids pressed for a winner during the second-half. Facundo Erpen headed a Cooke corner just wide and Howard denied Cooke with another fine save.

Three minutes from time, Osman surged forward to pick out Jose Baxter, who repaid the compliment and allowed the midfielder to make amends for his team's failure in Chicago and gain a morale-boosting 2-1 triumph.

**Everton:** *Howard; Neville, Jagielka, Lescott, Baines (Valente 46); Pienaar, Gosling (Jutkiewicz 64), Rodwell (Yobo 46), Arteta (Baxter 77); Yakubu, Osman.*

As for the five or six players required by David Moyes for the 2008/09 campaign, Marouane Fellaini, a 20-year-old Belgium international midfielder, was signed from Standard Liege for £15 million – a club record fee, Steven Pienaar's loan deal from Borussia Dortmund was made permanent for £2 million and Louis Saha was recruited from Manchester United for an undisclosed fee. In addition, Lars Jacobsen and Carlo Nash were recruited as free agents and Segundo Castillo arrived on loan.

Then in early-2009, Everton signed Jô on loan from Manchester City and Seamus Coleman, a 21-year-old right-back, from Sligo Rovers for a bargain transfer fee of £60,000. The latter was royal blue larceny.

With the new men requiring time to settle in, the opening of the 2008/09 season mirrored the discouraging pre-season. Everton won only two (both on the road) and drew four of its opening 12 fixtures. These results included a defeat in the Goodison derby and elimination from the League Cup by Blackburn and the UEFA Cup by Standard Liege.

Undaunted by injuries to Yakubu, results improved and the team recovered to finish in fifth place in the Premier League with 63 points. Also, it came close to lifting a meaningful trophy. After defeating Manchester United in the FA Cup semi-final at the new Wembley Stadium, thanks to saves by Tim Howard in a breathtaking penalty shoot-out, they lost the final to Chelsea by 2-1 – despite taking the lead through a Louis Saha goal after 25 seconds.

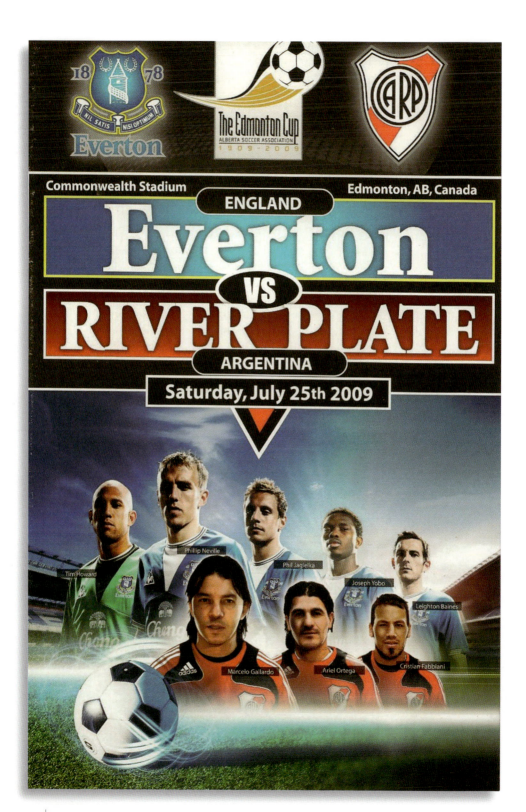

# 2.4

# VISITS TO CANADA AND THE USA
# IN 2009, 2011 AND 2013

David Moyes was so impressed by the advanced training facilities and resulting physical conditioning of his squad, the bonding experiences and the quality of the pre-season opponents during Everton's visit to Texas in 2004, that he returned to North America again and again.

In early 2009, the club reciprocated by inviting the Columbus Crew – the recent winners of the 2008 MLS Cup – to kick off their pre-season training at Finch Farm. Coached by Everton old boy Robert Warcycha, the American visitors played a behind-closed-doors game against Everton Reserves. Understandably match details are unclear, but it is known that the home side was coached by Andy Holden and featured youngsters like Hope Akpan, Kieran Agard and Jose Baxter. Holden recalled: 'It was a decent run-out for us. Columbus were a good side with a few internationals in their ranks, including Frankie Hejduk who had 85 or so USA caps. We won 1-0. But what I remember most about the day is the conversation David Moyes and I had with Robert Warzycha over a cup of tea. It was clear to us that he had a lot of affection for the club.'

Some North American fans argue that the Merseyside club's only success during the Moyes era was capturing the prestigious MLS All-Star fixture, albeit on penalties in 2009. Indeed, Everton were the first overseas club to win the trophy.

## PRE-SEASON TOUR 2009

Just seven weeks after Everton had lost to Chelsea in the FA Cup final, the team arrived at their pre-season camp in Seattle. In preparation for matches with River Plate in Alberta and the MLS All-Stars in Utah, David Moyes pushed his men through his brutal pre-season regimes to the limit of their physical capabilities. Jimmy Gabriel attended the first training session. The former Goodison favourite, who had been Colin Harvey's assistant and also served two spells as caretaker-manager, divulged, 'I found out a few months ago that the lads were coming here, and I've been counting down the days since. The club is in your blood – that's what happens when you play for Everton.'

Throughout their stop-over, the manager urged his charges to savour the contest against the 33 times champions of Argentina. He said, 'River Plate are a world name in football. The boys need to keep testing themselves against all manner of sides.' The members of Everton party left their Seattle base on 22 July thinking the club was to confront River Plate. However, the numerous billboards around Edmonton demanded they think again. Apparently, the match was more than just football. It was England versus Argentina; two historical enemies going head-to-head. It was war.

## Game 30
## 25 Jul 2009: RIVER PLATE 1 EVERTON 0

Only 15,800 fans turned up to celebrate the 100th anniversary of the Alberta Soccer Association at the 60,000-capacity Commonwealth Stadium. Even though their crown might have slipped after a couple of fallow seasons, the Argentinians were still a joy to watch with their subtle flicks and two-touch passing. Everton – minus Mikel Arteta, Phil Jagielka, Victor Anichebe and Seamus Coleman – started brightly. In the opening minutes, Steven Pienaar steered Jô's powerful cross wide of the target and the on-loan Brazilian drilled a free-kick at keeper Mario Vega. At the other end, goalkeeper Carlo Nash saved from Rodrigo Archubi and Matias Abelairas shot narrowly wide. Next, Tim Cahill had a great scoring opportunity. After Jô gained possession, his centre was met crisply by the Australian's right boot – only for goalkeeper Daniel Vega to smother it.

Overall, the Merseysiders had given as good as they received against the maestros from Buenos Aires but were defeated by a moment of brilliance from Ariel Ortega, nicknamed 'El Burrito'. He scored the game's only goal in the 27th minute with a strike that would have graced any occasion. Seizing a loose ball, Ortega dashed in behind Jack Rodwell, skipped away from Joleon Lescott and, in the same movement, chipped keeper Carlo Nash from 20 yards.

River Plate continued to pile on the pressure. First winger Rodrigo Archubi went close. Then Ortega's pass to Matias Abelairas caught the Everton goalkeeper out of position, but midfielder hit the post. After the resumption, the Merseysiders almost equalised when Jô danced past a pair of defenders and rounded Vega before sending his shot into the side-netting. Also, Leighton Baines powered a free-kick just wide. Few would disagree that the South Americans were worthy winners.

As for the advertised hostilities? The match against River Plate exploded mid-way through the first-half after Jack Rodwell had fouled Christian Fabbiani. Eye-witness reports indicate that the resulting skirmish involved Rodwell and Marouane Fellaini being surrounded by six angry Argentinians. No fatalities were reported.

**Everton:** *Nash; Hibbert, Yobo, Lescott, Baines; Cahill, Pienaar (Wallace 75), Fellaini (Saha 69), Rodwell; Baxter (Neville 69), Jô (Vaughan 69).*

Moving onto Utah and the newly-built Rio Tinto Stadium in Sandy – located some 15 miles south of Salt Lake City – where the MLS All-Star game was promoted as a big deal. Make that, a really big deal for North American soccer. Conceivably, there were more open training sessions, press conferences and other events in the run up to the game than the FA Cup final. The All-Stars had triumphed all five previous times they had met foreign opposition. Everton would have to be their best if they were not to follow the examples of Chelsea and West Ham. David Moyes noted, 'The MLS has improved greatly over the years since we have been coming here. It is getting better and now so many of the clubs have their own stadiums, it has made a big difference. We were in Seattle last week and I was really impressed with what I saw. It is going to be a difficult game.'

### Game 31
### 29 July 2009: MLS ALL-STARS 1 EVERTON 1 (3-4 on penalties)

Outside, the stadium complex lay in the shadows of the snow-capped Wasatch Range. Inside, hundreds of youngsters emerged waving flags from all over the globe, US Marines marched onto the pitch with the star-spangled banner and two skydivers descended from a cloudless sky with the official match ball.

On the other occasion when David Moyes' men ventured to Utah in July 2007, they had failed to cope with the altitude and the dry heat. That did not seem to be the case two years on. Everton opened brightly and took the lead in the 12th minute when Louis Saha seized on a mistake by Stuart Holden (Houston Dynamo) and nonchalantly slid his effort past goalkeeper Kasey Keller (Seattle Sounders). While they rode their luck on occasions, the Merseysiders controlled the game until winger Conor Casey (Colorado Rapids) held off Leighton Baines and slipped the ball across the six-yard box for Brad Davis (Houston Dynamo) to tap in. That goal in the 24th minute gave the MLS team increased confidence and Tim Howard was required to make saves from Conor Casey and Fredy Montero (Seattle Sounders) in quick succession before the interval.

The second-half began inauspiciously until a careless mistake by Joleon Lescott was nearly punished by substitute Landon Donovan (Los Angeles Galaxy). Many observers claimed that it was further proof that Manchester City's public courtship was having a detrimental effect on the central-defender. With the MLS All-Stars now on top, they should have taken the lead on 76 minutes when, after an unforced error by Louis Saha, the ball landed at the feet of Landon Donovan who struck the woodwork from six yards. Dead on his feet, Tim Howard came to the rescue in the closing minutes and saved a powerful header from Davy Arnaud (Kansas City Wizards).

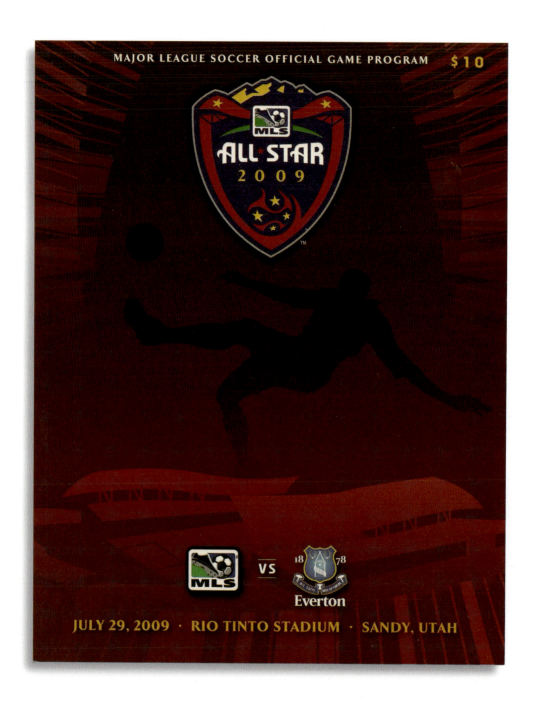

Cue the penalty shoot-out. The situation looked bleak when both James Vaughan and Jô missed, but the Everton goalkeeper excelled by thwarting Brad Davies, making a stunning block from Davy Arnaud and catching the embarrassing effort from Freddie Ljungberg (Seattle). To their credit, Leighton Baines, Phil Neville, Joleon Lescott and Jack Rodwell scored to claim a 4-3 victory and the 2009 transatlantic excursion ended with Phil Neville lifting a trophy. Tim Howard was named Most Valuable Player, which capped an outstanding year for the goalkeeper.

'I didn't realise that it was such a massive game in North America,' recalled James Vaughan. 'I came on for Leon Osman some 15 minutes from the end, along with Jose Baxter, and sensed that we were headed to penalties. Because of my heroics in the heart-stopping shoot-out against United at Wembley months earlier, I volunteered to take our first spot-kick. I missed, as did Jô with the second. Once again it was left to Tim Howard to grab the glory.'

**Everton:** *Howard; Hibbert, Yobo, Lescott, Baines; Cahill (Wallace 76), Rodwell, Fellaini (Jô 56), Neville; Osman (Vaughan 76), Saha (Baxter 76).*

Reserve keeper Carlo Nash participated in the trip and recalled: 'In 2009 pre-season we flew straight to Seattle – where we had a training camp. The players knew it would be tough, David Moyes was a hard taskmaster and we were not going over there to enjoy the sights. On pre-season tours the gaffer wanted us to share rooms so that we got to know each other. My roommate on that tour was Seamus Coleman, a great lad. Because he had a nasty infection in his foot, Seamus had to stay in his room – I felt sorry for him. He was struggling and had to see a specialist out there.

'Then we flew onto Edmonton, Alberta for the game against River Plate. Tim Howard had joined up with the rest of the squad in Seattle after his international duty for the USA. Because he had only a couple of days of training, it was a bit too early for him to play in the game. Therefore, it was a great opportunity for me to show what I could do against top-class opposition. The stadium had a capacity of 60,000 but there were maybe only 15,000 watching the game. Wherever you go in the world you meet people with an Everton allegiance and Edmonton was no exception. We bumped into fans from many different corners of North America and Merseyside. As for the action on the pitch, the defining moment was the goal scored by Ariel Ortega, the Argentina playmaker. He got through our defence and chipped the ball over me into the far top corner – it was a great finish that I could do absolutely nothing about. Sometimes, you just have to acknowledge the class that you are up against.

'Next, we travelled to Salt Lake City to play the MLS All-Stars in front of a capacity crowd. The MLS side was part-way through its season and was firing on all cylinders whereas we were trying to get match fit. Prior to the game, we trained at a ski resort in the Rocky Mountains. The altitude there caused the goalkeepers a few problems in the finishing sessions as, due to the difference in atmospheric pressure, the flight of the balls was unpredictable. But the MLS All-Star game was a fantastic experience.

'Everton Football Club and Goodison Park have always been special for me. My first game as an Everton fan was the Merseyside derby in 1981 – that's what got me into football. Alan Wright, Billy's brother used to take me to the games. But I have Big Nev to thank for getting me interested in goalkeeping at an early age. Therefore, when the opportunity came around for me to join Everton in 2008 there was no hesitation. I thoroughly enjoyed my time there. My only regret is not playing many first team games, but it was difficult with someone like Tim Howard in front of you. He was a great keeper at the top of his game.'

Seamus Coleman's memories of the tour were painful and unpleasant: 'I had only been with the club for about six months, so I was really looking forward to the pre-season trip to Seattle, Salt Lake City and Edmonton. We had played a friendly game at Rochdale before we left and I came off the bench to replace Shane Duffy after about an hour. I developed a blister but thought nothing of it. My foot was sore on the flight to Seattle though and I mentioned it to Doc Irving. He had a look at it and straight away put me on some strong antibiotics. The infection had nearly reached the bone. It was only when it started to heal that they told me that the antibiotics may well have saved my career. It was that serious.

'The trip was a nightmare because I couldn't leave my hotel room. I was so bored and was missing out on my first real chance to bond with the lads in the first team. I was allowed out once, to join the rest of the squad and staff for a slap-up dinner at Buca de Beppo in Salt Lake City. The restaurant was one of many owned by club director, Robert Earl. It was a fantastic place. I had never seen so much food! I was sitting with Jack Rodwell, James Wallace and James Vaughan – the young lads sticking together – and we were amazed that the food just kept coming and coming! At least being confined to my hotel room spared me the agony of having to sing in front of everyone! Since then though, I've been back several times with Everton and the experience has been much better than in 2009. The USA is the perfect base for pre-season training.'

No little credit for the club's involvement in the fixture belongs to Graham Smith. 'As an event organiser, I had been involved with Mayor League Soccer for several seasons and had no hesitation in recommending Everton's participation in the MLS All-Star game,' he recalled. 'As a licensed agent, I had enjoyed many interactions with the club. That year, I had represented Anton Peterlin and Cody Arnoux in their ambitious sojourns at Goodison. It was a great opportunity and a giant leap for both. Looking back, I've introduced several players to Everton. In addition to Predrag Radosavljevic and Robert Warzycha, I recommended several other North American and European youngsters. The ones that come immediately to my mind are goalkeeper Brad Friedel of the Columbus Crew and Liverpool, midfielder Zvonimir Soldo of Dinamo Zagreb, who progressed to represent Croatia on 60 or so occasions, and another midfielder, Zvonimir Boban of Dinamo Zagreb and AC Milan, who became deputy secretary general of FIFA. But for one reason or another, the club did not recruit them.'

Back at Goodison, Everton kicked off the new season with a 6-1 loss to Arsenal. After selling Joleon Lescott for £22 million to Manchester City in late-August, manager David

Moyes strengthened his squad by adding Diniyar Bilyaletdinov from Lokomotiv Moscow for £8.5 million, Sylvain Distin from Portsmouth for £5 million and Johnny Heitinga from Atletico Madrid for £6 million. In January, he recruited Landon Donovan from the Los Angeles Galaxy on loan. Everton improved to finish in eighth place in the Premier League with 61 points. In Europe, the club was eliminated from the Europa League by Sporting Lisbon 4-2 on aggregate.

## PRE-SEASON TOUR 2011

For the sixth time in eight years, Everton travelled to the North America continent. During David Moyes' reign, the US cities of Houston, Salt Lake City, Los Angeles, Chicago, Denver, Columbus, Dallas and Seattle had already hosted his players. However, the latest trip saw them seeking the springboard for a successful league campaign in the City of Brotherly Love as well as the nation's capital. Everton were based at the NovaCare Complex, the cutting-edge residence of the NFL's Philadelphia Eagles. The training sessions at the magnificent complex were hard and the tartan taskmaster pushed all of his men to the limit. Some of them to the point of vomiting.

The opening game was against Philadelphia Union, one of the most successful of MLS franchises, at PPL Park located at Chester on the banks of the Delaware River before moving onto Washington DC. Sadly, the Merseysiders suffered a public relations own-goal when Tim Howard – the USA goalkeeper, World Cup hero and the face of soccer in North America – did not make the trip to Philadelphia.

The host's chief executive Nick Sakiewicz was shocked by the news. 'We're really surprised,' he said. 'We he didn't learn about Tim's status until a few days ago. We understand the need to rest players and have no issue with that. It just would have been nice to know. Why would we put him in our advertising? Had we known Howard wouldn't be playing, the Union would have invited a different opponent.' In response, David Moyes claimed that his goalkeeper was resting following his involvement with the USA in the Gold Cup final against Mexico some three weeks earlier. It would be an understatement to say that the Philadelphia public was displeased.

Neil Jones of the *Liverpool Echo* reported, 'Real Madrid are in town at the weekend and should sell out the 60,000 Lincoln Financial Field in the city centre. Not that you would guess that Ronaldo and friends were enroute. A quick glance at both local newspapers – *The Inquirer* and the *Daily News* – shows little soccer coverage. The Women's World Cup, which the USA lost to Japan is mentioned. Real Madrid's visit to Philadelphia? Marouane Fellaini's recovery from an ankle knock? Nothing.'

David Moyes was eager to judge the fitness levels of his side after a few days in the Pennsylvania heat and fielded a strong side without Fellaini. By contrast, their opponents, perched at the top of MLS' Eastern Conference, chose to rest a number of their key players and reduce the average age of their line-up to 22 years.

**TIM HOWARD**
*U.S. NATIONAL TEAM GOALKEEPER*

**CHARLIE DAVIES**
*D.C. UNITED LEADING GOAL-SCORER*

**MIKEL ARTETA**
*EVERTON'S SPANISH PLAYMAKER*

**TIM CAHILL**
*AUSTRALIAN WORLD CUP STAR*

**ANDY NAJAR**
*2010 MLS ROOKIE OF THE YEAR*

**JOSH WOLFF**
*TWO-TIME WORLD CUP VETERAN*

 **VS.**

# D.C. UNITED VS. EVERTON

Sat. July 23, 7:30pm – RFK Stadium

dcunited.com | 202-587-5000

Presenting Partner

On to the action. With temperatures hovering around 95F, both teams laboured to find cohesion in the first-half and it was the home side who mustered the first meaningful attempt on goal when, in the seventh minute, Carlos Valdes headed Sheanon Williams' long throw onto the top of Jan Mucha's net. The hosts also enjoyed the final chance of the opening period when Valdes met Justin Mapp's corner with a side-footed volley which flashed wide.

Both sides rang the changes at the interval. Ross Barkley and Conor McAleny were introduced, having spent the first part of the summer with the club's youth team in Moscow, along with Jack Rodwell, Sylvain Distin and Apostolos Vellios. The teenage Greek striker, eager to impress in a squad lacking attacking options, wasted little time in robbing Roger Torres and smashing a bold right-foot strike wide from 35 yards. Then with Everton exerting control, John Heitinga went even closer with a curling effort. In response, Danny Mwanga, the Congolese-born forward who was first pick in the 2010 MLS draft, lashed the ball into the side-netting and then shot wide left from 10 yards. In the 74th minute, Everton responded with Vellios' instinctive flick drawing the save of the match from substitute goalkeeper Thorne Holder.

Despite the noise generated by the infamous 'Sons of Ben' among the crowd of 18,582 providing a colourful backdrop, the game looked to be heading for a scoreless draw. Then in the 88th minute, substitute Christian Hernandez – a 17-year-old high school player – was afforded time and space to sweep his right-footed strike beyond goalkeeper Mucha for the winning goal. Cue bedlam amongst the home support, especially moments later when John Heitinga was dismissed. The defender was shown a red card after clashing with the goalscorer during stoppage time. Referee Jorge Gonzalez admitted afterwards that he got the decision wrong and would not include the incident in his match report.

**Everton:** *Mucha, Coleman, Baines, Jagielka, Heitinga, Bilyaletdinov (Barkley 63), Arteta (Rodwell 46), Cahill (McAleny 78), Neville, Gueye (Distin 46), Beckford (Vellios 46).*

Philadelphia, sitting top of the MLS Eastern Conference after 19 games, were deserving winners. Manager Moyes noted, 'It was an unbelievable workout. The Union play at a high tempo. They are a very fit team with some good players. We were tested to the full. In the last 15 minutes, physically we were dead. We didn't have enough people we could change and ran out of energy. But we have no complaints, I thought Philadelphia deserved it. The 1-0 score-line was a fair one.'

Next stop Washington DC. Everton travelled 150 miles south to the Robert F Kennedy Memorial Stadium. The venue, which boasted a capacity of 45,000, had hosted five games during the 1994 World Cup. Again, Tim Howard's absence took the shine off the fixture. Although the presence of a Premier League club was deemed exciting, the USA star was expected to be the main attraction. The Everton boss explained, 'Given his commitments to the national team during the summer, we've had to make sure that he got some holiday time with his family. He'll be here to say hello but won't be playing.' In promoting the friendly, DC United had featured Howard in its newspaper and online marketing. United spokesman Doug Hicks said, 'We'll do something with him pregame and intend to make him accessible in some manner to fans. That, too, is subject to the Everton manager's discretion.'

The squad was worse for wear. Injuries had prevented Louis Saha and Tony Hibbert from making the tour. Mikel Arteta had arrived in Washington DC on crutches. Marouane Fellaini, Leon Osman and Victor Anichebe had picked up knocks in training. At the same time their hosts wrestled with the dilemma of mid-season friendlies against superior opponents – play the regulars for competitive purposes and risk injury or play the second-string and risk a lopsided outcome. The Union decided to field five reserves.

## Game 33
## 23 July 2011: DC UNITED 1 EVERTON 3

The Merseysiders started quickly in difficult conditions. For the first 20 minutes the most successful club in MLS history, with four MLS Cups, played like a team in awe of its opponents. It was Merseyside men versus American boys. Everton waltzed to a fourth minute lead when Leighton Baines threaded a pass down the left channel for Victor Anichebe to bolt past Brandon McDonald and chip goalkeeper Bill Hamid from a prohibitive angle.

Everton did not have to wait long for their second goal. Rodwell's willingness to get on the ball, Vellios' awareness and Barkley's football brain combined to release Diniyar Bilyaletdinov. The Russian kept a cool head to drive a low finish between keeper Bill Hamid's legs. In the 27th minute, DC United looked to get a foothold in the contest. First, Honduras international Andy Najar powered a free-kick wide from 25 yards. Then moments on, Joseph Ngwenya sent a delicate chip over Mucha onto the crossbar.

Goalscorer Victor Anichebe recalled: 'More than anything, I remember it being extremely hot and humid in the RFK Stadium. The conditions sapped our energy and we had to adapt our approach to the game against DC United. I scored the opening goal when Leighton Baines played a long ball forward and I managed to get there first, open up my body and knock it past the keeper from a tight angle. Of course, it wasn't my first goal during an American tour. Back in 2006, I scored against Columbus Crew. I recall that we had a South African guy called Delron Buckley on trial who passed the ball infield to me and I hit it first time with my right foot into the far corner to level the scores. It was no fluke. I was really pleased because, the club had just signed Andy Johnson for a big fee from Crystal Palace and, at that stage of my Everton career I needed to show the boss what a local teenager could do if called on.'

The hosts made eight replacements at half-time. Immediately after the break, substitute Chris Pontius cut the deficit to 2-1. With the steamy conditions taking their toll on the visitors and inspired by the 12,789 attendees, DC United sought an equaliser. Chris Pontius hit the post and Josh Wolff blasted his shot wide from two yards. Still Everton created chances, Seamus Coleman should have made it three after he ran onto Apostolos Vellios's cut-back but lashed his effort over the bar. Then following enterprising play by Conor McAleny, Jack Rodwell's curling effort was deflected over and Tim Cahill's header from the ensuing corner was hacked off the line and Diniyar Bilyaletdinov's follow-up effort hit the bar. Finally, Everton sealed the victory in the 82nd minute when winger Magaye Gueye volleyed in Jermaine Beckford's cross at the back post.

**Everton:** *Mucha; Coleman, Distin, Jagielka (Heitinga 70), Baines (Neville 70); Rodwell, Barkley (Osman 46), Bilyaletdinov, Cahill (Beckford 72); Anichebe (McAleny 52), Vellios (Gueye 46).*

Surprisingly, in his post-match interview, David Moyes questioned the methods used to promote soccer in the USA, 'It's a little bit razzmatazz for my liking. In Europe the football people earn their money and go to see the football. That's what they do. They don't eat popcorn or drink Coca-Cola. They're there to watch the football, and they have a passion about it.'

In the eyes of many, Everton had developed a strong core augmented by a decent crop of youngsters emerging from Finch Farm. But prior to the start of the season, the club sold Mikel Arteta to Arsenal for £10 million and recruited Royston Drenthe from Real Madrid and Denis Stracqualursi from Tigre on loan. At mid-season, it conscripted Landon Donovan from the Los Angeles Galaxy for a second loan spell, Darron Gibson from Manchester United for £500,000 and Nikica Jelavic from Rangers for £5.5 million.

While many fans shook their heads at the thought of Gibson replacing Arteta in midfield, Everton finished seventh in the table with 56 points, four ahead of Liverpool. But like so many times before, the Reds had the last laugh. The 2011/12 season ended in disappointment when Everton were defeated in the FA Cup final by their neighbours with Andy Carroll scoring the winner in the 87th minute. Football can be so cruel.

A key member of the backroom staff who has participated in seven North American tours is kitman Jimmy Martin. He reflected: 'I loved every transatlantic trip and have so many great memories of the places that I have visited and the people I have met. One of my favourites was in 2011, when we were in Washington DC, James McFadden and I went to Arlington National Cemetery to see the graves of US President John F Kennedy and world boxing champion Joe Louis. It was quite an emotional experience.

'Then there was the time that Tim Howard hired a Hummer and drove us around the streets of Hollywood and Santa Barbara. I loved Tim – even though he could be a bit fussy at times! He was such a magnificent professional. Everything had to be just right. One day he would be a medium and the next day he would be a large! Previously in 2009, when we were in Seattle, I met my old mate Jimmy Gabriel. I love the man. We had a fantastic night out and Jimmy gave me the gold ring he had won with Seattle Sounders. It is one of my most treasured possessions.'

## GUINNESS INTERNATIONAL CHAMPIONS CUP 2013

At the conclusion of the 2012/13 campaign, before he took over from Sir Alex Ferguson at Manchester United, David Moyes and his team finished sixth in the Premier League with 63 points, two more than Liverpool, but failed to qualify for participation in Europe. Most surprisingly, they were eliminated in the sixth round of the FA Cup by Roberto Martinez's Wigan Athletic by 3-0. While Wigan progressed to win the competition and suffer relegation, their manager inherited the Goodison hotseat. Following the appointment of Martinez, Everton took part in the inaugural Guinness International Champions Cup. They were in good company. The other participants were Chelsea – UEFA Europa League winners, Juventus – Serie A champions, AC Milan, Internazionale, Real Madrid – La Liga runners-up, Valencia and Los Angeles Galaxy – MLS Cup winners.

Prior to the clash with Juventus before an enthusiastic crowd of 22,208 at ATT Park in San Francisco, Phil Jagielka – now captain – noted, 'As far as the teams we're going to play, we couldn't have asked for better pre-season opponents. Sometimes it can be more of a fitness session, but when there is something to play for you get those competitive vibes going. When you speak to the manager, he's so positive that you can't wait for the next training session or game to come.'

Roberto Martinez revealed that he planned to adopt a 3-5-2 formation against Juventus, 'It is a glamorous game against a team I have admired for the last few years. From a tactical point of view, they are the best at playing a back three. It's going to be a big test. This is as good as it gets in terms of games for us.'

### Game 34
### 31 July 2013: JUVENTUS 1 EVERTON 1 (5-6 on penalties)

Both teams began cautiously and jostled for control of midfield. Everton's new formation served them well in the opening exchanges as they took the game to Juventus and even had the ball in the net after six minutes. Steven Pienaar's delivery into the box sailed past goalkeeper Marco Storari as Phil Jagielka attempted to make contact. However, referee Ricardo Salazar ruled the defender offside. Next, it was the turn of the Italians. Tim Howard was required to stop Arturo Vidal's searing free-kick from 20 yards. Luca Marrone was the first player to test the Everton goalkeeper on 17 minutes, rifling in a shot from 25 yards which was gathered at his far post. With the game opening up, Marrone again went close to breaking the deadlock. He missed a sitter at the back post. Then Arturo Vidal brought the crowd to life when he struck a volley marginally wide. At the other end, 19-year-old John Stones smacked the woodwork with a header just before half-time.

After the break, Juventus raised the tempo in their search for an opener. It almost paid instant dividends when Federico Peluso connected with Mauricio Isla's cross on 48 minutes, looping his header narrowly over the crossbar with Tim Howard well beaten. Whereas Everton focused on counterattacks and were only prevented from breaking the deadlock by the sharp reflexes of goalkeeper Marco Storari, who foiled Kevin Mirallas from close range. The Belgium winger excited the enthusiastic 2,000 or so Evertonians congregated in ATT Park with a solo breakaway but could not beat Storari. Then on the hour mark, he put Roberto Martinez's side in front by out-smarting defender Federico Peluso and sending his shot inside the near post.

Juventus countered. A flowing attack set up Arturo Vidal with a clear goalscoring opportunity on 68 minutes, only for the Everton goalkeeper to dash off his line and smother the ball before the Chile international made clean contact. Juventus were only prevented from restoring parity by the heroics of Howard when he dived low to his left to thwart Carlos Tevez's shot and pulled off a miraculous stop to deny Mirko Vucinic. Notwithstanding, the best chance fell to Steven Pienaar who should have sealed the victory when he capitalised on a defensive slip only to sweep the ball wide when one-one-one with the keeper with 14 minutes left. Finally, Everton cracked. Tim Howard, who had excelled on home soil, was powerless to prevent a rocket launched by Ghanaian midfielder Kwadwo Asamoah that earned a share of the spoils for Antonio Conte's men.

Onto the lottery of spot-kicks. Everton recovered from Leon Osman's unfortunate opening miss to secure a dramatic penalty shoot-out victory by 6-5. Alessandro Matri, Kwadwo Asamoah, Mirko Vucinic and Arturo Vidal as well as Ross Barkley, John Stones, Kevin Mirallas, Phil Jagielka and Bryan Oviedo were successful. Then Andrea Pirlo missed with his kick that would have given the Italian side victory. Thereafter, Seamus Coleman stepped up to score and Tim Howard dived to save Federico Peluso's effort. Immediately, the stadium reverberated with chants of 'USA! USA!'

**Everton:** *Howard; Baines (Oviedo 64), Stones, Jagielka; Gibson (Osman 64), Distin, Coleman, Pienaar; Mirallas, Fellaini, Anichebe (Barkley 88).*

The highlight of the shoot-out was an audacious effort from young Stones, who successfully executed a Panenka-style penalty by chipping the ball into the top left corner of the Juventus net as goalkeeper Marco Storari dived to his right. After admitting it was not his truest strike of a football, the 19-year-old defender – who had been signed from Barnsley for £3 million just seven months earlier – also revealed it was no quirk of fate, 'I did it a few months ago for the Everton Under-21 side. The lads have been saying that I wouldn't do it in front of a big crowd.'

'I had been practicing it in training. I wanted it to go straight down the middle, but I shanked it and the ball went right. I might have to mix it up now because other teams will be analysing who takes penalties and how we take them.' His moment of magic from the penalty spot may never have happened had he scored during normal time but his header hit the woodwork: 'Before the game some of the lads said "You're going to score" but I was just wanted to play well. The ball came off my head and clipped the post – an inch left and it would have gone in. While it would have been lovely to score, it was a privilege to play against such a good team. It was an unreal experience. It seemed so surreal.'

Buoyed by the success, Everton travelled south to Los Angeles. At the pre-match press conference, manager Roberto Martinez admitted that he relished the chance to test his team against one of the best in the world: 'When Real Madrid go into any sort of game they're expected to win. The test doesn't come any higher.'

## Game 35
## 2 August 2013: REAL MADRID 2 EVERTON 1

In front of an enthusiastic crowd of 40,681 at Dodger Stadium in Los Angeles, the Merseysiders kept their composure and gave Real Madrid more than a few headaches. From the opening whistle, Everton showed the same confidence and attacking conviction which saw them defeat Juventus. However, they were guilty of defending too high up the field in the early exchanges and were punished when Cristiano Ronaldo – who had already gone one-on-one with Tim Howard and missed – surged into area and opened the scoring on 18 minutes.

At the other end, Kevin Mirallas seemed to have been fouled in the penalty area on 24 minutes, but referee Baldomero Toledo – a charitable and overawed local official – waved away appeals. Then after the Belgian speedster had won another free-kick, Marouane Fellaini climbed high to meet Leighton Baines' delivery only for his firm header to hit the post. If that wasn't frustrating enough, Everton had the ball in the net shortly afterwards. This time Sylvan Distin's header was disallowed for pushing. The sense of injustice was compounded within minutes when Ronaldo, who appeared to have strayed offside, latched onto a defence-splitting pass from Luka Modric to square for Mesut Ozil to side-foot home. The Portugal wizard might have rubbed salt in the Everton wounds near the interval when he was clean through, but his delicate chip flew over the bar.

Nikica Jelavic came on for the second-half and within minutes had diverted a Kevin Mirallas cross-shot only for goalkeeper Diego Lopez to save. On the hour mark, Jelavic made no mistake with a snapshot after a superb knock-down from Steven Naismith who climbed above Daniel Carvajal. Phil Jagielka thought he had headed an equaliser when he stooped to meet a Leighton Baines free-kick but the effort went narrowly over. The introduction of Gerard Deulofeu and Ross Barkley gave Everton fresh momentum. But despite the young substitutes showing impressive self-belief and skills, Everton failed to find an equaliser.

**Everton:** Howard; Coleman (Stones 84), Distin, Jagielka, Heitinga (Gibson 68), Baines; Osman, Fellaini (Barkley 68), Naismith, Kone (Jelavic 45), Mirallas (Deulofeu 84).

At full-time, the Merseysiders were entitled to feel aggrieved after a narrow defeat by one of the best sides in the world. That said, the performance bode well for the upcoming Premier League campaign. The narrow victory earned Carlo Ancelotti's team a match-up against Chelsea in the final of the tournament in Miami.

Leon Osman has fond memories of California and the game against Real Madrid: 'It was a terrific experience, as much for the venue as for the quality of the opposition. Dodger

Stadium is so iconic. It was fantastic to play there but the pitch was shocking. It wasn't too bad where the baseball outfield would have been, However, where you normally expect to see the pitcher's mound and runners' lines they had just thrown down some grass rolls like you would put down in your garden. It was extremely bumpy to say the least. That's the excuse we used for being so rusty, although it didn't seem to have the same effect on the Spanish opposition.'

He continued: 'Real had their big-guns out and were managed by Carlo Ancelotti. With Ike Casillas, Sergio Ramos, Cristiano Ronaldo, Karim Benzema, Mezut Ozil, Luka Modric – it was by far the strongest line-up I ever faced in a pre-season game. We lost but felt a little hard done by because Sylvain Distin had a perfectly good header disallowed. Maybe it helped the tournament organisers if Real Madrid won the game, got to the final and lifted the trophy?' He continued: 'The Juventus game had been no less exciting. It went to penalties. Two of the players to miss both wore the number 21 shirt, so my disappointment was eased by the fact that the other one was Andrea Pirlo! I was in decent company at least. To play Juventus, Real Madrid and Valencia was great and, as it was Roberto Martinez's first pre-season, we were all very keen to impress. We were getting used to the way he wanted us to play. The training sessions, as well as the games, were very intense. None of us got to see much of California. But in Los Angeles we were in the same hotel as Matt Damon who was there to promote his latest film *Elysium*. So me, Leighton Baines and Kevin Mirallas had a photo taken with him. We were only with him briefly, but he seemed a very nice guy – although not nice enough to get me a part in his next film.'

Victor Anichebe, an unused substitute along with Joel Robles and Apostolos Vellios concurred: 'It was a pleasure to be around the likes of Cristiano Ronaldo and Sergio Ramos. To see them up close was great for a young player like me. Kitman Jimmy Martin had warned us all not to swap shirts at full-time because he needed them for the last match of the tour. "Even if it's Ronaldo, you don't swap shirts lad," he warned me. In the end, it didn't matter because we wore the new away kit against Valencia in Miami, so I could have tried to get Ronaldo's shirt. But, like most young players, I was scared of Jimmy!'

Another La Liga outfit was up next in fifth-place play-off. Valencia had finished fifth in the Spanish top-flight. In the USA, they had defeated Internazionale but lost to AC Milan in their previous games. The match took place at the Sun Life Stadium – the impressive mansion of the Miami Dolphins which had hosted six NFL Super Bowls.

### Game 36
### 6 August 2013: VALENCIA 1 EVERTON 0

The tournament slogan was 'No friendlies, just football'. And that certainly rang true after five minutes when Valencia's Antonio Barragan scythed down Bryan Oviedo before being promptly booked. With Marouane Fellaini, who was being courted by Manchester United's new manager David Moyes, playing alongside Darron Gibson and the exciting duo of Ross Barkley and Gerard Deulofeu, Everton created and wasted a host of first-half openings.

With the humidity stifling and Valencia adept at retaining possession, Everton were required to do plenty of running. After an opening shot from Oviedo blazed wide, Everton should have broken the deadlock the 15th minute, but Ross Barkley decided against sliding the ball to the well-placed Gerard Deulofeu and the chance went begging. As expected, the La Liga side had their moments too. Goalkeeper Joel Robles was required to thwart Roberto Ibanez. Also, Issa Cissokho let fly from close range only for the ball to scrape the outside of the post. At the half-hour mark, Everton produced their most incisive attack. Bryan Oviedo fed an on-running Steven Naismith, but the Scottish midfielder could not apply a quality finish to beat goalkeeper Diego Alves. Next Victor Anichebe outpaced the Valencia defence before losing control of the ball, then went much closer when he missed the target from 12 yards with Alves beaten.

Valencia went ahead in the 52nd minute when marauding left-back Aly Cissokho squeezed a pass to Mikel Herrero whose shot from outside the box left Joel Robles flat-footed. Everton responded but failed to find a way back into the match – creating but wasting good openings. In hindsight, perhaps the most memorable feature of the night was the extravagant laser show which entertained the crowd of 38,513 at the interval. The 1-0 loss dropped them to sixth-place finish in the eight-team tournament.

**Everton:** *Robles; Stones (Jelavic 47, Kone 88), Distin, Jagielka; Oviedo, Fellaini, Gibson (Osman 84), Barkley; Naismith (Baines 56), Deulofeu (Mirallas 56), Anichebe (Coleman 45).*

Manager Roberto Martinez had inherited the club's involvement in the tournament. Greg O'Keeffe, then at the *Liverpool Echo*, recalled: 'Kenny Moyes, the former-manager's brother who was a football agent and middle-man, had organised the tour – arranged everything. As you would expect at the MLB stadiums in California, the press facilities were high-tech and compared with those at Arsenal, the finest in the Premier League. The sightlines were unobstructed and there were hundreds of staff only too willing to help. We didn't interact much with the US or Italian media in San Francisco, but everyone was respectful. Whereas in Los Angeles, there was a perception that we were merely making up the numbers. Our players were anonymous, as an army of journalists from across the globe plus a dozen or so Hollywood celebrities, including a certain Jenifer Lopez, swarmed around the Real Madrid players.'

The journalist continued: 'By the time we had reached Miami, Roberto Martinez had changed the club. He had lifted everyone's spirits with his relaxed manner, genuine friendliness and unwavering optimism. Everton were back – well at least for that season. Coincidentally, the club decided to unveil its striking new sunshine yellow-and-blue away strip there. Much like the home kit, it was made from recycled plastic water bottles in accordance with Nike's commitment to produce athletic wear with a low environmental impact. As a sports journalist, it remains my favourite overseas trip. I remember sitting under the palm trees by the hotel pool as Phil Jagielka modelled the kit and thinking to myself that I had chosen the ideal profession. As an Evertonian, I travelled back brimming with confidence.'

Thousands of Evertonians had flown from Europe and all corners of North America to attend the matches. The club's players' life president Graeme Sharp recalled the abundance of friendly faces: 'We would bump into them everywhere. Always friendly, enthusiastic and well-behaved, many would use the visits to North America as their annual holidays. Certainly, this was the case during the International Champions Cup competition in 2013 when thousands descended on San Francisco, Los Angeles and Miami. The organised meet and greet nights were always chock a block with Blues of all ages. Meeting fans has always been an important part of our trips, but I'm always impressed by the sheer number of Evertonians who follow the club in the good as well as not so good times. For example in California, there may have been more Juventus supporters than Evertonians in the stadium, but there were certainly more Everton fans from England than Juventus fans from Italy.

'The players and staff know that engaging with the fans is an important part of a pre-season tour and most enjoy the banter and – let us call it – feedback. As for the fans, particularly the US-based ones, the get-togethers give them an unrivalled opportunity to meet their heroes. I have always been taken by their devotion and knowledge – especially those who had never been to Goodison. As a player and a club ambassador, I must have met thousands of supporters over the years in the USA, usually in local bars, nightclubs and restaurants. More often than not, they have turned into memorable nights out!'

Jimmy Martin found the 2013 trip demanding: 'We supply fresh kit every day to every member of the touring party. Therefore, the most important room in any hotel is the designated kit-room. As soon as we arrived, we would unpack everything and lay it out. Obviously, we need a lot of space. The hotel normally provided a lounge to use or two adjoining rooms that we could convert into a big one. When that happens, we have to use every available space – including the baths!'

'Without question, the toughest trip was in 2013. It was Roberto Martinez's first pre-season as manager and so everyone was on their toes. Weeks before, I had to work out how much kit was required for each city and then ship it across the Atlantic. We had sent one load to San Francisco, another to LA and yet another to Miami. The mountain of used kit was sent back to Merseyside before we moved onto the next city. We were in the USA for two weeks and the total amount of gear was unbelievable – training kit, equipment, match kit, leisure wear, the lot. Also, we had to cater for all kinds of weather. Although we knew it would be warm, we would have to include heavy training kit in case of bad weather.'

His assistant Tony Sage elaborated: 'Prior to our arrival in San Francisco in 2013, we had sent out 25 sets of four different training kits for the players and another 15 sets for the staff, so that is 160 items straight away. Then there were 40 sets of two different leisure outfits for them to wear in and around the hotel. For training, we had 12 sets of four different coloured bibs, three sets of different coloured cones, 20 poles and 40 footballs. The only items we took over with us were the players' footwear – boots, training shoes, flip-flops – and their shin-pads, because they were obviously needed for training and the friendlies against Accrington Stanley and Blackburn Rovers before we travelled. For the games in the USA, each player was issued three shirts, three pairs of shorts and three pairs of socks. Clearly, a kitman's life is not an easy one.'

The tour had been worthwhile, but would it provide the catalyst for Premier League glory? Upon returning home, the club sold Marouane Fellaini to Manchester United for £27.5 million and then signed Antolin Alcaraz and James McCarthy from Wigan and arranged loans for Chelsea's Romelu Lukaku and Manchester City's Gareth Barry. Everton finished a respectable fifth in the table with a haul of 72 points – a total that would have secured Champions League qualification in eight of the previous 10 seasons.

As for the club's record on North American soil? Overall, it has played 35 games against an assortment of local and overseas opponents. Teams overseen by the directors, Harry Catterick, Howard Kendall, David Moyes and Roberto Martinez have notched 18 wins, 6 draws and 11 defeats. Further scrutiny reveals that the results are skewed by the one-sided score-lines during the 1956 tour. In the opening six fixtures against mostly semi-professional hopefuls, Everton won five and lost to Schwaben with a goals total of 23-4. Whereas in the concluding games against Aberdeen, the club won three and drew one with an aggregate of 14-8. In the 1961 American Soccer League Challenge Cup. Everton played seven ties mostly against the representatives of weaker European nations. They won six of them and lost one to Bangu with a goals total of 23-5. Of course, they were hammered by Dukla Prague in both legs of the final with an aggregate of 2-9.

More important, performances and results have been even less convincing in the MLS era during which the club has contested 14 matches. Against international peers from Europe and South America they have featured in seven games, recording one win, two draws and losses to Club America, River Plate, Real Madrid and Valencia. Of the games to date against MLS sides, the visitors have won only two games, drawn one and lost to Real Salt Lake, the Chicago Fire and the Philadelphia Union. Of course to its credit, the club defeated the MLS All-Stars in 2009 – albeit on penalties.

It is often suggested that the first club of Merseyside should tour regularly to enhance its reputation in North America. Be that as it may, it is essential that future tourists perform well against all opponents, especially those representing Major League Soccer. Many claim that pre-season jaunts should focus on the physical conditioning required for the Premier League season, but some of the club's more recent performances have eroded its long-term standing in American eyes.

One Everton team has returned triumphant from North America. That was in March 2016, when the clubs' Under-18 side, under the tutelage of ex-players Kevin Sheedy and Phil Jevons, won the Gordon Jago Super Group final of the Dr Pepper Dallas Cup. The club had been a regular participant in the tournament which, at one time or another, had showcased the rare talents of promising youngsters such as Edu, Maicon and Edmílson from Brazil, Raul from Spain, Beckham, Owen and Rooney from England, Dempsey, Donovan and McBride from the USA, and many others.

# NORTH AMERICAN RESULTS

| **1956** | 18 May | Newark Select at Newark, NJ | 4-0 |
| | 29 May | American Soccer League at New York, NY | 7-0 |
| | 25 May | Lusitania at Ludlow, MA | 4-1 |
| | 30 May | Schwaben (Augsburg, Germany) at New York, NY | 0-1 |
| | 2 June | St Louis Catholic Youth at St Louis, MO | 5-0 |
| | 5 June | Chicago All-Stars XI at Chicago, IL | 3-2 |
| | 9 June | Aberdeen at Vancouver, BC | 3-3 |
| | 13 June | Aberdeen at Edmonton, Alberta | 2-1 |
| | 16 June | Aberdeen at Toronto, Ontario | 3-1 |
| | 17 June | Aberdeen at New York, NY | 6-3 |
| **1961** | 23 May | Montreal Concordia at Montreal, Quebec | 1-0 |
| | 25 May | Kilmarnock at Montreal, Quebec | 2-1 |
| | 4 June | Karlsruhe at New York, NY | 5-2 |
| | 7 June | Dinamo Bucharest at New York, NY | 4-0 |
| | 11 June | Bangu at New York, NY | 0-2 |
| | 14 June | Beşiktaş at New York, NY | 4-0 |
| | 17 June | Americans of New York at Montreal, Quebec | 7-0 |
| | 2 August | Dukla Prague at New York, NY | 2-7 |
| | 6 August | Dukla Prague at New York, NY | 0-2 |
| **1985** | 1 August | Inex at Toronto, Ontario | 1-1 |
| | 4 August | Canada at Toronto, Ontario | 1-0 |
| **2004** | 29 July | Pachuca at Houston, TX | 5-2 |
| | 1 August | Club America at Houston, TX | 1-3 |
| **2006** | 26 July | Columbus Crew at Columbus, OH | 1-1 |
| | 29 July | Club America at Dallas, TX | 1-1 |
| **2007** | 21 July | Real Salt Lake at Salt Lake City, UT | 0-2 |
| **2008** | 30 July | Chicago Fire at Bridgeview, IL | 0-2 |
| | 3 August | Colorado Rapids at Commerce City, CO | 2-1 |
| **2009** | 25 July | River Plate at Edmonton, Alberta | 0-1 |
| | 29 July | MLS All Stars at Sandy, UT | 1-1 (4-3 pens) |
| **2011** | 20 July | Philadelphia Union at Chester, PA | 0-1 |
| | 23 July | DC United at Washington, DC | 3-1 |
| **2013** | 31 July | Juventus at San Francisco, CA | 1-1 (6-5 pens) |
| | 3 August | Real Madrid at Los Angeles, CA | 1-2 |
| | 8 August | Valencia at Miami, FL | 0-1 |

Coach Sheedy noted: 'Travelling, representing your club, keeping yourself occupied, staying focussed and looking after yourself properly on tour is all part of being a top professional footballer and the Dallas Cup is of tremendous value to youngsters. I've been over for the tournament on four occasions and win or lose it was a great experience for the players and staff. It's a massive tournament involving teams from all over the world and so well organised. The facilities and accommodations are excellent.

'As for our success in the 2016 tournament, it was one of the best things I have achieved in my football career. I don't say things like that lightly. I could just see how determined the boys were to get the results. The camaraderie, friendship and the will to succeed was unbelievable. That's what helped us pull through in the end. They gave everything for the blue shirt.'

Everton recovered from losing their opening game against Tigres UANL (Mexico) by beating Kyoto Sanga (Japan), Real Salt Lake, the hosts FC Dallas before winning the final against Fulham by 2-1. Delial Brewster scored both goals.

The former Ireland international star noted: 'The lads grew in confidence as the games went on. In the final, we got our tactics right and Beni Baningime man-marked their best player. We were the best team and I really enjoyed seeing the boys celebrate. I said to them "Wherever your careers take you from here you can always look back on this achievement with immense pride. You've given everything and it's a big tournament to win."

Baningime recalled fondly: 'It was a great experience. We travelled to Texas not expecting to win because the year before we'd had a really strong team which included Tom Davies and Kieran Dowell, but somehow didn't return with the trophy. Our team spirit was brilliant. When the final whistle went, I was well aware that, as Everton captain, I must be respectful, so I made sure that I shook the hands of every one of the Fulham players ... and then I celebrated!'

Strangely, only three members of the victorious side – Pierce, Yates, Lees, Yarney, Harrington, Baningime, Denny, Kiersey, Morris, Broadhead, Brewster and unused substitutes – Johnson, Virtanen, Corke, Moore, Mellen – graduated to the Everton first team. Beni Baningime played 12 senior games, Nathan Broadhead was an 82nd minute substitute in the Europa League match at Apollon Limassol and Alex Denny was a 91st minute substitute in the same match.

# PART THREE

# TOFFEEMEN AND TOFFEEWOMEN

# TIME-LINE OF NORTH AMERICAN LEAGUES

| | |
|---|---|
| 1894 | American League of Professional Football |
| 1906-1921 | National Association Foot Ball League |
| 1907-1939 | St Louis Soccer League |
| 1914-1921 | Southern New England Soccer League |
| 1909-1910 | Eastern Professional Soccer League (Mark 1) |
| 1921-1933 | American Soccer League (Mark 1) |
| 1922-1997 | Canadian National Soccer League |
| 1923-1977 | German-American Soccer League |
| 1928-1929 | Eastern Professional Soccer League (Mark 2) |
| 1926 | International Soccer League (Mark 1) |
| 1934-1983 | American Soccer League (Mark 2) |
| 1960-1965 | International Soccer League (Mark 2) |
| 1961-1966 | Eastern Canada Professional Soccer League |
| 1967 | United Soccer Association |
| 1967 | National Professional Soccer League (Mark 1) |
| 1967-1984 | North American Soccer League (Mark 2) |
| 1983 | Canadian Professional Soccer League |
| 1984-2008 | Major Indoor Soccer League (Mark 2) |
| 1984-2001 | National Professional Soccer League (1984-2001) |
| 1984-1985 | United Soccer League |
| 1986-present | United Soccer Leagues (formerly USISL) |
| 1987-1992 | Canadian Professional Soccer League (Mark 1) |
| 1987-1992 | Lone Star Soccer Alliance |
| 1990-1996 | American Professional Soccer League |
| 1995-2004 | A-League |
| 1991-2001 | National Professional Soccer League (Mark 2) |
| 1996-present | Major League Soccer |
| 1998-2006 | Canadian Professional Soccer League (Mark 2) |
| 2003-present | National Premier Soccer League |
| 2007-present | Canadian Soccer League (Mark 2) |
| 2008-present | Major Indoor Soccer League (Mark 3) |
| 2011-present | North American Soccer League (Mark 3) |
| 2011-present | United Premier Soccer League |

# 3.1
# LEAGUES OF YESTERYEAR

The development of North American soccer has been undermined by its constantly changing structure. The first league, the American League of Professional Football, was founded in 1894 but folded after just one season. Since then, there have been more than 50 outdoor and indoor leagues. In the absence of a national framework, soccer remained popular in many parts of the USA thanks to the National Challenge Cup which was first contested during the 1913/14 season and is still going strong as the Lamar Hunt US Open Cup.

By 1920, there were numerous semi-professional leagues. The most influential was the original American Soccer League (ASL: 1921-1933), which covered Boston, New York and the industrial northeast. Many of its leading clubs were sponsored by local companies with deep pockets and successfully attracted several players from overseas by sidestepping international contract protocols such as transfer fees. That was until the 1929 stock market crash wreaked havoc on these companies and the financial backbone of the league.

Nevertheless, scores of leagues continued to be formed – only to collapse. In the post-war era, US soccer suffered from a lack of public interest and was even referred to as 'a game played by communists and fairies in short pants.' Indeed, it was not taken seriously by the bulk of the regional newspapers and their baseball obsessed sports readers. Rarely featured on the back pages, most soccer teams consisted of a mix of immigrants, part-time enthusiasts and college students playing, more often than not, in near-empty high school stadiums. Over time the better teams turned professional and competed in the reincarnation of the American Soccer League (ASL: 1933-1983), and later the United Soccer Association (USA: 1966-1967). The latter consisted of European and South American teams given local names.

Cue the United Soccer Association. In the afterglow of the 1966 World Cup, two rival leagues were formed – the United Soccer Association, which was recognised by FIFA, and the unaccredited National Professional Soccer League (NPSL) which had a contract with CBS Television. The former had intended to launch its league in 1968 but, given the expected competition, fast tracked its launch by importing whole teams for the inaugural season.

In the summer of 1967, Roy Vernon – the ex-Everton captain – and his Stoke City teammates morphed into the Cleveland Stokers for six weeks. Other franchises included ex-Everton goalkeeper Pat Dunne and the Boston Rovers (Shamrock Rovers), Chicago Mustangs (Cagliari), future manager Walter Smith and the Dallas Tornado (Dundee United), future Everton midfielder Tommy Jackson and the Detroit Cougars (Glentoran), Houston Stars (Bangu), future signing Ernie Hunt and the Los Angeles Wolves (Wolverhampton Wanderers), New York Skyliners (Cerro of Montevideo), San Francisco Gales (ADO Den Haag), Toronto City (Hibernian), future defender Colin Todd and the Vancouver Royal Canadians (Sunderland) and the Washington Whips (Aberdeen).

## MEMORIES OF THE UNITED SOCCER ASSOCIATION

### Ernie Hunt – the £80,000 practical joker

*In the eyes of many teammates, Hunt was a character who rarely thought before he spoke or misbehaved. There wasn't much he wouldn't say or do to get a laugh. His Everton teammate Alex Young recalled …*

'The practical joker had arrived from Molineux after they had won the Second Division title and some American trophy (the United Soccer Association title) which he made sound like the European Cup. He had been the top-scorer of an exciting attack which included centre-forward Derek Dougan, winger Dave Wagstaffe and the incredibly gifted Peter Knowles. When Wilf Dixon introduced him to his new teammates at Bellefield, Ernie pointed at me and proclaimed: "Alex Young? The Catt bought me to replace you!" Instantly, the dressing room fell silent as the coach cautioned him not to talk that way to someone who had celebrated league and cup triumphs with Everton and north of the border with Hearts.

'It got worse. The next day he upset Gordon West by hiding itching powder in his socks. The big goalie, known for his gentle disposition and wicked sense of humour, wasn't too pleased and yelled a derivative of the joker's surname coupled with an unflattering reference to the Mickey Mouse American trophy that Hunt liked to brag about.

'Then there was his exchange with Alan Ball during a League Cup game at Goodison. After I had scored two in the opening minutes, we lost our way and Sunderland had drawn level by halftime. Then with 10 minutes left, we were awarded a penalty. Vividly, I remember Ernie upsetting Alan by complaining that at his old club someone who had netted twice would be given the chance to complete his hat-trick. The World Cup winner's response was predictable: "Well, you're at Everton not bloody Wolves and you won't be here long if you do pipe down." Not only did the red-haired dynamo miss his spot-kick but he blamed Ernie when Sunderland scored the winner in the last minute.'

## Tommy Jackson and the 1967 Detroit Soccer Riot

*Shortly before joining Everton, the Glentoran midfielder was exposed to the dark side of the Brazilian beautiful game in the USA …*

'We were just a bunch of football-mad lads from Belfast who felt honoured to represent the Detroit Cougars in the United Soccer Association tournament. As part-time underdogs, we had surprised everyone – including ourselves – with our unbeaten run against a handful of more prestigious sides; that was until we encountered Bangu who were known as the Houston Stars. My recollection of events is a bit rusty. I remember us falling 2-0 behind and being frustrated that the shameless diving, flagrant play-acting, incessant petulance and over-the-ball tackles of the Brazilians had gone unpunished by the referee. I remember Danny Trainor being kicked in the head and retaliating by butting his aggressor. I think that I stepped in to separate them but have no recollection of being kicked in the back so hard that some South American coward left his stud-marks down my spine. After that, I understand that things deteriorated into a violent on-pitch brawl.'

Ian Thomson of the *Washington Post* filled in the details: 'Club president Johnston Nelson led the charge from the sidelines as a mass of Glentoran bodies joined the ruck from all angles. Bangu's players uprooted corner flags to use as weapons as they came under attack from the furious invaders. Nelson, a former Irish Guard, unleashed combinations of lefts and rights at the retreating Brazilians. With Jackson receiving treatment to his kidney area, the fighting continued for 10 minutes before the police restored order and the referee abandoned the game.

'Ironically, the United Soccer Association tournament – which did not have a television deal – had made it into US living rooms as highlights of the scrap were broadcast on the national news. Not that tournament commissioner Dick Walsh was celebrating the exposure: "This is a black mark on American soccer. We are trying to launch the game here and such incidents are not doing it any good."'

### The cultured Colin Todd

*Probably England's most polished central-defender in the 1970s, Colin Todd had two spells in British Columbia during his time with Sunderland before joining Everton …*

'Back in 1967, four or five British clubs travelled over to North America to promote soccer with the United Soccer Association. My team, Sunderland, went as the Vancouver Royal Canadians. At age 17, it was my first time abroad. We played in an old open-air ground (The Empire Stadium) and on very solid Astroturf. They were like exhibition games and I don't recall the attendances being that great. As for a favourite memory? We stayed in the same hotel as Little Richard. Jim Baxter had a drink with him and they argued over whether Richard had more gold discs than Jim had Scotland caps! "Slim Jim" was a drinker and gambler but a wonderful man and top player – we didn't see the best of him at Sunderland.

'I went back to Vancouver 17 years later – having played for Brian Clough's Derby, Jim Smith's Birmingham, Brian Clough's Forest and Gordon Lee's Everton. Alan Hinton was the manager and Terry Hennessey was the coach at the Whitecaps – they had both been with me at Derby. The Whitecaps played at a brand-new stadium (BC Place) with a very appreciative crowd and the football was much better than in the 1960s. We had Peter Ward, Franz Thijssen, Paul Bradshaw, David Cross and Carl Valentine.

'Unfortunately for me, I got injured in one of my first games. I played the full 90 minutes but was in horrendous pain. Because the X-ray didn't reveal anything, Terry and Alan thought that there was nothing wrong with me. So we went on the road trip and I played – even though I wasn't fit. Back in British Columbia I went for another scan and they found a stress fracture, so my leg went in plaster and that was me finished. My wife loved Vancouver and would have happily stayed out there. I recall that it was a bit chaotic at the end – we were urged to get our salaries and get out quick. But I believe that Canadian soccer is doing extremely well now.'

### Roy Vernon and the United Soccer Association

*After leaving Everton for Stoke City, the former-club skipper became a Cleveland Stoker during the summer of 1967. Again, Alex Young recalled …*

'I was Taffy's closest pal and roommate at Everton and, in private and public, he avoided discussing his dismissal from the 1961 tour. But he loved to recount his return to the North America as a Cleveland Stoker. Everyone knows that Taffy was a smoker, a drinker, a gambler and a bit of a lad and Cleveland was his kind of town.'

Vernon's antics were detailed in his biography: 'Settled in at the prestigious Pick Carter Hotel, Roy and his pals used the local university's sports field and the Cleveland Athletic Club's gym and pool for training. Off the pitch, they were known to enjoy afternoons tanning on the hotel roof and, needless to say, nights out at the hotel bar. Vernon's pal John Moore recalled: "Jackie March, Bill Bentley and I went to Taffy's room – he had been a drinking a bit too much. We picked him up along with his mattress and put them on the floor in the foyer and ran off. He never woke up. I don't know what happened, but he got his own back. He wrecked our room – he tipped it upside down.'"

While the Cleveland Stokers were pipped by Washington Whips to the Eastern title, Roy Vernon was named in the USA's All-Star Select XI. Of course, he was not your typical athlete. Aside from his tobacco addiction and legendary refuelling habits, the inside-left was slender in build – or as another teammate Terry Conroy eloquently put it: 'If he turned sideways you would mark him as absent.'

The United Soccer Association lasted just two seasons. In 1968, some degree of order was established when the top provincial leagues merged to form the North American Soccer League (NASL:1968-1984). The original intent was to slowly build the league towards financial viability while establishing and maintaining a presence on the US sports scene.

That changed when the New York Cosmos, backed by Warner Communications, pulled off the transfer coup of the century by luring the world's greatest player to North America in 1975. The arrival of Pelé dominated the media's attention and attendances soared nationwide – at least for a short-time.

The NASL was replete with marketing and football innovations which seemed impossibly alien to European eyes. To provide more excitement, the league's powers that be took the liberty of fiddling with the FIFA rules and introduced shoot-outs in the place of spot-kicks to decide draws. Commencing some 35 yards out, the dribbler would barrel down on the goalkeeper who would usually charge off his line towards him. Though popular in the NASL, the innovation did not take off elsewhere.

Just as Pelé had kick-started soccer in the USA, his retirement in 1977 coincided with its decline in popularity. After the league's television deal with ABC was not renewed, a belated salary cap caused many overseas stars to defect. Unfortunately, the NASL had failed to control costs which bankrupted one team after another until its death certificate was dated Thursday, 28 March 1985.

To many European observers, the league was little more than a retirement home for wrinkled stars to receive a final paycheque. Indeed, some of Everton's biggest names from the 1960s and 1970s chased the NASL dollar.

## MEMORIES OF LIFE IN THE NASL

### Alan Ball and the NASL

*One of The Old Lady's favourite sons, Ball was the youngest member of England's 1966 World Cup winning team. During the twilight of his career at The Dell, he enjoyed a couple of NASL summers ...*

'In 1978, I was appointed player-coach at Philly. My teammates included Johnny Giles, who was even older than me, and Peter Osgood, who looked older than the Irishman. Our team had a great time off the pitch but weren't very good on it. For me, it was eerie playing in front of 5,000 fans in the 60,000-seater Veterans Stadium.

'The following summer, I joined the Whitecaps. And believe me it was no holiday. Under the determined guidance of Tony Waiters, we upset Johan Cruyff and the LA Aztecs and Franz Beckenbauer and the New York Cosmos to nab the National Conference and then beat the Tampa Bay Rowdies in the NASL Soccer Bowl. We had a great bunch of lads. All British except for two or three Canadians. There was my old Everton pal Roger Kenyon, plus Tony Parkes (Queens Park Rangers), John Craven (Blackpool), Ray Lewington (Chelsea), Jon Sammels (Arsenal), Trevor Whymark (Ipswich Town), Willie Johnson (Rangers), Peter Daniel and Kevin Hector (Derby County) and a novice keeper named Bruce Grobbelaar. While our gates averaged 25,000, our victory parade through downtown was the largest gathering in

Vancouver history. The crowds were even bigger than those assembled to welcome the Queen and the Duke of Edinburgh.'

### Dave Clements in the eyes of his club and national manager

*Clements was appointed captain for the 1974/75 campaign, an extraordinary season during which Everton imploded during the run-in. His former boss Billy Bingham recalled in 2010 ...*

'I was an inexperienced manager under a lot of pressure to win a trophy, actually to capture the First Division title. I recall that after Bill Shankly had left Liverpool, our fans approached the new season with heightened optimism. I had assembled a quality team, one that was difficult to beat, and had added Bob Latchford, Martin Dobson and Dave Clements – one of the most underrated players in Everton's history who was handpicked to replace Howard Kendall. Although I thought of him as a young lad from Larne, he was mature beyond his years. Dave was my voice on the pitch and, thanks to his drive, we topped the table for most of the season. I remember his facial expression after we had chucked away a 2-0 lead to lose against Carlisle around Christmas. He was distraught. I reassured him that all teams stumble and the great ones recover quickly.

'We didn't lose again until we visited Middlesbrough in March. This set back was followed by a 3-0 disaster at – you guessed it – Carlisle. I can assure you that the chairman, manager and captain were as upset as the fans. We talked at length about our hiccups, but things continued to go against us at already relegated Luton Town and at Goodison to Sheffield United after leading 2-0 at the interval. Dave and the rest of the lads were shell-shocked.

'This late slump saw us finish fourth, three points behind Derby. The players and fans who remember that season still cannot believe how we chucked away such a golden opportunity to re-establish Everton as the top team on Merseyside. We all deserved better. I was delighted when the lad from Larne flew to New York to play alongside Pelé and some of the biggest names in the game. In my eyes, he wasn't out of place.'

### Terry Darracott – the rugged Roughneck

*Underrated as a player but celebrated as one of the club's greatest ever-servants, Darracott embraced soccer and life in the USA ...*

'America was brilliant – what an experience. I can talk about it until I go blue in the face. Everton were going to let me go in 1979. I was devastated as I never thought that I'd leave. Gordon Lee had offered me the job of reserve trainer, but I was only 29 and thought that I'd carry on until I was 35. Tulsa Roughnecks manager Alan Hinton and his assistant Terry Hennessey offered me a two-year contract. I thought that it would be a great experience for the family, living in North America. Tulsa paid £25,000 for me. The franchise had been in Hawaii before Tulsa so just I missed out! A lot of the lads were from Derby County and Nottingham Forest. Also we had Rubén Astigarraga, an Argentine left-footed magician, whilst our left-winger was an Iranian called Iraj Danifard – a superb footballer and a real grafter. We had four or five American kids who could be relied upon whenever they came in for the odd game or two – their attitude was superb. I was thrilled when Alan asked me to be captain. The experience of being a spokesman for players who had problems with the club helped me to grow.

'The club owner was Ward Lay, the man behind the internationally famous crisp company. We were in good hands but realised that the team had to be successful. The Roughnecks averaged crowds of 17,000 – which wasn't bad for a city that didn't know too much about soccer. Matchdays were remarkable. The fans parked up hours before kick-off and got out their BBQ grills, food and drinks to create an unbelievable family atmosphere at the Skelly Stadium.

'One-night Billy Epstein and Ella Fitzgerald sang the national anthem – they were sensational and brought the crowd to tears. Another time, a stuntman named Captain Dynamite dressed as Evel Knievel and lay down in a coffin on the centre spot. Next thing, there was an almighty explosion which blew it to bits. When he got to his feet, the whole place erupted. Off the pitch, the players went into the local community twice a week to coach boys and girls - it was brilliant.

'The Tulsa Roughnecks were good at home but a bit hit-and-miss away. As skipper, I was delighted to shake hands with Johan Cruyff for the coin toss-up before the game against the Los Angeles Aztecs. I remember that the Dutchman played everywhere on the pitch and everyone had to give him the ball. When we played at Fort Lauderdale, George Best had been missing for days – where he had been, goodness knows. So their manager put him on the bench. As I stood for the national anthem, my teammate Sammy Chapman said, "Can you believe we're on the pitch and he's a substitute?" The match finished 2-2 – Best came on and scored a brilliant winner in overtime.

'After every game, the host club put on a party for the fans to meet the players. I went over to George and asked if the Tulsa lads could have a chat with him. He was brilliant. One lad said, "George, we couldn't believe that you were sub tonight." He replied, "It's the coach, he's a right so and so – he wants me to train every day!" We all stood there with mouths open, flabbergasted and more or less nodded in agreement that the coach was out of order!

'Tulsa reached the NASL play-offs in 1979 but drew the New York Cosmos – the best and most popular team in North America. The city was buzzing when we beat them 3-0. The return game was in the massive 80,000-seater Giants Stadium in New Jersey. We got battered 3-0 and then lost in overtime. After I received a booking for fouling Johan Neeskens, his teammate Carlos Alberto smashed me in the face, out of view of the officials. I accepted it because he'd won the World Cup with Brazil! That was my last game in North America as I was beginning to feel pain in my right cartilage due to playing on the evil artificial turf. Within two weeks of coming home, I signed for Wrexham in the Third Division as they were able to pay the £25,000 that Tulsa wanted.'

## Jimmy Gabriel – Mr Soccer in Seattle

*'The Angel Gabriel' won the league and cup with Everton and also served the club as caretaker manager in 1990 and 1993 before driving the growth of soccer in Seattle and the Pacific North West …*

'My first exposure to US soccer was when my good friend and old teammate Alex Young told me about the mouth-watering offer he had received to play for the New York Generals. Even though it sounded like an exciting and very profitable way for him to wound down his glorious playing career, Alex rejected the deal to manage a bunch of part-timers in Belfast. I know, it doesn't make sense. That New York club folded at the end of the season but the NASL was born the next year and the New York Cosmos absorbed many of its best players. Alex could have been 'The Golden Vision of New York' and worshipped like Pelé is today.

'Some six years later, I got my own chance to move to the USA and join the recently formed Seattle Sounders – first as a player and then as player-manager. The team, which included two old foes – Mike England and Jimmy Robertson – won the Pacific Conference and reached NASL Soccer Bowl '77 in Portland only to fall to the New York Cosmos. I think Giorgio Chinaglia scored the winner. After the final-whistle, Pelé came into our dressing-room and presented me with the match-ball.

'Many NASL featured teams contained older players from the leading First Division clubs who had travelled to North America to pick up their final paycheque. There are too many to mention but off the top of my head there was George Graham and Frank McLintock from Arsenal plus the long-haired London kid (Charlie George) who broke Liverpool hearts at Wembley. Also, there was the cream of Stamford Bridge – Alan Hudson, Peter Bonetti, Charlie Cooke and Peter Osgood. Then there were top professionals such as Johnny Giles, Peter Lorimer and Terry Yorath from Leeds and Jim Holton, David Sadler and Alex Stepney from United. And how can I forget the big stars like George Best, Bobby Moore and Rodney Marsh. Many of them were as hard-working in the USA as they had been in England and earned their wages.

'While other clubs may stake a claim to some of our men, Everton were very well represented by Alan Ball, Roger Kenyon, Terry Darracott, Duncan McKenzie, Jimmy Husband, Colin Todd, Dave Thomas and my good friend Bruce Rioch. I almost forgot about Gary Jones, George Telfer and Cliff Marshall. And, of course, there was Steve Seargeant, Dave Clemence, Dave Irving, Brian Quinn and yours truly who decided to settle in North America. Apologies, if I've missed anyone.

'Not only did Everton Football Club provide more players than any other British club to aid the development of the NASL and Major League Soccer, it also provided some top-class coaches especially when you think of recent additions such as Preki, Bob Warzycha in the MLS and Adrian Heath in the USL. Without any doubt, the club has done its bit for North American soccer.'

# Richard Gough – a Goodison hero, an Ibrox icon

*At the dawn of the new millennium, Scotland international Richard Gough was at a crossroad in his illustrious playing career, but it was safe to say that Everton was not on his radar as a potential next-stop …*

'At age 36 and after a dozen years at Ibrox, my life with the San Jose Clash was very different. It was a big step down, there was this strange MLS play-off system and little edge to the games. I missed the type of intensity associated with being a Rangers or an Everton player. Off the field though, California felt right and my kids were going to school there. I had played in the USA previously with the Kansas City Wizards but had been called back to Ibrox in an emergency to help the club's 10-in-a-row bid when Lorenzo Amoruso and Alan McLaren were sidelined with injuries.

'At the end of the 1999 MLS season, I was playing for Nottingham Forest on loan from San Jose and was in the process of taking over the USA Under-20 team when I got an invitation from Harry Redknapp to play alongside a young kid at West Ham called Rio Ferdinand, who he wanted to learn from me. I called Walter Smith for his advice about what money I should be asking. Walter proposed that I join him and Archie Knox at Goodison and said that I would enjoy Liverpool more than London. So I went to Everton and played shoulder to shoulder with Dave Watson first and then David Weir, who I knew from his days at Hearts. Aside from having won lots of silverware with Rangers, I still had to prove myself to my new teammates. Looking back, I think I did that.'

*Gough brought leadership. His teammates still speak of him asking Walter Smith and Archie Knox to leave the dressing room so that he could address the players …*

'I only did that a couple of times in my whole career as the captain of a football club. I just said to the players "We're doing the same training as we did last year but now you're blaming the coaches and other things. We need to have a look at ourselves first." I told them to look at themselves in the mirror after every game and ask if they could have done any better or helped a teammate out of a difficult situation. I wanted us, as players, to look at ourselves. Afterwards, Mark Hughes declared, "That was absolutely brilliant, I've never seen anything like it." The bottom line is – it doesn't matter who is in charge, what matters is how you perform when you go out onto that field.'

In July 2020, Archie Knox – Walter Smith's assistant manager at Rangers and Everton – briefed the *Daily Record*: 'Experienced defenders are like experienced strikers – a couple of yards in the head are often better than a couple of yards in the feet. Richard Gough played for us at Everton when he was 39 and his central defensive partner, Dave Watson, had turned 40. He was at the heart of the defence in 1999 when Everton defeated Liverpool at Anfield. That day, he was up against Robbie Fowler and Michael Owen, two boys half his age, and they couldn't get near him. It's a great shame that players like Richard Gough are so few and far between these days.'

## Jimmy Husband in Memphis, Tennessee

*One of the young stars of 1969/70 title-winning side, 'Skippy' lit up the home of The Beatles in the late-1960s and the home of Elvis in the late-1970s …*

'I'd spent four great years at Luton but when David Pleat came in as manager I knew it was time for a change. After receiving a call from Eddie McCreadie, who had been appointed as the manager at the Memphis Rogues, we discussed a move to the NASL. I thought, "This is what I fancy doing." My wife Val was surprised but supportive. The Rogues were generous. They provided us with a three-bedroom condo and a company car – I just had to pay for the gas. Memphis was a great city; we'd go downtown to the bars playing live music. I built up my musical knowledge and became a fan of Willie Nelson, Waylon Jennings and the boys. Also Tennessee was fantastic for our kids, Jilly and Jamie, as there was so much for them to do.

'The team struggled. In addition to Alan Birchenall and Phil Beal, it included two Yugoslavians who couldn't stand each other. It was some years on – during the civil war in Yugoslavia – that I learned about the ethnic tensions and hatred there. The club's support was great and we had a lovely stadium – what they called a bowl. The average matchday temperatures were around 80F, so you couldn't run around British-style. We had to adapt – like foreign players do in the United Kingdom.

'Anyway, after two years the owner had money problems and the franchise was transferred to Calgary, Alberta. Negotiations for the Husband family to go there did not work out but Eddie McCreadie approached me as he'd got the manager's job at the Cleveland Force in the indoor league. Ohio was a total contrast to Memphis – there was little social life in the winter because there could be eight inches of snow, so you were not going to drive out to a restaurant at night.

'Football-wise, I did not enjoy the indoor game at all – it was more like ice hockey but without the sticks: Wham bam! Some teammates had been involved in that sort of soccer for years and would be playing one-twos off the walls. But it was all new to me and it was difficult to get used to the tactics. If you went over you would graze yourself, so you had to grease your knees and elbows before the game.

'After one season I moved on. The new ASL franchise in Oklahoma was being managed by Brian Harvey who had been in the USA for some years and knew the ropes. He got in touch with me and we immediately agreed terms. I had two good years in Oklahoma City. It has lots of history, good food, great music, Route 66 and all that, but by the end I was getting a bit knackered. Also, the franchise was struggling financially so I decided to get out while I was getting paid. But looking back we had five great years in North America.

'Other favourite memories? I would travel back after the NASL season had closed and maintain my fitness at Bellefield. I was in my early-thirties and beginning to ache all over. Usually after a bit or running I would seek a rub-down for one of the massage experts. Few people spoke to me. The person who kept me company was Bill Shankly who had retired and lived nearby in West Derby. He would lie on the adjoining table and talk for hours about coal mining, the Glenbuck Cherrypickers, his wife Nessie, the art of tackling, the beauty of Scotland, Dixie Dean and Tommy Lawton, Tom Finney and Preston North End and, of course, the colossus named Ron Yeats and his beloved Liverpool Football Club. I recall that before his death in 1981, Shanks wrote that he had been received more warmly by Everton Football Club than you know where.'

### Dave Irving and wet T-shirts

*After departing Everton, Irving joined Oldham Athletic in a move that would change the direction of his life. Subsequently, he spent four years playing and another 26 years coaching and managing in the USA …*

'Maurice Whittle, the Oldham captain, liked to travel to the USA in the off-season and invited me to join him at the Fort Lauderdale Strikers in 1979. I stayed for four months and played in the NASL with the legendary Gordon Banks. I loved Florida. It was a totally different lifestyle and I was like a kid in a candy shop. There was sunshine and beaches. I loved it. So much so that I opened a bar called "David Irving's Back of the Net Pub" and had a great time with my mates who included George Best. We judged many wet t-shirt competitions!

'During the next four decades, I played for teams in Tulsa, Atlanta and San Jose and also manged teams in Miami, Charlotte, Myrtle Beach, Wilmington and Tulsa. The highlight of my time on the pitch was a game against the New York Cosmos – whose line-up included Pelé – in front of 77,000 spectators. We lost, but it was an unbelievable experience.'

### Gary Jones and good times

*Jones illuminated Goodison with his portfolio of exciting skills but never realised his potential on either side of the Atlantic Ocean …*

'I was only 27 when I signed for the Fort Lauderdale Strikers, previously known as the Miami Toros. For a lad from Prescot, sunny Florida was the stuff of dreams. Surf, sand and good times – all year round. Even though Lockhart Stadium was no better than those used for high school kids and was thousands of miles away from what I had grown up with, my teammates included Gordon Banks, George Best, Ian Callaghan and Gerd Müller – some of the biggest names I've had the good fortune to play with in the Eastern Division of the NASL's American Conference or anywhere else for that matter. Our crowds of around 10,000 would drop to 1,000 if the fans got wind that Best or Müller weren't playing.

'Did I mention that it was a time of permed hair, sun blessed bodies and some really good times? Florida was a fantastic experience but the one thing that really bugged me about the Fort Lauderdale Strikers was that the squad was numbered alphabetically. Banks was No 2, Best was No 3 and I was unlucky No 13.'

## Roger Kenyon in BC

*Plagued by work-related injuries, the 'Goodison Assassin' moved to the NASL and powered the Vancouver Whitecaps to victory in Soccer Bowl '79. In 2001 he recalled his time in Canada …*

'I had fallen down the pecking order at Everton and was making only a few appearances per season. So, when Gordon Lee told me about an opening in Canada, I jumped at the chance. After all, if the Pacific Conference of the NASL was good enough for my old mate Alan Ball, then it would be good enough for me. Life in Vancouver was a mind-blowing experience. It is such a beautiful city. Back then, it was very British. The locals said it was more British than England.

'Our squad was definitely British. We featured only three locals – Buzz Parsons, Bob Bolitho and a young centre-half named Bob Lenarduzzi who went onto manage the Canada national side for an eternity. The only down-side to my three years in British Columbia was the thousands of miles we travelled to away games. We wasted so much time in airports, planes, hotels and US Customs.'

## George Kirby by The Golden Vision

*Chalk and cheese, the powerful centre-forward paved the transatlantic path for an icon – well almost. Back in 2000, Alex Young recalled his conversations with George Kirby about moving to the New York Generals …*

'Even though George had left Goodison before I moved down south from Hearts, I was almost a teammate of his in New York. It would have been an unusual coupling. His bustling approach and powerful shooting had been productive in the Second Division and well suited to the NASL type of football. I remember Freddie Goodwin – the New York boss, no doubt egged on by Harry Catterick – flattering me by saying that I was the answer to his need for a big British star to illuminate the biggest soccer club in the New York television market and offering me an unbelievably lucrative deal. He would think nothing of waking me at 3.00am to tell me about the size of the air-conditioned house, the depth of the swimming pool and the length of the luxury American automobile – it was an Oldsmobile, a make I had not heard of.

'Freddie was persistent. The next morning he would try to entice me with details of the likely bumper weekly pay-packet containing 2,500 greenbacks – which was about 10 times more than my wages and bonuses at Everton. He was insistent that I chat with the owners namely RKO General, Inc about sweetening the deal, George Kirby about life in New York and Phil Woosnam, then manager of the USA national side and soon-to-be commissioner of the NASL, about the growth of the game in North America. I recall that George revealed that his teammates were mostly from Argentina, Brazil, Germany and Trinidad and were a great bunch of lads. They also included Geoff Sidebottom from Aston Villa who had been a big pal of Freddie's when they were at Scunthorpe together. George chatted about the likely opponents and revealed that most of the defenders that he had played against in the USA were slow on the turn, crude in the tackle even by Scottish standards and would be mesmerised by my dainty footwork on the ground.

'The Generals were getting a bargain. The fee was only £7,500 but, and in the event of me returning home to join either an English or Scottish League club within two years, they would have to fork out another £12,500 to Everton. Even though the letters to cancel my Football League registration had been drafted, I declined the offer as I didn't want to disrupt my family. Also I didn't fancy the air travel to cities scattered across North America. Years earlier, I had toured Canada with Hearts and had hated everything about flying. Even so, I kept an eye on New York's results. That July, George and his pals played an exhibition match against Pelé and Santos. Such is life, while he was defeating the best of Brazil at Yankee Stadium – I was on my way to manage the semi-professionals at Glentoran. My timing could not have been worse. It was shortly before the onset of the sectarian conflict now known as "The Troubles" in Belfast. I lasted about three months, the violence went on for three decades.'

### Cliff Marshall and Pelé at Yankee Stadium

*A trailblazing winger on Merseyside, Marshall moved to the USA and met his football hero but not his music hero …*

'I was an out-and-out striker and played football for the love of the game, with a smile on my face. But, after one of the Everton coaches insisted that one of my priorities was to defend, I'd had enough and told Billy Bingham that I wanted to leave. I didn't know what I was going to do next but within two weeks I had a phone call inviting me to play for the Miami Toros. Getting there was a challenge. First, the US Consulate in Liverpool kept refusing to grant me a visitor's visa, so I phoned Everton. Within an hour, the visa was ready – that's the power of football clubs on Merseyside. Then, I was held at US Immigration for four hours with my new club's officials waiting outside. I think it had something to do with me having a visitor's visa and a pair of football boots in my suitcase. My uncle, an ex-military man, lived over there so I gave the immigration officers his number and they called him. He went ballistic and they soon let me in.

'The club gave me a good wage, a Corvette and a very nice apartment, which I shared with Gordon Fearnley (ex-Bristol Rovers) and one of my mates from home. We were always partying. We'd go deep-sea fishing then cook the catch on the beach. Barbeques, wine, women and song – what more could a single man want? My mate would tell people that he was a cousin of one of the Beatles; so we'd end up with free drinks. They were great times. The Miami Toros hierarchy, Joe and Elizabeth Robbie, also owned the Miami Dolphins – and soccer was something new for them to dabble in. The city was very Hispanic but for some reason the franchise found it difficult to attract supporters and moved to Fort Lauderdale for the next season. Therefore, I was shocked when it was announced that David Beckham was financing a Miami franchise and wondered if he had researched what had happened to the Toros. Maybe things have changed dramatically since 1976?

'Back then the standard was mediocre all round – below that of the Central League. Chris Lawler (ex-Liverpool) and Jim Holton (ex-Manchester United) had come over, plus we had a Peruvian and a Chilean along with a number of young Americans. I played about 10 or 12 games and, although on the wing, was given freedom to roam. Unlike at home, there wasn't any unpleasantness from supporters – but the game was taken less seriously. In Miami, it was all razzmatazz with enthusiastic cheerleaders and the stadium organ playing the Jaws theme as we were getting closer to the goal.

'For years I've been telling people that I had played against my hero Pelé at Yankee Stadium, but they'd look at me as if I was making it up. Recently, I found footage of his bicycle kick against the Toros (we lost 8-2) on YouTube and if you freeze the picture you can see me with "Marshall" on my back. Yes, it's me in that flash shirt!

'As for my music idol, Marvin Gaye was staying at our Rhode Island hotel. A few of us tried to sneak into his after-show party upstairs but there were some giant security guards on the lift. We thought they were for Marvin but found out that it was for Sammy Davis Jnr who had booked the whole of the 10th floor. Sadly, I never got to meet Marvin. I was gutted. Hand on heart, I still am.'

### Duncan McKenzie – a magical Roughneck

*In the mid-1970s, the Gwladys Street terraces resonated with thunderous chants of 'We all agree, Duncan McKenzie is magic.' But within 24 months, he had moved onto Chelsea, Blackburn and Tulsa …*

'After Peter Taylor, who had been with Brian Clough at Nottingham Forest, had heard about Blackburn needing to raise funds by selling me, he encouraged Terry Hennessey to sign me for the Tulsa Roughnecks in 1981. It was an attractive deal for a 31-year-old. On arriving in Oklahoma, Terry said, "Don't unpack, we are going to Bermuda tomorrow." The squad flew to Hamilton and checked into a grand hotel where Miss World was a receptionist – I thought "Wow". But for me, the most wonderful thing about the NASL was that I was being well paid to see the whole of continental North America in style – visiting fascinating places I never dreamt that I would see.

'Tulsa was fabulous. The club threw me a big welcome party which the mayor came to. I'd take my wife out for a meal and when I'd ask for the bill, somebody had already paid it (and left). Such incredibly nice people – I was a bloody idiot for coming back! My six-year-old son became best pals with a boy called Joe-Max – yes that one! His father Carl Moore co-owned Tulsa Roughnecks. He was a lovely guy who had grown up in poverty but made a fortune in the oil industry. He lent me a DeLorean car. Our families played golf, tennis and enjoyed each other's company. There were wondrous moments like playing at Tulsa Golf and Country Club which cost $40,000 to join but Carl told me I could play there any time that I wanted. The city had a floodlit course so that the workers at McDonnell Douglas could have a round after finishing their shift at midnight.

'As the Roughnecks started winning, the crowds grew. The club would give the young fans little gifts before each game like a dollar bill or one of those big pointy hands. The players did loads of soccer clinics in nearby towns. To encourage local kids to play soccer, we were required to have six Americans in the side. Those that were good were generally born and bred in Germany (their parents being in the US military stationed there) and grew up playing soccer or were naturalised US citizens originally from Central and South America. The others included players considered not quite good enough for league football in the United Kingdom and, of course, some of the biggest names that the soccer world had ever seen – who were on their last legs.

'I also played indoor soccer. In truth, I made one appearance during which I ripped my medial knee ligaments. The problem was that you played in hockey arenas and they would lay Astroturf on top of the ice. It was like bagatelle – whacking the ball off the walls. After I had strengthened my knee, I spent a year with the Chicago Sting. But coming to a big city from a friendly club like Tulsa was just not for me. I will never forget one incident in Chicago. After I had scored a winning goal, Karl Heinz Granitza (the NASL's second all-time leading scorer) came up to me in the showers and said, "You make the goals – I am the one who scores them in this team." I replied, "Well, I'm not stopping you."

'Nevertheless, we enjoyed some success. I recall that we drew 0-0 with Nacional of Uruguay, defeated Napoli 3-1 and the New York Cosmos 4-3 to win the 1982 Transatlantic Challenge Cup. The final was played at the New York Giants Stadium in front of 20,000 enthusiastic Italians, as Giorgio Chinaglia was the main man at the Cosmos. Our winner in overtime didn't go down too well with them. So, the organisers had to present us with the trophy in a pub down the street.'

### Tony McLoughlin and the 148th minute goal

*The first Everton former player to hook the NASL title died in August 2012. His youth team pal Jimmy Husband recalled the muscular striker ...*

'Tony was a big and powerful lad – often unplayable in the air – who would have excelled in an earlier era of British football. He did well across the pond and won the NASL title – which I can assure you was no small accomplishment. Tony deserves to be remembered and celebrated by Evertonians for that feat alone.'

McLoughlin played for Dallas at the time that the NASL indulged its passion for changing the long-established procedures for deciding competitions. Rather than arranging a showpiece at a neutral venue with possible replays or a two-legged format with aggregate scores, the NASL borrowed the play-off approach used in other American sports – especially baseball. Therefore in 1971, the NASL introduced a best-out-of-three system in which there would be no draws. Games tied after 90 minutes were settled by sudden death in favour of the first team to score the 'golden goal' in overtime periods lasting 15 minutes each – no matter how many periods it took for someone to score.

Consequently, Tony McLaughlin's Dallas Tornado and the Rochester Lancers and engaged in a war of attrition in the 1971 play-off semi-finals. In the first-leg at Rochester, the winner was scored by the hosts in the 176th minute – during the sixth period of overtime. The Texas side stormed back to claim the second game at home. The third game at Rochester was another defensive marathon which was settled in the 148th minute by McLaughlin. In the NASL final, Dallas lost the opener of the three-game series against the Atlanta Chiefs but won the second and third games convincingly to claim the 1971 NASL title.

## Bruce Rioch and Seattle

*The kilted warrior, who was born in Aldershot, enjoyed a tremendous playing career with Luton, Aston Villa, Derby and Everton but considers Seattle to be a special place ...*

'By 1980, I knew that Derby wanted to part company with me. So when Alan Hinton, my old teammate came to England to speak to me and asked, "Why not join me in Seattle?" I agreed to go for six months. I remember flying in on St Patrick's Day – over the Rocky Mountains on the approach to Seattle airport – and thinking that it looked absolutely amazing. It proved to be an incredible place to live and a great footballing move for me.

'The other lads from the old country helped me settle in and we had an incredible season, Breaking the record for wins in a NASL campaign. Our average gate that season was around 26,000. We played in the Kingdome Stadium – which was later demolished. We had 54,000 Against the New York Cosmos and 38,000 in our derby against the Vancouver Whitecaps. The games got better and better as our season progressed and the fans realised that this was a team that was entertaining and getting results.

'I recall playing for the Sounders in Tulsa, Oklahoma for the very time. It was 120F. We had a giant industrial oscillating fan to cool the dressing room but as soon as you stepped outside the sweat poured off you. My teammates Roger Davies and David Nish, who had played there previously for the Tulsa Roughnecks, cautioned, "If you hear the siren, get off the pitch as quickly as you can." I asked them, "What siren?" And they went, "The tornado warning siren." Holy moly, they marked my card with that! Also during the game, the trainers threw packs of crushed ice onto the pitch so you didn't know whether to stop to pick one up or continue to play the ball.

'In Seattle I had become extremely good friends with Jim Gabriel, who had been having been a tough and accomplished player. He was ingrained in Seattle football culture and was a true gentleman. After the Sounders and the NASL collapsed, I went back out there in 1985 and, with Jim, set up a soccer organisation called FC Seattle. We worked closely together to set up men's and women's teams and also establish a league on the Pacific Coast called the Western Alliance Challenge Series (WACS). In addition, we brought in teams from the United Kingdom and South America to play in guest fixtures. Nine of our girls were in the US women's national team. Sadly, the club imploded when the funding evaporated almost overnight so I came back to the old country looking for work.'

## Steve Seargeant and the Choo Choo cheerleaders

*'Sarge' was an ever-present for Everton during the 1974/75 season before being injured in the run-in. Without him, Billy Bingham's league leaders picked up only three points in the last four games and finished fourth. In 1978, he moved to the USA where he still lives …*

'When Gordon Lee bought England international Mike Pejic I thought that I had no chance of getting back in the team and asked for a transfer. Manager Ken Furphy, a one-time Everton reserve who had coached Pelé at the New York Cosmos, saw me play for Everton Reserves and sold me on the idea of playing in the Silverdome which was shared with the NFL Detroit Lions. I signed a two-year contract and planned to return to the United Kingdom. Detroit is a down-to-earth blue-collar city and the people are great – it's a lot like Liverpool. As I flew into the airport, I was looking out for soccer goalposts on the sports fields – there were none.

'The Detroit Express was co-owned by Jimmy Hill, the former PFA boss, Coventry chairman and host of the BBC's *Match of the Day*, but the club was as American as apple pie, hot dogs and Chevrolet. We played on artificial turf at the 80,000-capacity Pontiac Silverdome. Our modest crowds, usually around 10,000, were entertained by the razzmatazz of the Choo Choo cheerleaders. Our radio jingle, which went something like "Catch Detroit's Express … it's our new soccer team … now we have everything," was played ad-infinitum on the local stations.

'Our line-up had a British core. We had a decent defence with the likes of Eddie Colquhoun and Graham Oates, which was reinforced by Tony Dunne and Jim Holton of Manchester United fame. Up front, we had Alan Brazil and Mark Hateley. The arrival of Trevor Francis from Birmingham City, however, changed the face of the franchise. He was a revelation, scoring 36 goals in his 33 games for the Express. His awesome skills stole the hearts of Detroit soccer fans. Also, his movement made me look like a very good passer of the ball! Trevor was coming back from injury but was still the best player in the NASL. Lethal inside the area, he had a terrific turn of speed – a fifth gear. Also, Trevor was a top-class guy. We all signed autographs after a match, but he would stop behind for another 30 minutes signing them. Of course, Trevor would become the first £1 million Englishman when he later joined Brian Clough's Nottingham Forest.

'At the end of one season we went on tour to Austria, Luxembourg and Kuwait. Contractually, we were required to have a big-name player, so George Best joined us in Linz. The next morning, he came down with his suitcase and announced, "Well I'm off back to the States, I'm fed up." Somehow, they managed to get Bobby Moore out to Kuwait for our next match and I ended up playing at centre-back alongside one of my heroes. I did all the running and he did all the passing! He was phenomenal.

'In addition, I played in the indoor league – on Astroturf in ice hockey rinks. The crowd loved it as it was more like an American sport. It was fast – backwards and forwards all the time. The action didn't stop – you would do short shifts then touch the other guy and he'd jump in.

It was all on the fly. Our keeper, Slobe Ilijevski, was unbelievable. He scored 20 goals. I had enjoyed three seasons outdoors and another two indoors and was settled in Michigan but after Jimmy Hill moved the franchise to Washington DC, I left for California among the chaos.

'The Express had sold 6,000 season-tickets and lined up agreements with the local radio and television stations to carry games for the 1981 outdoor season. We had no warning. Though our families were waiting for us back in Detroit, we were told that would be flying to RFK Memorial Stadium to play our first game as the Washington Diplomats. Ken disclosed that he would not be taking me to DC so I went to Anaheim and teamed up with Carlos Alberto at the California Surf. Then at age 31, I joined the Phoenix Inferno in a new league called the Major Indoor Soccer League. I loved it there – living near the famous red rock mountains from September to May. It was swimming pool weather on Christmas Day. After I got my green card, I went back to Detroit to run soccer camps and clinics. American kids are funny. Some are mad about watching the game. They know the name Everton but don't have much of a clue about what's happened in games.'

### George Telfer and the dreaded Astroturf

*Telfer spent nine seasons in the senior squad at Everton but going to North America in 1981 was not the best decision in his career …*

'After I left Everton in May 1981, I was contacted by several decent English clubs but received an excellent offer from the San Diego Sockers of the NASL – it was a four-year contract at a very good salary. I flew out to Georgia to join the Sockers who were about to play against the Atlanta Chiefs. After I landed there, I had a problem with US immigration as I only had £50 in my pocket. The authorities kept me at the airport until someone from the club came to rescue me. I didn't play in that match, nor in the next one against the Washington Diplomats, who had Johan Cruyff in their line-up. I made my debut on Independence Day at Tampa Bay. I don't remember too much about the game but recall having a fitness test on the local beach. Looking on were Lawrie McMenemy, Glenn Hoddle and Steve Archibald. I was dripping in sweat when Lawrie said, "George, you look like a Greek god!" The matchday heat was unbelievable – even for a Greek god – and I couldn't continue after half-time. I was exhausted.

'From Tampa we went back to San Diego, where I did a couple of television interviews as they wanted to know the difference between British and American soccer. Back then, one key thing was the variety of nationalities at San Diego. We had Kaz Deyna – the Poland midfielder who had played for Manchester City, Volkmar Gross – the German keeper who had been suspended for two years from the Bundesliga and banned for life from the national team because of his involvement in match fixing – and Juli Veee – a Hungarian who went onto play for the USA national team and was one of the best players I have ever seen. Being right next to the border, we played in several tournaments in Mexico. Some of my teammates lived in Tijuana and crossed the border to play. For me, it was staggering going from such shocking poverty to the beauty and luxury of California.

'We travelled all over the country living out of our suitcases. At home, we played at the Jack Murphy Stadium – the abode of the San Diego Chargers of the NFL and the San Diego Padres of MLB – which retained the markings for the baseball diamond. We got to the semi-final of the Soccer Bowl and were beaten in the third game by the Chicago Sting at Comiskey Park. Sadly, I had a bit of a nightmare with injuries having torn a cartilage playing against the Jacksonville Tea Men. My agreement allowed me to turn out for an English club in the winter – but the Sockers wanted me to play indoors. To be honest, I was never the best five-a-side player. So, we had a bit of a dispute and I returned home. The only club I could get fixed up with was Scunthorpe United – which shows how quickly you are forgotten.'

### Dave Thomas sans shin-pads

*With his socks rolled down, the left-winger helped Bob Latchford net 30 league goals in 1978 before spending one season in the NASL. Recently, he became the first ex-England star to be registered blind and receive a guide dog – a Labrador named Hannah …*

'After leaving Everton, a club that I still love, my career went downhill. I felt like I was falling out of love with the game and the people in it. Then in 1981 Johnny Giles signed me for Vancouver Whitecaps from Wolverhampton Wanderers. Looking back, it was a great experience for me, my wife Brenda and our two girls – even if things were a bit "Mickey Mouse" at times. They loved their football in Vancouver – there were 30,000 fans for every home game. The pitch was an Astroturf carpet with concrete underneath. It took some getting used to. If you knocked the ball past the full-back in order to get a cross in, the ball would run so quick that, more often than not, it would go out of play. So it needed to be a game to feet rather than knocking the ball ahead of anybody.

'I had signed for three years but because the NASL rules allowed only six places for foreigners, I didn't play some of the time. As for my teammates? Peter Beardsley was signed from Carlisle. You could tell that he was going to be a very good player. Also, there was Roger Kenyon – another good player. My old Everton teammate was quiet and humble but tough, he wasn't someone you wanted to get in a fight with!'

### Ray Veall – the first NASL Toffee

*Following spells at Preston and Huddersfield, the dashing winger embarked on an exciting footballing odyssey which took in three continents including North America ...*

'I was too hasty to leave Doncaster. The opportunity came around too quickly. It was a hell of a big jump for a naive boy. At Everton, we had a very good side and I played with great footballers. I just wish it had lasted longer. I got disheartened and disillusioned. I had a niggling injury that held me back. So, I faded out of the scene.

'Somehow Ray Wood, the former Manchester United goalkeeper who had been appointed coach at the Los Angeles Wolves, knew that I didn't want to continue at Huddersfield and approached me about playing in the NASL. I thought that a change was as good as anything. Ray scoured England for players and picked up a couple of Brazilians then brought everyone together in Leeds during the middle of winter. While he was away, I was left in charge of training. I went round to their hotels in the morning, but it was so freezing that they didn't want to get out of bed.

'Then we went to Los Angeles. We would meet at the Kings' Forum every day and train at a nearby park. On a Saturday or Sunday we'd get the bus to the Pasadena Rose Bowl to play our home games. It had a capacity of 100,000 – we had crowds of 5,000. Most fans came as families. They thought that we were wonderful because we were English professionals. They treated us as stars. Also, the club looked after us. We got to see the LA Lakers (basketball), the LA Kings (ice hockey), boxing matches and big shows – they made us feel important.

'We played in the stifling summer heat. I vividly remember coming off at half-time one day and having to go on the oxygen bottle – it was so hot and humid that I couldn't breathe. But the NASL gave me a new lease of life. The lower tempo suited me. There were some good players – some up to English First Division standards. The league was split into sections of four. We were in the one along the West Coast but played other teams. At Dallas, one of their lads approached me, 'Are you Ray Veall?' It was Brian Harvey, Colin's brother. Based on his recommendation, I received a call asking if I would like to play for them. After the Wolves folded, my wife and I didn't really want to leave. We had made a lot of friends and enjoyed a lovely lifestyle. The USA was a tremendous experience. We lodged with Ruth's sister in Leyland until I received information that South Africa wanted players, so that's where we went next. Then it was onto New Zealand where we have been very happy.'

### Defender Mike Walsh and the Sunshine State

*One of Howard Kendall's infamous 'Magnificent Seven', the central-defender failed to settle on Merseyside before leaving for sunny Florida in 1983 …*

'Brian Kidd, who I knew at Bolton, put in a word with his manager at Fort Lauderdale. The Strikers had some great players including Ray "Rocky" Hudson who was the "Gazza before Gazza" at Newcastle, Keith Weller, Ricky Villa and Jan Van Beveran, who had been Holland's top goalkeeper. After arriving in Florida, I had one week to acclimatise to the humidity. At first you think that you will not be able to cope, but you adjust to it.

'I'll never forget my first game in North America – I was on the subs' bench in Montreal. The players ran onto the pitch when their names were read out and waved to the fans. When the announcer got to the substitutes and read out my name, Brian Kidd, who was sat next to me, said: "Right, get on!" So, I ran onto the pitch waving enthusiastically as he and the other substitutes laughed at me. Of course, it was only the starting eleven who were supposed to do that. I had to go off at the far side and walk around the pitch with them in stitches. Eventually, when I came on as substitute, I went in for a sliding tackle on the Astroturf and ripped my skin from my knee to my hip. I did not do it again!

'It was different to English football – the grass pitches were better than the muddy ones at home and you could play with the ball a bit more. The heat and humidity – even at night – was a big disadvantage to the teams coming to play Fort Lauderdale. Players had to keep taking water on board. The pace was much slower than in England where it was a million miles an hour. What I found difficult was the bodychecking around the edge of the box. In England you would be awarded indirect free kicks for obstruction, but the North American referees did not award them.

'Florida was really enjoyable. I had penned a two-year deal, bought a house and thought that we would settle there. It was a beautiful place and the people connected to the club were fabulous. But at the end of the season, the owners Joe and Elizabeth Robbie pulled the plug claiming that soccer was not financially viable and dispatched the franchise to Minneapolis – a place I knew nothing about. I could have gone there but Manchester City came in. It was was a chance to get back to the city of my birth – even though I was a United fan. I found it strange at Maine Road as I was half-thinking about the American way of defending. I wish I had gone to Minnesota now!'

### Bruce Wilson in the Central League

*Canada's greatest-footballer had successful trials with Everton in 1975 but returned to the NASL to flourish in Vancouver, Chicago, New York and Toronto …*

'The try-out at Everton at the end of the 1975 NASL season was organised by Jim Easton, my coach at Vancouver, with help from John Best and Jimmy Gabriel, who were coaches in Seattle. I had Scottish and English grandparents, so my heritage allowed me to come over for the trial. I had travelled over alone and was fortunate that Barrie Mitchell – who played for Tranmere Rovers – had me stay with him. I definitely felt welcome at Everton. I was able to hook a ride to training with Dave Clements. He was a captain and also a very nice fellow. I picked up a number of good little tips from him as the days went on. My first impression of Bellefield was that it looked tremendous. The fields were fabulous whereas those in North America were artificial. Training was very physical in terms of amount of running at each session.

'I played in four reserve team matches with the younger players and others coming back from injury. I did well. When I was offered a contract in early-November – Billy mentioned that if I signed he would give me a chance with the first team sometime in December. I had to weigh up a lot of issues related to England and giving Everton a real go. In the end, my wife was unable to get a work visa for the United Kingdom and I was offered a teaching job in conjunction with carrying on with the Whitecaps. So, I decided to go back to the NASL.'

After the demise of the NASL, many so-called experts saw outdoor soccer as alien to the average North American sports fan who demanded more action, more goals and lots more razzmatazz. They believed that the future of lay indoors with the Major Indoor Soccer League (MISL).

## OTHER MEMORIES OF YESTERYEAR

### Indoors with Brian Monaghan

*The diehard Blue moved from the fringes of the Everton first team to the USA to become an indoor goal king and a highly respected coach …*

'I remember my career at Everton like it was yesterday. As one of Billy Bingham's blue-eyed boys, I was privileged to captain the youth team in both legs of the 1977 FA Youth Cup final. We had a very good side which included Mark Higgins, Martyn Murray – cursed as the next George Best – and Joe McBride and almost picked up the prestigious trophy. 1977 was a tough year for Evertonians. We lost both the League Cup final second replay to Aston Villa and the FA Cup semi-final replay to Liverpool in April after being robbed by a certain referee from Treorchy, then surrendered the FA Youth Cup to Crystal Place in May.

'Throughout my two-year professional career at Everton, I was on the verge of the first team and travelled with them on six occasions as 13th man – the one that pushes the skip. When I was released at the end of the following season, manager Gordon Lee said: "Don't give up son. You'll score goals wherever you go but you're not my kind of player." Like many youngsters before me, I was gutted by the news. Absolutely gutted.

'Thanks to John Benison, the youth coach at Liverpool, I enjoyed a couple of spells in Australia and then a new life in the USA. At age 28, I joined the Austin Sockadillos. Established by Fernando Marcos, who in my eyes is the man who put modern soccer on the North American map, the team was managed by Tony Simões, the former Benfica and Portugal star, with the help of Wolfgang Sühnholz. We played in the United States Interregional Soccer League (USISL), which was established initially to develop players for the Major Indoor Soccer League (MISL). With lower operating costs, the league was financially stable whereas both the MISL and the American Professional Soccer League (APSL) failed. The Sockadillos played at Tatu's All-Star Indoor Soccer Place which resembled an abandoned aircraft hangar. The pitch was artificial turf of one type or another. The crowds were extremely modest – typically around 500.

'Nonetheless, I scored goals for fun – 71 in 22 games and was voted MVP of the USISL in 1989. Not bad for a lad from Bootle. In the summer we ventured outdoors as the Capital Sockadillos and played initially in the Southwest Outdoor Soccer League. But around 1992 I decided to concentrate on coaching and, as a result, have supervised several of the biggest youth soccer clubs in Texas. Also as head coach of the US Youth Soccer Olympic Development Program (Region III) between 1989-2007, we made many trips to play against Europe's finest and accelerated the development of some big names including Stuart Holden (Houston) and Clint Dempsey (Dallas).

'As executive director of soccer at Lonestar Soccer Club, we have in excess of 7,000 members from ages 4 to 19. We are coaching the children of the kids that I had coached. In some geographical locations, soccer is pushing American football, basketball and baseball for the hearts and minds of sports fans. Nowadays, Austin is a soccer-mad city and a local MLS franchise is building a soccer-specific stadium and an ultra-modern training complex. All European clubs want a North American footprint but, at this time, I fear that Everton is in the middle off the pack. That said, I look forward to my beloved club playing against Austin – I would consider it compensation for being released by Gordon Lee.'

### Asa Hartford and the Bogota Connection

*Acknowledged as having one of the finest turbo-charged engines in British football in the 1970s, some three years after leaving Everton, Hartford powered the Fort Lauderdale Sun to the USL title in 1984 …*

'In my final season at Manchester City, manager Billy McNeil and I didn't really see eye to eye. So going to the United States seemed to be a great way of keeping fit. I had met Ronnie Sharp, the Fort Lauderdale Sun owner, and another guy – who seemed a bit "wide" – in a hotel just off the M56 near Manchester Airport. I doubted that anything would come of it – but it did. And in 1984, I went to sunny Florida, made about 30 appearances in the United Soccer League and loved every minute of it. I was pleased to be playing, feeling fit and injury free. The Sun played at the Lockhart Stadium, which was on the site of where David Beckham's franchise is based now. Back then there was no roof and the stands were temporary bleachers made from scaffolding. It was a far cry from Goodison and Maine Road.

'Keith Weller was the coach. There was a New York guy called Tommy Mulroy who was whiter than white apart from his red raw left arm as he had driven down to Florida with it hanging out of the car window. We had Dave Watson (ex-Sunderland and Manchester City) and Teofilo Cubillas, a top Peruvian player who we called him "El Nene" because of his boyish looks. Then there were three guys from Haiti – it was the first time that I had seen players warming up in the changing room before kick-off by jiving and dancing with their Sony Walkman headphones on.

'Early in the season, Ronnie Sharp got done for smuggling a couple thousand pounds in weight of marijuana from Columbia. We read the headline in the *Miami Herald* – "Sun owner in drugs swoop." He did a deal with the DEA, I believe – I didn't much care for his chances of living after that. All the American lads were saying it was a pity that he got caught, as they would have definitely got their bonus that year!'

### Billy Kenny Senior in the Eyes of a Corinthian

*In 2004, Brian Labone reflected on some of the local teenagers who had failed to fully realise their potential at Everton. They included his former-teammate Billy Kenny Snr…*

'Billy was a tidy midfielder who had the misfortune to play in a depleted midfield in a markedly average Everton side. I had watched him come through the junior ranks and had expected him to provide cover for Colin Harvey and Alan Ball, both of whom were struggling with a series of injuries in 1971. He made his first team debut about 10 days after my final appearance when the side was in a state of flux. Instead of the revered "Holy Trinity", Harry Catterick was required to select a midfield featuring the likes of Henry Newton, Terry Darracott and Billy Kenny.

'Shortly after Mick Buckley, who was a younger version of Colin Harvey, made his breakthrough, Billy – like so many Everton youngsters before him – left for Tranmere. Then he drifted into the American Soccer League with some obscure team in Cleveland, Ohio and finally the Cheshire League. From Everton to Ashton United in three years! On the subject of a rapid decline, there can be no sadder example than his son who, in the eyes of many, was the type of creative teenage genius that an Everton manager could build a successful team around. Sadly, his promising career was terminated by serious addictions. What a waste!'

### David Weir – a product of the American collegiate soccer system

*Weir's time at Everton was bookended by spells in Scotland with Hearts and Rangers where he was voted Player of the Year at age 40. But his playing career began at a small private university in Indiana in 1988 …*

'To be honest, Evansville wasn't my choice. They picked me! I was playing in a tournament for Scotland schoolboys in Skegness, where we competed against the best county sides in England. A lot of American colleges were there looking for recruits. Anyway, I got a tap on the shoulder from the man from the University of Evansville. At that time, I was seriously thinking about going to university but also wanted to be a professional footballer – so the offer ticked both boxes … and they were going to pay for it. The move was a massive leap for me because prior to going to the USA I had never been on a plane! The standard of soccer at Evansville was very good, we played the best NCAA teams and we were consistently ranked in the top 20 college teams in the USA.

'I suppose that I could have stayed in North America but at that time the only professional option was the indoor soccer league and that wasn't for me. I wanted to make a career out of football, so I moved back to the United Kingdom. I joined Falkirk and made my first team debut at the age of 22. Possibly my four years at Evansville and my late introduction to the professional game allowed me to play until I was 40. Maybe it helped my mindset. Certainly, it gave me a greater perspective on life and probably made me appreciate being a professional footballer a bit more because I wanted to squeeze every single second out of my playing career for club and country.'

*Goodison lore has it that the 2004/05 season, when the team qualified for the Champions League, was constructed on the foundations of a pre-season trip to Houston …*

'It was difficult time for us as a group of players, and for the manager, because things weren't right and there were issues on both sides that needed to be tackled. There wasn't a full and frank discussion every day, but we all got to know each other a little bit better, players and staff, and the lads got a few things off their chests. We came back from Houston knowing exactly what to expect from each other. We had a lot of fun, trained really hard and played a couple of really good games. As a pre-season trip, it genuinely could not have gone any better.'

*All of the Toffeemen who played in the leagues of yesteryear are profiled with pen-pictures and caricatures. They appear in alphabetical order. Some names are more familiar than others but none is greater than World Cup winner Alan Ball ...*

# Alan Ball

**played for**

Ashton United,

Blackpool,

Everton,

Arsenal,

Hellenic (South Africa) (loan),

Southampton,

Philadelphia Fury (loan),

Vancouver Whitecaps,

Blackpool,

Southampton,

Floreat Athena (Australia) (loan),

Eastern AA (Hong Kong),

Bristol Rovers

**coached at**

Philadelphia Fury,

Blackpool,

Portsmouth,

Colchester United,

Stoke City,

Exeter City,

Southampton,

Manchester City,

Portsmouth

Well equipped with sublime skills, swaggering self-confidence and a finely-tuned Rolls-Royce engine, Ball was proof that red hair is no bar to greatness. He was lured from Blackpool for £112,000 after his indefatigable man-of-the-match display in the 1966 World Cup final at Wembley. With his white-hot Hummel boots in perpetual motion Everton's 'Ball of Fire' combined tireless tenacity and hatred for losing with timely goals to convert 'The Holy Trinity' of Kendall, Harvey and Ball into the most dominant midfield unit of its era. The 1970 coronation was scant reward for their superiority. Ball's exit to Arsenal at age 26 for a UK record fee of £220,000 remains one of football's mysteries. While at Southampton, the then veteran enjoyed two productive summers in North America – winning the 1979 NASL title with the Vancouver Whitecaps.

| Everton 1966/67–1971/72 | | |
| --- | --- | --- |
| | games | goals |
| League | 208/0 | 66 |
| Total | 251/0 | 79 |

# Geoff Barnett

**played for**
Everton,
Arsenal,
Minnesota Kicks

**coached at**
Minnesota Kicks

A sought-after schoolboy prodigy, the Northwich-born shot-stopper won the FA Youth Cup in 1965 as well as England Under-23 recognition alongside Jimmy Husband and John Hurst. Solid displays by Gordon West and Andy Rankin limited Barnett to just 10 League outings during his seven seasons at Goodison. An agile goalkeeper who controlled his goalmouth with no little courage, Barnett was sold to Arsenal for £35,000 in October 1969 as an understudy to Scotland regular Bob Wilson. Even though he missed out on that club's 1970/71 double-winning season, Barnett played around 50 first team games for the Gunners including the 1972 FA Cup final against Leeds United before joining the NASL's Minnesota Kicks in early-1976.

| Everton 1962/63-1969/70 | | |
|---|---|---|
| | games | goals |
| League | 10/0 | 0 |
| Total | 10/0 | 0 |

# Peter Beardsley

**played for**
Wallsend Boys Club,
Carlisle United,
Vancouver Whitecaps,
Manchester United,
Vancouver Whitecaps,
Newcastle United,
Liverpool,
Everton,
Newcastle United,
Bolton Wanderers,
Manchester City (loan),
Fulham,
Hartlepool United,
Melbourne Knights

**coached at**
England,
Newcastle United

The football virtuoso featured in over 800 first-class matches during his 20-year playing career – including 73 outings in his two spells at Vancouver. Wherever he played, Beardsley was an expert at unlocking defences with his near flawless technique. No more so than at Liverpool, where the England ace helped the Reds claim League titles in 1988 and 1990 and the FA Cup in 1989. After falling out of favour at Anfield, he was picked up by manager Howard Kendall for a bargain £1 million in 1991. Even at age 30, his guile and timeless skills continued to create chances for his teammates and bag goals for himself. But with Everton suffering financial woes, he re-joined Newcastle for £1.4 million in 1993. David Johnson and Beardsley are the only men to have scored for both clubs in the Merseyside derby.

| Everton 1991/92-1992/93 | | |
|---|---|---|
| | games | goals |
| League | 81/0 | 25 |
| Total | 95/0 | 32 |

# Mick Bernard

**played for**

Shrewsbury Town,
Stoke City,
Cleveland Stokers (loan),
Everton,
Oldham Athletic

Alongside Roy Vernon and his other Stoke City mates, Bernard played for the Cleveland Stokers in the United Soccer Association during the 1967 season. Some five years on, the tough-tackling midfield bruiser – who was often prone to physical excess – was signed by manager Harry Catterick for £140,000 to fill the gigantic void created by Alan Ball's sensational exit. Having failed the unenviable challenge, he was converted into an unyielding full-back by new manager Billy Bingham. Though often sidelined by injuries, Bernard was a member of squad that lost the League Cup final to Aston Villa in 1976 – appearing in the first replay at Hillsborough. He joined Second Division Oldham Athletic for £25,000 in 1977 but retired almost immediately due to calf problems.

| Everton 1971/72-1976/77 | | |
| --- | --- | --- |
| | games | goals |
| League | 139/8 | 8 |
| Total | 160/11 | 8 |

# Ian Bishop

**played for**
Everton,
Crewe Alexandra (loan),
Carlisle United,
Bournemouth,
Manchester City,
West Ham United,
Manchester City,
Miami Fusion,
Barry Town,
Rochdale,
Syracuse Salty Dogs,
Burscough,
New Orleans Shell Shockers

**coached at**
Evergreen (Virginia)

Bishop was a local teenager whose rebellious nature masked his astute football brain, precise passing, and crisp tackling. Curiously, the midfielder made only one substitute appearance for Everton before being discarded by new manager Howard Kendall. It was a bizarre decision. Regardless, he rebuilt his career in the Second Division at Carlisle United and Bournemouth before joining Manchester City in 1989 for £465,000. Months later, after a change in manager, the budding cult hero was sold by his old nemesis Kendall to West Ham United where he sparkled for a decade before returning to Maine Road in 1998, aged 33. After his second spell in sky blue, which involved relegation to the third tier and amazing back-to-back promotions to the top-flight, Bishop enlisted with the short-lived Miami Fusion in Major League Soccer.

| Everton 1983/84 | | |
| --- | --- | --- |
| | games | goals |
| League | 0/1 | 0 |
| Total | 0/1 | 0 |

# Dave Clements

**played for**
Millbrook,
Portadown,
Wolverhampton Wanderers,
Coventry City,
Sheffield Wednesday,
Everton,
New York Cosmos,
Colorado Caribous

**coached at**
Northern Ireland,
Colorado Caribous,
Denver Avalanch,
St Louis Steamers,
Kansas City Comets,
University of Denver Pioneers

An important member of the Coventry City side that advanced to the top-flight in 1967, Clements decided to stay in the Second Division with Sheffield Wednesday where he developed into a solid full-back and a no-frills midfielder. He was transferred to Everton for £80,000 in 1973. Though no teammate won the ball more or passed it more often, the captain failed to halt the unfathomable implosion of manager Billy Bingham's side during its quest for First Division glory in 1975. While still at Goodison, the intrepid 29-year-old replaced Terry Neill as player-manager of Northern Ireland before being tempted by the riches of the NASL. He continued his influential form alongside Pelé at the New York Cosmos and was selected as a member of the star-spangled Team America in the Bicentenary Cup competition against Italy, Brazil and England.

| Everton 1973/74-1975/76 | | |
|---|---|---|
| | games | goals |
| League | 81/4 | 6 |
| Total | 97/5 | 8 |

# Terry Darracott

**played for**

Everton,

Tulsa Roughnecks,

Wrexham,

Prescot Cables

**coached at**

Everton,

Manchester City,

Blackburn Rovers,

Wrexham,

Bolton Wanderers (scout),

Hull City (scout)

Strong, brave and honest in the tackle, Darracott made his senior debut for his boyhood club against Arsenal in 1968 at just 17 years and 122 days as the back-up for World Cup winning left-back Ray Wilson. Possibly more effective as a no-nonsense man-marker against the likes of Manchester City's Colin Bell, Manchester United's George Best and Arsenal's Alan Ball, he was Everton's first-choice left-back throughout the 1973/74 season. Sadly, his place in Merseyside football lore was cemented by a fatal error in the dying seconds of extra-time in the second replay of the 1977 League Cup final against Aston Villa. The lifelong Evertonian moved to the NASL in 1979 to give similar steadfast service as captain of the Tulsa Roughnecks.

| Everton 1967/68-1978/79 | | |
| --- | --- | --- |
| | games | goals |
| League | 138/10 | 0 |
| Total | 168/11 | 0 |

# Chris Dunleavy

**played for**

Everton,
Southport,
Philadelphia Atoms,
Chester,
Halifax Town,
Wollongong City

Despite his lack of inches, the 5ft 10in centre-half enjoyed a 15-year playing career involving more than 400 first team games for clubs in northern England plus spells in North America and Australia. After failing to progress beyond the Central League side, the 19-year-old defender – like so many local youngsters before him – dropped down to Third Division (South) port in 1969 only to taste relegation at the conclusion of his first season at Haig Avenue. In 1973, Dunleavy moved to the NASL for the first of his two seasons with the Philadelphia Atoms. Composed mostly of unheralded North Americans, the team clinched the NASL title at the end of their first-ever season. After his second stretch, which coincided with Philadelphia introducing professional indoor soccer to the USA, the resolute defender signed for Fourth Division Chester.

| Everton 1967/68-1968/69 | | |
|---|---|---|
| | games | goals |
| League | 0/0 | 0 |
| Total | 0/0 | 0 |

# Pat Dunne

**played for**

Stella Maris,

Everton,

Shamrock Rovers,

Manchester United,

Plymouth Argyle,

Boston Rovers (loan),

Shamrock Rovers,

Thurles Town,

Shelbourne

**coached at**

Thurles Town,

Shelbourne,

Shamrock Rovers

The Dublin teenager spent three years as back-up to Albert Dunlop without making his debut. Known for having one arm longer than the other, he moved to Shamrock Rovers where he completed the League of Ireland double. Dunne was signed by Matt Busby for £10,500 in 1964 and, with Best, Charlton and Law, won the league title in his first season. Though capped by Ireland, the emergence of John Gaskell resulted in his sale to Plymouth for £5,000. Shortly after his arrival, he became a guest player for Boston Rovers in the 1967 United Soccer Association fixtures and was voted keeper of the tournament. At age 27, Dunne rejoined Shamrock Rovers only to become the first man to be shown a red card in League of Ireland football. He wound down his 20-year playing career at Shelbourne.

| Everton 1959/60–1961/62 | | |
| --- | --- | --- |
| | games | goals |
| League | 0 | 0 |
| Total | 0 | 0 |

# Jimmy Gabriel

**played for**

Dundee North End,

Dundee,

Everton,

Southampton,

Bournemouth,

Swindon Town (loan),

Brentford,

Seattle Sounders,

San Jose Earthquakes

**coached at**

Seattle Sounders,

San Jose Earthquakes,

Seattle Storm,

Bournemouth,

Everton,

Seattle Sounders,

University of Washington Huskies

Recruited from Dundee by manager Johnny Carey for £27,000 in 1960, the 19-year-old kilted warrior instantly endeared himself to the Goodison faithful with his wholehearted and unselfish toil. 'The Angel Gabriel' was a linchpin of the sides that captured the league title and the FA Cup in the 1960s. Following the arrival of Howard Kendall, the popular right-half and occasionally swashbuckling forward moved to Southampton and then to the NASL as player-coach with the Seattle Sounders and coach with the San Jose Earthquakes. After returning to Everton as assistant-manager to Colin Harvey and serving as caretaker-manager on two occasions, he resettled to the Pacific North West in 1997 to coach the Seattle Sounders and the University of Washington. In retirement, Gabriel is rightly celebrated as 'Mr Soccer' in his adopted city.

| Everton 1959/60-1966/67 | | |
|---|---|---|
| | games | goals |
| League | 255/1 | 33 |
| Total | 302/1 | 37 |

# Brian Godfrey

**played for**
Everton,
Scunthorpe United,
Preston North End,
Aston Villa,
Bristol Rovers,
Newport County,
Portland Timbers,
Bath City

**coached at**
Bath City,
Exeter City,
Weymouth,
Gloucester City,
Shortwood United,
Cinderford Town

Godfrey made his only first team appearance out of position on the left-wing against Fulham in 1960. With Everton poised to make massive buys in the British transfer market, the 20-year-old inside-forward swiftly departed to Scunthorpe United for a bargain fee of £250. In October 1963, Godfrey was sold to Preston for £8,000 where, after netting 10 times in his first 13 games, he was capped by Wales. Everton apart, his entire career was spent outside the top-flight. His two biggest disappointments were being excluded from the Preston side that contested the FA Cup final against West Ham United in 1964 and being part of the Aston Villa side relegated to the Third Division in 1970. After leaving Newport County, he captained the Portland Timbers to the NASL final, then known as Soccer Bowl '75, which the expansion team lost to the Tampa Bay Rowdies.

| Everton 1958/59-1959/60 | | |
| --- | --- | --- |
| | games | goals |
| League | 1 | 0 |
| Total | 1 | 0 |

# Asa Hartford

**played for**

West Bromwich Albion,

Manchester City,

Nottingham Forest,

Everton,

Manchester City,

Fort Lauderdale Sun,

Wolverhampton Wanderers,

Norwich City,

Bolton Wanderers,

Stockport County,

Oldham Athletic,

Shrewsbury Town,

Boston United,

Bury

**coached at**

Bolton Wanderers,

Stockport County,

Shrewsbury Town,

Boston United,

Blackburn Rovers,

Stoke City,

Manchester City,

Blackpool,

Manchester City,

Macclesfield Town,

Accrington Stanley,

Birmingham City (scout)

Subsequent to the headline-grabbing collapse of his £177,000 transfer from West Bromwich Albion to Don Revie's Leeds United in late-1971 when a medical examination discovered a hole in-the-heart condition, the Scottish midfield dynamo enjoyed a long career of some 800 senior games. After helping Manchester City snatch the 1976 League Cup, the Scotland ace joined Brian Clough's Nottingham Forest for £500,000, only to be dispatched to Everton for £400,000 after three appearances. At Goodison, he was acclaimed for his abilities to graft, win the ball cleanly, glide past foes and spray passes across the pitch. Though his second stint at Maine Road involved relegation from the top-flight, the 33-year-old found time to help the Fort Lauderdale Sun seize the championship of the new United Soccer League.

| Everton 1979/80-1981/82 | games | goals |
|---|---|---|
| League | 81/0 | 6 |
| Total | 98/0 | 7 |

# Ernie Hunt

**played for**

Swindon Town,
Wolverhampton Wanderers,
Los Angeles Wolves,
Everton,
Coventry City,
Doncaster Rovers (loan),
Bristol City,
Atherstone Town,
Ledbury Town

The stocky striker left Swindon Town, his local club, in 1965 to join Wolverhampton Wanderers where his goals propelled them to the First Division in 1967. That summer, Hunt was part of the Wolverhampton squad disguised as the Los Angeles Wolves which snared the inaugural United Soccer Association title. Immediately afterwards, the 24-year-old was signed by manager Harry Catterick for £80,000 but failed to settle – lasting just six months. His displays were so poor that some fans claimed Satan had sent him to steal Goodison's sanity. By contrast at Coventry City, his next club, he is remembered fondly for his stunning goal absurdly against Everton. His teammate Willie Carr took a free-kick by gripping the ball between his heels and flicking it up for Hunt to volley expertly past goalkeeper Andy Rankin.

| Everton 1967/68 | games | goals |
|---|---|---|
| League | 12/2 | 3 |
| Total | 14/2 | 3 |

# Jimmy Husband

**played for**

Everton,

Luton Town,

Memphis Rogues,

Cleveland Force,

Oklahoma City Slickers

The exhilarating product of manager Harry Catterick's nursery was baptised at 17 years 186 days. Husband was an unorthodox winger who possessed a passion for making long mazy runs through even the tightest and toughest defences. At his very best, 'Skippy' was an unplayable forward and, alongside centre-forward Joe Royle, scored goals for fun throughout the 1968 FA Cup run and to a lesser extent during the breathtaking 1969/70 League campaign. Sadly, his confidence and form were impacted by a vicious foul by Derby's Dave Mackay in late-1968. No longer the fearless forward sprinting across the pitch into open spaces and terrifying his markers, Husband switched to Luton Town and then wound down his career playing both indoors and outdoors in the USA.

| Everton 1964/65-1973/74 | games | goals |
|---|---|---|
| League | 158/7 | 44 |
| Total | 191/8 | 55 |

# David Irving

**played for**

Workington,

Everton,

Sheffield United (loan),

Oldham Athletic,

Fort Lauderdale Strikers,

Shamrock Rovers,

Fort Lauderdale Strikers,

Tulsa Roughnecks,

Atlanta Chiefs,

San Jose Earthquakes,

Oulun Palloseura (Finland)

**coached at**

Oulun Palloseura,

Fort Lauderdale Strikers,

Miami Freedom,

Carolina Vipers,

Myrtle Beach Boyz,

Myrtle Beach Seadawgs,

Wilmington Hammerheads,

Tulsa Roughnecks

Snatched from the anonymity of Workington in the Fourth Division for £30,000 in 1973, the physically imposing forward made only eight first team outings during his five seasons on Merseyside before moving to play at Fort Lauderdale and three other NASL teams. Some six years later, Irving returned to the USA to commence a productive 16-year career coaching the Fort Lauderdale Strikers who he guided to the Pro Soccer League National Championship title in 1989. Highly respected throughout North American soccer, Irving has served as head-coach at a half-dozen clubs in the American Professional Soccer League (APSL), the now defunct Continental Indoor Soccer League (CISL) and the United Soccer League (USL).

| Everton 1972/73-1975/76 | games | goals |
|---|---|---|
| League | 4/2 | 0 |
| Total | 6/2 | 1 |

# Tommy Jackson

**played for**

Glentoran,
Detroit Cougars (loan),
Everton,
Nottingham Forest,
Manchester United,
Waterford United

**coached at**

Waterford United,
League of Ireland,
Crusaders,
Glentoran,
Ballymena United

Before joining Everton for £8,000, the midfield terrier had played for the Detroit Cougars in the United Soccer Association and was a key participant in the infamous 1967 Detroit Soccer Riot. At Goodison, though not blessed with the tremendous vision and skills of Howard Kendall, Colin Harvey or Alan Ball, his efforts were such that he should be mentioned in any discussion of 'The Holy Trinity'. The fearless grafter excelled when required to deputise for Kendall and Harvey. In late-1970, he moved to Nottingham Forest in a part-exchange deal involving Jackson plus £150,000 for midfielder Henry Newton. Some five years on, he joined the newly-promoted Manchester United on a free transfer. A top manager in Ireland, his haul at Glentoran alone was 16 trophies including two Irish League crowns, three Irish Cups and two Irish League Cups.

| Everton 1967/68-1970/71 | | |
|---|---|---|
| | games | goals |
| League | 30/2 | 0 |
| Total | 34/4 | 0 |

# David Johnson

**played for**

Everton,

Ipswich Town,

Liverpool,

Everton,

Barnsley (loan),

Manchester City,

Tulsa Roughnecks,

Preston North End,

Barrow,

Naxxar Lions (Malta)

**coached at**

Barrow

Though blessed with the Midas touch, netting on his Everton debuts in the League, FA Cup, League Cup and European Cup, the lively 21-year-old forward was traded to Ipswich Town in a baffling exchange deal involving the more experienced Rod Belfitt and a miserly £40,000. After a decade away, the England international rebounded to Goodison via Anfield where he had helped Bob Paisley's side amass four League crowns, two League Cups and three European Cups and become the very first man to net a winner for both clubs in the Merseyside derby. Of course, by then he had lost his cutting edge and blistering pace. While on the books of Second Division Manchester City, Johnson spent the 1984 NASL season with the Tulsa Roughnecks.

| Everton 1970/71-1971/72 & 1982/82-1983/84 | games | goals |
|---|---|---|
| League | 79/11 | 15 |
| Total | 92/13 | 20 |

# Gary Jones

**played for**

Everton,

Birmingham City,

Fort Lauderdale Strikers

Without doubt, the Prescot-born left-winger was one of Everton's most naturally-gifted footballers in the post-war era. Sadly, Goodison's incandescent beacon of hope exhibited his amazing ball skills too infrequently. But in his pomp, he could illuminate The Old Lady with his dazzling ball skills and array of football magic. No more so than in late-1975 when he tormented a meanspirited AC Milan defence in the UEFA Cup. Like several other Everton players around that time, he was offloaded by manager Billy Bingham to Birmingham City, in the case of Jones for £110,000 in 1976. He concluded his career in the NASL with a Fort Lauderdale Strikers side that featured World Cup-winning heroes Gerd Müller and Gordon Banks as well as another richly gifted entertainer named George Best.

| Everton 1968/69-1976/77 | | |
| --- | --- | --- |
| | games | goals |
| League | 76/6 | 13 |
| Total | 90/8 | 15 |

# Billy Kenny Snr

**played for**

Everton,

Tranmere Rovers,

Cleveland Cobras,

Ashton United

After three seasons on the fringes of the first team at Goodison and another two seasons as a regular at Prenton Park, the local-born midfielder joined the Cleveland Cobras. At age 25, Kenny was one of the more experienced members of a squad drawn mainly from the local Lake Erie Soccer League, which included teams composed of immigrants from Eastern Europe. Though talented footballers, his young teammates lacked cohesion and often failed to put aside their nationalist loyalties. Given his silky skills, Kenny adapted effortlessly to the synthetic grass installed at the George Finnie Stadium in Berea and made 23 appearances during the 1977 ASL season before joining Ashton United in the Cheshire County League.

| Everton 1967/68-1974/75 | | |
| --- | --- | --- |
| | games | goals |
| League | 10/3 | 0 |
| Total | 10/3 | 0 |

# Roger Kenyon

**played for**
Everton,
Vancouver Whitecaps,
Bristol City,
Blackpool,
Altrincham

The 20-year-old central-defender was a ready-made replacement for Brian Labone. More of a ruthless Barbarian than a sporting Corinthian, the ferocity of his tackles would echo around Goodison. Called 'The Assassin' behind his back, his promising career was undermined by many injuries, including those sustained in a horrific car accident. With his face and throat filled with glass, the resolute defender and popular club captain was initially pronounced dead at the crash scene. Kenyon spent 14 years at Goodison but, despite being named a substitute on several occasions by manager Don Revie, was never capped by England. After leaving Everton in 1979, Kenyon enjoyed rewarding spells, involving 60 NASL games, with the Vancouver Whitecaps.

| Everton 1964/65–1978/79 | | |
| --- | --- | --- |
| | games | goals |
| League | 254/14 | 6 |
| Total | 291/18 | 9 |

# Brian Kidd

**played for**

Manchester United,

Arsenal,

Manchester City,

Everton,

Bolton Wanderers,

Atlanta Chiefs (loan),

Fort Lauderdale Strikers,

Minnesota Strikers,

Barrow,

Preston North End

**coached at**

Barrow,

Preston North End,

Manchester United,

Blackburn Rovers,

Leeds United,

England,

Sheffield United,

Portsmouth,

Manchester City

The teenager grabbed the international headlines by netting for Manchester United in the 1968 European Cup final. In the wake of United's decline and subsequent demotion to the Second Division, he moved onto Arsenal and then Manchester City. As a £150,000 replacement for Bob Latchford, the now near 30-year-old striker joined Everton in 1979 and, though a decent marksman with a keen eye for goal and a powerful shot, he is often remembered for his dismissal during a fiery FA Cup semi-final against West Ham United. Following a period at Bolton, he became a prolific scorer in the NASL with the Fort Lauderdale Strikers, the Minnesota Strikers and the Atlanta Chiefs before flourishing as assistant manager at Manchester United, Manchester City and many others.

| Everton 1978/79-1979/80 | | |
| --- | --- | --- |
| | games | goals |
| League | 40/0 | 11 |
| Total | 51/0 | 19 |

# George Kirby

**played for**
Everton,
Sheffield Wednesday,
Plymouth Argyle,
Southampton,
Coventry City,
Swansea Town,
Walsall,
New York Generals,
Brentford,
Worcester City

**coached at**
Halifax Town,
Watford,
Íþróttabandalag Akraness
(Iceland),
Halifax Town,
Íþróttabandalag Akraness

A robust target man who was physically imposing on the ground and equally commanding in the air, Kirby was a regular scorer wherever he played and totalled 119 goals in 309 League games during his career. Even though the local-born centre-forward featured in fewer than 30 first team games in his seven seasons at Goodison, he experienced both Second and First Division football. In 1967, at age 33, he defected from Third Division Walsall to the New York Generals of the National Professional Soccer League. Kirby stayed at that club for the inaugural NASL season before it folded. At New York, the centre-forward netted 23 times in his 47 outings. Thereafter, he returned to Europe to manage clubs primarily in the Fourth Division.

| Everton 1952/53-1958/59 | | |
| --- | --- | --- |
| | games | goals |
| League | 26 | 9 |
| Total | 27 | 9 |

# Cliff Marshall

**played for**

Everton,

Miami Toros,

Southport,

Winsford United

The left-winger, whose speed of thought matched his amazing speed of foot, joined his boyhood favourites in 1973. Within about 18 months, Marshall had made an inspiring First Division debut against Leicester City. Impatient and frustrated at finding further game-time limited, he decided to bolt to the Miami Toros of the NASL in 1976. Though held in high regard for his skills, pace and general hustle, he left North America at the end of his first season when the Florida-based club folded. Back in England, the 21-year-old enlisted with a woeful Southport side that finished next to the bottom of the Fourth Division. As all trivia experts know, Marshall was the first black footballer (not mixed race) to turn out for Everton Football Club.

| Everton 1973/74-1975/76 | | |
|---|---|---|
| | games | goals |
| League | 6/1 | 0 |
| Total | 7/1 | 0 |

# Duncan McKenzie

**played for**

Nottingham Forest,
Mansfield Town,
Leeds United,
Anderlecht,
Everton,
Chelsea,
Blackburn Rovers,
Tulsa Roughnecks,
Chicago Sting,
Ryoden (Hong Kong)

Celebrated for his abilities to hurdle British Leyland Minis, throw Dunlop golf balls the length of a football pitch and take away the collective breath of Everton fans rather than net simple tap-ins, the 26-year-old entertainer was capable of outwitting most defenders with his audacious repertoire of magic tricks. Signed from Anderlecht for £200,000 in late-1976, he was extremely unlucky that manager Billy Bingham was dismissed almost immediately and replaced by the more dour Gordon Lee, who sought consistency rather show-stealing tricks. Despite his special bond with The Old Lady, McKenzie was offloaded after only 21 months. At Chelsea, Blackburn, Tulsa and Chicago, he continued to dazzle his vociferous fans, taunt robust opponents and frustrate managers.

| Everton 1976/77–1978/79 | games | goals |
| --- | --- | --- |
| League | 48/0 | 14 |
| Total | 61/1 | 21 |

# John McLaughlin

**played for**
Gowanhill United,
Falkirk,
Everton,
Seattle Sounders,
Falkirk

His follically-challenged scalp, short stature and frail frame made the left-back one of the most implausible looking footballers to have played professionally for any British club in any era – never mind Everton in the 1970s. That said, the 23-year-old Scot was a tenacious defender who made well-timed tackles with courage and commitment. Signed in late-1971 by manager Harry Catterick from Falkirk for £65,000 to replace the cultured veteran Keith Newton, he became something of a cult hero and was nicknamed 'Tiger' by the Gwladys Street faithful. After five seasons on Merseyside, he teamed up with Jimmy Gabriel, Geoff Hurst and Harry Redknapp at the Seattle Sounders in the NASL before winding down his career in the third tier of Scottish football.

| Everton 1971/72-1975/76 | games | goals |
|---|---|---|
| League | 59/2 | 1 |
| Total | 70/2 | 1 |

# Tony McLoughlin

**played for**

South Liverpool,
Everton (youth),
Wrexham,
Chester,
Wigan Athletic,
Dallas Tornado,
Altrincham

A bustling centre-forward who taped his knuckles before each contest, McLoughlin did not take up the game until age 16, just before he turned out for South Liverpool of the Lancashire Combination in 1964. The following year, he moved to Everton and, along with Jimmy Husband and John Hurst, became a decisive member of the 1965 FA Youth Cup-winning side – scoring in every round. In fact, he netted the opener in the second-leg of the final in front of 30,000 fans at Goodison as Everton beat Arsenal 3-2 on aggregate. After spells in the lower leagues, he moved to Texas where he became the goalscoring hero when Dallas Tornado's scooped the 1971 NASL Championship Series.

Everton youth player: 1963/64-1965/66

# Steve Melledew

**played for**
Rochdale,
Everton,
Aldershot,
Bury,
Crewe Alexandra,
Boston Minutemen (loan),
Hillingdon Borough

**coached at**
Thatcham Town,
Newbury,
Abingdon United,
Newbury

By age 23, the Rochdale-born forward had helped his hometown club advance to the Third Division and also caught the eye of manager Harry Catterick during a pre-season friendly against Everton in 1969. Within two weeks, he had moved to Goodison for £15,000. Though Melledew netted plenty of goals playing next to Mick Lyons in the Central League, he failed to advance beyond the fringes of the first team as Catterick's side, powered by Kendall, Harvey and Ball, dominated the 1970 League campaign. In due course, his robust approach helped both Aldershot and Bury gain promotion to the Third Division. In 1975, he was loaned by Crewe to the NASL's Boston Minutemen and as an ever-present scored six times in 22 games alongside Eusebio.

| Everton 1969/70-1970/71 | | |
|---|---|---|
| | games | goals |
| League | 0/0 | 0 |
| Total | 0/0 | 0 |

# Brian Monaghan

**played for**

Everton,

Pharan Slavia (Australia),

Mansfield Town,

Pharan Slavia,

Burscough,

Pwllheli,

Austin Sockadillos/
Capital Sockadillos

**coached at**

Westlake (Austin),

Austin Flyers,

Austin Capitals,

Classics Soccer Club
Houston,

Texas Heatwave (Kingwood),

CC United Austin,

Houston Texans Soccer,

TSC Texans,

San Antonio Scorpions,

Lonestar (Austin)

Four years after joining Everton's youth academy, the Bootle-born forward – along with Kevin Ratcliffe, Mark Higgins and Steve McMahon – played in the 1977 FA Youth Cup final. He had netted six times in earlier rounds but failed to score in either leg, as Crystal Palace won 1-0 on aggregate. Following brief spells with Haran Slavia in Melbourne, Australia and Billy Bingham's Mansfield Town in the Third Division, Monaghan moved to the USA to focus on indoor soccer – where he holds the record for most goals in a USISL season – and coaching. Nationally respected with over 35 years of experience at school, collegiate and professional levels, he has been involved in the development of several men and women who progressed to represent the USA national teams.

| Everton 1975/76-1977/78 | | |
|---|---|---|
| | games | goals |
| League | 0/0 | 0 |
| Total | 0/0 | 0 |

# Brian Parkinson

**played for**

Everton,

Los Angeles Skyhawks,

Santa Barbara Condors (loan),

Los Angeles Skyhawks,

Miami Americans,

California Sunshine

The unused deputy for keeper David Lawson moved to the USA to represent four different sides during his five seasons in the American Soccer League. Almost instantly, Parkinson became a crowd favourite at the Los Angeles Skyhawks, conceding just 0.70 goals per game and helping them clinch the ASL Championship. The Liverpool-born custodian was loaned to the Santa Barbara Condors but returned to Los Angeles after that club folded halfway through its inaugural campaign. Nicknamed 'Superstop' by the fans, he conceded an average of 1.17 goals per game during the next two years. After his next club, the Miami Americans, collapsed following its first season, he switched allegiances to the California Sunshine, based in Orange County. To entice younger fans, his new club was renowned for promoting two core philosophies – to field as many Americans as practical and to keep profanity off the pitch.

| Everton 1971/72-1975/76 | | |
| --- | --- | --- |
| | games | goals |
| League | 0/0 | 0 |
| Total | 0/0 | 0 |

# Bruce Rioch

**played for**

Luton Town,

Aston Villa,

Derby County,

Everton,

Derby County,

Birmingham City (loan),

Sheffield United (loan),

Seattle Sounders,

Torquay United,

Gresley Rovers

**coached at**

Torquay United,

Seattle,

Middlesbrough,

Millwall,

Bolton Wanderers,

Arsenal,

Queens Park Rangers,

Norwich City,

Wigan Athletic,

Odense Boldklub (Denmark),

Aalborg (Denmark)

After capturing the 1968 Fourth Division title with Luton Town, the 1972 Third Division crown with Aston Villa and the 1975 League title with Derby County, the 29-year-old midfielder joined Everton for £200,000 in late-1976. Respected for his ferocious – sometimes sinister – tackling and powerful shooting, the first England-born footballer to captain Scotland moved back to Derby within 11 months. By 1980, he was playing in the NASL for the Seattle Sounders. After coaching Torquay in the Fourth Division and then Seattle in the Western Alliance Challenge Series, he enjoyed success as a manager by guiding both Middlesbrough and Bolton Wanderers from the third tier to the top-flight and laying the foundations for Arsène Wenger's dynasty at Highbury.

| Everton 1976/77-1977/78 | | |
|---|---|---|
| | games | goals |
| League | 30/0 | 3 |
| Total | 39/0 | 4 |

# Steve Seargeant

**played for**
Everton,
Detroit Express,
California Surf,
Phoenix Inferno

**coached at**
Oakland University
Golden Grizzlies,
Lawrence Technological University
Blue Devils,
United FC Michigan

At around 5ft 8in on his tip-toes, Seargeant lacked the height to be a First Division centre-half and was converted by manager Billy Bingham into a tidy left-back to replace John 'Tiger' McLaughlin. Known for his intelligent positioning, solid tackling and sound distribution, Seargeant showed moments of genuine class during the 1974/75 season until he was injured against Burnley and was forced to miss the final four League fixtures. In his absence, his top-of-the-table teammates imploded and finished only fourth in the table. Unable to regain his first team place, he joined the NASL's Detroit Express for a nominal fee of £22,500 in early-1978, playing both outdoors and indoors. After three years, Seargeant moved onto the California Surf before concluding his days indoors with the Phoenix Inferno in the MISL.

| Everton 1968/69-1977/78 | | |
| --- | --- | --- |
| | games | goals |
| League | 77/3 | 1 |
| Total | 86/4 | 1 |

# Gary Stanley

**played for**

Chelsea,

Fort Lauderdale Strikers (loan),

Everton,

Swansea City,

Portsmouth,

Wichita Wings,

Bristol City,

Bath City,

Waterlooville

Born in Burton-upon-Trent, the talented midfielder launched his career with Second Division Chelsea where his efforts helped the club gain promotion in 1977 but failed to save it from relegation in 1979. Following a summer involving 20 games in the NASL alongside Gerd Müller and George Best at the Fort Lauderdale Strikers, the now 25-year-old was signed by manager Gordon Lee for £300,000. Renowned for his strength on the ball and unselfish industry, Stanley failed to sparkle at Everton and is most remembered for being dismissed with Ray Kennedy for their parts in the 1980 Anfield mass brawl. Sold to Swansea City for £150,000, he moved back to North America in 1986 to spend three seasons in the MISL with the Wichita Wings where he mustered only two goals in his 51 indoor appearances.

| Everton 1979/80-1980/81 | games | goals |
|---|---|---|
| League | 52/0 | 1 |
| Total | 61/2 | 1 |

# George Telfer

**played for**

Everton,

San Diego Sockers,

Scunthorpe United,

Preston North End,

Altrincham,

Runcorn,

Barrow,

Formby

At age 18, the homegrown left-winger made a very impressive senior debut in late-1973 against Arsenal. A finely balanced athlete, he scorched the Goodison turf with his scintillating pace. Even so, he faced stiff competition for the first team spot from the likes of John Connolly, Gary Jones, Ronny Goodlass, Dave Thomas and young Joe McBride throughout the next eight seasons. Eventually, Telfer conceded defeat and moved to the San Diego Sockers in 1981. He made only two appearances in the NASL before joining lowly Scunthorpe United who finished next to the bottom of the Fourth Division table in 1982. With his assistance, they recovered to gain promotion to the Third Division at the conclusion of the following 1982/83 campaign.

| Everton 1972/73-1980/81 | | |
|---|---|---|
| | games | goals |
| League | 81/18 | 20 |
| Total | 91/25 | 22 |

# Dave Thomas

**played for**

Burnley,

Queens Park Rangers,

Everton,

Wolverhampton Wanderers,

Vancouver Whitecaps,

Middlesbrough,

Portsmouth

Thanks to the exit of Willie Morgan to Manchester United, the gifted left-winger became a first team regular at Burnley. Although sold to Queens Park Rangers for £165,000 in 1972, he was awarded a Second Division winners' medal by the Lancashire club and a runners-up medal by their West London rivals at the end of that season. Having illuminated the First Division throughout the 1976/77 campaign, the 26-year-old was bought by manager Gordon Lee for £200,000. Without shin-pads and with his socks wrapped around his ankles, Thomas would slalom down his wing like an Alpine skier before supplying pin-point crosses towards Bob Latchford. After two seasons at Wolverhampton Wanderers, he spent the 1981 NASL season with the Vancouver Whitecaps playing with the likes of Roger Kenyon and Peter Beardsley.

| Everton 1977/78-1979/80 | games | goals |
| --- | --- | --- |
| League | 71/0 | 4 |
| Total | 84/0 | 6 |

# Colin Todd

**played for**

Sunderland,

Vancouver Royal Canadians (loan),

Derby County,

Everton,

Birmingham City,

Nottingham Forest,

Oxford United,

Vancouver Whitecaps,

Luton Town,

Whitley Bay,

Ashington

**coached at**

Middlesbrough,

Bolton Wanderers,

Swindon Town,

Derby County,

Bradford City,

Randers (Denmark),

Darlington,

Randers (Denmark),

Esbjerg (Denmark)

Born in Chester-le-Street, the classy central-defender racked up two Football League crowns with Derby County and was voted 1975 PFA Players' Player of the Year before moving to Everton in 1978. The 29-year-old England star was acquired by Gordon Lee for £290,000 and converted into a right-back in order to retain the manager's favoured defensive axis of Mike Lyons-Billy Wright. Technically-advanced and ice-cool with the ball at his feet, he rarely forfeited possession when under pressure. Perplexingly, the Goodison favourite was offloaded to Birmingham City for £275,000 in 1979. Todd had two spells in British Columbia during his 700-game career. As a teenager, he had been loaned by Sunderland to the Royal Canadians in 1967. Then as a 35-year-old veteran, he joined the Vancouver Whitecaps in 1984.

| Everton 1978/79 -1979/80 | | |
|---|---|---|
| | games | goals |
| League | 32/0 | 1 |
| Total | 35/0 | 1 |

# Ray Veall

**played for**

Skegness Town,
Doncaster Rovers,
Everton,
Preston North End,
Huddersfield Town,
Los Angeles Wolves,
Maritzburg (South Africa),
Gisborne City (New Zealand)

Less than 24 months after playing non-League football for his hometown club Skegness Town, the 19-year-old outside-left was starring for the First Division's champions-elect. Bought for £10,000 by manager Harry Catterick from Second Division Doncaster Rovers in 1961, the lively forward excelled alongside Roy Vernon and Alex Young until replaced by the more battle-hardened Johnny Morrissey. An old-fashioned winger, who would out-pace full-backs and get to the by-line before delivering his crosses, he made 11 senior appearances as Everton romped to the league title in 1963. Unable to secure a first team place, Veall moved onto Preston for £8,000 and then became one of the first British imports to the NASL when he joined the Los Angeles Wolves during the league's inaugural season in 1968.

| Everton 1961/62-1964/65 | | |
|---|---|---|
| | games | goals |
| League | 11 | 1 |
| Total | 11 | 1 |

# Roy Vernon

**played for**

Mostyn YMCA,
Blackburn Rovers,
Everton,
Stoke City,
Cleveland Stokers (loan),
Halifax Town (loan),
Cape Town City,
Great Harwood,
Hellenic (South Africa)

An ultra-confident maverick who was no respecter of authority, the Wales star was one of the game's most prolific goalscorers of his generation. Signed by manager Johnny Carey from Blackburn Rovers in 1960, the sinewy forward netted in over half of his Everton outings and was the club's top scorer for four seasons. With his keen sense of anticipation, devastating acceleration and venomous shooting, the fiery inside-left dovetailed beautifully with the sublimely skilled Alex Young to capture the 1963 League title in style. Notorious for his expulsion from Everton's 1961 North American tour, he revisited the USA as a key member of the Stoke City side that, camouflaged as the Cleveland Stokers, took part in the United Soccer Association tournament.

| Everton 1959/60-1964/65 | | |
|---|---|---|
| | games | goals |
| League | 176 | 101 |
| Total | 200 | 111 |

# Mike Walsh

As Sam Allardyce's trusted side-kick at Burnden Park, Walsh was an uncomplicated central-defender who was more imposing in the air than on the ground. In 1978, he led Bolton to the top-flight, but after the Lancashire club had slipped back into the Second Division, he was signed by manager Howard Kendall for £90,000 plus Jim McDonagh. One of the exalted 'Magnificent Seven' arrivals in mid-1981 – the others were Alan Ainscow, Jim Arnold, Alan Biley, Mick Ferguson, Neville Southall and Mickey Thomas – he and five others never lived up to the hype. Walsh joined the Fort Lauderdale Strikers in 1983. At the end of that NASL season, his club bolted to Minnesota and the Ireland defender left for Lancashire.

| Everton 1981/82–1982/83 | | |
|---|---|---|
| | games | goals |
| League | 20/0 | 0 |
| Total | 22/0 | 0 |

# David Weir

**played for**

University of Evansville
Purple Aces,

Falkirk,

Heart of Midlothian,

Everton,

Rangers

**coached at**

Everton,

Sheffield United,

Brentford,

Rangers,

Nottingham Forest,

Brighton & Hove Albion

After being selected as an All-American by the National Soccer Coaches Association of America (NSCAA) while at the University of Evansville, Weir returned to scotland to join Falkirk in 1990 before excelling at Heart of Midlothian in the Scottish Premier Division. Then, in 1999, the now 29-year-old defender was signed by manager Walter Smith for £250,000 – preferring Everton to Liverpool because of his admiration for the acclaimed Scottish boss. A top-class defender – formidable in the air, adept at reading the unfolding action and powerful in the tackle – and a highly respected captain, he became a pivotal fixture at Goodison for eight years before teaming up again with his mentor Smith at Ibrox. Six years on, Weir was interviewed for the Everton manager's job which went to the more experienced Roberto Martínez.

| Everton 1998/99-2006/07 | | |
|---|---|---|
| | games | goals |
| League | 223/12 | 9 |
| Total | 254/15 | 9 |

# Bruce Wilson

**played for**

Vancouver Spartans,
Vancouver Columbus,
Vancouver Inter-Italia,
Vancouver Italia,
Vancouver Whitecaps,
Chicago Sting,
New York Cosmos,
Toronto Blizzard,
Inex Canada

**coached at**

University of Victoria Vikes,
Victoria Vistas

The future Canadian soccer icon was invited for trials at Bellefield in September 1975. An exciting overlapping full-back, the then 24-year-old Canada international enjoyed several accomplished outings in the Central League. So much so that the Vancouver Whitecaps were approached about a possible deal. But unable to secure a work permit for his wife, he returned to North America to play 299 games in the NASL and receive 57 Canada caps. After spells in Chicago, New York and Toronto, Wilson became player-coach at the Inex Canada. For the past three decades, he has served as head-coach at the University of Victoria. Bruce Wilson was inducted into the Canadian Soccer Hall of Fame in 2000 and its USA equivalent in 2003.

Everton trialist: 1975/76

# TEAMS ASSOCIATED WITH FEATURED PLAYERS

Atlanta Blackhawks • Atlanta Chiefs • Atlanta United • Austin Aztex • Austin Sockadillos
Boston Beaneaters • Boston Breakers • Boston Minutemen • Boston Rovers
Brookhattan • Brooklyn Wanderers • Brooklands Athletic • Burnaby Villa
California Cougars • California Sunshine • California Surf • Canada Inex
Cape Cod Crusaders • Capital Sockadillos • Carolina Dynamo • Carolina Vipers
Charleston Battery • Charlestown • Chattanooga Red Wolves • Chicago Fire
Chicago Sting • Chivas USA • Cleveland Cobras • Cleveland Force • Cleveland
Internationals • Cleveland Stokers • Colorado Caribous • Colorado Rapids
Columbus Crew • Connecticut Bicentennials Connecticut Yankees • Dallas
Dallas Sidekicks • Dallas Tornado • DC United • Denver Avalanche • Detroit Cougars
Detroit Express • El Paso Locomotive • Fort Lauderdale Strikers • Fort Lauderdale Sun
Fresno • GPS Portland Phoenix • Hamilton Steelers • Houston Dynamo • Inter Miami
Jersey Blues • Kansas City Comets • Kansas City Wiz • Kansas City Wizards
Las Vegas Lights • Long Island Rough Riders • Los Angeles Aztecs • Los Angeles Galaxy
Los Angeles Salsa • Los Angeles Skyhawks • Los Angeles Wolves • Memphis 901
Memphis Rogues • Miami Americans • Miami Freedom • Miami Fusion
Miami Toros • Milwaukee Rampage • Minnesota Kicks • Minnesota Strikers
Minnesota United • Montreal Carsteel • Montreal Impact • Montreal Manic
Montreal Maroons • Myrtle Beach Boyz • Myrtle Beach Seadawgs • Nanaimo City
New Bedford Whalers • New England Revolution • New Jersey Americans
New Jersey Imperials • New Jersey Wildcats • New Orleans Shell Shockers
New York Americans • New York City • New York Cosmos • New York Express
New York Generals • New York Red Bulls • New York Rockets • New York Soccer Club
New York/New Jersey MetroStars • Northern Virginia Royals • North Jersey Imperials
North Shore Carling's • North Shore United • North York Rockets • Nova Scotia Clippers
Ocean City Nor'easters • Oklahoma City Energy • Oklahoma City Slickers
Orlando City • Orlando Pride • Pfaelzer • Philadelphia Atoms • Philadelphia Fury
Philadelphia Union • Phoenix Inferno • Pittsburgh Miners • Pittsburgh Riverhounds
Portland Rapids • Portland Thorn • Portland Timbers • Real Salt Lake
Richmond Kickers • Royal Canadians • Sacramento Gold • Sacramento Republic
Saint Louis • San Diego Sockers • San Francisco Bay Seals
San Francisco United All Blacks • San Jose Clash • San Jose Earthquakes
San Jose Grizzlies • Santa Barbara Condors • Seattle Sounders • Seattle Storm
Sporting Kansas City • St Catharines Roma Wolves • St Louis Steamers
St Louis Storm • Syracuse Salty Dogs • Tacoma Stars • Tampa Bay Mutiny
Tampa Bay • Tampa Bay Rowdies • Toronto • Toronto Blizzard • Toronto Italia
Tulsa Roughnecks • Vancouver City • Vancouver Columbus • Vancouver Continentals
Vancouver Firefighters • Vancouver Inter-Italia • Vancouver Italia
Vancouver Royal Canadians • Vancouver Spartans • Vancouver St Andrew's
Vancouver Whitecaps • Ventura County Fusion • Washington Diplomats
Washington Spirit • Westminster Royals • Weston • Wichita Wings
Wilmington Hammerheads

# 3.2
# LEAGUES OF TODAY

It has been claimed that before the advent of Mayor League Soccer (MLS) in 1996, the game in North America mirrored the spot kick attempted by Diana Ross to start the 1994 World Cup – it seemed like a great idea at the time but never went to plan.

Unlike its counterparts elsewhere in the world, Major League Soccer is a fixed membership competition with no promotion or relegation in which the regular campaign is followed by a knockout tournament. While the season concludes with the MLS Cup game in November, it is punctuated by the annual MLS All-Star game – an exhibition game which features the league's top players.

Learning from the demise of the NASL, MLS was designed as a single entity corporate structure with teams existing as separate franchises. The central organization shares the revenues and holds all player contracts. As of late-2020, there are 26 teams – 23 in the USA and another three in Canada – with an expansion to 30 teams planned for the 2023 season. To support and accelerate the development of North American-born footballers, the squads are limited to five foreigners. In addition, there is a salary cap per team with top wages of $175,000 – except for those of the four designated marquee players per team, some of whom have royal blue roots.

Buoyed by gates averaging above 20,000 per game and long television contracts, Major League Soccer appears stable. As of 2020, its matches are broadcast in the USA by the ESPN networks and Fox Sports in English and the Univision networks in Spanish. North of the border, they are broadcast by the TSN networks in English and by TVA Sports in French. With Major League Soccer at the top of the pyramid, the other professional leagues in the USA are the United Soccer League Championship (USLC) at level 2 which was started in 2011 and the recently introduced USL League One (USL1) at level 3.

North of the border, the Canadian Premier League (CPL) began play in 2019. It consists of eight teams from Alberta, British Columbia, Manitoba, Nova Scotia and Ontario.

## MEMORIES ON LIFE IN MAJOR LEAGUE SOCCER

### Tim Cahill in New York

*Cahill was always a big game player. The higher the stakes the more the Australian led from the front. So, he understood the questions that would be asked of him when he swapped the Premier League for the MLS in 2012 …*

'I had a big opportunity to join a great project with the New York Red Bulls organisation under Gerard Houllier (head of global football) and Andy Roxburgh (sporting director). I wanted to help them win a trophy. They had a $250 million stadium just for soccer and the training facilities were getting built in New Jersey. I knew about the growth of the game in the USA and went there with my eyes wide open ready to embrace it. I knew what was expected from me on the pitch and what was expected commercially, too.

'I always knew I would play in the MLS one day; I just didn't know when. It was perfect timing because I still had personal goals that I wanted to achieve. I never wanted to be a bit-part player at Everton because it's in my DNA that I want to play. It was right for me and my family, also it was right for what Don Garber (commissioner of Major League Soccer) wanted for the league and what New York Red Bulls wanted to do.'

*Cahill was named in the MLS Team of the Year in 2013, played for the MLS All-Stars in their victory against Bayern Munich and won the MLS Best Player award in 2014. It was total vindication of his decision to exchange Goodison for the Red Bull Arena …*

'During my time in North America, I played in the 2014 World Cup, and scored one of the best goals of my career for Australia against Holland. Also, I won the Asian Cup in 2015. Winning the Supporters' Shield and the Best MLS Player ESPY Award in my second season was massive in regard to people questioning whether I'd made the right move in leaving such a massive club like Everton.'

*Having played club football in England, the USA, China, Australia and India, he's clearly not afraid to 'up sticks' and follow any challenge dangled in front of him – but the one constant during his global tour was the omnipresence of Evertonians …*

'Every game, home and away! They were everywhere, the American Evertonians. When we played in Dallas or Los Angeles or Canada, anywhere within the league, I was blessed to be welcomed with open arms by Evertonians from all around the world. After the games, the players walk around the pitch signing autographs and throwing footballs and T-shirts into the crowd and if I saw Everton jerseys I'd go over and hang out with them. It was nice to see Evertonians at the games and a pleasure for me to spend a few minutes with them.

At Goodison, if kids see you on the street and they want an autograph, it's a big honour so I would spend half an hour before games and up to an hour after games with the Everton fans signing autographs.

'I played against Mikel Arteta at the Red Bull Arena when he was on pre-season with Arsenal in 2014. We are the best of friends, but when you're on the pitch there are no lines. We were constantly on at each other. At Everton, we had to be on the same team in training because we were so competitive. The boss realised that very early!'

*Cahill's commitment could be defined in the aftermath of the MLS Cup Eastern Conference semi-final defeat by 1-0 to DC United in 2012. A contributing factor was a penalty miss by Kenny Cooper, whose first effort was denied for encroachment. His retake was saved. After the final whistle, Cooper was distraught and the media were waiting for him …*

'I told them that I had missed penalties in my time and that not for an instant was anybody blaming Kenny. Thierry Henry was our captain, but I've always been a leader. I've always protected players in my team on the park and know that at times you have to take a shot for your teammate. I've always done that, and I felt that it was the right thing to do. When I go to battle, I'm in it until the end.'

**Anders Limpar – an FA Cup winner**

*A deadline day signing in March 1994, the Sweden international winger played a pivotal role in the infamous Wimbledon game six weeks later when Everton needed a miracle to retain its top-flight status. Limpar knew how the Goodison faithful felt that day because he, too, was an Evertonian …*

'It was around about 1979/80 when I first watched Everton. I liked a player called Imre Varadi mainly because he was from Hungary as was my father. And, of course, I was in awe of Bob Latchford. When I signed for Arsenal in the summer of 1990, the club held a press conference at Highbury which attracted lots of sports journalists and photographers from the national newspapers. I was standing there, next to manager George Graham, holding my brand-new Arsenal shirt when a reporter asked me if I was an Arsenal supporter. Without any hesitation, I shook my head and said "No, I am an Evertonian!" My time in North London was definitely the best period of my career. Arsenal won the title in 1991 – losing one game. It was against Chelsea at Stamford Bridge. Four years later when I signed for Everton, that very same reporter was at Bellefield. He said to me "You are happy now!"'

'I was signed by manager Mike Walker on transfer deadline day in March 1994 and could never have imagined that just six weeks later my beloved club would be in the bottom three, one point behind Southampton, Sheffield United and Ipswich Town and teetering on the brink of relegation. Before the final game against in-form Wimbledon everyone was terrified – the management, the players and the fans. Things look bleak – even a win would not guarantee our survival. We were 1-0 down after three minutes. Wimbledon had a corner at the Gwladys Street End and I took the ball with my hand inside the box – for some unknown reason. I just wanted to push it away from Robbie Earle. Anyway, Dean Houldsworth scored the penalty. Things got even worse. We were 2-0 down after 20 minutes following a mix-up in defence that led to an own goal by Gary Ablett. It was a horrible feeling. So to make amends for my moment of madness, I went up the other end and fooled the ref, I am sorry to say, and Graham Stuart scored the penalty. That was the gasoline for us.'

*The following April, Limpar played in the FA Cup semi-final against Tottenham Hotspur at Leeds, in a game that is rated by many as the greatest and most vibrant Everton performance in the 1990s ...*

'Three sides of Elland Road ground were packed with noisy Everton fans. Their support was almost deafening. We were so fired up in the dressing room and went onto the pitch wanting to do them proud with nothing to lose. We outplayed and smashed Tottenham Hotspur by 4-1. It could have been many, many more. As for the showpiece at Wembley Stadium, only Evertonians thought we could win – the rest of the football world said that we had no chance. While Alex Ferguson's Manchester United had one of the finest sides in England, we had an amazing team spirit that was hard to beat. We were a family; it was like you were playing with your brothers. Defeating United, thanks to Paul Rideout's well-taken goal, and capturing the FA Cup were the best feelings ever.

'I moved to AIK in 1998 because I wanted my son Jesper to go to school in Sweden. My time there was productive. We won the cup and the league. Then I got a call from Glenn Myernick, who was the coach of Colorado Rapids, asking if I wanted to join them in the MLS. I didn't know much about the league, which was only a few years old, but decided to go. It was a pretty good league back then. I played for the Rapids for two years and I enjoyed it. Our team included two experienced American internationals – Marcelo Balboa (127 caps) and Peter Vermes (66 caps) – and we reached the final of the US Open Cup. There weren't that many big names in Major League Soccer at that time, but I was privileged to play against the great Carlos Valderrama of the Tampa Bay Mutiny.

'The football was different with far less pressure. Sometimes we played in front of 1,500 fans at American football stadiums that could hold over 100,000 people, so there was no atmosphere. The fans were new to soccer and didn't have anything like the knowledge they have now. For example, in one of my early games in Colorado, I remember playing a pass to one of my forwards. When the linesman flagged him offside, the stadium announcer used the tannoy system to explain the offside rule to the spectators!

'After two years in Colorado, I was ready to settle in Sweden after playing abroad for 16 years. I had no regrets about leaving the USA – my biggest regret was when Everton had asked me to sign for another three years and I said "No". I love the club, and that's from my heart. I love the Everton fans. I love the atmosphere they create. When I come back to Goodison, I see people who were working at the club 25 years ago. I feel like I'm at home. It's such a nice feeling.'

## Paul Rideout – an FA Cup hero

*Today, Rideout coaches youngsters at the Arizona branch of MLS club, Real Salt Lake. After a nomadic career including a spell at Kansas City, he has found a place to settle …*

'I've always loved the United States. I used to go on vacations here and liked the lifestyle, it's more laid back than the old country. The people are friendly and it's safe where we live in Phoenix. My kids enjoy it. They are college soccer coaches and wouldn't have received such job opportunities back home. Personally, I like coaching kids. I'm committed to treating them the right way and making them better footballers.'

*No chat with Paul Rideout can be conducted without a detour to the famous victory over Manchester United. Fans will recall that Anders Limpar launched a swift counterattack as Matt Jackson galloped up the right-wing. The Swede waited for the perfect moment before releasing the ball to the full-back, who teed up Graham Stuart. Wembley held its breath as his shot struck the bar. But waiting was Rideout who planted a firm header into the back of the net. Three years later, the fifth man in Everton's history to score an FA Cup winner was heading across the Atlantic …*

'I grabbed the opportunity to come to Major League Soccer in 1998. Mo Johnston was already with the Kansas City Wizards, so that helped. I signed a three-year contract. Back then only the international players had guaranteed contracts, the rest could have been cut at any point. I was impressed by their desire to learn from the overseas players. After training, the younger American players in the squad always wanted to do more. We had a few wanting to improve their heading – so Mo and I stayed behind because, back then, the team's coaches didn't want to know. The general set-up was pretty poor, there was little enthusiasm or professionalism.

'In contrast, the way they do things now is superb. It's as good as any professional set-up and we've come a long way with the academy. There are a lot of very good, young American players coming through. It's down to coaching as there are a lot of very good American coaches who have all their badges. Both my sons are coaching at junior colleges in Kansas. I've been down a few times to help them out and watch how they work. I must confess that they're much further ahead than I am with all the science that's involved in football these days.'

*Rideout was signed by Howard Kendall, played under Mike Walker, won the FA Cup with Joe Royle and left when Dave Watson was in temporary charge. He takes a bit of them all into his own coaching sessions in the USA …*

'There's nothing wrong with taking best bits from the people you've worked with. I played for several clubs and every coach had something to offer. At Everton, Howard and Joe were fabulous man-managers. That's what you need when you're coaching youngsters. Each kid is different with a different mentality to how they work.

'As for Everton in 2020. Alan Ball was right – once Everton touches you, nothing is ever the same again. I have parents who travel around the country and tell me they had been talking to someone who is an Evertonian! Of course, I never miss an Everton game on the television. In particular, I loved watching Duncan Ferguson when he was in charge for a few games. I loved his enthusiasm. I knew he'd be like that! He really got the boys going again. Duncan is a fantastic character. He's all heart. Also, he has a fantastic knowledge of the game.'

### Wayne Rooney – the greatest footballer developed by Everton

*Rooney was only 18 years and 312 days when he left Everton in 2004 for Manchester United, where he became the club's record goalscorer, a feat he also achieved for England. Some 13 years on he returned to his boyhood favourites on a free transfer. After one season, however, he joined DC United in Major League Soccer. The then 32-year-old gave everything during his year in Washington DC. Initially, Rooney hit the national headlines for his performance against Orlando City in August 2018. In the 96th minute of the game, Rooney rolled back the years and sprinted 40 yards to chase down Will Johnson. The Orlando midfielder was primed to secure a victory after DC United's head-coach Ben Olsen had pushed his goalkeeper forward for a stoppage time corner-kick. Rooney tackled Johnson, then took a few touches into the opposing half before unleashing an inch-perfect cross for Luciano Acosta to nod home.*

'I scored my first goal in the States against Tim Howard and the Colorado Rapids! I'd played a few games for DC (against Vancouver Whitecaps, Atlanta United and New York Red Bulls) without scoring and it was Tim up next – and I just knew I was going to score. I went through and put the ball through his legs. It was nice to catch up with him though. It was always good when there was someone from back home over there who I knew. I played against Adrian Heath's team two or three times and I spoke to him after the games. Also, I met up with the Everton masseur Jimmy Comer when he was in Boston visiting his daughter (the *Killing Eve* actress, Jodie Comer). I often saw Everton shirts and an Everton flag in the crowd. It was nice seeing fans from Everton, and from Manchester United, who were in DC for a holiday and decided to come and watch the game. They'd wait outside the stadium for a picture or an autograph.'

*Wayne Rooney enjoyed his time playing and living in North America, but admits that he never thought about plying his trade in Major League Soccer until the opportunity to move to Washington DC presented itself ...*

'When I came back to Everton in 2017, I never had any plans to play in the States. Obviously, I had been watching the league over there, taking a bit more interest when the likes of Becks (David Beckham), Steven Gerrard, Frank Lampard and Robbie Keane played, but I never thought about playing there myself. After speaking to the owners of DC United and the manager, I went there with an open mind ready to embrace the experience. DC United were bottom of the league and I didn't really know what to expect in terms of the standard. But it surprised me. The standard, and particularly the American lads, was better than I thought it was going to be.

'The atmosphere at DC United was good, with the section behind the goal who make a lot of noise, but the expectations in the USA are different – you don't feel the same pressure to win the games. A lot of people are there for a day out and to enjoy watching the game whereas in England, and especially at Goodison, you feel the pressure from the fans who want you to do well in every game. Obviously, the US fans want their teams to do well but the pressure is nowhere near what it is in England. And there are very few, if any, away fans at the games, mainly due to the distance they'd have to travel. When we played in New York we'd maybe get twenty or so fans, and vice-versa when they came to Washington.'

*The global reach and coverage of the English Premier League meant that Wayne could keep himself fully up to date with what was going on back home …*

'A lot of the DC games were played in the evening so on a Saturday I could get up early and watch the Premier League games. More often than not I'd be up with the kids and would be able to see the early kick-off, the 3.00pm game and the 5.30pm kick-off before having a little sleep before our own match.

Andy Hunter, now a seasoned sports journalist with *The Guardian*, reflected on Rooney's introduction to the USA and his involvement in the Dallas Cup in 1999: 'After capturing the FA Youth Cup in 1998, the club was invited to send an Under-15 team to take part in the tournament. As a writer at *The Evertonian* magazine, I was asked to accompany the squad on its 10-day trip to Texas. Like today, it was an important youth competition – possibly the most prestigious in the world – with the pomp and circumstance of choreographed opening and closing ceremonies. Prior to our departure, I joined the staff and the players for an orientation session at Bellefield which involved interviewing and taking mugshots of the young teenagers. One of them – a schoolboy from Croxteth – asked me: "If I do well, can you put my picture in the newspaper?" At age 13, Wayne Rooney was the youngest and most gifted member of an impressive team which also included Jay McEveley – who went onto play for about a dozen League clubs, England Under-21 and Scotland and Darren Potter – who played for Liverpool and the Republic of Ireland.

'Even though Everton were eliminated from the competition by Santos, the Dallas Cup introduced Wayne Rooney to the football world outside of Merseyside. I recall that he scored most of his side's goals in the tournament and celebrated his first with an extravagant cartwheel which not surprisingly got his picture in the *Liverpool Echo*.'

### Robert Warzycha – Bob the Pole

*In July 2004, following Everton's victory over Pachuca, the former Everton winger was interviewed by Houston radio host Glenn Davies …*

'Everton fans know football and love skilful players – especially wingers. I had a great relationship with them. Gwladys Street nicknamed me "Bob the Pole". It was a term of friendship. They made me feel welcome. In good times and not so good times, they follow the team around country and around the world – look at tonight's massive turn out of men, women and kids who have travelled from the Merseyside for a pre-season match. I was one of the first overseas players at Everton and one of the first in the Premiership. The others weren't bad either – Peter Schmeichel, Eric Cantona, Andrei Kanchelskis and Anders Limpar. The last two were highly talented wingers who went onto play for Everton.'

*In 2006, prior to Everton's game against Columbus Crew, he noted …*

'When I moved to Columbus about 10 years ago, there weren't many Premiership games on television. But now I am able to watch Everton every week. Win, lose or draw, I love watching them. When you have played such an illustrious club steeped in so much history, who do you think I am going to support? Manchester United? Chelsea? Arsenal? No way. Everton Football Club is the only one for me.'

Graham Smith, who had helped recruit Warzycha, recalled: 'As a licensed agent, I had worked closely with Howard Kendall – a most honest and honourable football manager – and brought in two of the first overseas players to appear in the English top-flight – Predrag Radosavljevic and Robert Warzycha. I remember taking Howard to see Robert, then with Górnik Zabrze, play for Poland against Billy Bingham's Northern Island at Windsor Park. The Everton boss was so impressed with his skills and bargain price that he wanted to sign him then and there. There was one problem, Robert did not speak a word of English. Not a single word. In due course, the negotiations were concluded over one of Howard's infamous get-togethers in Chinatown. Looking back, Robert Warzycha was a tremendous talent whose star shone brightly at Goodison throughout the 1991/92 season. Sadly, he started to struggle after Howard Kendall's team had begun to flounder and slip into the lower half of the table.'

## MEMORIES OF LIFE IN THE OTHER LEAGUES

### Gary Ablett in the A-League

*In 2002, one of Merseyside's favourite sons and the only player to win the FA Cup with both Liverpool and Everton reflected on winding down his playing days in North America with the Long Island Rough Riders …*

'In the eyes of many, I was the grandfather of the Rough Riders, which had lost many of its established stars after the introduction of Mayor League Soccer. Often, we played at small university stadiums and converted baseball fields which had little in common with Anfield, Goodison and Wembley. Most of my teammates were young and formidable athletes. They loved to train and their enthusiasm for playing soccer was contagious. Our main man was Eddie Buddle who later did so well with the Columbus Crew and the Los Angeles Galaxy that he was capped by the USA national side. Perhaps equally as important, my time in New York introduced me to coaching and regenerated my love for the beautiful game. I enjoyed my football in the A-League. The experience helped me land a job with the Everton juniors at Bellefield.'

## Jose Baxter – reborn in the USA

*If life really is a roller-coaster then it's not inaccurate to suggest that the gifted Everton youngster suffered a few derailments along the way. Baxter had become the youngest player in August 2008 and was on the bench for the 2009 FA Cup final. But after joining Sheffield United in 2013, his career began to unravel ...*

'I was young, stupid and hanging out with the wrong crowd. I didn't know the real world. I was in a bubble, being on quite a lot of money at a young age. I didn't have boundaries in terms of money and doing silly stuff. Things began to spiral out of control at Bramall Lane where I received two suspensions in nine months for using ecstasy and cocaine. It was a tough time. I was really low, crying a lot and staying in my bedroom for days at a time in total darkness. My world had flipped upside down until one morning I went to a local gym. It was the best thing I have ever done. I met some unbelievable lads, really positive people. They brought routine back into my life and I loved it. I was getting fitter and getting my confidence back.

'I was in a chippy in Huyton on a Friday night when I got a telephone call. I don't normally answer withheld numbers, but I recognised the voice straight away. Bill Kenwright said: "It feels like yesterday that we spoke son." He added that he wanted to help me turn my career, and my life, around. We kept in touch, but I thought it would be a case of me using the facilities at Finch Farm to get fit then try and find a new club. Never in my wildest dreams did I think I would be going back on a 12-month contract. What the chairman did for me is something that I will take to my grave. At the training ground, I was absolutely terrified about what everyone who knew me there would think of me. But they all welcomed me with open arms. I was privileged to play 10 games for David Unsworth's Under-23 team during the 2017/18 season. I was handed a lifeline by Everton. It truly is the People's Club and one day I would love to give a little bit back.

'Then at age 27, I signed for Memphis 901 who play in the USL Championship. I received a call from an agent who asked me about my relationship with Tim Howard. I said that we got on well. I've always felt that with the Everton lads, you don't need to be on the phone every day to have a great relationship, we're just always here for each other, players and staff alike. Then Tim called to say that his club would like to sign me on a free transfer. He said it was a no-brainer for them if I fancied it. I had always thought that one day I would play abroad, not necessarily in America. I'm loving it in Memphis! Obviously, the circumstances aren't the best right now – I came here in February 2020 and then everything turned upside down with Covid-19. But it's great to have Tim around, there are always a few laughs in training and I'm still learning from him. He's been there and done it and he's always sharing information about his experiences, which is great. Before I first came over here a lot of people said that I'd find it easy but that's not the case. The standard of play is very good.'

*Caricatures and pen-pictures of the Toffeemen associated with Major League Soccer and the other leagues of today are presented alphabetically. They start with Gary Ablett, one of Merseyside's favourite sons ...*

# Gary Ablett

**played for**

Liverpool,
Derby County (loan),
Hull City (loan),
Everton,
Sheffield United (loan),
Birmingham City,
Wycombe Wanderers (loan),
Blackpool,
Long Island Rough Riders

**coached at**

Everton,
Liverpool,
Stockport County

After enjoying success at Anfield, including two League titles and an FA Cup, the versatile defender was snapped up by manager Howard Kendall for £750,000 in 1992. An underrated footballer, Ablett is remembered fondly for his inch-perfect cross from the left-wing which enabled substitute Daniel Amokachi to net the fourth goal in the 1995 FA Cup semi-final against Tottenham Hotspur at Elland Road. Having snared the famous trophy with Liverpool in 1989, he became the only player to win the FA Cup with both Merseyside giants. Following a spell in the USL A-League with the Long Island Rough Riders, he re-joined Everton as a youth coach before moving onto manage Liverpool Reserves and Stockport County. Sadly, Ablett died at age 46 from non-Hodgkin's lymphoma.

| Everton 1992/93-1995/96 | | |
| --- | --- | --- |
| | games | goals |
| League | 128/0 | 5 |
| Total | 156/0 | 6 |

# Daniel Amokachi

**played for**

Ranchers Bees (Nigeria),
Club Brugge,
Everton,
Beşiktaş,
1860 Munich,
US Créteil-Lusitanos (trial)
(France),
Colorado Rapids,
Nasarawa United (Nigeria)

**coached at**

Nasarawa United,
Nigeria,
Enyimba (Nigeria),
Nigeria,
Ifeanyi Ubah (Nigeria),
Hercules (Finland)

Following his pivotal performances in the African Nations Cup and the World Cup in 1994, Amokachi was snapped up from Club Brugge for £3 million by manager Mike Walker. Although the Nigerian star was a misfit, 'The Bull' entered Merseyside folklore when he infuriated manager Joe Royle by bringing himself on as a substitute and netting twice in the 1995 semi-final against Tottenham. Amokachi went on to win Olympic gold in 1996. But by then, he had moved to Besiktas for £1,750,000. After helping his club capture the 1998 Turkish Cup, his playing days petered out. He signed for 1860 Munich but failed a medical test, then joined MLS's Colorado Rapids but, hindered by knee injuries, was released before making a senior appearance. Recently, Amokachi was named as his country's football ambassador by President Muhammadu Buhari.

| Everton 1994/95-1995/96 | | |
| --- | --- | --- |
| | games | goals |
| League | 34/9 | 10 |
| Total | 42/12 | 14 |

# Epsen Baarsden

**played for**

San Francisco United All Blacks/
San Francisco Bay Seals,
Tottenham Hotspur,
Watford,
Everton (loan)

A product of the US Interregional Soccer League, the colossal goalkeeper – 6ft 5in tall with an equally massive wingspan – arrived on loan from Watford as a back-up for the increasingly error-prone Richard Wright in late-2002. Although born in San Rafael, California and selected to play for the USA Under-18 team, Baarsden switched his international eligibility and represented Norway in four senior games. In his only first team outing for Everton, he conceded four soft goals in a 4-3 loss at Tottenham Hotspur, one of his former clubs. Both the player and manager David Moyes were dissatisfied by his error-strewn performance. So much so that Baardsen elected to retire from football at age 25 claiming he had lost interest the game.

|  | Everton 2002/03 | |
|  | games | goals |
| --- | --- | --- |
| League | 1/0 | 0 |
| Total | 1/0 | 0 |

# Jose Baxter

**played for**

Everton,

Tranmere Rovers (loan),

Oldham Athletic,

Sheffield United,

Everton,

Oldham Athletic,

Plymouth Argyle,

Memphis 901

At the time the club's youngest-ever first team player, Baxter made his debut as a substitute against Blackburn Rovers in 2008, aged 16 years and 191 days. The local boy seemed to have all the major prerequisites – excellent technique, adroit positioning and irrepressible enthusiasm – to conquer the hype associated with his break-though. Regardless, the attacking midfielder lingered on the fringes of David Moyes' first team before switching to Oldham Athletic in 2012 and to Sheffield United for £500,000 in 2013. His stay in Yorkshire was disrupted by suspensions related to drug use. In 2017, Everton handed him a lifeline and he turned out on 10 occasions for the Under-23 side before rejoining Oldham Athletic in League Two. Most recently, Baxter has played for Tim Howard's Memphis 901 in the USL Championship.

| Everton 2008/09-2011/12 & 2017/18 | games | goals |
|---|---|---|
| League | 1/6 | 0 |
| Total | 2/13 | 0 |

# Alan Biley

**played for**
Luton Town,
Cambridge United,
Derby County,
Everton,
Stoke City (loan),
Portsmouth,
Brighton & Hove Albion,
New York Express,
Brest (France),
Panionios (Greece),
Fisher Athletic

**coached at**
Ely City,
Potton United,
Barton Rovers,
Diss Town,
Spalding United,
Wootton Blue Cross,
Kettering Town,
Spalding United,
Rothwell Town,
Corby Town,
Spalding United,
Hemel Hempstead Town,
Bedford Town

Though a prolific marksman at Cambridge where he had won the 1977 Fourth Division title and Portsmouth where he had won the 1983 Third Division title, manager Howard Kendall's first signing had a frustrating time at Goodison. After scoring in both of his first two games, the £300,000 recruit from Derby is remembered more for his rock-star hairstyle than his matchday efforts. Increasingly lacklustre, he was offloaded to Portsmouth for £125,000 after just 13 months. Thereafter, the much-travelled forward turned up at the Uniondale-based New York Express in the Major Indoor Soccer League. The club played only part of the 1986/87 season before folding due to both football and financial woes. Subsequently, over the course of more than a decade, Biley endured managerial spells with a seemingly neverending list of non-League clubs.

| Everton 1981/82 | games | goals |
| --- | --- | --- |
| League | 16/3 | 3 |
| Total | 18/3 | 3 |

# Tim Cahill

**played for**

Sydney Olympic,
Sydney United,
Millwall,
Everton,
New York Red Bulls,
Shanghai Shenhua,
Hangzhou Greentown (China),
Melbourne City,
Millwall,
Jamshedpur (India)

**coached at**

Everton

Having played an indispensable role in the Millwall side that had romped away with the 2000/01 Second Division title, the 24-year-old attacking midfielder was signed by manager David Moyes for a bargain £1.5 million shortly after the Londoners lost the 2004 FA Cup final. Courtesy of his priceless headed goals, trademark celebrations and never-say-die approach, the Australian became a Goodison cult-hero as well as a versatile member of the teams that finished regularly in the top third of the Premier League table. After eight years on Merseyside, Cahill was sold to the New York Red Bulls for £1 million in 2012. The Australian featured in 64 games during his two full seasons in the USA and scored the fastest goal in Major League Soccer history (clocked at 7.0 seconds) against the Houston Dynamo in 2013. Born in Sydney, Cahill appeared at four World Cup finals and remains his country's all-time leading marksman with 50 goals.

| Everton 2004/05-2011/12 | games | goals |
|---|---|---|
| League | 180/16 | 56 |
| Total | 256/22 | 68 |

# David Carney

**played for**

New South Wales
Institute of Sport,

Everton,

Oldham Athletic,

Halifax Town

Hamilton Academical,

Sydney,

Sheffield United,

Norwich City (loan),

Twente,

Blackpool,

Alcorcón (Spain),

Bunyodkor (Uzbekistan),

New York Red Bulls,

Newcastle Jets,

Sydney

Born and raised in Sydney by his Merseyside-born and Everton-loving parents, the midfielder/full-back was signed at age 16. On Merseyside, he advanced quickly to play alongside Wayne Rooney in all eight of the 2002 FA Youth Cup ties, which ended in a 4-2 aggregate defeat to Aston Villa in the final. Though talented, hard-working and a regular in the Everton Reserves, he was released and joined Oldham Athletic in 2003. During the next 15 years, his travels took in various clubs located in England, Scotland, the Netherlands Spain, the USA and even Uzbekistan. Prior to joining his compatriot Tim Cahill in New York, he had spent 11 months without a pro club. After nine games with the New York Red Bulls in 2013, Carney wound down his playing career with Newcastle Jets and Sydney in his country of origin.

| Everton 2001/02-2002/03 | | |
| --- | --- | --- |
| | games | goals |
| League | 0/0 | 0 |
| Total | 0/0 | 0 |

# Jan Eriksson

**played for**

Sundsvall (Sweden),
AIK,
Norrköping (Sweden),
Kaiserslautern,
Everton (trial),
AIK,
Servette Genève,
Helsingborgs (Sweden),
Sunderland,
Tampa Bay Mutiny

Having secured the club's top-flight status against Wimbledon, manager Mike Walker sought defensive reinforcements. As a result, the central-defender – who had been awarded the 1992 Guldbollen (the Swedish Footballer of the Year award) as well as 35 Sweden caps – was enlisted for pre-season games against Fram, Hassleholm and Bjarreds in 1994. After no deal was agreed, the player joined AIK. Two years on, Eriksson signed for Sunderland. Though declared 'an absolute bargain' at £250,000, he made just one senior appearance in two seasons. Following his release, he moved to the Tampa Bay Mutiny to rediscover his form alongside Carlos Valderrama. Eriksson succeeded in the USA and was selected to take part in the 1998 MLS All-Star game.

Everton trialist: 1994/95

# Ramiro Funes Mori

**played for**

Dallas (youth),
River Plate,
Everton,
Villarreal

The Argentina star emigrated with his family to the USA as a child and joined the Dallas youth team at age 17 after his twin brother Rogelio had won 'Sueño MLS' – a nationally-televised player search organised by Major League Soccer. A year later, the versatile defender returned to Buenos Aires and signed for River Plate. After helping them capture the Argentina Primera Division in 2014 and the Copa Libertadores in 2015, he was recruited by manager Roberto Martinez for £9.5 million to rival centre-halves Phil Jagielka and John Stones. Lauded as a cultured ball-playing defender, his gloss soon dulled – his progress being impacted by a knee injury picked up while on international duty. In mid-2018, the Argentina star joined Villarreal in La Liga for about £9.5 million.

| Everton 2015/16 – 2017/18 | | |
|---|---|---|
| | games | goals |
| League | 41/14 | 4 |
| Total | 53/14 | 5 |

# Richard Gough

**played for**

Charlton Athletic,
University of the
Witwatersrand Wits
(Johannesburg),
Dundee United,
Tottenham Hotspur,
Rangers,
Kansas City Wizards,
Rangers,
San Jose Clash,
Nottingham Forest (loan),
Everton

**coached at**

Livingston

Born in Stockholm and raised in Johannesburg, the confident and classy defender had won the Scottish League title with Dundee United before his transfer to Tottenham Hotspur for £750,000 in 1986. The next year, Gough became the first £1 million Scottish footballer when he moved north of the border to Glasgow and captained Rangers to a amazing haul of nine League crowns, three Scottish Cups and six Scottish League Cups. At age 37, following spells in Major League Soccer with the Kansas City Wizards and the San Jose Clash, Gough was recruited by his old Ibrox mentor Walter Smith. Appointed Everton captain, he rolled back the years and was near flawless next to Dave Watson and David Weir. Now residing in San Diego, Gough serves as the global ambassador for Rangers.

| Everton 1999/00-2000/01 | | |
|---|---|---|
| | games | goals |
| League | 38/0 | 1 |
| Total | 41/1 | 1 |

# Matteo Ferrari

**played for**

SPAL,

Internazionale,

Genoa,

Lecce,

Internazionale,

Bari (loan),

Parma,

Roma,

Everton (loan),

Genoa,

Beşiktaş,

Montreal Impact

Born in Aflou, Algeria, the confident defender had been capped 11 times by Italy and turned out for a half-dozen Serie A clubs before joining Everton on loan from Roma in 2005. The terms included a €200,000 annual fee, with an option to purchase at €5.5 million. Sadly, his cultured contributions were halted by persistent hamstring injuries and limited to just 13 first team outings. In the twilight of his career, Ferrari joined the Montreal Impact prior its participation in the inaugural MLS season and was rewarded with Canadian titles in 2013 and 2014. Of course, Ferrari was no stranger to highly polished silverware. Previously, he had lifted the Coppa Italia with Parma in 2002 and Roma in both 2006 and 2007 as well as the Turkish Cup with Beşiktaş in 2011.

| Everton 2005/06 | games | goals |
| --- | --- | --- |
| League | 6/2 | 0 |
| Total | 11/2 | 0 |

# Mo Johnston

**played for**

Milton Battlefield,

Partick Thistle,

Watford,

Celtic,

Nantes,

Rangers,

Everton,

Heart of Midlothian,

Falkirk,

Kansas City Wiz/
Kansas City Wizards

**coached at**

New York/New Jersey MetroStars
(New York Red Bulls),
Toronto

In 1989, the Scotland ace split the city of his birth when he shattered an unspoken taboo to become the highest-profile Roman Catholic to turn out for Rangers. Respected for his uncanny knack for converting half-chances, he snapped up two Scottish League titles at Ibrox before moving to Everton for £1.5 million in 1991. Though talented, the restless striker failed to endear himself to the Goodison faithful and, within two years, was granted a free transfer. After stints in Scotland, Johnston resurfaced at the Kansas City Wiz (later renamed the Kansas City Wizards), where he helped them lift the MLS Cup in 2000. After hanging up his playing boots at age 38, Johnston became assistant-coach at the New York/New Jersey MetroStars (later renamed the New York Red Bulls) and then the director of football at Toronto.

| Everton 1991/92-1993/94 | games | goals |
| --- | --- | --- |
| League | 28/6 | 10 |
| Total | 32/7 | 10 |

# Anders Limpar

**played for**
Brommapojkarna (Sweden),
Örgryte (Sweden),
Young Boys Berne,
Cremonese,
Arsenal,
Everton,
Birmingham City,
AIK,
Colorado Rapids,
Djurgårdens (Sweden),
Brommapojkarna,
Sollentuna United (Sweden),

**coached at**
Djurgårdens ,
Sollentuna United

A £1.6 million acquisition from Arsenal by under-pressure manager Mike Walker, the enigmatic winger struggled to display his best form during Everton's flirtation with relegation in 1994. The low-point of that period was his handling of a harmless cross to concede a penalty in the final-day dogfight with Wimbledon. Afterwards, of course, he made amends by throwing himself to the ground, in a manner that scored highly for artistic merit, to grab the lifeline of a penalty. The following season, his sublime skills added creativity to Joe Royle's 'Dogs of War'. No more so than his lung-busting breakaway which led to Paul Rideout's FA Cup winner against Manchester United. The Sweden ace concluded his career with two less eventful seasons in Major League Soccer with the Colorado Rapids.

| Everton 1994/95-1996/97 | | |
| --- | --- | --- |
| | games | goals |
| League | 51/15 | 5 |
| Total | 64/18 | 6 |

# Jim McDonagh

Conceding just 33 goals in 42 matches, the Ireland goalkeeper had been a flawless and ever-present shot-stopper when Bolton Wanderers secured the Second Division title in 1978. Two years on, after that club's relegation, the 27-year-old was signed by manager Gordon Lee for £250,000 to replace Highbury-bound George Wood. However, within 12 months, during which the increasing error-prone McDonagh was ousted by Jim Arnold — with a raw Neville Southall waiting in reserve — he reverted to Burnden Park in a part-exchange deal for defender Mike Walsh. Thereafter, he enjoyed stints with seven other League clubs, six non-League sides and three North American outfits. Between 1985-1987, he shone for the Wichita Wings — making 998 saves in the Major Indoor Soccer League.

| Everton 1980/81-1981/82 | | |
|---|---|---|
| | games | goals |
| League | 40/0 | 0 |
| Total | 48/0 | 0 |

# Terry Phelan

**played for**

Leeds United,
Swansea City,
Wimbledon,
Manchester City,
Chelsea,
Everton,
Crystal Palace (loan),
Fulham,
Sheffield United,
Charleston Battery,
Otago United (New Zealand)

**coached at**

Otago United,
Kerala Blasters (India)

The Manchester-born left-back was a vibrant member of the Wimbledon 'Crazy Gang' that defeated Liverpool to win the 1988 FA Cup before leaving for Manchester City for £2.5 million – then a British record fee for a full-back. After failing to shine at Maine Road and then Stamford Bridge, the 29-year-old moved on to Goodison. Signed by manager Joe Royle for around £850,000 in 1997, he was known for his blistering pace and unselfish industry until his contributions were hampered by a series of injuries. Phelan made just 28 senior appearances in three years before being granted a free transfer. After helping Fulham advance to the top-flight in 2001, the Republic of Ireland defender joined the Charleston Battery and turned out in the A-League (now known as the USL First Division) for two seasons.

| Everton 1997/98–1999/00 | | |
| --- | --- | --- |
| | games | goals |
| League | 23/2 | 0 |
| Total | 25/3 | 0 |

# Paul Rideout

**played for**
Swindon Town,
Aston Villa,
Bari,
Southampton,
Swindon Town (loan),
Notts County,
Rangers,
Everton,
Qianwei Huandao (China),
Kansas City Wizards,
Chongqing Huandao (China),
Shenzhen Jianlibao (China),
Tranmere Rovers

**coached at**
Tranmere Rovers,
Kansas City Wizards,
Sporting Blue Valley,
University of Missouri Tigers,
Sereno (Phoenix),
Real Salt Lake Arizona

The Bournemouth-born forward turned out for a dozen or so clubs worldwide during his illustrious career. Some 10 years after becoming Swindon's youngest-ever first teamer, he was transferred from Rangers to Everton for £500,000 in 1992. Under managers Howard Kendall and Mike Walker, injuries often sidelined the deceptively skilful striker as the club flirted with relegation. Later, inspired by the arrival of new manager Joe Royle, he scored several key goals to maintain the club's top-flight status and also lift the FA Cup in 1995. Sandwiched between two lucrative stints in China, he played for the Kansas City Wizards. Upon retiring, Rideout has specialised in youth coaching and player development – first at Tranmere Rovers and then at soccer academies in Missouri and Arizona.

| Everton 1992/93-1996/97 | | |
|---|---|---|
| | games | goals |
| League | 86/26 | 29 |
| Total | 111/29 | 40 |

# Wayne Rooney

**played for**
Everton,
Manchester United,
Everton,
DC United,
Derby County

**coached at**
Derby County

Without question, Rooney is one of the greatest British footballers of all-time. The 16-year-old prodigy made his debut for his childhood favourites against Tottenham in 2002 and proceeded to illuminate every Premier League stadium in the land with his skills, strength, work ethic, aggression and much more. With Everton struggling financially, he was sold to Manchester United for £25.6 million in 2004, where he went on to win five Premier League titles and the UEFA Champions League. After returning to Goodison on a free transfer for a brief reunion in the 2017/18 season, England's record goalscorer exited to DC United after 12 months. Whereas some ageing super-stars enter Major League Soccer purely for the money, Rooney worked hard for his team and enjoyed clearly his football – netting 23 times in 48 games.

| Everton 2002/03-2003/04 & 2017/18 | games | goals |
|---|---|---|
| League | 81/31 | 25 |
| Total | 102/33 | 28 |

# Philippe Senderos

**played for**

Servette Genève,

Arsenal,

Milan (loan),

Everton (loan),

Fulham,

Valencia,

Aston Villa,

Grasshopper (Switzerland),

Rangers,

Houston Dynamo,

Chiasso (Switzerland)

The 6ft 3in commanding centre-half was recruited from Arsenal where he had missed the entirety of their undefeated 2003/04 season due to a series of injuries but had lifted the FA Cup in 2005. After falling out of favour, Senderos was loaned to AC Milan. Despite having several central defenders in his senior squad, manager David Moyes added the Switzerland mainstay on loan in January 2010. The 24-year-old defender made only three senior outings – totalling 140 minutes before signing for Fulham on a free transfer. In 2019, after a five-year stretch in which he played for six teams in five different countries, Senderos retired from football. One was the Houston Dynamo where, despite being plagued by hamstring injuries, he won the 2018 Lamar Hunt US Open Cup.

| Everton 2009/10 | | |
| --- | --- | --- |
| | games | goals |
| League | 1/1 | 0 |
| Total | 2/1 | 0 |

# John Spencer

**played for**

Rangers,

Morton (loan),

Lai Sun (Hong Kong) (loan),

Chelsea,

Queens Park Rangers (loan),

Queens Park Rangers,

Everton (loan),

Everton,

Motherwell (loan),

Motherwell

Colorado Rapids

**coached at**

Houston Dynamo,

Portland Timbers,

Colorado Rapids,

San Jose Earthquakes

After enjoying a productive spell at Stamford Bridge, during which he earned Scotland full international recognition, Spencer moved to Queens Park Rangers for £2.5 million in 1996. Despite his goalscoring efforts, the West Londoners failed to gain promotion to the top-flight and the 27-year-old striker joined Everton to help stave off relegation fears. Signed initially by manager Howard Kendall for an infertile six-game loan spell in March 1998, he was bought for £1.5 million before the arrival of new manager Walter Smith that summer. It was an odd deal. Playing in an underperforming side, he struggled before departing to Motherwell for £500,000 and then to the Colorado Rapids. As assistant-coach, he helped to guide the Houston Dynamo to MLS Cup glory in 2006 and 2007 and, as a result, was appointed head-coach at Portland.

| Everton 1997/98-1998/99 | games | goals |
|---|---|---|
| League | 5/4 | 0 |
| Total | 5/4 | 0 |

# Mickey Thomas

**played for**

Wrexham,
Manchester United,
Everton,
Brighton & Hove Albion,
Stoke City,
Chelsea,
West Bromwich Albion,
Derby County (loan),
Wichita Wings,
Shrewsbury Town,
Leeds United,
Stoke City,
Wrexham,
Inter Cardiff,
Porthmadog

Born in Mochdre near Colwyn Bay, the prototypical workhorse joined Manchester United shortly after helping Wrexham to the 1978 Third Division title. Some three years on, the 27-year-old midfielder was signed by manager Howard Kendall in an exchange deal involving full-back John Gidman. Though admired for his attacking flair, he lasted just three months before being offloaded swiftly to Brighton for £400,000 after refusing to turn out for the Central League side. Changing clubs frequently, Thomas moved to the MISL's Wichita Wings in 1986. There he played 76 games in two seasons alongside Gary Stanley and Jim McDonagh. His whistlestop tour was terminated abruptly by an 18-month stay at HMP Liverpool following his involvement in a money forgery scam.

| Everton 1981/82 | | |
| --- | --- | --- |
| | games | goals |
| League | 10/0 | 0 |
| Total | 11/0 | 0 |

# Robert Warzycha

**played for**

Górnik Wałbrzych,
Górnik Zabrze,
Everton,
Pécsi Mecsek (Hungary),
Kispest Honved (Hungary),
Columbus Crew

**coached at**

Columbus Crew,
Górnik Zabrze,
Ruch Chorzów (Poland)

The exciting right-winger was signed by manager Howard Kendall from Górnik Zabrze for £500,000 in March 1991 and became the club's only overseas footballer to play on the opening weekend of the Premier League in August 1992. Equipped with superior power, pace and eye-catching pitch-craft, he would breeze past defenders, beating man after man with effortless ease, during his honeymoon period. Sadly, the Poland international seemed to lose his hunger and his sparkle faded. So much so that he was allowed to leave for Hungary for an unknown fee in 1994. He rebuilt his career with the Columbus Crew during Major League Soccer's inaugural season. Warzycha spent seven seasons in Ohio as a player. In 2002, aged 39, he hung up his boots before embarking on a wide range of coaching roles at Columbus over the next 11 years, replacing the legendary Sigi Schmid as head coach in 2009.

| Everton 1990/91-1993/94 | | |
| --- | --- | --- |
| | games | goals |
| League | 51/21 | 6 |
| Total | 60/26 | 8 |

# Abel Xavier

The flamboyant defender played for professional clubs in eight different countries – never over-staying his welcome at any of them. Signed by manager Walter Smith from PSV Eindhoven for £1.5 million in 1999, Xavier was considered a capable, confident and charismatic right-back until he perpetrated the unforgiveable act of treachery by crossing the great divide located in Stanley Park in 2002. Consequently, the 28-year-old became the first man to feature in both Merseyside derbies for different sides during the same season. He played for Everton at Goodison and Liverpool at Anfield. After being banned for 14 months for using performance-enhancing anabolic steroids during his time with Middlesbrough, the Portugal star and his outlandish bleached hair and beard joined David Beckham in Los Angeles.

| Everton 1999/2000-2001/02 | | |
| --- | --- | --- |
| | games | goals |
| League | 39/4 | 0 |
| Total | 45/4 | 0 |

# EVERTON AND NORTH AMERICAN HALLS OF FAME

The National Soccer Hall of Fame is located at Toyota Stadium in Frisco near Dallas. It celebrates soccer achievements in the USA and membership is widely considered the highest honour in American soccer. Established in 1950, the bar for USA players is high. The one for their foreign-born counterparts is sky-high bordering on prohibitive. Candidates for election as a player must have been retired for three full calendar years, but for no more than 10 years, and must have made at least 20 appearances for the USA or played at least five seasons in the American top professional league and have been named to that league's All-Star team. As of 2020, the 156 inducted players include 13 women. Its members include:

| | |
|---|---|
| **Teddy Glover** | inducted 1951 |
| **Predrag Radosavljević** | inducted 2012 |
| **Joe-Max Moore** | inducted 2013 |
| **Brian McBride** | inducted 2014 |

Its Canadian counterpart was established in 1997 and boasts a membership of 129 players, including 19 women. These include:

| | |
|---|---|
| **Sam Chedgzoy** | inducted 2004 |
| **Gordon Stewart** | inducted 2004 |
| **Tomasz Radzinski** | inducted 2018 |

Also, it includes Dick Howard, the legendary coach, respected broadcaster and lifelong Evertonian, who was inducted in 2002.

It should not be overlooked that Bruce Wilson, a successful trialist who made four Central League appearances for Everton in 1975, was enshrined into the Canadian Soccer Hall of Fame in 2000 and the National Soccer Hall of Fame in 2003.

Although indoor soccer dates back to the Major Indoor Soccer League in 1978, there are only – 34 members of the Indoor Soccer Hall of Fame, which was introduced to celebrate the history of indoor/arena soccer and set the standard for future achievements. The members include:

| | |
|---|---|
| **Predrag Radosavljević** | inducted 2013 |
| **Brian Quinn** | inducted 2013 |
| **Roy Turner** | inducted 2019 |

# 3.3
# NORTH AMERICAN BLUES

In return for being blessed by a legion of Everton stars, North America reciprocated with significant contributions to the welfare of Everton Football Club during the past couple of decades. Granted some are relatively unknown to even the most ardent supporters and some links are fleeting and perhaps tenuous, however others include top-class footballers such as Joe-Max Moore, Brian McBride, Predrag Radosavljević of the USA and Tomasz Radzinski of Canada. Then there is Tim Howard – the most recognizable face and beard of US soccer and Landon Donovan – the finest USA-born soccer player of all-time. Collectively, these six North American stars have been awarded more than 500 senior caps.

Then there are the men who signed professional contracts or were invited for extended trials and special training at Bellefield and Finch Farm but did not advance to the first team. These include Gregg Berhalter and Brian Quinn for the USA and Bruce Wilson for Canada. Though most were deemed not ready for Everton, the dozen footballers were good enough to earn 248 senior caps between them. Also, when you consider the timely financial investment made by Robert Earl coupled with the glamour of his Hollywood pal Sylvester Stallone, there appears to be some merit to rebranding Everton as 'North America's Club'.

### NORTH AMERICAN MEMORIES OF EVERTON FOOTBALL CLUB

#### Cody Arnoux from North Carolina

*A decade after spending the 2009/10 season at Everton, Arnoux revealed his continued support for the Toffees …*

'I didn't know what I was getting into and there's no getting round it – I wasn't good enough. But it was some experience. The level was just so much higher than I could have imagined.

I'll never forget the tempo of our first training session, there wasn't a minute to switch off or rest. I remember playing in a pick-up game between the young guys and the first team regulars. We didn't have the ball for 15 minutes. The likes of Pienaar and Arteta were laughing at us. Finishing sessions were the same. If I scored one in three I'd be happy, but you'd have Yakubu and Saha who didn't miss. Seriously, they never missed. I've no big regrets. Just to have the opportunity was amazing. I'll always be an Evertonian.'

### Gregg Berhalter – an Everton reserve

*The career of the current USA head-coach commenced with the Raleigh Flyers and ended with the Los Angeles Galaxy – two spells bookended his time in Holland, England and Germany. Along the way, Berhalter found himself at Everton in 2000 …*

'I was out of contract in Holland and on trial with a couple of clubs in England. I had offers but I didn't like the terms so my agent, Paul Stretford, contacted the folks at Everton to see if I could train with them and keep fit before an upcoming USA international game. Everton were really gracious in allowing me to train and play. Of course, if they had loved me, then they would have signed me. But I wasn't the sort of centre-back that coach Walter Smith wanted. When you look at the profile of the experienced central-defenders at the club such as Richard Gough, Dave Watson and David Weir, it wasn't me.

'I didn't get a chance to play with the first team, which was unfortunate, but I did well training and the club invited me back for another month. I played in some the reserve games, but the schedule was impacted by bad weather and some games were cancelled. It was fun though. The squad was a cast of characters! Mark Hughes, Duncan Ferguson, Kevin Campbell, Francis Jeffers, David Weir, Paul Gascoigne, Alan Stubbs, David Unsworth, Alex Nyarko and my compatriot Joe-Max Moore who was instrumental in making me feel comfortable. He had told me great things about the club before I arrived. It was a great dressing room.

'For a change, there were no jerks in the team! I got on really well with everyone. I remember being surprised that everyone at the club was so nice. My wife and I really enjoyed the city, too. We stayed in the Marriott Hotel in Liverpool city centre and would walk everywhere – it's a special place.

'Walter Smith and Archie Knox were great guys to work with. Walter was a man of few words. But Archie wasn't! I really enjoyed training alongside some phenomenal soccer players at Bellefield. It gave me confidence and the feeling that I had that level in me. The experience convinced me to want to stay in the United Kingdom. I knew that if I could find a club similar to Everton then I'd be in good hands. Everton is a special football club. It really is. It's a family-orientated club with great supporters.

'I'm a big fan of the English Premier League. The more players that the USA has gaining experience in the best league in the world then the better we will become as a national team. Everyone has a different pathway. Major League Soccer is good for developing players at certain stages and then as the players progress the EPL is a great league for their further development.'

*Making the reverse trip across the Atlantic was Wayne Rooney. Gregg Berhalter enjoyed having the former Everton striker in the MLS …*

'You can sum up Wayne Rooney's time in Major League Soccer with one piece of play shortly after he had arrived from Everton. With Orlando City looking sure to score in the very last minute, he sprinted back defensively, made a crisp tackle, won the ball and then delivered an incredible pin-point cross from around the halfway line for a teammate to score and win the game. It was amazing. Simply amazing. Wayne did whatever was needed to be done for DC United to be successful.'

### Landon Donovan – a USA icon

*The greatest North American soccer player of all time, Donovan won the US Player of the Year award in 2002, 2003, 2004, 2007, 2008, 2009 and 2010. He joined Everton in early-2010 for the first of two exhilarating loan spells …*

'I have fond memories of my times at Finch Farm. On my very first morning, I had enjoyed a great training session and was buzzing when we came back to the locker room. Then Phil Neville shouts, "Landon, why didn't you train today pal? Are you injured?" I didn't understand the banter, so I was like, "What do you mean? I was out there … you didn't see me?" Of course, the whole locker room lost it laughing at my expense.'

*Donovan credits the Everton coaches with emphasising the importance of hard work …*

'Alan Stubbs told me, "If you run and work your ass off, the people here will love you. You don't always have to score but if you work hard, they will appreciate it." While it stuck with me, I only really got it when I made a tackle and the Goodison crowd went crazy! Throughout games, I kept saying to myself, "Run, tackle and fight. Run, tackle and fight." I played 13 games during my first loan spell but each time I was absolutely exhausted at the end.

'I was so appreciative of the way that people took to me. The fans inspired me. They knew that in an evening game they could make Goodison electric. It was unlike anything I've experienced in my life. We would score and the roof would come off the iconic stadium.'

*He was already an established USA star who had tried his luck in the Bundesliga when the Premier League, namely Everton, first came calling in January 2010 …*

'Tim Howard and I had a lot of conversations about European soccer, including the one when he let me know that Everton were interested, but I have to be honest having the opportunity to play for that football club in the English Premier League was an easy decision. The question was "How are we going to make it work?" but we found a way, thankfully. I flew to the United

Kingdom and arrived at Goodison during the half-time interval of an FA Cup game against Carlisle United. I had never known an atmosphere quite like it. The crowd was intimidating and it was inspiring.

'Any American who has ever been to Goodison wouldn't come away as anything other than a die-hard fan. There is no way you couldn't fall in love with that place after watching a match there. Everyone was so accepting of me, even though I'd only just arrived and felt I didn't deserve the way they were with me, and I was so determined not to let them down.'

*Donovan's introduction came on a wet, windy, snowy day in North London. The travelling Blues were interested to see how the boy from Los Angeles would cope …*

'David Moyes didn't name the team until we got to the stadium and so there was no time for me to think too much about it, which I thought was quite clever of him. The manager told me to just get out there and do my stuff for as long as I could. It went well until I began to cramp up around 70 minutes. That game is a really special memory. I always preferred playing in cold weather and that's part of the reason why I enjoyed playing in England. I remember thinking that 2-2 at The Emirates was a good result but I vividly recall going into the locker room after the game and Tim Howard, Phil Neville, Tim Cahill and others were absolutely livid that we had conceded a late goal and drawn the game. That said a lot about what Everton Football Club was about.'

*Landon Donovan loved Everton and Everton loved Landon Donovan. Although the loan spell went well, the man with strong principles resisted the opportunity to extend the love affair …*

'Towards the end, David Moyes brought me into his office and told me that he wouldn't be doing his job if he didn't ask me to stay. But I had made a pact with Los Angeles Galaxy that in exchange for the letting me join Everton, I had promised them that I would go back. It was really tempting in the United Kingdom because from a soccer point of view it was three of the best months of my career, but I did want to keep my word to the Galaxy.

'To be honest, I had some hesitations the second time because I didn't want to ruin what had happened before. Sometimes the sequel to a good movie can be terrible! But I couldn't turn down the opportunity to go back to Everton. It was odd because I had never joined a team that was in the middle of their season, so that was an interesting dynamic for me. But fortunately, I had a great reception from everyone and having Tim Howard there helped immensely. The staff, the fans and the rest of the players were great, so I was able to settle in quickly. Tim put Everton on the map in the USA and made the team a household name, which launched fan groups across the country.'

### Nico Defreitas-Hansen – an American schoolboy

*Finch Farm is over 4,000 miles from Miami, Florida where an adolescent Defreitas-Hansen had a big decision to make when he was still at high school …*

'As a teenager, I was playing both baseball and soccer and it got to the stage where I had to choose between the two because my life was getting too busy. I chose soccer. I realised that I was quite decent when I started playing for my local club and got called up to the US national team for my age when I was 14. I had played a bit of basketball too when I was younger and was always quite good with my hands, so I figured that being a goalkeeper was going to be my best bet. After my local team, Weston FC in Miami, travelled to the United Kingdom to play in the Manchester Cup, which I don't think is around anymore, Everton asked my older brother to come back for a trial. Without hesitation, we took the initiative and sent the club a video of me in action. They must have really liked what they saw because I was invited to come across with Luca.'

*Signing a two-year professional contract with the Merseysiders in the summer of 2019 was the fulfilment of a soccer dream for the youngster from Miami who had made major sacrifices to pursue his career ambitions …*

'The deal was a proud moment. It was everything I'd been working towards. Since I first arrived here, it's been fantastic – like a family. It's a great environment to be in and everyone is so supportive. Leaving my parents to travel such a long way at that stage in my life was a pretty big deal. At first, I moved in with one of the host families for six months. I wasn't really homesick because I was more excited about the future than anything. It was a new chapter in my life and a new challenge for me. I was just happy to be here and I wasn't thinking too much about home to be honest. I knew how big Everton was as a club because I have always followed Premier League football.

'The standard of play was unbelievable and such a massive difference from America, especially the level I had been playing at. You just couldn't compare it. To be honest, it took me a few sessions to get used to the pace and the intensity, but I felt that I quickly caught up. There have been ups and downs but for the most part it's been brilliant, getting used to the culture and playing and training day in, day out. I enjoy working with David Unsworth and the Under-23 side. He's hard on you because he knows that, at the end of the day, it'll be good for you. He expects maximum effort and if he's hard on you, it's a good thing because it means he cares and thinks you've got a chance of making it to the Premier League. The time to worry is when he's not having a go!'

*The teenage keeper made his first team debut in the last-minute of the pre-season friendly against Preston in 2020. Although he scarcely had time to touch the ball …*

'Being on the bench and then coming on was an amazing feeling. Just to be able to get that first team experience, being around the senior players and seeing the preparation was incredible. Even though I was only on the pitch for a minute, it was an experience that I'll never forget. I had played at Goodison before in December 2017. It was an FA Youth Cup game against Ipswich Town and even though we lost 2-1, being able to just play in the iconic stadium was truly brilliant. Anthony Gordon was in the team that night and he has gone onto play for the first team under manager Carlo Ancelotti.'

### Robert Earl and Rocky Balboa

*In January 2007, Sylvester Stallone accompanied the USA-based Everton director and Planet Hollywood restaurant mogul to Goodison. Interestingly, after the draw with Reading, little was seen of either of them again …*

Almost eight years later, Robert Earl appeared on NBC's *Late Night with Seth Meyers* and was introduced by the show's host as 'the owner of Everton Football Club in the English Premier League'. While the claim was something of an exaggeration, the Anglo-American business tycoon was a member of the board of directors having acquired 23% of the club's shares via a company registered in the British Virgin Islands.

Often referred to as a 'passive investor in Everton' and a 'mogul who makes things happen', that Tuesday evening, he promoted Merseyside's senior club to US television viewers with no little enthusiasm. Previously, Everton had embraced his advocacy of relocating to Kirkby, some nine miles from Liverpool city centre, yet failed to fully benefit from his world-class expertise related to global branding.

### Brian McBride and Everton

*The fearless USA international striker has the scars to prove it. Shattered cheekbones and Broken orbital bones are just some of the souvenirs from his 16-year playing career. But it was a problem during his loan spell at Preston that was by far the most serious … it was a life-threatening pulmonary embolism …*

'I took an elbow in the arm during a night game but didn't think very much of it. I remember that we were at Sheffield Wednesday the next weekend. When I took my shirt off after the game, my right arm was about twice the size of my left arm. Immediately, I was taken to the local hospital where they saw there was a clot and put me in a bed pretty much straight away. I was on the phone back to the United States and our doctor, Dr Edwards, told me I needed to get the blood clot out. That was the first time – they were able to angioplasty it out. The second time it happened, I had a rib removed to solve the problem. It is part of the job. If you do not take the hits you are showing a lack of respect to your teammates and, for a large part, the game itself.

'In 2003, I accepted an opportunity to join Everton on loan from the Columbus Crew. I had worked previously with David Moyes at Preston North End and had really enjoyed that experience. Actually, I had already been to Goodison Park to watch a Premier League game in which my good friend Joe-Max Moore was playing, so I had experienced the atmosphere and had a bit of knowledge of what the place was like. On my first day at the Finch Farm training ground, David Moyes called me into his office and said: "I really appreciate you coming here and helping us, but I've made a statement to the Everton board of directors that I'm not planning on signing anyone over the age of 30! Especially one that's in the same position as two of the club's highest earners."

'He asked me to give him what I had and enjoy my time at Everton. Because I had not played for two months, I found the speed of the games much quicker than the MLS. So, when the manager said he was going to start me at White Hart Lane I was in shock. Ironically, I scored on my debut past probably my best friend in soccer, Kasey Keller who was at Tottenham.

'I have to say that it was pretty amazing how people were so receptive of me, especially Big Dunc and Kev Campbell. Both were excellent from the day I got there until the day I left. I got some good advice on my first day, not to close the door when I used the toilet or a bucket of ice-cold water would come over the top! I enjoyed playing for Everton and after my sixth game, the manager said that there could be something on the table but I said, "Let's not worry about that right now."'

*Following a career that encompassed three World Cups and 95 appearances for the USA, McBride is putting his experience to use as general-manager of the USMNT ...*

'I am incredibly honoured to represent the USA and the US Soccer Federation once again. It's critically important for everyone to understand the privilege and pride that goes with wearing the jersey, and I'm excited about the opportunity to build relationships with players and clubs that align with the philosophy and values of US Soccer. In this position, part of my job is to help Gregg Berhalter and his staff in fostering a growth mentality for the US men's national team (USMNT) and to help Earnie Stewart ensure that this mindset is present in all of our national youth teams.

'The opportunity to help grow and nurture the sport in my homeland is something I couldn't turn down. Today, the standard is great, and it continues to get better. The young players have a better understanding of what it takes to be a soccer player. It's down to us at US Soccer and our coaches to work hard to continue to maintain the standards.'

### The first American – Joe-Max Moore

*A star of the USA national team joined Everton just before the turn-of-the century and forced his way into the affections of the Goodison faithful with a late equaliser against Tottenham which sparked a run of six goals in seven games ...*

'Without my Dad's help, support and guidance, there's very little chance I would have become a professional soccer player. He had been a college athlete and therefore I grew up around or playing just about every sport you could imagine. It had a positive effect on my overall athletic ability. My Dad became a part owner of the Tulsa Roughnecks in the early-1980s and for that reason I had exposure to the highest level of US soccer. Believe it or not, soccer was a big deal in Tulsa. Duncan McKenzie was one of the Roughnecks best players and biggest characters.

'When I was 23, my friend and US Soccer teammate Eric Wynalda recommended me to Saarbrucken. Though we finished sixth in the table, they were relegated because of licensing issues and I moved to Nuremberg, which was truly an amazing city and club. I had always dreamt of playing in the Premier League. But between work permit issues and maybe a slightly negative stigma attached to US players, I wasn't sure my chance would ever come. Thanks to Richard Gough and my agent Paul Stretford, I was given the opportunity to train with Everton in October 1999. My training went well and I was offered a three-year contract.

'There is no question that it was the right move for me. Manager Walter Smith and the guys made me feel welcome from the very beginning. It was a lot different from my spells in Germany where I found it hard to get to know the people. Most of them spoke English but didn't want to. Whereas in England, my wife and I settled in quickly. We lived with Liverpool's Brad Friedel until we found our own place in Heswall. That probably sounds weird, but Brad and I had played together since we were 18. We loved living in England – everyone spoke English and liked to laugh.

'The Premier League was all I had expected it to be. The pace is different to anywhere else in the world and the level of intensity is very high. Everybody has to give 110% for 90 minutes. Everything about Everton was amazing: the people at Bellefield, the supporters, the city itself. I enjoyed every minute of it. To feel the noise at stadiums like Goodison, Old Trafford and Highbury was incredible.

'I don't remember a great deal about my home debut against Sunderland but it's always nice to be part of a big 5-0 win. However, my first goal against Spurs brings back great memories. I came on as a late substitute. We had a throw-in. Mark Pembridge took it. He could basically throw it to the back post. For some reason, I was one of the only guys moving in the box and was just first to react. The goal got us a point and made me feel as though I belonged.

'The first nine months were special. We had a team and style that fitted my game very well. We had Nick Barmby, John Collins, and Don Hutchinson in a midfield that liked to keep the ball on the deck. I came in and made the most of my chances early on and was given quite a bit of playing time. Things couldn't have been better. Unfortunately, our team changed that summer, as did our playing style. As a result, I was looking for balls that were being nodded down by Duncan Ferguson and Kevin Campbell. That didn't quite fit my style of play and I went through a lengthy spell without scoring. With injuries mixed in, it became harder to get any significant playing time. It wasn't easy, for sure. I played part of the second-half against Fulham, which was David Moyes' first match in charge in March 2002. We were down to 10 men and didn't make it out of our own half much. I never saw the field again for Everton.

'Looking back, it was an incredible experience. I loved playing with Kevin. He was a real personality in the locker room. Big and strong, he had a good nose for the goal. Duncan was probably the toughest player I played with during my whole career. I remember the morning he came into training a little scratched up and told us the story about the guys who tried to break into his house. Paul Gascoigne was an idol of mine growing up – a tremendous talent and biggest character I've ever been around. I sat next to him in the locker room and he was always messing with someone. Gazza decided to wear my socks home on his first day of training. Thomas Gravesen was one of top two or three players I ever played with. Strong, hard and great on the ball. I wasn't surprised to see him move to Real Madrid.

'The 2002 World Cup finals and my time at Everton, were the highlights of my career. I always check Everton's results, and watch when I can. I took my family back to a game in 2010 and they loved it.'

### David Moyes and the Americans

*Not only did the Everton manager experience the first-class training facilities in the USA, but he enjoyed having the best North American players in and around his senior squad ...*

'We signed the three best American players of recent times. Brian McBride was awesome and it was unfortunate that we didn't sign him permanently. Tim Howard, who went on to be great for us and is tremendously respected in his homeland for what he achieved during his playing career.

'Landon was great too. He was the USA's best player at the time and did well in the World Cup. Landon hadn't trained much with us before he started playing for us, but he did really well. The USA star might not have fancied Liverpool as much as Los Angeles, but he enjoyed being with us. I always thought that the addition of the American boys was good for the team and for the club.'

### Dr Anton Peterlin

*The son of a Danish pilot mother and a Slovenian doctor father, Peterlin enjoyed the 2009/10 season at Everton before studying medicine and working as an A&E doctor in Copenhagen ...*

'There wasn't much soccer when I was a boy in San Francisco. They didn't have academies and parents of the players were often the coaches. I was fortunate to get a scholarship to the University of California when I was 17. During the off-season, I played for the San Francisco Seals and then Ventura Fusion. That's where I met Graham Smith, who alerted David Moyes. I had a trial that Everton for 10 days in March 2009. There was a draft system and the San Jose Earthquakes owned the rights to me. But I loved Europe and wanted to play in Europe. I was with Cody Arnoux but he was homesick and didn't feel the same way. The hardest thing was living in a hotel for two months. Life was much better when I moved into an apartment in Liverpool city centre. There, I spent time with Seamus Coleman, Kieran Agard, Hope Akpan and goalkeeper Lars Stubhaug. We'd play FIFA together and stuff like that. Seamus was a good friend. He's one of the most genuine people I know. I got on very well with Victor Anichebe, too, and spent some time at his house.

'The coaches Taff Holden and Alan Stubbs were great. I'll never forget that during training one day, Taff said: 'For a lot of you guys, this is the best club you'll ever be at, so enjoy it.' That was certainly true for me. I knew that I was four years too late getting to the level of the other lads, so I enjoyed every minute of it. It showed me just how far behind soccer in the USA was at the time.

'Players like Steven Pienaar, Tim Cahill and Mikel Arteta were incredible with their awareness and speed of play. They never ever made mistakes in their own half and knew what they were going to do with the ball before they got it. Arteta passed it forward all the time, always clever, into space. After every training session with them, I was exhausted mentally and physically.

'I played reserve team football but when the first team was in the Europa League, we'd help them train under Moyesy. It was a cut-throat environment. True Darwinism – the survival of the fittest. For every Ross Barkley or Tom Davies that come through the ranks there are scores of other young talented lads with their dreams crushed. I'm thankful just to have had the chance at Everton. I told manager David Moyes that when he let me go.'

### David Prentice and the engaging Yanks

*Now the sports editor of the Liverpool Echo, David Prentice has met and interviewed every North American to have played for Everton …*

'Evertonians didn't know quite what to make of Joe-Max Moore when Walter Smith snagged him on Richard Gough's recommendation in the final few weeks of the last millennium: not least what to call him! Was Max his middle name? Did he have a double-barrelled surname, Max-Moore – or was it the unusual Joe-Max? The latter was the correct outcome.

'But if the fans were unsure what to make of the sparky little striker, Joe-Max could have been forgiven for not knowing what to make of English football. He was baptised in an FA Cup tie at third-tier Exeter City – on the coldest day of the year on a frozen pitch. But the son of Tulsa who spent his formative years in California acclimatised magnificently – on and off the pitch.

'Mature beyond his 28 years, Joe-Max impressed me and many others at Bellefield. I had never met such a respectful and cooperative professional footballer. I put it down to his natural charm and apple pie upbringing. The next time I interviewed him was after his late equaliser against Tottenham that January, he was modest and shared the credit with the other members of Walter Smith's side. I think he scored another five times during the next six league and cup games and ultimately spent three years at Goodison – a cleverly clipped equaliser in an FA Cup quarter-final against Aston Villa underlining the technical quality he possessed. Typical of Everton in that era, though, Villa came back to win.

'But Joe-Max's attitude and demeanour whetted the appetite for Everton's next American acquisition. Brian McBride arrived with a reputation for being one of the USA's most aerially efficient players – suggesting he would adapt to the notoriously physical English game quickly. He did – but not in the manner that Evertonians had expected. Brian scored four goals in his first five games – all with his feet!

'Also, his arrival caused a bit of a stir, not least because he had married Dina Lundstrom, who had appeared as a swimwear model on the cover of Sports Illustrated. But Brian showed model professionalism himself at both Finch Farm and Goodison, not least because he was aware that, aged 30 he had arrived at a time when David Moyes was trying to lessen the average age of the squad and he was never destined for a lengthy Goodison spell.

'Tim Howard was an American for whom longevity was as much a part of his tenure as quality. No player has made more Premier League appearances for the Blues than the USA's Secretary of the Defence, a nickname deservedly bestowed following a stellar display in the 2014 World Cup against Belgium that led to worldwide recognition. Tim was equally highly regarded at Goodison throughout his 354 games – and one goal. I spoke to him many times throughout his tenure there – and he was always charming and entertaining company. After one sit down chat I commended him on how forthright and interesting he had been. 'I always try to be as engaging as possible,' he said. And he was.

'Landon Donovan, meanwhile, was the most popular American ever to pull on the royal blue jersey. He flew in from a Californian summer to make his debut in a blizzard at Arsenal's Emirates Stadium – and gave Evertonians a warm glow with the quality, penetration and commitment he displayed. Donovan wore the club's iconic number nine shirt – and the greatest compliment you could pay him is that he justified that decision.

'Evertonians would have loved him to have signed permanently. But he explained to me: "Before I signed, the Galaxy by no means had to let me go to Everton – it was at their discretion, I was under contract there so I asked them if they would allow me to go on loan for three months. They said the only way they would allow it is if I gave my word that I was definitely coming back to Los Angeles. In football you never know, things change all the time, but I am a man of my word and I like to honour that." But he added: "It was really hard for me because I wanted to stay at Everton. How could I not want to? It was some of the best times of my life as a football player." Of course, Landon Donovan did come back for a second spell in 2012, and again was adored by the Goodison faithful.'

### Brian Quinn – Mr Soccer in San Diego

*Born in Belfast and preened at Bellefield, Brian Quinn developed into an indoor soccer super-star and then a key member of the USA men's national team, making his first international appearance at age 31 ...*

'I loved Everton, I loved Merseyside, and would have stayed there forever if I had been a little bit better footballer. In May 1979, I was a teenager studying to be a schoolteacher and playing for Larne in the Irish League. I had already had unproductive trials with Arsenal, Middlesbrough and Queens Park Rangers when I was spotted by Everton playing for a Northern Ireland youth team in France. After a successful trial at Bellefield, I was signed on the same day as £250,000 Gary Stanley and joined the reserve squad which included some tremendous young players such as Kevin Ratcliffe, Steve McMahon, and Gary Stevens.

'To be close to the training ground, I stayed in digs with Mrs Parker in West Derby where my roommate was Kevin Richardson – another future international. I trained with the first team on several occasions but my progress was blocked by big money signings like Gary Stanley, Trevor Ross, Asa Hartford and Andy King plus the emergence of Steve McMahon and Paul Lodge – all great players. It was dog-eat-dog survival of the best and hungriest, but I've many fond memories of my Everton teammates.

'For example, around 1981 I was recovering from a pelvic strain under the watchful eyes of trainer Jim McGregor. Full-back John Barton, who was signed from Worcester City for a then record non-League fee of £25,000, was recovering from a broken ankle. After our treatments, we would soak in the big bath and John would sing to me. It was the same Lionel Richie song every day: "You're once, twice, three times a lady …" I'll let you finish the song's lyrics.

'Towards the end of my two-year contract, I was thinking about joining Bolton but was approached by Glentoran. Their top men came to Goodison and suggested that I play part-time and finish my teacher training studies, which made sense. That afternoon, I bumped into Mike Lyons. He said, "Don't go back to Belfast son. You have a future in the game." His words of encouragement changed my life. He was right, but like him I had no idea it was over 5,000 miles away. One day I received a call from Brian Halliday, my old mentor at Larne. He asked, "Do you fancy playing for the Aztecs in Los Angeles?" So in March 1981, my wife Sharon, young baby Nicola and I headed to the sunshine of California.

'Previously managed by the legendary Rinus Michels, who had overseen Ajax and Barcelona, the club had once fielded Johan Cruyff. However during my time there, it was in transition under the guidance of ex-Brazil manager Cláudio Coutinho and the new ownership of Grupo Televisa, the Mexican television giants. The manager appeared to be impressed by my abilities to win the ball and to play at an intensive tempo and I slotted into the first team alongside mostly youngsters from South America. Unfortunately in the absence of Cruyff, the home attendances plummeted, and the club folded at the end of my first season.

'Hence, I went into the NASL dispersal draft and was signed by the Montreal Manic, previously known as the as the Philadelphia Fury. "Le Manic", as they were called locally, were managed by Eddie Firmani who had steered the New York Cosmos, which included Pelé, Franz Beckenbauer, Carlos Alberto, Giorgio Chinaglia and Everton and Northern Ireland's Dave Clements, to success. In Montreal, we played outdoors at the iconic Olympic Stadium and indoors at the Montreal Forum, which had hosted dozens of Stanley Cup finals.

'Having only ever played 11 v 11, the indoor game was a new world. But I soon adapted to playing six-a-side on an NHL rink-sized pitch (200ft x 85ft) and smaller goals (12ft x 6.5ft high compared with the regular dimensions of 24ft x 8ft). It was football on steroids and my approach, which had been instilled into me by Colin Harvey, was "get the ball down to my feet then play it and go." After two seasons the club folded and I was back in the NASL dispersal draft. Next, I won the lottery and was selected by the San Diego Sockers. We had a great side which included Cas Denya. Alongside the Poland star, who was my room-mate, we seized the NASL title before the league folded in 1984. It was a massive shock but that was North American soccer in those days – unstable.

'My teammates either went home or, like me, stayed to play for the San Diego Sockers in the Major Indoor Soccer League. With a large squad of about 24 players, we dominated the MISL. I scored 180 goals in 287 games as we amassed eight consecutive titles. By 1990, my wife and I had five children (we now have six children and 12 grandchildren) – one was born in Belfast, another in Montreal and the others in California and, concerned about their futures, we decided to apply to became US citizens.

'At that time, I was a 31-year-old with no ambition to play international football. Even though I had not played on a regular pitch for three years, I was invited to train with the USA national team and then selected to play the Republic of Ireland, which included Everton's Kevin Sheedy, at Foxboro Stadium. I am proud and honoured to have gone onto represent my adopted country on 48 occasions shoulder to shoulder with the likes of Tony Meola, Marcelo Balboa, Earnie Stewart, Hugo Pérez, Jeff Agoos, Eric Wynalda, Cobi Jones, John Harkes, Alexi Lalas and, of course, Everton's Joe-Max Moore.

'After winding down my playing career, I was appointed head-coach of the San Diego Sockers, then in the Continental Indoor Soccer League. Later, at age 37, I became the youngest coach in MLS history when I accepted the same job at the San Jose Clash. After three seasons there, I reverted to the Sockers until the team folded in 2004. Almost immediately, I launched the Brian Quinn School of Soccer in sunny San Diego.

'Turning to professional soccer in North America, the future looks bright. There have been enormous changes since my days in the NASL – especially in the ownership of franchises. Back then, the clubs were sponsored by enthusiastic millionaires. Today, they are owned and operated by billionaires. The standard of football, however, has remained about the same. The best of the MLS are equivalent to the top of the English second tier. As for Everton's profile in Southern California, with the explosion in televised coverage we seem to be slipping farther and farther behind Liverpool, Manchester United, Bayern Munich, Juventus, Barcelona and Real Madrid. Even so, I look forward to the day when I visit the old country and cheer the Blues at the Bramley-Moore Stadium on the banks of the royal blue Mersey.'

### Predrag Radosavljević – the footballer better known as Preki

*In the 1980s, Yugoslavians like Preki could not play overseas until age 28. It was a rule to keep the best talent in the domestic league. He got around this by signing up for US indoor soccer in 1985, at the age of 22 …*

'The opportunity arose for me to play indoor soccer in the USA. The game was very fast and competitive with some incredible players who had played at the highest level. I was at Tacoma for five years and then St Louis for a couple more but was always kept an eye open to see if I could go back to Europe to play 11-a-side.

'Things did not change until I was 29 when Bobby Robson's PSV Eindhoven invited me for 17 days of training and decided to sign me. So my wife and I sold everything, moved to Serbia and waited for the paperwork to be completed. Unfortunately, St Louis and PSV could not agree on a price and the deal fell through. Then former-Arsenal and England full-back Bob McNab, my first coach in the USA, introduced me to Graham Smith who arranged for trials at Everton and then Tottenham Hotspur. Both clubs invited me back for pre-season training. I decided on Everton – I knew all about its rich history and what a massive club it was.

'I really enjoyed my time there although it was not always easy. Howard Kendall was great – his managerial style was different to that in Serbia. Running around without the ball at my feet was alien to what I had been brought up with. I am not knocking it, the approach was just different and I had to adapt to a new way of playing. Then I dislocated my shoulder and had to put everything on hold for six weeks. Afterwards, I was often sat on the bench – the coaches make their decisions and all you can do is train to the best of your ability. As a player you just think about what is good for you. Now, as a manager, I understand the reasoning. You think of what is better for the group – a player may be good technically but doesn't do the things you ask of him off the ball.

'The Everton players were all good guys. Peter Beardsley was the most naturally gifted. He was always thinking ahead about what he was going to do with the ball. Tony Cottee was a good reader of situations – it was easy to find him. Peter Beagrie was another great talent. But we did not have enough players able to move the ball fluidly along the ground. So, we had to play to our strengths, work hard and grind out results. Their drinking was one thing that I did not take on board, as alcohol does not go hand in hand with performance. If you become someone who spends too much time gambling in the bookies or drinking in the local pub, it becomes a distraction. I hear that today is different – English players are more responsible and take care of themselves.

'After Mike Walker came in, he tried to instil a different way of playing, with the ball on the ground, but the question was whether we had the players to do that. I don't think that the pieces were there. When my contract expired in 1994, I had the chance to go to Greece with Howard Kendall but joined Jim Smith at Portsmouth. I really enjoyed my year there, as I was finally starting to find my "outdoor legs". I was informed that a couple of Premier League teams wanted me, but I was 32 and decided to go back to the USA, sort out my citizenship and play in the MLS.

'One thing I took with me from England was the players' fitness levels, commitment in training and competitive edge. I knew that if I was going to continue to play, I needed to be in top shape. I changed the way I ate and trained. I took up yoga and found a different gear. It was a really proud moment to first represent the USA at 33 and go to the 1998 World Cup – but I wished that they had happened when I was younger. Then at age 40, I broke my left leg and dislocated my left ankle. It took 17 months to recover. I was stubborn and didn't want to quit, so I played a few more games and retired at 42.

'Coaching is the next best thing to playing. It is fascinating when you are making crucial decisions. You may want to play a certain way but with the players on your roster can you do that? I've always been attack-minded and like my teams to press. I ask a lot from them. I have always wanted to coach in the UK but there are way too many coaches and not enough clubs. The standard of the MLS has improved, they have signed a few good players from other countries. But I don't recall one player from a top league coming over before he is 32 because he will never get called up by their country again.

'MLS is a difficult league to play in with the different time zones, flights of 5-6 hours, going from nice weather to extreme heat and then to snow. The game here is evolving, the stadiums, the fans – but when it has a long way to go. It's still not close to the top five leagues in Europe or even the English Championship. Djimi Traoré, who played for Liverpool, is on my staff at Seattle so we have a go at each other. My son was born in Liverpool, but we are not on the same page – he's a Liverpool fan. I'm starting to question if he is really my son!'

Football agent Graham Smith who arranged for Preki's move to Premier League from the obscurity of the St Louis Storm reflected: 'He was an intelligent and tremendously talented footballer who adjusted quickly from his indoor background. Thanks to the best left peg to bless Goodison since the days of Kevin Sheedy, Preki responded well to having quality players around him but I do not think that Everton fans saw him at his very best. Like most footballers, he was not happy about spending so much time on the bench. Of course, there can be no such guarantees in the English Premier League.'

### Tomasz Radzinski – a goalscoring Canadian

*Born in Poland, Radzinski was brought up in Germany and Canada, where he played in the Canadian Soccer League, the National Soccer League and the Canadian National Soccer League. At age 21, the forward returned to Europe and played in Belgium, where his form earned him Canada caps. In 2001, he was signed from Anderlecht by manager Walter Smith for the highest fee ever paid for a Canadian soccer player ...*

'When I was growing up in Poland, life was not as easy. My parents were trying to find a better life for me and my younger brother, so when I was about 11 they decided to emigrate. The two choices were South Africa or somewhere in North America – and Canada got the vote. We moved out to Toronto – I still remember that cold April day when we arrived. I'd been playing soccer since a young age and was keen to continue. My Dad was looking for any soccer teams there – he would buy all of the local newspapers just to find mention of a team that I could play for – but the soccer competition didn't start until May. Via some friends he got to know Grzegorz Lato, a legendary player and coach who had a fantastic World Cup for Poland in 1974. So I got to play for North York Rockets in the Canadian Soccer League. The club was owned by Italians and the stadium had a capacity of 3,000. We'd get 2,000 at best.

'The league consisted of eight teams spread all over Canada. We would play two or three weeks of games at home and then go on the road for another two or three weeks – flying to places like Winnipeg, Calgary and Vancouver. The average player's contract was probably about $10,000 per year – therefore most of them were part-timers who worked during the day and trained in the evening. Therefore, you could put your money on the home teams winning their games because the visitors could never scramble together enough players to go on the road – the older and more experienced players couldn't afford to miss their regular jobs and wages.

'For me it was great – I was missing school! But both my parents were teachers so for them it was most important that I got my diploma and that soccer came second. The principal of the school was okay with it as I was playing a professional sport – I had to do my homework on the road and catch-up when I got back. I was already a year behind at school and my first priority was learning the English language – which was far more difficult than learning German. In Canada we had a local Polish community with the church, shops – even the school was made up of 25% of Polish students – so you could live there without learning or using a word of English.'

'I got my Canadian citizenship a little bit quicker than the rest of my family due to my soccer talent – they wanted me to be in the Olympic soccer team, so someone fast-tracked it. Playing for that team was my ticket to play back in Europe. When I was about 19, the Olympic team played in the 1994 Jeux de la Francophonie in Paris (a French version of the Commonwealth Games). My Dad contacted another Polish legend named Włodzimierz Lubański, who was living in Belgium and working as an agent. I had a really good tournament and then Lubański took me for three weeks of trials with Lokeren, a big Belgian team back then. For whatever reason they could not agree on the contract, but it took Ekeren only one game and training session to take me on, initially for one season.

'Were it not for the Jeux de la Francophonie, I would not have made the jump, as it was difficult to convince anybody in Europe to consider someone playing in the Canadian league. After four seasons I moved to Anderlecht. To be honest, if it wasn't for scoring a few goals in the Champions League and becoming Belgian champions, I wouldn't have had the chance to go to the Premier League in 1999. That was my most important season but my three years at Everton were second to none as an experience.

'As a kid only international games were shown on the televison and I dreamt of playing for Poland. Of course there was no possibility of Tomasz Radzinski playing for Poland – no Polish scouts would even have heard of me, being over in Canada. I was under no illusions and I never had any regrets – I had a fantastic time with the Canadian national team. It is too bad that the recent FIFA changes about when international games are played were introduced just a few years ago. Before that you would play for Canada on the Wednesday, fly back to Europe on the Thursday night, and arrive back on the Friday. No club manager in his right mind would put you in the team on Saturday.

'Therefore, many times I chose club over country. I said, "If this is the way it has to be, then don't call me up until further notice." This is why I was awarded less than 50 caps over 16 years. Maybe it was a bit selfish but for me the priority had to be the Premier League – I knew how few Canadians had played in it and I didn't want to be a failure. I wanted to keep my place and play in every single game – the only way to do that was if I could be available for David Moyes – fit and ready to go.

'When the new Canada national team coach came in, I started to play again. The most memorable thing for me in the whole of my career was in 2009 – my very last game for Canada, and it was against Poland in a town approximately 20km from where I grew up as a young child. The regular Canada captain came to me before the game and told me that I would be the skipper. So, it was very emotional for me – I shed a tear of two during both national anthems as it was surreal. Here I was captaining Canada against Poland. I did not have the best game as I was coping with so many emotions that day – even 11 years on I am still thinking about that game.'

### Antonee Robinson – a USA international from Milton Keynes

*Robinson joined Everton at age 11 and departed to Wigan Athletic a decade later with the rare distinction of being an international footballer who had never made a first team appearance for the Merseyside club …*

'Everton's assistant secretary, Jonathan Williams, had told me that he'd heard the USA was thinking of calling me up, but I thought he meant an Under-21 camp. I was sat in my mother's house in Liverpool when I first got a phone call from Dave Sarachan, the USA interim-manager, inviting me to join the full squad. My Mum was just a few doors away, so I ran to tell her and she got the champagne out!

'It was a week before the camp and I had yet to go get my American passport sorted. I was nervous going out there because I did not know what the standard of football was going to be like. However, I discovered that It was a young group of players so it was quite easy for me to settle in. The camp was in North Carolina and there was a friendly against Paraguay at the end of it. I didn't take part. In fact, I didn't make my senior debut until the end of my second camp in May 2018. It was against Bolivia in Philadelphia. We won 3-0. I would say that being an international footballer helped me to push on. As soon as you get that international tag, it helps your confidence and increases your market value. And, of course, it was a big country I was playing for, which also helped – it wasn't a small nation that nobody has heard of!

'I had good times and bad times at Everton. I was sidelined with injuries for a bit, but the club always stood by me and helped me to get back to the level I needed to be at. And the loan deals that Everton sorted out for me at Bolton Wanderers and Wigan Athletic helped me to be where I am today. When I was not in the USA squad, head-coach Gregg Berhalter was always checking up on me, especially when I had the issue with AC Milan after my big-money transfer broke down in early-2020. Gregg assured me that he was tracking my progress. I have got a lot of respect for him. But to this day, he has never mentioned the fact that he had trials at Everton and played for the Reserves.'

# Roy Turner and the Wichita Wings

*The defensive midfielder progressed from being a member of the Everton A team to a NASL star and then a USA international. As a coach, he is synonymous with the Wichita Wings who he coached for 485 games in the MISL and then NPSL …*

'I was raised an Evertonian and still follow them. When I left school and joined the post office, Mickey Lill used to watch me playing in Maghull and recommended me to Everton. My Dad was a bread man and, because I had no way to get to my first game, he took me to Bellefield in his van and then carried on with his round! Back then Everton were the best they had ever been. As a teenager, I turned out for the A-team with Tommy Wright and Colin Harvey. But I did not make it. I wasn't good enough, however, I went onto perhaps bigger and better things.

'I eventually got a chance to come to North America when the Toronto Falcons came to Merseyside looking to sign young players. They spoke to Tommy Jones, who was my coach at Bellefield, and he recommended me – for which I'm very grateful. It was the first time I'd been abroad and was an education in many ways. I realised that North America soccer was in its early years and offered a lot.

'The following year, I was fortunate to move to the Philadelphia Spartans, then after they folded to the Cleveland Stokers and finally to the Dallas Tornado, where I stayed for 11 years. I was known as "Iron Man" (and a few other names) and played alongside Tony McLoughlin – a good Evertonian, a great player and one hell of a character. When we won the NASL title in 1971, my Dallas teammates celebrated by taking a red double-decker bus from the Atlanta Stadium back to our hotel. Two years later, I was asked if I was interested in playing for the USA national team but responded that I wasn't a US citizen. Miraculously, a few weeks later I had become a naturalised citizen and was representing my new country!

'As for other highlights? I played for Toronto at New York in 1977. At home, I have a framed picture on the wall of Pele and me during that game. I bet Pele has the same picture on his wall. Also, I played at Soldier Field – the home field of the NFL's Chicago Bears. There were so few people at the 70,000-seater stadium, one of my teammates suggested that we should shake hands with everyone in the crowd and thank them for coming.

'Sometimes at Dallas we had crowds of 25,000 but, to be honest, they were mainly attracted by promotions like fireworks and parachute displays. The fans didn't take to soccer and we couldn't consistently keep them interested, so the club lost money. For a while, the indoor league offered the only professional soccer in North America and I became a coach in Wichita where I recruited Seamus McDonagh, Gary Stanley and Mickey Thomas from Everton. The Wings were a great success and would attract 10,000 fans to every game until the team folded in 2001. Then the outdoor game came back with a vengeance via Major League Soccer. Nowadays, people understand and appreciate soccer more than they did in my playing days.

'The last time I went over to England was five years ago for my father's funeral. It rekindled a lot of memories when I visited Goodison. I'm getting old now – I've turned 77, but it is my dream to visit the new waterfront stadium. I am just hoping that they finish it before I die!'

Of the 16 Americans and Canadians featured, only a half-dozen of them progressed to played first team football for Everton. Nevertheless, these six men made a total of 662 senior appearances, with 63% of them claimed by Tim Howard.

*Caricatures and profiles of the North American Blues are presented in alphabetical order. They kick off with young Cody Arnoux who was plucked from the fourth tier of US soccer ...*

# Cody Arnoux

**played for**

Wake Forest University
Demon Deacons,
Carolina Dynamo,
Everton,
Real Salt Lake,
Wilmington Hammerheads

The 21-year-old Wake Forest University graduate was yanked from the limbo of the semi-pro Carolina Dynamo in the USL Premier Development League – the fourth-level of the American soccer pyramid. Following a successful trial at Finch Farm in 2009, the former USA Under-15 and Under-18 spearhead made several appearances for Everton Reserves and also attended trials at Motherwell and Plymouth during the 2009/10 season before rebounding to North America. Arnoux, who was respected for his uncompromising and unshakable battering-ram approach, thought he had joined the Vancouver Whitecaps prior to the 2011 season. However, the MLS rejected his contract and he was assigned to Real Salt Lake in a lottery draft.

| Everton 2009/10 | | |
| --- | --- | --- |
| | games | goals |
| League | 0/0 | 0 |
| Total | 0/0 | 0 |

# Gregg Berhalter

**played for**

University of North
Carolina Tar Heels,
Raleigh Flyers,
Zwolle (Netherlands),
Sparta Rotterdam,
Cambuur Leeuwarden
(Netherlands),
Everton (trial),
Crystal Palace,
Energie Cottbus,
1860 Munich,
Los Angeles Galaxy

**coached at**

Los Angeles Galaxy,
Hammarby (Sweden),
Columbus Crew,
USA

The ambitious defensive kingpin left university after his junior year to gain playing experience in Europe. In late-2000, he was invited for trials at Everton and turned out alongside his USA compatriot and good friend Joe-Max Moore against Leeds United Reserves at Widnes. Though considered a calm and confident central-defender as well as a natural team leader, the trials were fruitless. Regardless, the 26-year-old USA international elected to stay in Europe with Crystal Palace, Energie Cottbus and finally 1860 Munich before returning to North America to help the Los Angeles Galaxy capture the 2011 MLS Cup. Following five years as head-coach at the Columbus Crew, Berhalter was appointed to same role with the US men's national team in late-2018.

Everton trialist: 2000/01

# Edson Buddle

**played for**

Long Island Rough Riders,
Columbus Crew,
New York Red Bulls,
Toronto,
Los Angeles Galaxy,
Ingolstadt 04 (Germany),
Everton (trial),
Los Angeles Galaxy,
Colorado Rapids,
Los Angeles Galaxy

**coached at**

Westchester Flames

Short of firepower and dependent on inexperienced youngsters like Victor Anichebe, Denis Stracqualursi and Apostolos Vellios, manager David Moyes turned to the veteran USA forward. Following his release by Ingolstadt 04 in the 2. Bundesliga, the then 30-year-old striker – who had the same US agent as Messrs Howard and Donovan – was invited for trials at Finch Farm in January 2012. They were not productive. Despite his enthusiasm, strength and athleticism, he failed to get the better of the Premier League quality defenders – let alone make them go weak at the knees. Consequently, Buddle spent rewarding second and third spells with the Los Angeles Galaxy and became one of only 11 men to have scored 100 goals in MLS history.

Everton trialist: 2011/12

# Landon Donovan

**played for**

IMG Soccer Academy,

Bayer Leverkusen,

San Jose Earthquakes (loan),

Los Angeles Galaxy,

Bayern Munich (loan),

Everton (loan),

Los Angeles Galaxy,

Everton (loan),

Los Angeles Galaxy,

León (Mexico),

San Diego Sockers

**coached at**

San Diego Loyal

North America's greatest ever soccer star is a seven-time winner of the Honda Player of the Year award. He captured two MLS Cups with the San Jose Earthquakes and another four with the Los Angeles Galaxy. As the big shot of the national team, until sidelined by manager Jürgen Klinsmann, Donovan helped the USA win four CONCACAF Gold Cups. Shortly after featuring in the 2009 MLS All-Star game against Everton, he joined the Merseyside club on loan for three months. At age 28, the attacking midfielder – who was widely respected for his scintillating pace, football intelligence, positive attitude and rare work ethic – was at his peak and terrorised Premier League opponents. In 2012, he returned to Everton for another two-month loan. Soon afterwards, Donovan announced his desire to take a break from soccer citing exhaustion.

| Everton 2009/10 & 2011/12 | | |
| --- | --- | --- |
| | games | goals |
| League | 14/3 | 2 |
| Total | 19/3 | 2 |

# Robert Earl

**associated with**

Everton

The acclaimed entrepreneur is a prominent figure in the worldwide hospitality, food and beverage industries. So much so that, along with the likes of Senator John McCain, billionaire George Soros and film producer Harvey Weinstein, Earl was selected as one of 'The 25 Most Influential Americans' by *Time* magazine in 2001. Some five years later, he became an Everton director after buying the 23% shareholdings of Paul and Anita Gregg via his BCR Sports investment vehicle registered in the British Virgin Islands. During Earl's turbulent term, which included the proposed ground move to Kirkby, he provided guarantees to enable the club to extend its bank borrowings, sign new players and end most seasons in the Top 6. But in the eyes of some fans, Earl's biggest masterstroke was inviting a blue and white clad Sylvester Stallone, the Rocky and Rambo movie star, to Goodison. In 2016, Earl – a naturalised US citizen – sold his stake in Everton Football Club to Farhad Moshiri for no small profit.

Everton director: 2006/07-2015/16

# Marcus Hahnemann

**played for**

Seattle Pacific University Falcons,

Seattle Sounders,

Colorado Rapids,

Fulham,

Rochdale (loan),

Reading (loan),

Wolverhampton Wanderers,

Everton,

Seattle Sounders

Association football has a long tradition of eccentric goalkeepers, that is people who choose the one position where they use their hands. A Pacific North West native and MLS star, the 6ft 3in giant joined Fulham from the Colorado Rapids for about £80,000 in 1999. Unable to displace Maik Taylor and Edwin van der Sar, Hahnemann moved onto Reading on a free transfer and helped them land the League Championship title in 2006. Next, the USA keeper – often picked as a back-up for either Kasey Keller or Tim Howard – joined Wolverhampton Wanderers in the Premier League and then Everton on an eight-month deal. Though the 39-year-old veteran never played a first team fixture, he was selected as substitute goalkeeper throughout the 2012 FA Cup run which ended with a dramatic last-minute loss to Liverpool in the semi-final at Wembley.

| Everton 2011/12 | | |
| --- | --- | --- |
| | games | goals |
| League | 0/0 | 0 |
| Total | 0/0 | 0 |

# Nico Defreitas-Hansen

**played for**

Weston (Florida),
Everton

Born in Southwest Ranches, Florida and a graduate of the famous Weston Soccer Academy, the novice keeper moved to the United Kingdom to join Everton as a 16-year-old boy. Admired as a confident and agile shot-stopper who had represented the USA at Under-14, Under-15 and Under-16 levels Hansen possessed tremendous potential to follow in the giant footsteps made for his club and his country by Tim Howard. Indeed, after several encouraging displays or Everton's junior sides, he signed a two-year pro contract in July 2019. Then some four months later, the talented youngster changed his national affiliation to that of his father and played for the Denmark Under-19 team. After handful of appearances for the Everton Under-23 side, he made a fleeting first team debut in a pre-season friendly in 2020.

|  | Everton 2019/20 games | goals |
|---|---|---|
| League | 0/0 | 0 |
| Total | 0/0 | 0 |

# Tim Howard

**played for**
North Jersey Imperials,
New York/New Jersey MetroStars,
MLS Pro-40 (loan),
Manchester United,
Everton (loan),
Everton,
Colorado Rapids,
Memphis 901

**associated with**
Dagenham & Redbridge,
Memphis 901

The most recognisable face of men's soccer in North America joined Everton from Manchester United for £3 million in 2007, after a highly productive season on loan. The bald, chiselled Adonis suffering from Tourette syndrome, then minus his trademark body tattoos and luxuriant beard, displayed feline reflexes and superior confidence during most of his decade at Goodison. Brave to the point of being foolhardy, the American dived in where others hesitated to place a boot. The goalkeeper made 210 consecutive League appearances between 2007-2013, a record bettered only by Neville Southall. Lauded as a gifted spot-kick saviour, he was also a fortunate goalscorer – netting with a wind-assisted kick against Bolton Wanderers in 2012. Howard represented the USA at two World Cup finals and became an American hero when his record-breaking 15 saves against Belgium in 2014 electrified his nation.

| Everton 2006/07–2015/16 | | |
| --- | --- | --- |
| | games | goals |
| League | 354/0 | 1 |
| Total | 414/0 | 1 |

# Brian McBride

**played for**

St Louis University Billikens,
Milwaukee Rampage,
Wolfsburg,
Columbus Crew,
Preston North End (loan),
Everton (loan),
Fulham,
Chicago Fire,
Wembley

**coached at**

USA

Having failed to find his top form in the German second tier, the former All-American centre-forward from Arlington Heights, Illinois returned to North America for the inaugural MLS season as the first overall draft pick. Towards the end of his successful eight years at Columbus Crew, the USA international forward was loaned to David Moyes' Preston and subsequently to Moyes' Everton. Signed as a stopgap in 2003, due to an injury crisis, the 30-year-old forward impressed the Goodison faithful with his battling and hard-working approach. After netting four times in eight games during his two-month loan period, he became a firm favourite. Recognised as one of the USA's finest strikers, McBride was appointed general manager of the US men's national team in 2020.

| Everton 2002/03 | | |
| --- | --- | --- |
| | games | goals |
| League | 7/1 | 4 |
| Total | 7/1 | 4 |

# Joe-Max Moore

**played for**

University of California at
Los Angeles Bruins,
Saarbrücken,
Nuremberg,
New England Revolution,
Emelec (Ecuador),
Everton,
New England Revolution

Born in Tulsa, Oklahoma where his father had been a part-owner of the NASL's Roughnecks, the All American forward spent much of his career in Europe yet scored most of his goals in North America. After two spells in Germany, he joined the New England Revolution and netted 49 goals in 90 games – many from acute angles. Then in late-1999, the increasingly versatile 28-year-old was signed by manager Walter Smith after a brief successful trial. Sharp and plucky, he made an explosive start with a spell of six goals in seven outings. Unfortunately, knee injuries plagued his further progress and, after missing all of the 2001/02 season, the USA favourite – who played in the 1994, 1998 and 2002 World Cups – returned to New England. In 2013, Joe-Max Moore was elected to the National Soccer Hall of Fame.

| Everton 1999/00 – 2002/02 | | |
|---|---|---|
| | games | goals |
| League | 22/30 | 8 |
| Total | 27/37 | 10 |

# Anton Peterlin

**played for**

University of California at Santa Cruz Banana Slugs, California Polytechnic State University Mustangs, San Francisco Seals, Ventura County Fusion, Everton, Plymouth Argyle, Walsall, Hellerup (Denmark)

A neat and tidy rather than an extravagantly skilful footballer, the rise of Peterlin was amazing. Everton scouts noticed his potential during a friendly game against the Ventura County Fusion, in the fourth-tier of US soccer, amidst the club's trip to North America in 2008. After making an equally positive impression throughout his trials at Finch Farm, the defensive midfielder agreed to a 12-month pro contract and moved to Merseyside. Even though the 22-year-old never reached first team standard, he appeared in eight reserve team games during the 2009/10 season and captained the club in a semi-final of the Liverpool Senior Cup – which it somehow managed to lose to Skelmersdale United. At the end of his Everton contract, his fairytale continued with another 12-month stretch at Plymouth Argyle, then managed by Peter Reid.

| Everton 2009/10 | | |
|---|---|---|
| | games | goals |
| League | 0/0 | 0 |
| Total | 0/0 | 0 |

# Brian Quinn

**played for**

Larne,

Everton,

Los Angeles Aztecs,

Montreal Manic,

San Diego Sockers,

Hamilton Steelers,

US Soccer Federation,

San Diego Sockers

**coached at**

San Diego Sockers,

San Jose Clash,

San Diego Sockers,

University of San Diego Toreros

After his stunning display against Everton in a youth tournament in Le Havre, the 19-year-old midfielder was signed from Larne of the Irish League by manager Gordon Lee for £30,000 in 1979. Though skilful and nippy, he struggled to adapt to the robust nature of professional football and had departed to the Los Angeles Aztecs by 1981. When the NASL collapsed, Quinn's skills lit up the indoor arenas like a pinball machine and helped the San Diego Sockers harvest eight consecutive MISL titles. After gaining his US citizenship, he re-focused on the outdoor game and was awarded 48 USA caps. In retirement, Quinn coached at clubs, colleges and academies throughout California and was tagged as 'Mr Soccer' in San Diego. In 2012, he was inducted into the Indoor Soccer Hall of Fame.

| Everton 1979/80-1980/81 | | |
| --- | --- | --- |
| | games | goals |
| League | 0/0 | 0 |
| Total | 0/0 | 0 |

# Predrag Radosavljević

**played for**

Čukarički Stankom
(Yugoslavia/Serbia),
Red Star Belgrade,
Dallas Sidekicks,
Tacoma Stars,
Råslätts (Sweden),
St Louis Storm,
Everton,
San Jose Grizzlies,
Portsmouth,
Kansas City Wiz,
Miami Fusion,
Kansas City Wizards

**coached at**

Chivas USA,
Toronto,
Sacramento Republic,
Saint Louis,
Seattle Sounders

Born in Belgrade, 'Preki' was blessed with an amazing left foot. After moving to the USA, he spent seven seasons in the MISL where he netted 322 goals in his 338 games. In 1992, the attacking midfielder was sold to Everton for £100,000. As expected, it was a massive leap from North American indoor soccer to the English top tier. Though acclaimed – or perhaps cursed – as the 'Next Kevin Sheedy', he was used primarily as an impact player. With the advent of Major League Soccer, Preki excelled at the Kansas City Wiz and was voted the MLS MVP in 1997 and 2003. He first appeared for the USA national team at age 33 and hung up his playing boots nine years later to focus on coaching in the USL and MLS. Predrag Radosavljević was elected to the National Soccer Hall of Fame in 2012 and the Indoor Soccer Hall of Fame in 2013.

| Everton 1992/93-1994/95 | | |
|---|---|---|
| | games | goals |
| League | 22/24 | 4 |
| Total | 25/28 | 4 |

# Tomasz Radzinski

**played for**

Cuiavia Inowrocław (Poland),
Osnabrück (Germany),
North York Rockets,
St Catharines Roma Wolves,
Germinal Ekeren (Belgium),
Anderlecht,
Everton,
Fulham,
Skoda Xanthi (Greece),
Lierse (Belgium),
Waasland-Beveren (Belgium)

**coached at**

Lierse

The Poznań, Poland-born speedster had played for both the North York Rockets of the Canadian Soccer League and the St Catharines Roma Wolves in the Canadian National Soccer League before returning to Europe. There, the Canada international forward won the Belgium Cup with Germinal Ekeren and then consecutive Belgian First Division titles with Anderlecht before moving to Everton for £4.5 million. On Merseyside, the 27-year-old striker displayed his scintillating acceleration but missed many gilt-edged opportunities. After confirming that football is the only profession where a man can succeed one time out of three and still be considered a prolific goalscorer, he submitted a transfer request and made a controversial and acrimonious exit to Fulham in 2004.

| Everton 2001/02-2004/05 | | |
|---|---|---|
| | games | goals |
| League | 78/13 | 25 |
| Total | 85/16 | 26 |

# Antonee Robinson

**played for**

Everton,

Bolton Wanderers (loan),

Wigan Athletic (loan),

Wigan Athletic,

Fulham

Robinson was blessed with terrific football ability but cursed by horrendous bad luck. Born in Milton Keynes, the left-back progressed quickly through Everton's junior ranks until a serious knee injury sidelined him for the 2015/16 season. He recovered to become a key member of David Unsworth's Under-23 team that won the Premier League 2 title in 2017. During impressive loan spells at Bolton and Wigan, Robinson was selected to represent the USA – his father's homeland. In total, he made seven pre-season appearances – mostly as a substitue. His final first team outing for Everton was in the July 2019 friendly against the Kariobangi Sharks. Later that month, Robinson was sold to Wigan Athletic for £1.9 million. Six months on, he agreed to join AC Milan for five-times that fee until his medical examination revealed heart rhythm irregularities. After Wigan's administration and demotion in 2020, he was traded to Fulham for £1.9 million.

| Everton 2014/15 – 2019/20 | games | goals |
| --- | --- | --- |
| League | 0/0 | 0 |
| Total | 0/0 | 0 |

# Roy Turner

**played for**
Everton,
Bangor City,
Philadelphia Spartans,
Toronto Falcons,
Cleveland Stokers,
Dallas Tornado

**coached at**
Wichita Wings

A very late developer, the 24-year-old former-youth player travelled to North America in 1967 to join the Toronto Falcons and then the Philadelphia Spartans of the National Professional Soccer League. The following season, the tough midfielder – nicknamed 'The Iron Man' – signed for the Cleveland Stokers in the newly-formed NASL but soon moved onto the Dallas Tornado. During his 10 productive seasons in Texas, Turner captured the 1971 NASL title, earned USA caps and set the record for most consecutive NASL appearances at 131. In 1979, he joined the Wichita Wings of the Major Indoor Soccer League where he spent eight seasons as head-coach. Roy Turner was added to the exclusive membership of the Indoor Soccer Hall of Fame in 2019.

| Everton 1961/62-1964/65 | | |
| --- | --- | --- |
| | games | goals |
| League | 0 | 0 |
| Total | 0 | 0 |

# TEAMS ASSOCIATED WITH FEATURED COACHES

Austin Aztex • Austin Capitals • Austin Flyers • Calgary Storm
Carolina Vipers • Charlotte Chivas USA • Cleveland Cobras • Cleveland Force
Cleveland Stokers • Colorado Caribous • Colorado Rapids • Columbus Crew
Denver Avalanche • Detroit Express • Fort Worth Panthers • Fresno
Grenadier Guards • Hartfield Athletic • Houston Dynamo • Inter Miami
Kansas City Comets • Kansas City Wizards • Los Angeles Galaxy • Miami
Miami Freedom • Miami Toros • Minnesota Kicks • Minnesota United
Montreal Carsteel • Myrtle Beach Boyz • Myrtle Beach Seadawgs
New York/New Jersey MetroStars • New York Red Bulls • Nova Scotia Clippers
Oklahoma City Energy • Oklahoma City Slickers • Oklahoma City Spirit
Oklahoma City Stars • Orlando City • Philadelphia Fury • Portland Timbers
Richmond Kickers • Sacramento Republic • Saint Louis • San Antonio Scorpions
San Diego Loyal • San Diego Sockers • San Jose Clash • San Jose Earthquakes
Seattle • Seattle Sounders • Seattle Storm • St Louis Steamers
Tacoma Stars • Toronto • Toronto Italia • Tulsa Roughnecks • Tulsa Tornados
Victoria Vistas • Washington Diplomats • Westchester Flames
Wichita Wings • Wilmington Hammerheads

# 3.4
# COACHES AND GURUS

This chapter profiles the Toffeemen who took the expertise and practical experience that they gained during their careers at Everton across the pond to benefit North American soccer and also those groomed in other American sports who transferred their advanced know how to Merseyside.

Men associated with Everton Football Club have coached at 62 soccer clubs in Canada and the USA. Many of them arrived as players and never returned home. The first professional coach was Norman Low, a wartime guest at Goodison, who took charge of the Cleveland Stokers in 1968 for their only NASL season. He was followed by Ken Furphy, the one-time Everton reserve, who progressed to coached Pelé and Giorgio Chinaglia at the New York Cosmos and four other NASL teams.

While some well-known coaches, such as Alan Ball, Jimmy Gabriel, Mo Johnston, Predrag Radosavljević, Bruce Rioch, John Spencer, Robert Warzycha and most recently Adrian Heath, have managed clubs at the highest levels, others have only tenuous associations with Everton Football Club and/or North America soccer. Notwithstanding, all have helped in raising the Merseyside club's international profile.

Then there are the former-youth players – all blue to the core – such as Leigh Cowlishaw, Brian Harvey, Brian Monaghan, Adam Smith and Tommy Wheeldon, who travelled to North America as players only to make significant and long-term contributions to the development of professional, collegiate and local youth players.

For completeness, the chapter also includes the North American performance gurus and specialist coaches who introduced advanced techniques into the training regimes employed at Finch Farm.

# MEMORIES OF COACHES AND GURUS

## Gordon Banks and Neville Southall at Bellefield

*Harry Catterick tried to sign Banks in the early-1960s. After the deal fell through, the keeper advanced to World Cup glory and legendary status on both sides of the Atlantic. He played for the Cleveland Stokers in 1967 and sought to resurrect his career with the Fort Lauderdale Strikers a decade later. Banks went on to coach Neville Southall at Everton in the 1980s. In 2019, the Everton and Wales icon eulogised …*

'He was a perfectionist with a fantastic temperament for big games. Gordon wasn't a shouter or a screamer; he just did his job with incredible efficiency. For me, he was the perfect goalkeeper and ideal goalkeeping coach. It was an honour to train with him at Bellefield, I would go home thinking, "I can't believe Gordon Banks is training me." It was simply fantastic to talk about football with him. But to train with him was an education you could not buy. Gordon was way ahead of his time by focusing on technical aspects rather than working you into the ground like so many goalkeeping coaches did back then. It was a joy for me to have worked with him.'

## Earl Barrett in Texas

*Nicknamed 'Earl the Pearl', much of the England full-back's spell at Everton was dogged by injuries. In 2016, Barrett moved to Texas to coach youngsters at Rise/Houston Express …*

'I was enjoying coaching the under-16 team at Stoke but looked into my crystal ball and could not see progression – not that I blame anyone. My wife and I have always thought about moving to America, so we went to California and visited my friend Robbie Earle, who works for ESPN, and met some of his contacts. I wanted to keep the iron hot so I returned and did a bit of coaching at different clubs. Back home, I got a call from Colin Chesters who was at Houston Express (which is now known as Rise Soccer Club). It was an opportunity I jumped at. We came in October 2016. It was a challenge for my daughters but they've come through it.

'At Rise we have up to 4,000 players associated with both the recreational and competitive teams, from the ages of 9 to 18 years old. At some levels you have two or three teams which are banded into different ability levels. It is a "pay to play" system over here – and it is all about getting your kid into college. Essentially, you send your son or daughter to our club and we develop him or her to get a soccer scholarship to college – and, as a result, you avoid the massive burden of $20,000 to $30,000 fees per year. So if you are good at sport you can play your way to an education. I think that it's a great system as it makes people do their education as well as play sports.

'It costs from $500 to $2,500 per year at Rise – it goes up the scale depending on the level that the individual plays at. The MLS Next, Girls Academy and ECNL are the highest levels that we compete in – every parent wants their son or daughter to be in the top leagues. As well as coaching hours, you get to go to "showcase" tournaments. The club will target the tournaments where we know that the college coaches will be at. We even produce biographical brochures of our players with the stats, age, position played, etc. College coaches might track a player for two years to determine their progression and judge if he/she will fit into their college team.

'During the week, I work mostly from home during the day and then get to training at 5:30pm and never leave before 9:30pm. Friday is a day off, but I usually spend my time preparing for the weekend game and then on Saturday we have to set everything up – such as the kits, tents, benches, nets, etc. Last weekend, I arrived at the pitches for 7.00am and did not get home until around 7.00pm. We have back-to back games, and I like to support the other coaches during their games.

'I love coaching and managing the teams – it is different than in the United Kingdom but I am enjoying it and passing something onto the young Texans. It would be nice to develop some of them into professional soccer players but, realistically, the majority are being prepared for US colleges.'

### Jim Barron at Yale University

*As an Everton coach, the experienced goalkeeper helped the very best in Neville Southall and more recently, as an Everton scout, spotted and recommended a couple of raw goalkeeping prospects to the club …*

'After leaving Swindon Town in 1976, I could have gone to the St Louis Stars but Bobby Thompson, who was at Wolverhampton Wanderers with me had just got the job of coach at the Connecticut Bicentennials, so I went with him. I did some coaching there – both for the team and at clinics in the local area – which was what I wanted. It was an extremely interesting and enjoyable six months.

'The NASL teams always put on a show at their games. At Dallas, they had an orchestra playing at one end and skydivers descending before the game. At Fort Lauderdale, they had Gordon Banks and Eusebio coming into the ground on fire engines. It was just the way that they promoted soccer back then. As for attendances, the stadium was heaving at Minnesota on Independence Day. But at other places, we only attracted 4,000. Our owners had no great knowledge of the game but saw that soccer was big worldwide and were trying to help develop it in North America.

'Connecticut was something of a soccer backwater and the following year the owners switched the franchise to California as the Oakland Stompers and then the year after to Alberta as the Edmonton Drillers. I could have stayed in North America coaching. In fact, the agent for Giorgio Chinaglia asked if I would like to run clinics there, but I had already promised John Barnwell that I would join him at Peterborough United as player-coach.

'Right now, soccer is a lot more mainstream and the Premier League is massive. Until recently, I would go back to the USA every summer to do soccer clinics in Ohio with 200-odd kids from ages 6 to 18. I must admit that some of the girls were better players than the boys.

'My connection with Everton goes back to the 1980s when I had the privilege of coaching Neville Southall, Mickey Stowell and Jason Kearton three days a week. I also coached the Welsh squad's goalkeepers. Neville was phenomenal – the best keeper in the world in his pomp, but daft as a brush. He was a superb trainer – he wanted to do everything right. I remember when he was picked to play for the Football League against Serie A. It was dark by the time we got to Naples, but he wanted to do some training. So we spent 45 minutes on some concrete tennis courts in the city centre. By and by, Robbie Cooke – the chief scout at Everton, who had played for me at Peterborough, asked me to watch some games for him. Consequently, I scouted for a dozen years and uncovered some real talent. For example, I recommended teenage prospects and now England internationals such as Jordan Pickford and Nick Pope to Everton. I love Everton Football Club – it's a great club.'

### Leigh Cowlishaw in Virginia

*A youth team player at Everton during the late-1980s, Cowlishaw moved to the University of Richmond on an athletic scholarship and stayed in the Virginia area for some 30-odd years and counting ...*

'I was in the same Youth Training Scheme (YTS) intake as Eddie Youds, Phil Jones, and Mark Wright. They were offered pro contracts and went onto play about a dozen first team games between them for Everton, whereas I was not as fortunate and, after disappointing trials at Crewe, Chesterfield and elsewhere started work at as a clerk at Marston's Brewery in Burton-upon-Trent. Then out of the blue, I was offered an athletic scholarship to attend the University of Richmond.

'Immediately, I was impressed by the modern sports facilities which were possibly better than those at Bellefield. Virginia was a different way of life. I attended business administration classes in the morning and soccer training in the late afternoons. In addition, we played in tournaments against some decent sides including the University of Virginia Cavaliers who featured two future USA stars in Claudio Reyna and Jeff Agoos. They must have amassed 250 international caps between them.

'By good luck, my graduation coincided with the formation of the Richmond Kickers, which were composed initially of the best players from the local universities. We adopted a composed, less physical style of play and, guided by Dennis Violett – the former Busby Babe and England international, bagged the American double (USISL Premier League and US Open Cup titles) in 1995. An incredible accomplishment. It is and always has been a tremendous club which organises summer camps and community initiatives. One year, I had the great pleasure of meeting two big names from Everton's past – Mike Lyons and Bobby Collins – who were coaching local youngsters.

'Around 1999, I had become troubled by knee injuries and began to look at the business side of soccer when, again out of the blue, I was appointed head-coach. I served the Richmond Kickers in that role for 18 very enjoyable years. As for the standard of our football? Well, we were competitive against Crystal Palace, West Bromwich Albion and Swansea City during their pre-season tours and, in general, are equivalent to the Football League Championship/League One level. The future of US soccer appears strong. As for Everton's standing in North America? There is no substitute for winning silverware and boasting about it.'

### The Everton Way with Tosh Farrell

*Farrell was the primary driving force behind the trail-blazing initiatives, known as 'The Everton Way,' throughout North America …*

'In the early 2000s, an Evertonian named Jeff Tipping – the technical director of the National Soccer Coaches Association of America – invited me to Kansas to speak at an NSCAA conference. It went really well and resulted in a clamour for more information from clubs across North America. When I approached chief executive Keith Wyness with the idea of selling it all online, his ears pricked up and Everton became pioneers – the first club to develop an online coaching programme on a global scale.

'In total, we had a dozen clubs, from Florida to Ottawa, associated with what we branded "The Everton Way". Consequently, I made presentations at seven NSCAA conferences and made a massive input into coach and player development in North America as well as getting the Everton brand out there. With the backing of people at the club – David Moyes, Alan Irvine, Keith Wyness and then Robert Elstone – I felt confident that I was delivering a programme that was well thought of.

'Certainly, the Ontario Soccer Association saw the benefits and commissioned a television series from GolTV. It was filmed over eight weeks. Unfortunately, we couldn't agree on copyright, so it was never aired. Perhaps if it had been, Everton would have been the biggest English club in North America. "The Soccer Dream" television programme evolved from it. The winner, Abe Donzo came over and trained at Everton. In the other direction, we took Jose Baxter, John Nolan and Adam Forshaw to Boston for some presentation games, playing the region's top Under-14 sides. Joe-Max Moore and his son turned up to watch – which gave us great kudos.

'In 2008, an American bank was interested in investing into "The Everton Way" – but the stock market crashed. We had all the pieces in place but not the resources or nous to see it through. It was generating expectations that we weren't ready for.'

Ray Hall, former-manager of the Everton academy, spent 22 years developing and guiding young footballers before retiring in 2011. He was also instrumental in establishing The Everton Way: 'Jim Canavan – the director of coaching at Ontario Soccer Association came over to meet me. He wanted to affiliate with a Premier League club. After we had spoken,

I asked Jim why he chose Everton – apparently, I was the only one to return his call. Anyway, I told Keith Wyness that we should do something as it would give us access to thousands of youngsters in a growing market. He said, "Off you go." Tosh and I made a presentation at the Toronto Soccer Coaching Conference. The next time we were there a guy from Thunder Bay near the Arctic Circle asked, "How do I get my team better, as only I come down here?" At Toronto airport, we concurred that the way forward was an online affiliate scheme to give us a presence in US and Canada from a marketing and recruitment point of view. Tosh became the club's international youth development officer.

'The plan was to establish a permanent presence in the US market. Everton would maintain control of the strategy and help the local clubs grow. Tosh would be on the ground over there. He really set the place alight. We got a foothold at a club that became known as Everton Connecticut. Then there was Everton Texas and Everton New Jersey. Before I knew where I was, I was getting telephone calls and faxes from all over USA and Canada. Tosh became so popular that he was invited to take over a club in Boston, Massachusetts. After he left us, I tried to keep it all together but ended up having to close the whole thing down. The affiliates weren't getting their value for money. If we could turn back the clock, I would have gone to the club's chief executive officer and asked him to recruit someone to take over from Tosh.'

### The International Academy Affiliate Programme with Paul Harris

*Harris was a popular youth coach at Finch Farm where, alongside Ray Hall and Tosh Farrell, he helped form partnerships with junior clubs in North America …*

'I began coaching at age 21. Thanks to Everton's Nick Chadwick, an old school-friend, I was introduced to Tosh Farrell and worked with the Under-12 players including Jack Rodwell, Ross Barkley, John Lundstram, Tom Davies and the tremendously gifted Kieran Dowell. In due course, I focused on introducing "The Everton Way" initiatives and forming partnerships with junior clubs in North America and elsewhere. We promoted our "People's Club" image and the impressive fact that 16-year-old boys, such as Jose Baxter, James Vaughan and Wayne Rooney, had progressed to the Premier League. As a consequence, many clubs changed their names to reflect their affiliation with Everton.

'In addition to offering knowledge and expertise related to young player development, we helped to promote the club's image and generate income at about $30,000 per partnership. Unfortunately, we were unable to unearth any exceptional American talent and our partnerships petered out.

'Therefore, I was pleased to learn that the club has launched a new initiative – The Everton International Academy Affiliate Programme – as part of its global growth strategy. In 2012, I left Finch Farm for Ottawa. Though we strive to promote a love for soccer and the pursuit of excellence at all ages, Canada is something of a soccer wilderness, compared to hockey, with few opportunities for teenagers to progress professionally.'

**Wayne Harrison – inspired by Harold Moffatt and Alan Ball**

*An internationally recognised youth coach, Harrison has written numerous books on coaching and player development emphasising the 'One Touch Mentality' …*

'Everton is in my family. My grandfather, Harold Moffat, played for first team on three occasions in the 1920s. A right-winger, he made his debut alongside a young Dixie Dean. It was the centre-forward's first game after fracturing his skull in a motorcycle accident. I can't say that my grandfather taught me everything that I know about football but as a child, he would take me out into the streets of Cleator Moor to practice – every night, rain or shine. I think he enjoyed it even more than me.

'After I joined Everton as a schoolboy, the club allowed me to continue playing Rugby Union locally. I was half-decent scrum-half and an even better goal-kicker and represented England at Under-16 level. At only 5ft 2in, I always knew that I would struggle to reach the very top in professional football, so after three years at Everton I left to continue my education at Chester College and graduated with a degree in sports psychology. While there, I was selected to represent Great Britain at the 1979 World Student Games in Mexico. Prior to the tournament, we played a friendly at Bloomfield Road and Blackpool snapped me up. Initially, I played for manager Stan Ternent and then player-manager Alan Ball. The red-haired one was my inspiration. A genuine hero. Besides his remarkable engine, he was three – sometimes four moves – ahead of everyone. Like a Russian chess master.

'Having played 90 or so games for Blackpool in the Third and Fourth Divisions, I moved to Finland and the lower English Leagues and also tried indoor soccer with the Baltimore Blast. Then at age 38, I turned to coaching and enjoyed stints in northern England, the Middle East and North America. Most recently, I've concentrated on coaching coaches. I encourage a one-touch approach to football – inspired by Alan Ball. Through Soccer Awareness, my Minneapolis-based company, I organise clinics, publish books and much more to teach soccer intelligence, promote tactical and cognitive training and develop the thinking player who is aware of space, time and movement before he receives the ball. My biggest thrill as an author occurred in 2002, when my publisher rang to say that Real Madrid's Jose Mourinho had ordered a couple of my books. Jose was so impressed that he penned an endorsement. Possibly Alan Ball and I taught him everything – well not everything – he knows?'

**Brian Harvey in Oklahoma**

*Better known in England as the younger brother of 'The White Pelé', Harvey has spent over 40 years playing and coaching in Oklahoma and Texas …*

'We're a family of blues. I have followed Colin as a player, youth coach, head-coach and manager – he has been an unbelievable club servant. At the end of my coaching career in Oklahoma City, they named a sports field after me; then the following week Colin, Alan and Howard had their statue unveiled at Goodison. Our Mum and Dad would have been proud.

'Having Colin as my brother made me a much better player. He'd drag me out every night to play in the street where we lived in Fazakerley. We had a street team – it was good fun. He was already training at Bellefield on Tuesday and Thursday nights when his coach Les Shannon invited me for a try-out. I went down one Tuesday night, but it was a case of "You're alright but you're never going to be as good as Colin." So, I went to Sheffield Wednesday and finished up at Chester.

'The Dallas Tornado manager Bob Kap had been sent over to sign footballers from the North West. I ended up in a training camp in Spain with players from Germany, Norway and Holland. I secured a place and went to play in the USA in 1968. I was there for three years but didn't think the NASL was going to take off so headed to Australia and Hong Kong. I played for Rhyl in the Welsh League before coming to Oklahoma City. There were no soccer-specific stadiums – clubs were tenants in baseball diamonds and American football stadiums. The Skelly Stadium in Tulsa had a very bad playing surface. Whereas the artificial pitch at the Astrodome in Houston was concrete with a plastic carpet laid over it. It was pretty dangerous.

'Everton has a fantastic history and there's great potential with the new stadium, but the club needs to be more global. We're overshadowed by Liverpool and have developed an inferiority complex – not just on the field. Bayern Munich have opened a New York office and Liverpool and Manchester United have US offices. We need to promote ourselves. When Ian Callaghan did a question-and-answer session in Dallas, the pub was choc-a-bloc. He did something similar in Los Angeles, North Carolina and New York. Everton have never done anything like that. "The People's Club" is a good slogan but we need to get in among the people. There are huge markets overseas, but first Everton have to think about challenging for honours.'

### Adrian Heath – the MLS head-coach

*It is some 3,800 miles from Merseyside to Minnesota, where he now coaches, but 'Inchy' never misses an opportunity to watch his beloved Everton in action …*

'We get access to every Premier League game over here in Minnesota, so I watch every single game that Everton play. Michael (Keane) keeps me updated because he is a part of the family now with his twin brother being married to my daughter. If Everton are playing when we are at a hotel and I walk into the dining-room and if the match is not on the television, one of our analysts will quickly switch channels to get it! They all know where my love and loyalties lie when it comes to football in England.

'I've been in the USA for more than 12 years and Everton has always been a name here. Look at the players – Tim is huge, Landon is one of the best players the US has ever produced and Brian McBride is loved for the way he played the game. I know a few people who follow Everton because of those connections. I had over six years in Orlando and used to meet up with the Evertonians in the bar they went to. There is a good Everton following in Minnesota as well. And we had Wayne Rooney over here. He had a great time at DC United and left his mark on Major League Soccer. What they loved about him was that he did not act like a big-time superstar. He rolled his sleeves up and got on with it. Many of the DC United staff are friends of mine and they loved having him around. Wayne rarely did an interview without mentioning Everton!'

*Heath's focus is now firmly on establishing Minnesota United as an MLS force, but his heart will always be in L4 and relishes his visits to the place he calls home …*

'I dread the day that the club no longer plays at Goodison. I never take the reception I get for granted. I am just proud because it shows that the supporters know that when I played, I gave them everything. I always look forward to going back there. I'll be back for the last game because it will be a day that people will remember for the rest of their lives.'

*Then there was 10 May 1998, a date that makes Heath shudder. He was assistant manager when the club, at home to Coventry, needed a better result than Bolton Wanderers at Chelsea to avoid relegation …*

'Burnley had offered me a five-year contract and, of course, after one season Howard and I got fired – so with hindsight it doesn't look like my best decision! But that was the lure of Everton and I could never turn the club down. If we had got relegated, I would never have got over it. I know what the club means to so many people and it would have been a devastating blow. It was certainly the most emotional day I have ever had in football. When we left our hotel on the Wirral, I looked at some of the players' faces and I thought "some of these might not be able to cope with the pressure that's coming." It's not something I would want to go through again. It was the most relieved I have ever felt inside a football stadium. Relegation would have hit Howard really hard.

'I used Howard as a reference point. If I wanted to speak to someone for advice or to bounce ideas off, he was the logical choice. I had known him since I was 15. I used to look after his boots at Stoke and would babysit his son. I would like to think that I have developed relationships with players in the way that he did. He was the best man-manager that there's ever been.'

### Coach Tommy (TE) Jones

*One of Everton Football Club's greatest-ever servants, after hanging up his playing boots TE Jones coached youngsters at Bellefield and later guided the Toronto Italia to success in the 1960s. Around 2000, he reflected on his brief spell in North America …*

'For me, coaching was the next best thing to playing. At Everton and Toronto, I encouraged versatility. I believe that a professional footballer should be able to play anywhere – at least in an emergency. In the days before subs, the more positions a player had mastered – the more valuable he was to his team. To mix things up in training in Canada, I would put full-backs up-front, inside-forwards in defence and move the big centre-forward and crazy goalie to centre-half. In hindsight, many of my old teammates started their careers in different positions. To extend my own career, I made the easy move from uncomplicated centre-half to uncomplicated left-back but, like many others, longed to play in goal and make a game-changing penalty save in front of the Kop.'

*Coincidently, Jones was asked to be ready to fill a new demanding role during Everton's visits to the United States and Canada in 1961 …*

'It was odd that we took only one goalie with us. I was no longer considered as a first team regular and was along to make up the numbers, basically, should anybody get injured. Therefore, I was nominated as Albert Dunlop's proxy. Despite my dreams of saving a spot-kick at Anfield, I had never played in goal in my life. I recall that we were playing six-a-side in one of our training sessions when the boss took me to one side, "You'd better go in goal to get a feel of the ball." I beamed with confidence between the posts until Roy Vernon hit his first shot in my direction. Showing the prowess of an enthusiastic novice, I dove to stop the ball. It struck the end of my index finger – and nearly broke it in two. I was in agony, I really was. Fortunately, I was never required to deputise for Albert!'

### Coach Mike Lyons

*Another of Everton's greatest ever servants, Lyons enjoyed his brief spell coaching in Canada before spending almost three decades in warmer climates …*

'It's that long ago that I almost forgot about my shift in Canada with the Nova Scotia Clippers. When I'd been playing in the top division at Everton, we wouldn't have been allowed just to head off to Canada or the USA for the off-season – we were expected to concentrate on Everton and only Everton. By 1991 I was coaching, so when I was offered the chance to go over to Canada at the end of the English season, I decided to give it a go. I knew the manager, Gordon Hill, who had played for Manchester United. I went over as assistant-coach and quite enjoyed it – it was certainly different to English football.

'Everyone at the club was fine and we were well looked-after. Soccer was not the major sport, it lagged behind Canada's two national passions namely ice hockey and lacrosse, but the standard was not bad. To be honest. I even played in a couple of games – I don't know if I was fit enough but I did alright. The franchise ended after just one season but a year or two on I was given the opportunity to continue my travels by coaching in Brunei. As of 2020, I have spent almost three decades in that part of the world and Australia.'

### Adam Smith in California

*Raised in a loyal royal blue family, Smith was thrilled to be selected as the goalkeeper of the club's youth team in the late-1980s before enjoying a long career playing and coaching in the USA …*

'Everton has always been an important part of my life. I was fortunate to spend two years as a goalkeeper in the club's junior sides under the guidance of Graham Smith (the youth coach and not the agent, who is also my father, with the same name) and benefitted from specialised instruction from two recognised experts – Jim Barron and World Cup winner Gordon Banks. My progress was hampered by a lack of inches, I am just under 6ft, and a lack of consistency. I discovered that these limitations weren't quite as problematic in the USL where the standard was equivalent to League Two/Conference football.

'As a result, I've had the pleasure of rubbing shoulders with several former-Everton players. First, there was Gary Ablett, my teammate at Long Island and then Dave Irving, my boss at Wilmington. That's where I commenced my coaching career. Next there was John Spencer at Portland, where my diverse roles ranged from academy director to reserve team coach, and then I worked as Preki's head-assistant at Sacramento. All were helpful co-workers and great friends.

'I've witnessed major changes during the past 20-odd years. Even though some franchises have struggled in their immature markets, soccer enjoys unprecedented television coverage and an expanding fanbase. Currently, the top MLS teams are on a par with those in the English Championship. I remain a staunch Evertonian and have been fortunate to follow the club during all of its North American tours, many of which were arranged by my father's company. It has been in my heart always. So much so that when I married my wife Venessa in a quiet ceremony in Ventura, California, she walked down the aisle to the rousing sounds of the pipes and drums of "Z-Cars."'

### Steve Tashjian – the performance expert

*The highly-acclaimed performance expert for the USA national team served as a fitness coach at Everton from 2009 to 2014 …*

'In 2009, the Columbus Crew trained at Finch Farm for a week. At the time, Phoenix-based Athletes' Performance Inc, who had done good work with the German national team, had a contract to provide integrated physical therapy, performance training, and nutrition programs at Everton. During our stay, I was advised that the American expert had moved on and was asked if I would be interested in the role. Eventually in July 2009, I got the call to confirm that I had the job. Incredibly, I was at the White House in Washington DC at the time with the winners of the MLS Cup! So, on that day I met the President Barack Obama and got the Everton job!

'I flew to Seattle to meet up with head-coach Robert Warzycha and the Crew squad and prepare for a game against the MLS All-Stars before heading over to England. I went directly from the airport to the Ricoh Arena for a friendly match against Coventry. It was Marcus Hall's testimonial which ended 2-2. That group of Everton players were great at making me feel comfortable. Tim Howard was obviously a big help, so were Phil Neville and Tim Cahill. I had guys like Ossie and Hibbo to teach me about the fabric of the club. I consider the relationships and friendships to be biggest highlights of my five-year stay. It's that sort of club. I had to come back to the USA in 2010 for family reasons and the club was fantastic about it. I wasn't rushed to come back. David Moyes urged me to take care of my family first.

'I loved my time on Merseyside and will always have a huge affection for Everton Football Club. With regards to my favourite matches, I recall the 2-2 draw with Tottenham Hotspur in December 2009 when Seamus Coleman exploded onto the scene as a substitute, Tim Cahill equalised in the 86th minute and Tim Howard saved a penalty from Jermain Defoe in the 95th minute. The 4-4 draw in April 2012 against soon-to-be champions Manchester United in front of 76,000 at Old Trafford was another favourite. That afternoon we fought back to score two goals in the final five or six minutes.

'Also, the FA Cup quarter-final replay at the packed Stadium of Light sticks out. We triumphed 2-0 against Sunderland to advance to a dramatic semi-final clash with Liverpool at Wembley – much to the delight of the thousands of jubilant Blues who were present. That night taught me a lot about Scouse superstition and English football etiquette. After I had changed seats shortly after we had taken the lead through Nikica Jelavic, our assistant-kitman, Tony Sage, went mad at me: "What are you doing? You don't switch seats when we're winning!" He was genuinely upset. The dressing room banter could be brutal but there was always charm to it and no shortage of Merseyside wit. I found the atmosphere both spirited and brotherly. The more stick you got, the more you felt accepted by everyone. For example, on my second day at Finch Farm, kitman Jimmy Martin called me a "Yankee-Doodle dickhead!"

'After five years, I felt that it was time to hop back across the pond. It had been a wonderful learning experience. Previously, I had been a head- fitness coach and a head-strength coach, but Everton gave me the chance to dive into sports science. I had access to excellent resources at Finch Farm and my mind opened to new ways of working. Danny Donachie, the head of medical services, wanted me to lead the end-stage rehabilitation process as a bridge for the players who were between finishing rehab and being ready to join in training. In addition, I learned how to deal with some very big personalities.'

### Kyle Thorne – another American expert

*The American coach helped to introduce advanced training programmes at Finch Farm in 2007 and departed about one year later with a much deeper understanding of Everton and match-going Blues …*

'Premier League soccer? The closest comparison you can make is American college football such as the Big Ten and Pac-12 where you have die-hard fans ranting, raving and chanting. There's nothing like it in US professional sports. From an American perspective, you sit in the stands – having a beer or eating a hot dog – and maybe you turn to your neighbour to ask them a question, and it's not a big deal. At Everton, they'd rather slap you in the face than talk to you during a big match. They're locked into their football. It's no joke.'

## Tommy Wheeldon Snr in Alberta

*An Everton youth product who is now hailed as 'Mr Soccer in Alberta', Wheeldon spent some 15 years coaching at the Calgary Storm in the USL A-League …*

'Along with Peter Reid, I had been part of the midfield engine of a successful Huyton Schoolboys team and spent spells at West Ham, where I played for the first team in a friendly against Morecambe, Tranmere Rovers and St Helens Town before enjoying two wonderful seasons at Everton. For me, it was a dream come true.

'I was signed by Billy Bingham and then two years later was released by Gordon Lee who did not fancy me and had plenty of experienced midfield options in Mick Buckley, Trevor Ross, Mick Bernard, Bryan Hamilton, Martin Dobson, and the high-spirited Andy King. Hampered by persistent Achilles problems, I wound down my playing days in Devon and Cornwall before concentrating on coaching, first with Ray Hall at Everton and then Steve McMahon at Swindon Town. I was working at Exeter City when I was invited by Michael Vandale – a Canadian director – to assist his development initiatives at the Calgary Storm.

'It was a quantum leap into the unknown. By chance, my arrival coincided with the 10-day Calgary Stampede, the annual rodeo and festival. I will never forget McCall Field, now known as Calgary International Airport, because I was lassoed in the Arrivals Hall – seriously, some local cowboy threw a rope around me – and stayed that way until my host Mark McLaughlin showed up with his son dressed from head to toe in Everton's colours. Unbeknown to me, Mark was from the Moss Cross area of Huyton. Also, he was a national celebrity, being the place-kicker for the Calgary Stampeders of Canadian Football League where he had secured three Grey Cups.

'Initially responsible for the youth development set-up, I was appointed head-coach within 12 months. Even though the standard at that time was equivalent to League Two football, Calagary produced some excellent young talent including goalkeeper Lars Hirschfeld who we sold to Tottenham Hotspur for £30,000 and later earned 48 Canada caps, Nick Ledgerwood who joined Munich 1860 and was awarded 50 Canada caps and Owen Hargreaves who won trophies galore with Bayern Munich and Manchester United as well as a small mountain of England international caps.

'I was an enthusiastic coach. In June 2003, I was serving a ban having been sent off during the clash with the Vancouver Whitecaps but had used a walkie-talkie from the stands to the bench to help the boys in the next match. The USL A-League disciplinary committee deemed it illegal and banned me for two more games. The *Calgary Herald* reported the incident: "Something about this Calgary Storm match seemed odd. Slightly off kilter. Only a few minutes after the kick-off against the Portland Timbers, that undefinable, elusive difference smacked you in the face. The sideline entertainment was down, And the noise level was way down. Things were quiet. Too quiet." After the Storm had lost 2-0, midfielder Nick Zuniga said, "We wanted to do well for Tommy. He is an emotional guy. We know it hurts him to miss this game." And where pray tell, he was asked, would Tommy have sat during his suspension? Zuniga blinked, shrugged. "I heard he might be over there." He pointed to the north, on a now deserted grassy hill looking down on the pitch.

'Wheeldon had been banned from the bench the previous game, sat in the stands and following more shenanigans was warned by the A-League that he was persona non grata on Sunday. Locally, there was much joking that he might sneak through the gate in high heels, heavily rouged, Jackie O glasses and wearing a padded halter top or pay the Global TV cameraman a fiver to lend him his gear or might surface in the bleachers strapped with pillows and dressed as Elvis Presley in his heavier period. No came the assurance, Wheeldon is nowhere in sight. It must have killed him to stay away.'

Wheeldon recalled: 'Of course, I did not miss the game. I followed the action from a rooftop adjacent to the main stand, which was supposedly dangerous. Yes, I was mirrored those kids famously pictured on the roof of St Luke's church following the action at Goodison. Like them, I was oblivious to the danger as long as I could watch the game. After 15 years in Canada, I bounced back to the old country. My sons – both diehard Evertonians – are still there. Jonathan is a talented defender and Thomas is his astute manager at Calvary, arguably the best side in the newly-formed Canadian Premier League. With great enthusiasm, both claim that we are entering a golden era for Canadian soccer.'

### Chris Woods – the USA goalkeeping coach

*The goalkeeper won 43 England caps but, before hanging up the gloves for good, he was keen to experience soccer in the USA and joined Colorado Rapids. Sadly, things didn't develop as planned …*

'I was 36 and reaching the end of my playing days. Major League Soccer was quite new and I was looking to start a new life in the USA, but it didn't work out like that. After my first MLS season had finished, I signed for Southampton on loan but unfortunately I broke my leg and displaced my ankle in my sixth game. As I didn't want to do my rehab in the USA, it put an end to my time with the Colorado Rapids. I had enjoyed it though. The only downside was that games tended to be played in the gigantic American football stadiums. The Rapids played at the Mile High Stadium, the home of the Denver Broncos, which had a 70,000 capacity but we averaged just over 10,000 fans.'

*Woods turned to coaching and joined manager Walter Smith, at Everton in 1998. He stayed for 15 years before following David Moyes to Manchester United. His working relationship with Tim Howard helped to reignite his connection with US soccer …*

'In 2011, Jurgen Klinsmann was the head coach of the US men's national team but didn't have a goalkeeping coach. He spoke to Tim who put my name forward. Jurgen asked me to help out for a game against Belgium in Brussels. Everton boss David Moyes said he was fine with it and I did the game. To be honest, I didn't think it would lead to anything until Jurgen phoned me again a couple of weeks later and asked if I would be interested in the job. Jurgen is a fantastic person. He is extremely enthusiastic and a really good guy to work for. He leaves no stone unturned.

'Obviously, I had to go back to David Moyes and the Everton boss allowed me to take the opportunity. The USA role also gave me the chance to watch American players and if any caught my eye, I could report back to him. His one stipulation was that once the games had finished, I needed to get back to Finch Farm as soon as possible. I enjoyed the job so much that the transatlantic travel didn't bother me. It was great to be able to see how things worked over there.

'Knowing Tim Howard helped an awful lot. He was terrific – his handling and his reading of situations, his speed and his decision making were first-class. If anybody says that a goalkeeper is a good shot-stopper, it's because he should be! The top ones can pull out match-winning saves more regularly but it all boils down to making good decisions at the correct times and Tim was really good at that. He was a great leader on the pitch as well. With working with him at Everton, we knew what we wanted from each other. When we were with the USA it was a case of making him as sharp and prepared as we could.

'There were several other good US goalkeepers in that era – Kasey Keller, Brad Friedel, Marcus Hahnemann and Brad Guzan. Growing up playing basketball and American football, US youngsters tend to have good "eye-hand-ball" coordination. Today, there's a young lad at Manchester City called Zack Steffen. He's the number one now, which I am pleased about because I always thought he had great potential.'

*Caricatures and brief profiles of the coaches and gurus are presented in alphabetical order. They unfold with Sam Allardyce...*

# Sam Allardyce

**played for**
Dudley Town,
Bolton Wanderers,
Sunderland.
Tampa Bay Rowdies,
Coventry City,
Huddersfield Town,
Bolton Wanderers,
Preston North End,
West Bromwich Albion,
Limerick,
Preston North End

**coached at**
West Bromwich Albion,
Bury,
Limerick,
Preston North End,
Blackpool,
Notts County,
Bolton Wanderers,
Newcastle United,
Blackburn Rovers,
West Ham United,
Sunderland,
England,
Crystal Palace,
Everton,
West Bromwich Albion

Known for his industrial tackles and simple passes, 'Big Sam' helped Bolton and Preston to promotion. These successes sandwiched an 11-game spell at the Tampa Bay Rowdies in 1983. Moving into club management, he was highly regarded for steering Notts County to the Second Division, guiding Bolton and West Ham to the top-flight and ensuring Crystal Palace and Sunderland stayed there. As England manager, Allardyce's career nose-dived following an undercover investigation by the *Daily Telegraph* in 2016 and he quit after one game. After a spell at Crystal Palace, the 63-year-old embraced his seventh top-flight job and remedied Everton's depressing start to the 2017/18 season. Though an apostle of sports science and performance analysis, he was criticised throughout his six-month term at Goodison for his long-ball tactics.

Everton manager: 2017/18

# Gordon Banks

**played for**

Millspaugh,

Chesterfield,

Leicester City,

Stoke City,

Cleveland Stokers (loan),

Hellenic (South Africa) (loan),

Fort Lauderdale Strikers,

St Patrick's Athletic (loan)

**coached at**

Port Vale,

Telford United,

Everton

Banks had agreed to join Everton from Leicester for £27,500 in 1961. Six months after the deal collapsed, the club signed Gordon West and the Sheffield-born goalkeeper went onto enjoy global fame as a 1966 World Cup winner and 1972 FWA Footballer of the Year on top of his place in football history for his breathtaking save from Pelé in 1970. Respected for his strength, flawless handling and quick reflexes, he was sold eventually to Stoke City for £50,000 in 1967. His top-flight career was curtailed at age 35, when he lost his right eye in a car crash. Regardless, he played two seasons with the Fort Lauderdale Strikers in the NASL. In the late-1980s, he was engaged as a specialist goalkeeping coach working at Bellefield with Neville Southall and Bobby Mimms.

Everton goalkeeping coach: 1986/87–1987/88

# Earl Barrett

After aiding Joe Royle's Oldham side capture the Second Division title in 1991, the pacy defender was sold to Aston Villa for £1.7 million and helped them finish runners up in the Premier League in 1993 and nab the League Cup in 1994. Midway through the next season, Barrett re-joined Royle at Goodison for around £1.7 million but was cup-tied and unable to feature in the club's glorious run in the FA Cup. A supreme athlete equipped with amazing energy and stamina, the England full-back preferred to jockey rather than tackle wingers. Regrettably, his progress was dogged by knee injuries which caused him to miss most of the 1995/96 season. Upon hanging up his boots, 'Earl the Pearl' earned a sports science degree and focused on coaching youngsters – most recently in Missouri City near Houston, Texas.

| Everton 1994/95-1997/98 | | |
| --- | --- | --- |
| | games | goals |
| League | 73/1 | 0 |
| Total | 82/1 | 0 |

# Jim Barron

**played for**
Newcastle West End,
Wolverhampton Wanderers,
Chelsea,
Oxford United,
Nottingham Forest,
Swindon Town,
Peterborough United,
Connecticut Bicentennials

**coached at**
Wolverhampton Wanderers,
Íþróttabandalag Akraness
(Iceland),
Everton,
Cheltenham Town,
Birmingham City,
Northampton Town,
Aston Villa,
Everton (scout)

After more than 400 League games with Oxford United in the Second and Third Divisions and then Nottingham Forest in the First and Second Divisions, the veteran custodian, who was respected for his shot-stopping abilities, joined the New Haven-based Connecticut Bicentennials for their last NASL season in 1977. After short spells coaching at Wolverhampton Wanderers and Íþróttabandalag Akraness, he spent several years as a specialised goalkeeping coach at Bellefield, where he aided Neville Southall's quest for perfection. In 1990, as the manager of Cheltenham, Barron arranged a testimonial match for Nick Jordan and Ray Baverstock involving Everton, during which he convinced the Wales legend to switch sides. Southall gave an error-free and match-winning display for the Conference hosts. Throughout the past decade and more, Barron has served Everton as a scout.

Everton goalkeeping coach: 1987/88-1990/91

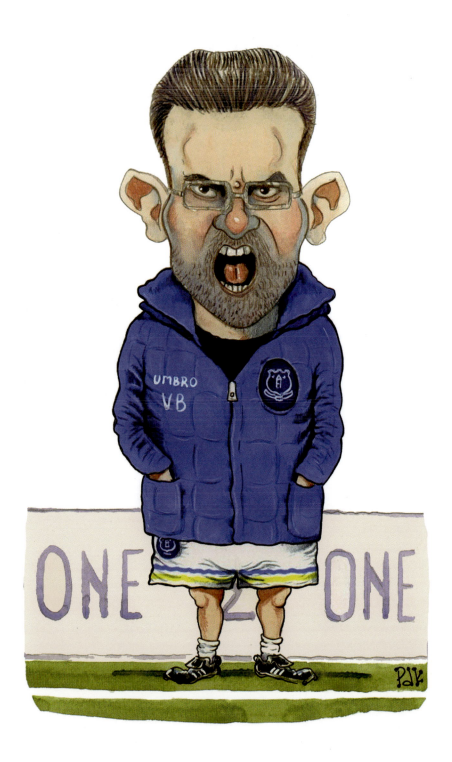

# Viv Busby

**played for**

Wycombe Wanderers,
Luton Town,
Newcastle United (loan),
Fulham,
Norwich City,
Stoke City,
Sheffield United (loan),
Tulsa Roughnecks,
Blackburn Rovers,
York City

**coached at**

York City,
Hartlepool United,
Sheffield United,
Everton,
Swindon Town,
York City,
Gretna,
Workington

Despite having gained promotion with Luton Town, Stoke City and York City during his 17-year playing career, the centre-forward is best remembered on Merseyside for scoring the two goals for Second Division Fulham that eliminated Everton, the high-flying league leaders, from the FA Cup in 1975. Five years on, after unrewarding spells at Norwich City and Sheffield United, Busby spent the 1980 NASL season with the Tulsa Roughnecks, scoring just one goal in his 19 senior outings. Back in the United Kingdom, he kicked off his coaching career at York and Hartlepool before teaming up with manager Howard Kendall at Sheffield United. In 1997, they switched to Goodison only to suffer a painful league campaign at the end of which the club narrowly avoided relegation on goal difference. In 2000, while coaching at Andy King's Swindon Town, he won his six-month battle against leukaemia.

Everton coach: 1997/98

# Tommy Casey

**played for**

Belfast YMCA,
East Belfast,
Bangor,
Leeds United,
Bournemouth,
Newcastle United,
Portsmouth,
Bristol City,
Gloucester City,
Toronto Inter-Roma,
Ammanford Town

**coached at**

Gloucester City,
Lisburn Distillery,
Everton,
Northern Ireland Youth,
Coventry City,
Grimsby Town,
Reykjavik,
Harstad (Norway)

Casey was a hard-working and ball-winning wing-half. The highlight of his playing days was Newcastle United's victory in the 1956 FA Cup final. Also with Northern Ireland, he featured in the 1958 World Cup finals and, alongside Jimmy McIlroy and Billy Bingham, produced high-octane performances at centre-forward against West Germany and inside-forward against Czechoslovakia. After relegations to the Second Division at Portsmouth and the Third Division at Bristol City, Casey dropped into non-League football with Gloucester City and spent the summer of 1965 with Toronto Inter-Roma in the Eastern Canada Professional Soccer League. Later, his coaching jobs including a stint at Everton. While Harry Catterick was recovering from a heart attack, he oversaw 10 league and cup games in early-1972 and is remembered for his rudimentary tactics.

Everton trainer-coach: 1971/72

# Leigh Cowlishaw

**played for**
Everton (youth),
University of Richmond Spiders,
Richmond Kickers

**coached at**
Richmond Kickers

Frustrated at failing to make a breakthrough as a youth player at Everton in the late-1980s, the Burton-upon-Trent teenager grasped the chance to relocate to Virginia and play National Collegiate Athletic Association (NCCA) soccer and study for a degree in business administration at the University of Richmond. After graduating, the hard-working midfielder joined the newly-established Richmond Kickers of the United Soccer League where he went on to feature in more than 150 first team games. The highlight of his career was helping the club win the US Open Cup in 1995. Afterwards, Cowlishaw was honoured by having his No 13 shirt retired and being appointed head-coach. He served the Richmond Kickers in that capacity for another 18 seasons, guiding them to the USL Championship title in 2013.

Everton youth player: 1987/88-1988/89

# Willie Donachie

**played for**

Manchester City,
Portland Timbers,
Norwich City,
Portland Timbers,
Burnley,
Oldham Athletic

**coached at**

Oldham Athletic,
Everton,
Sheffield United,
Manchester City,
Sheffield Wednesday,
Ipswich Town,
Millwall,
Antigua & Barbuda,
Newcastle United,
Hartlepool United,
Temecula,
Accrington Stanley,
Montserrat

The Scotland star's playing career spanned 22 years and involved some 700 first team games – making over half of his appearances for Mancheater City. The classy right-footed left-back became a reliable fixture at Maine Road and also enjoyed two summers in the NASL – playing 60 games for the Portland Timbers. After joining Norwich for £200,000, he returned to Oregon in 1982 to make another 31 outings. As a coach, he developed a productive partnership with Joe Royle. First, they steered Oldham into the Premier League and the League Cup final. Following their arrival at Goodison in November 1994, they drove Everton to safety and an FA Cup triumph in 1995. He returned to Maine Road as Royle's assistant and is often hailed for his role in Manchester City's back-to-back promotions in 1999 and 2000. Widely respected for introducing meditation and yoga exercises into modern training regimes, Donachie coached at Temecula in the fourth tier of the US soccer pyramid before continuing his football-related globetrotting in sunny Montserrat.

Everton assistant-manager: 1994/95-1996/97

# Tosh Farrell

**coached at**

Everton,

Tosh Farrell Soccer
Development Center (USA),

Kendal Town,

Tosh Farrell Soccer (UK),

Robbie Fowler Football Academy

Farrell is credited with overseeing the progress of a long list of local players in the 9-year to 12-year age groups at the Everton academy. They include internationals Victor Anichebe, Ross Barkley, Jack Rodwell and Wayne Rooney. He headed the club's initiatives to form partnerships with academies in the USA and Canada and played a principal role in the creation of 'The Everton Way', which allowed him to share his philosophies, methodologies and wisdom worldwide. In 2010, Farrell left Everton to establish his own soccer development business in Massachusetts. After five years he returned home to open Tosh Farrell Soccer which instructs clubs as well as individual players on the key technical, physical, mental, social and other skills required to succeed.

Everton youth coach: 1996/97-2009/10

# Ken Furphy

**played for**

Everton,

Runcorn,

Darlington,

Workington,

Watford

**coached at**

Workington,

Watford,

Blackburn Rovers,

Sheffield United,

New York Cosmos,

Miami Toros,

Detroit Express,

Washington Diplomats,

Bermuda,

Cleveland Force,

Exeter City (technical director)

The 19-year-old robust defender was snapped up by manager Cliff Britton from Evenwood Town of the Northern League for a fee of £50 in 1950. The right-back spent two seasons trying to dislodge rivals Eric Moore and Tommy Clinton – even after the club's relegation at the end of his first season. Instead, he moved to Runcorn in the Cheshire League and then onto enjoy a 15-year playing career involving over 500 games with Darlington, Workington and Watford. As player-manager, he oversaw the promotions of Workington and Watford. Then in 1976, after stints in charge at Ewood Park and Bramall Lane, he jumped to the NASL as head-coach of the New York Cosmos. Known for his Northern candour, at their first meeting he informed Pelé: 'I'm going to treat you just like any other player – don't expect anything special.'

| Everton 1950/51-1951/52 | | |
| --- | --- | --- |
| | games | goals |
| League | 0 | 0 |
| Total | 0 | 0 |

# Paul Harris

**played for**
Crewe Alexandra (youth),
Stafford Rangers,
Newcastle Town

**coached at**
Everton,
Ottawa South United

A graduate of Dario Gradi's highly-acclaimed youth academy at Gresty Road, which produced future internationals such as David Platt, Robbie Savage, Neil Lennon, Geoff Thomas, Danny Murphy and Seth Johnson, Harris failed to break into the Crewe first team. His modest playing career continued with semi-professional football in the Southern League Premier Division with Stafford Rangers and in the North West Counties League Division One with Newcastle Town. Thereafter, he was a member of the staff at Everton's academy for almost a decade, serving as the club's international development coach during his final four years. He moved to Canada in 2012 joining Ottawa South United, one of the top clubs in the capital city where he heads the club's advanced development programmes for players and coaches.

Everton youth coach: 2003/04-2011/12

# Wayne Harrison

**played for**
Everton (youth),
Workington,
Sheffield Wednesday,
Blackpool,
Preston North End,
Burnley (trial),
Oulun Palloseura (Finland),
Kokkolan Palloveikot (Finland),
Baltimore Blast,
Morecambe,
Barrow,
Carlisle United,
Cleator Moor Celtic

**coached at**
Workington,
Bamber Bridge,
Lancaster City,
Accrington Stanley,
Blackpool,
Al Ain (UAE),
Eden Prairie (Minnesota),
Dakota County College
Blue Knights,
San Diego Surf,
Soccer Awareness LLC

Born in Whitehaven, the teenager was on Everton's books for three years before returning to Cumbria and signing for Fourth Division Workington in 1975. Later, the 5ft 6in dynamo spent his best days at Blackpool playing alongside player-manager Alan Ball. After spells in Finland and the USA, he signed for Football Conference Barrow, Northern Premier League Workington and Fourth Division Carlisle United before moving into youth coaching. After four years as the academy director at Blackpool, Harrison relocated to the UAE and then the USA. A National Soccer Coaches Association of America (NSCAA) instructor, he owns Soccer Awareness LLC, which trains coaches and players worldwide and, from his base in Minnesota, has produced dozens of books and educational videos promoting his one-touch soccer approach.

Everton youth player: 1973/74-1975/76

# Brian Harvey

**played for**
Everton (trial),
Sheffield Wednesday,
Chester,
St Bonaventure University Bonnies,
South Coast United,
Dallas Tornado,
Caroline Hill (Hong Kong),
Kwong Wah (Hong Kong),
Melbourne Hakoah,
Urban Services (Hong Kong)

**coached at**
Urban Services,
Oklahoma City Slickers,
Tulsa Tornados,
Oklahoma City Stars,
Oklahoma City Spirit,
Oklahoma City University Stars

Having been passed over by his boyhood favourites as a young teenager, Colin Harvey's brother chose to join Sheffield Wednesday as an apprentice in 1963. After failing to make a breakthrough at Hillsborough, he joined Chester and then after one league outing he moved to the USA to study at St Bonaventure University – a small college in Allegany, New York. Post-graduation, the midfielder enjoyed a 10-year career playing in Hong Kong, Australia as well as the USA which included four seasons with the Dallas Tornado where, around the dawn of the NASL, he embarked on a six-month whistle-stop tour involving some 45 games in 19 countries. After hanging up his boots, Harvey returned to the USA to coach various Oklahoma-based clubs in the ASL and the USL before establishing the men's and women's soccer programme at Oklahoma City University.

Everton trialist: 1963/64

# Adrian Heath

**played for**

Stoke City,

Everton,

Espanyol,

Aston Villa,

Manchester City,

Burnley,

Sheffield United

**coached at**

Burnley,

Everton,

Sunderland,

Sheffield United,

Leeds United,

Coventry City,

Austin Aztex,

Orlando City,

Minnesota United

Statistics only tell part of the Adrian Heath story – 'Inchy' was a giant. Signed by manager Howard Kendall from Stoke City for £750,000 in January 1982, he could hover behind the front-men, forage in midfield or partner Graeme Sharp up-front. His intelligent off-the-ball movement meant that the patter of his boots was heard everywhere, especially at Oxford in the famous League Cup tie that changed the fortunes of Howard Kendall and his team. Though injury curtailed his involvement in the epic 1984/85 campaign, he played a key role in Everton's success in the mid-1980s. Heath left for Espanyol in 1988 but returned nine years later as Kendall's right-hand man. In 2008, he moved to North America to coach in the USL at Austin and Orlando, before taking over at the new MLS franchise in Minnesota.

| Everton 1981/82-1988/89 | | |
| --- | --- | --- |
| | games | goals |
| League | 206/20 | 71 |
| Total | 278/30 | 94 |

# Tommy Jones

**played for**
Everton

**coached at**
Everton,
Toronto Italia

TE Jones turned professional in 1948 and replaced the legendary TG Jones at centre-half during the woeful 1950/51 season after which the club dropped from the top-flight. A model of consistency, the defender succeeded Peter Farrell as club captain in 1957. However, with the emergence of an exciting teenager named Brian Labone, 'the penultimate Corinthian' – respected widely for his sportsmanship and impeccable football etiquette – wound down his career at left-back. Forced to retire at age 30 due to a severely damaged knee, the proud one-club man had a brief spell coaching the juniors at his beloved Everton before steering Toronto Italia to a Canadian league and cup double in 1963 with a cosmopolitan squad of semi-professionals from Argentina, Brazil, Denmark, England, Ireland, Italy, Mexico and Uruguay.

| Everton 1948/49-1961/62 | games | goals |
|---|---|---|
| League | 383 | 14 |
| Total | 411 | 14 |

# Norman Low

**played for**

Rosehill Villa,
Newcastle United,
Liverpool,
Newport County,
Bristol City (guest),
Everton (guest),
Liverpool (guest),
Swindon Town (guest),
Lovell's Athletic (guest),
Norwich City

**coached at**

Norwich City,
Workington,
Port Vale,
Witton Albion,
Cleveland Stokers,
Cleveland Cobras (scout)

Though registered with Second Division Newport County, the rugged defender was enlisted as a last-minute deputy for the injured TG Jones in 1944 and represented Everton at Southport in the game that doubled as a the first-leg of the Liverpool Senior Cup final and a War Football League Northern Division fixture. At the end of Second World War, Low was appointed manager of Norwich City in the Third Division (South) and then Workington in the Third Division (North). Skilled at unearthing bargains buys, the Aberdeen-born boss guided Port Vale to the Fourth Division title in 1959. Low had been chief scout at Anfield for many years before moving to the USA in 1968 and taking charge of the Cleveland Stokers for their only NASL season.

| Everton 1943/44 | games | goals |
| --- | --- | --- |
| League | 0 | 0 |
| Total | 1 | 0 |

# Ian Marshall

**played for**

Everton,

Oldham Athletic,

Ipswich Town,

Leicester City,

Bolton Wanderers,

Blackpool,

Pasadena Eagles

**coached at**

Ian Marshall Soccer Academy

(Canada)

Lionhearted, physically imposing and well-equipped to turn out at centre half or centre forward, Marshall made his debut against West Brom in 1985 and was part of the Everton first-team squad for the next few years. With his advancement limited by the arrival of Dave Watson, he joined Oldham for £100,000 in 1988. Converted into a striker by manager Joe Royle, his goals helped secure the Second Division title in 1991 before he moved on to Ipswich for £750,000 in 1993. Subsequently, the Liverpool-born player won the League Cup with Leicester City, promotion to the top flight with Bolton and the Football League Trophy with Blackpool. Upon retiring, he moved to North America where he established a soccer academy in St Johns, Newfoundland.

| Everton 1985/86 – 1987/88 | | |
| --- | --- | --- |
| | games | goals |
| League | 9/6 | 1 |
| Total | 17/7 | 2 |

# Mike Lyons

**played for**

Everton,

Sheffield Wednesday,

Grimsby Town,

Nova Scotia Clippers

**coached at**

Grimsby Town,

Everton,

Nova Scotia Clippers,

Brunei,

Canberra Cosmos,

Brunei,

Stirling Lions (Australia),

Cockburn City (Australia),

UWA Nedlands, (Australia),

Mandurah City (Australia)

The proud Evertonian compensated for a perceived lack of finesse with awesome athleticism, immense courage, tireless industry and a giant royal blue heart worn proudly on his sleeve. Totally committed to the Everton cause, he would not hesitate to run through a brick wall for his beloved club. As a solid centre-half or a robust centre-forward, he displayed the resulting mixture of blood and mud as a tribal decoration during all of his 473 appearances. An integral part of the Everton set-up throughout the 1970s, no player understood the passion of Gwladys Street like him. After a spell coaching at Bellefield, Lyons was appointed assistant-coach at the Nova Scotia Clippers in 1991 – their only season in the Canadian Soccer League (CSL) – before continuing his globe-trotting coaching/management career in Asia and Australia.

| Everton 1970/71-1981/82 | | |
|---|---|---|
| | games | goals |
| League | 364/26 | 48 |
| Total | 445/28 | 59 |

# Phil Neville

**played for**
Manchester United,
Everton

**coached at**
England Under-21,
Manchester United,
Valencia,
Salford City,
England Women,
Great Britain Women,
Inter Miami

A member of the 'Class of '92', Neville won six Premier League titles, three FA Cups and the 1998/99 UEFA Champions League during his 11 seasons at Old Trafford. In 2005, the full-back/midfielder was signed by manager David Moyes for £3.5 million. Hailed for his professional attitude, work rate and versatility, Neville served Everton for eight seasons – the final six years as captain. Capped 59 times by England, he left Goodison to coach at Manchester United and Valencia and was caretaker-boss at Salford City before being appointed head coach of the England women's team. In 2021, Neville moved to the USA as head coach of Inter Miami – the MLS franchise partly owned by David Beckham. Since 2014, Neville, Beckham and four other members of the 'Class of '92' have been co-owners of Salford City and have steered the club from the Northern Premier League (North) to the English Football League Two.

| Everton 2005/06-2012/13 | games | goals |
|---|---|---|
| League | 237/5 | 5 |
| Total | 295/8 | 5 |

# Adam Smith

**played for**

Everton (youth),
Chatteris Town,
Cambridge United,
Winsford United,
Crewe Alexandra,
Walsall,
Holywell Town (loan),
Mold Alexandra (loan),
Los Angeles Salsa,
Soham Town Rangers,
Harrogate Town,
Geylang United,
Motherwell,
Long Island Rough Riders,
Wilmington Hammerheads

**coached at**

Portland Timbers,
Sacramento Republic,
Elk Grove Youth (California),
Fresno

A young goalkeeper at Everton in the late-1980s, the Rainhill-native did not begin his professional career until after he had graduated from Manchester Metropolitan University. Then Smith made over 200 appearances in non-league football in England and Wales before moving to North America where he helped both the Long Island Rough Riders and the Wilmington Hammerheads claim USL titles. At age 38, he hung up his matchday gloves and was appointed goalkeeping coach at John Spencer's Portland Timbers during that club's inaugural MLS season. Later he assisted another Toffeeman, Predrag Radosavljević, at the Sacramento Republic before becoming head-coach at Fresno in 2017. The club ceased operations after two constructive seasons in the United Soccer League.

Everton youth player: 1988/89

# Walter Smith

**played for**

Ashfield,

Dundee United,

Dallas Tornado (loan),

Dumbarton,

Dundee United

**coached at**

Scotland Under-18,

Scotland Under-21,

Scotland,

Rangers,

Everton,

Manchester United,

Scotland,

Rangers

Walter Smith has a gossamer-thin association with North American soccer. Shortly after the solid and versatile defender kicked off his modest playing career with Dundee United, he turned out for the newly formed Dallas Tornado in the 1967 United Soccer Association tournament. In the Lone Star State, Smith made just three appearances before returning to Tannadice and becoming a key cog of the Second XI. In 1975, he switched to Dumbarton for £8,000 and returned for half of that figure two years later. After injuries forced his retirement, the 29-year-old turned to coaching at Dundee United and then at Rangers where he helped garner 10 League successes, five Scottish Cups and six League Cups. Accompanied by Archie Knox, the noted disciplinarian left Ibrox for Goodison in 1998 but was terminated after four lean years on Merseyside.

Everton manager: 1998/99-2001/02

# Steve Tashjian

**coached at**

Los Angeles Galaxy,
Azusa Pacific University
Cougars,
Columbus Crew,
Everton,
Columbus Crew,
USA

For five or more seasons, the California-native aided managers David Moyes and Roberto Martinez as the head of sports science and conditioning and also the director of end-stage rehabilitation responsible for reducing injuries, expediting recovery and improving performance. Previously, Tashjian had worked at the Los Angeles Galaxy, the Azusa Pacific University and was also the member of Sigi Schmid's staff at the Columbus Crew accountable for athletic performance when they won the MLS Cup in 2008. After leaving Finch Farm, he enjoyed a second stint in Columbus working for Gregg Berhalter. At that time, only the Seattle Sounders employed a similar expert in Major League Soccer. Then in 2019, he joined Berhalter at the USA national team and was tasked with developing data driven platforms related to health, wellness, sports medicine, sports science, strength, conditioning and recovery.

Everton coach: 2009/10 -2013/14

# Kyle Thorne

**coached at**

Everton,

Ottawa Fury,

San Francisco Delta

Thorne is credited with introducing the intensity of gridiron football training routines to Finch Farm. A graduate of Azusa Pacific University, who had gained experience as a strength and conditioning specialist with the NFL's San Diego Chargers, he was hired by manager David Moyes as a specialist fitness and performance coach in 2007. After some 20 months on Merseyside, Thorne was lured back to the National Football League by the New York Jets. Later he worked simultaneously at clubs involved in three different sports, namely the Ottawa Redblacks of the Canadian Football League, the Ottawa Fury of the new NASL and the Ottawa 67's of the Ontario Hockey League. Then he moved to the NASL's San Francisco Deltas before joining the CFL's Edmonton Eskimos as the director of human performance where his training workouts reduced injuries and achieved 95% player availability.

Everton coach: 2007/08-2008/09

# Dr Peter Vint

**coached at**

Everton

The American expert in high performance sport and biomechanics had served teams in the NBA, NFL, MLB and MLS as well as the US Olympic Committee. Having guided US athletes and swimmers to a haul of 64 medals at the 2012 London Olympics, Dr Vint joined Everton as head of the club's academy in August 2016. Despite his obvious dearth of a football background, Dr Vint was charged with propelling the academy from one of the most highly regarded in the land to the best in Europe. In order to do so, he introduced advanced programmes related to sport science, medicine, and analytics for the 160 players in the Under-9 to the Under-19 levels. Dr Vint left Everton after just 15 months. Most recently, he was appointed performance director for the INEOS 1:59 Challenge, in which Eliud Kipchoge ran the marathon distance in under two hours, and Chief of Sport at USA Volleyball.

Everton academy director: 2016/17-2017/18

# Steve Walsh

**associated with**

Bury,

Chester City,

Chelsea,

Newcastle United,

Leicester City,

Hull City,

Leicester City,

Everton,

Southampton,

Charlotte

Recruited as a special advisor by the MLS franchise planned for Charlotte in 2022, Chorley-born Walsh was employed as a schoolteacher while scouting for Chelsea when the London club signed Didier Drogba and Gianfranco Zola. As the full-time chief-scout at Leicester City, Walsh discovered Riyad Mahrez and N'Golo Kanté, players who inspired the East Midlands club to the 2016 Premier League title. Shortly afterwards, he was appointed Everton's first director of football. Throughout his two-year stint alongside managers Ronald Koeman and Sam Allardyce, the club spent a large chunk of its billionaire owner's fortune on 20-odd additions. These included Swansea's Ashley Williams (at £12 million) and Gylfi Sigurdsson (£45 million), Beşiktaş's Cenk Tosun (£19.5 million), Arsenal's Theo Walcott (£20 million), Ajax's Davy Klaassen (£23.6 million), Manchester United's Morgan Schneiderlin (£24 million) as well as Crystal Palace's Yannick Bolaise (£25 million). In mid-2018, with Everton loitering in mid-table, Walsh was replaced by Marcel Brands.

Everton director of football: 2016/17-2017/18

# Tommy Wheeldon

In late-1976, manager Billy Bingham announced a triple swoop of a football magician named as Duncan McKenzie, a midfield enforcer called Bruce Rioch and an 18-year-old novice named Tommy Wheeldon. Previously the ex-England Under-18 midfielder, who cost around £1,000, had been unemployed – turning out for St Helens Town in the Cheshire League on Saturdays and Newalls in his local league on Sundays. Even though he made a favourable Central League debut against Manchester United at Goodison in early-1977, his further progress was blocked by the wealth of midfielders on the club's books. After moving into the lower leagues, he turned to scouting and then coaching. Wheeldon spent some 15 years coaching at the Calgary Storm in the USL A-League and the highly-acclaimed Calgary Foothills academy.

| Everton 1976/77-1977/78 | games | goals |
|---|---|---|
| League | 0/0 | 0 |
| Total | 0/0 | 0 |

# Chris Woods

**played for**

Nottingham Forest,
Queens Park Rangers,
Norwich City,
Rangers,
Sheffield Wednesday,
Reading,
Colorado Rapids,
Southampton,
Sunderland,
Burnley,
Birmingham City

**coached at**

Everton,
USA,
Manchester United,
West Ham United

Peter Shilton's patient understudy eventually made his senior England debut against the USA in 1985. His 43rd and final international appearance also came against the USA, in 1993. At club level, the masterful and near imperious custodian gathered up League Cups with both Nottingham Forest and Norwich City as well as five Scottish League titles and five Scottish League Cups with Rangers, where he established a British record by playing 1,196 minutes without conceding a goal. Following short spells at Colorado, Sunderland and Burnley, the 600-game veteran hung up his boots and well-worn gloves at age 39 to become the principal goalkeeping coach at Everton, where he also helped the USA national team. After 15 years, at Everton Woods followed manager David Moyes to Old Trafford in 2013.

Everton goalkeeping coach: 1998/99-2012/13

# FEATURED MEN AND WOMEN
### international appearances

## Toffeemen

| | | |
|---|---|---|
| Landon Donovan | USA | 157 |
| Tim Howard | USA | 121 |
| Wayne Rooney | England | 120 |
| Tim Cahill | Australia | 108 |
| Joe Max-Moore | USA | 100 |
| Brian McBride | USA | 95 |
| Alan Ball | England | 72 |
| David Weir | Scotland | 69 |
| Richard Gough | Scotland | 61 |
| Peter Beardsley | England | 59 |
| Anders Limpar | Sweden | 58 |
| Philippe Senderos | Switzerland | 57 |
| Mickey Thomas | Wales | 51 |
| Asa Hartford | Scotland | 50 |
| Dave Clements | Northern Ireland | 48 |
| Robert Warzycha | Poland | 47 |
| Tomasz Radzinski | Canada | 46 |
| Daniel Amokachi | Nigeria | 44 |
| Terry Phelan | Ireland | 42 |
| Mo Johnston | Scotland | 38 |
| Tommy Jackson | Northern Ireland | 36 |
| Roy Vernon | Wales | 32 |
| Predrag Radosavljević | USA | 28 |
| Colin Todd | England | 27 |
| Ramiro Funes Mori | Argentina | 26 * |
| Jim McDonagh | Ireland | 25 |
| Bruce Rioch | Scotland | 24 |
| Abel Xavier | Portugal | 20 |
| John Spencer | Scotland | 14 |
| Tommy Casey | Northern Ireland | 12 |
| Matteo Ferrari | Italy | 11 |
| Sam Chedgzoy | England | 8 |
| David Johnson | England | 8 |
| Dave Thomas | England | 8 |
| George Wilson | Scotland | 6 |
| Epsen Baarsden | Norway | 4 |
| Mike Walsh | Ireland | 4 |
| Earl Barrett | England | 3 |
| Brian Godfrey | Wales | 3 |
| Jimmy Gabriel | Scotland | 2 |
| Brian Kidd | England | 2 |

## Toffeewomen

| | | |
|---|---|---|
| Rachel Unitt | England | 102 * |
| Rachel Brown | England | 82 |
| Lucy Bronze | England | 81 * |
| Hayley Raso | Australia | 46 * |
| Jody Handley | England | 38 |
| Claire Emslie | Scotland | 30 * |
| Natasha Dowie | England | 14 * |
| Olivia Chance | New Zealand | 11 |
| Jo Fletcher | England | 9 * |
| Lizzie Durack | England | 1 |

## Coaches, trialists and youths

| | | |
|---|---|---|
| Omar Daley | Jamaica | 75 |
| Gordon Banks | England | 73 |
| Phil Neville | England | 59 |
| Bruce Wilson | Canada | 57 |
| David Carney | Australia | 48 |
| Brian Quinn | USA | 48 |
| Gregg Berhalter | USA | 44 |
| Chris Woods | England | 43 |
| Willie Donachie | Scotland | 35 |
| Jan Eriksson | Sweden | 35 |
| Terry Cochrane | Northern Ireland | 26 |
| Stuart Holden | USA | 25 |
| Stefan Marinović | New Zealand | 25 |
| Collin Samuel | Trinidad & Tobago | 24 |
| Miklos Molnar | Denmark | 18 |
| Edson Buddle | USA | 11 |
| Marcus Hahnemann | USA | 9 |
| Sean Johnson | USA | 9 * |
| Troy Perkins | USA | 7 * |
| Antonee Robinson | USA | 7 * |
| Gordon Stewart | Canada | 4 |
| Danny Szetela | USA | 3 * |
| Roy Turner | USA | 2 |
| Kris Twardek | Canada | 2 * |
| Steve Zakuani | Congo | 1 |

* still active

# 3.5

# TRIALISTS AND YOUTHS

Many British teenagers who graduate through the club's academy fail to advance to first team football at Everton. Most seek clubs in lower leagues, others move on directly or indirectly to the USA and Canada. In the other direction, young North Americans are invited to Merseyside for extended training and/or formal trials at Finch Farm and possible participation in friendlies. Nowadays, many USA starlets are following this European pathway and side-stepping the typical four years of NCAA college soccer. Many of the top US teenagers are turning professional – more often than not with leading Bundesliga clubs. With the nation's reputation for developing top-class goalkeepers, goaltenders, shot-stoppers, custodians, etc., Everton have appraised six young US prospects at Finch Farm during the past decade. To date, only Nico Defreitas-Hansen has been engaged.

Of course, Premier League standards are high. Make that extremely high. As a result, relatively few North American soccer players have been offered professional contracts by leading English clubs. Some have recovered from the rejection by Everton to star in Major League Soccer and, as in the case of Stuart Holden, Sean Johnson and Troy Perkins, to appear for the US men's national side.

Then there are the North Americans that were never provided an opportunity to exhibit their talents. One exceptional 15-year-old midfielder from Calgary – a Canadian citizen with a mother from North Wales and a father from Lancashire – is not included in this sub-chapter. Oddly, the experts at Bellefield denied him a trial during his visit the United Kingdom because 'we have all the YTS players we need at this time.' Owen Hargreaves continued his search for a club to continental Europe and was snapped up by Bayern Munich. During his injury-blighted career, he won four Bundesliga titles and a Champions League crown with Bayern Munich and one Premier League title and another Champions League crown at Manchester United, plus 42 England caps.

## MEMORIES OF YOUTH AND TRIALISTS

### Ronnie Ekelund and Alan Ball

*The former Barcelona midfielder was invited for trials in 1999. Ultimately rejected by Walter Smith, he progressed to join the San Jose Earthquakes. As part of his inspiring and patriotic after-dinner talks, Alan Ball often mentioned how he signed him for Southampton ...*

'During Southampton's 1994 pre-season training in the Netherlands, we stayed at the same hotel as Johan Cruyff's Barcelona. After a couple of drinks in the hotel bar reminiscing about our days in the NASL and before retiring for the night, the Barcelona boss asked me: "Bally, is there anything I can get you?" With typical Farnworth wit, I replied, "How about a left-sided midfielder." We both laughed as the Dutchman waved goodnight. The next morning I went downstairs for breakfast to discover Ronnie Ekelund waiting for me and, as all Southampton fans know, we signed the left-footed Denmark Under-21 international on loan – with an option to buy for around £500,000.'

### John Robinson – brother of a vegan defender and an educationalist pioneer

*Spurned by his boyhood club, Robinson enjoyed his spell with the soccer-playing Yankees in the American Soccer League in the late-1970s ...*

'I was at Everton twice. The first time was as a full-back in 1973 when I was 19 and my brother Neil was 17, we both played in the B and C teams. After a few months Everton let me go but Neil signed professionally. When I was 20, I had been made redundant by Liverpool City Council so Neil asked Billy Bingham if I could come for another trial. This time as a forward, I trained with the reserves and the first team fringe players for a few months before the club released me again.

'In 1976 two smashing guys from the New Jersey Americans, Skip Roderick and Mike Angelotti, came over to Everton for extended trials. They were living in digs but, after Neil befriended them, lodged with us at 45 Queens Drive. Before they went back to the USA, they invited me to give them a shout if I ever fancied playing over there. So, after my Dad died in 1977 I just wanted to get away and got in touch with Mike who was at the Connecticut Yankees. He got me a trial there. I flew to the USA in June and caught the last two months of the season. The Yankees were in the American Soccer League, then the longest running in North America. It was effectively the second division below the NASL and was at a standard similar to the English Fourth Division.

'Bob Kratzer was the owner, general-manager and coach – it was a bit of a one-man-band. Like all ASL teams, we were a mix of foreigners like me who hadn't made the grade and young and enthusiastic Americans. We were based in Hartford and the fans were really invested in the team. We did a meet and greet after every game – no-one had seen that in England at that time. We would meet the fans at the supporters' clubs – mingle and sign autographs – which was great for me as I was not used to it! At every single club we went to there was a Scouser – usually an Evertonian – at the bar. They got everywhere!

'The Yankees hadn't taken out insurance on me so when I got phlebitis I had to come back to England. Then in 1979, I returned to the USA and went to work at Mercer County Community College in Trenton, New Jersey where Mike Angelotti was an alumnus and played for them as a sweeper. It was one of the top junior colleges in the country – the facilities and set-up were outstanding. While there, I went to several Cosmos games – the *Trenton Times* sponsored our college team so I got into Pelé's last game as an official press photographer. I had a press pass and a camera with no film! I remember being just yards from Muhammad Ali who had fought Ernie Shavers days before.

'Anyway, Mercer was due to play in the NCAA finals and the Washington Diplomats of the NASL wanted to sign me – but I tore my cartilage. With the operation costing $5,000 and the college having insured me for only $500, I had to go home again. That was the end for me.'

### Skip Roderick and the manager's daughter

*The young American chased his soccer dream to Bellefield. In the mid-1970s Roderick had extended trials with Billy Bingham's squad …*

'My time at Everton was extremely rewarding and kick-started my career as a soccer player, coach and leader. I had been playing for the Philadelphia Atoms in the NASL and then the New Jersey Americans in the ASL. But lacking the vision for midfield, I had become a centre-back – I was big, fast and good in the air. I came to England in the Fall of 1976 thanks to my soccer mentor, Barry Gorman – Billy Bingham had been his coach at Glentoran. So, I chased my dream – I just wanted to gain experience and to learn more about the game in England – and if anything came of it that would be a bonus.

'I went over with Michael Angelotti, who was a great defender. We didn't know what we were getting into, but the club put us up with the phenomenal Robinsons who opened their arms to us. They became our extended family. Dai Davis would pick Neil, Michael and I up for training every day as he drove past the house. Neil was a vegan, so his mother and sister were saints. They would make two lots of meals – one vegetarian and one with meat. Michael and I would spend many the afternoons with Neil's father who was a quadriplegic. He would spend hours watching soccer on television and he would say to me, "This is what keeps me alive – waiting to see my sons playing football on television."

'On our first day of training at Bellefield, we were overwhelmed to be surrounded by so many tremendous players, so many superstars. That morning, I played the best game of soccer in my entire life. It was a six-a-side game and I played upfront and scored a load of goals. The coaches seemed impressed – perhaps more by my personality than my ability. I would do impersonations of movie stars like John Wayne, tell American stories and soon fitted into the locker room.

'I was warned to lay off centre-forward Bobby Latchford in training as I would try to beat the crap out of him – which was the kind of thing we did back home. It was fantastic to workout with the first team in the morning and the younger players under Colin Harvey in the afternoon. I worked my tail off and was always top in the fitness exams – except on one day. I had laid off the booze except for one night when the lads took me out. It was just my luck that the next day was a fitness exam and instead of coming near the top I was near the bottom and puking. Billy Bingham was mad at me, but the other guys were in tears laughing – they'd snookered me.

'Bill Shankly lived around the corner from the training ground and would come in and hang out. One afternoon, I'd suffered a tweak and was sitting on the table waiting for treatment and spotted Bill getting a massage. He looked at me: "I know you. You're the kid who came over on tour and was at our training facility three years ago." What a memory! I had been in England with the President's Eleven – the top 15 or so college kids playing soccer on the East Coast – and he would get us tickets to Liverpool matches. When Everton were at home I would be behind the bench at Goodison and when they were on the road I would be watching the Reds at Anfield.

'Billy Bingham invited me to his home in Southport for Sunday dinner. It was the first time I had watched "Fawlty Towers" on the television. We laughed at it and had such a great time that I would come over every week. Slowly but surely, I built up enough courage to ask the manager if I could take his beautiful daughter out on a date to the movies. He said that he would think about it but two days later asked, "Skip, have you ever been to Ireland?" When I said "No", he replied, "Well, I have tickets for you and Michael on tonight's boat to Dublin. You're going to a town called Sligo." I asked if I had a choice. His answer was, "Not really." So, we said goodbye to everybody and crossed the Irish Sea.'

### Oliver Shannon at Clemson

*After the lifelong Evertonian was released by the club as a teenager in 2014, he accepted an athletic scholarship to study and play soccer at Clemson University and subsequently at Atlanta United …*

'I joined Everton at age five. My youth team colleagues included Chris Long and Gethin Jones plus younger lads like Joe Williams, Jonjoe Kenny and Tom Davies. When I was 16, I travelled to Texas for the Dallas Cup. But with Eric Dier, Ross Barkley and John Lundstram in midfield I was never going to make the team.

'At 18, rather than wait for the 2013/14 end of season meeting, I asked the powers that be if I was going to get a pro contract. The answer was negative, so I set my sights on the USA as I had a genuine interest in American sports. Everton lined up conversations with different US colleges and I received offers of athletic scholarships from the likes of Stamford, UCLA, Ohio State and Connecticut but fell in love with Clemson whose coach, Mike Noonan, had done his badges with Alan Irvine. I loved the US college system – I studied full-time for a degree in sports communication and business, and played for Clemson in the Atlantic Coast Conference (ACC) in front of huge crowds. Also, I had time for a bit of a social life whereas football in England is all-consuming.

'My aim was to become a professional footballer in the USA and I graduated in time for the January 2018 draft. This involved a week in Orlando, where I played three games in four days with players I had never met before. In between them, I had job interviews with MLS coaches like Patrick Vieira and Adrian Heath, obviously we chatted about Everton. Then I flew to Philadelphia for the draft where I would find out where I would be playing in. It turned out that I was the 36th pick and ended up in Georgia. Atlanta United was an amazing experience with its new Mercedes-Benz stadium and massive sell-out crowds. We had some really good players, 12 members of our 25-man squad were full internationals. Tata Martino, the former Argentina boss, was our coach. Together, they won the MLS Cup in 2018. I was a regular in the second team which played in the USL, the second division of North American soccer, but didn't earn an extension to my contract despite doing well. A new head-coach, Frank de Boer, came in and made it clear that I wasn't in his plans.

'I came home and Everton helped me to get trials at different clubs. Unfortunately, I didn't get any offers. As a result, I made the decision to stop playing and got a job with Team Ineos in cycling. Work is my priority now, but I play part-time for Bala Town. It's just one night of training per week with a game at the weekend. We're in the Europa League this season (2020/21), which will be a new experience. Since coming back, I have enjoyed watching Everton at Goodison and sometimes away. I hope to work for the club one day.'

*Caricatures and pen-pictures of the youths and trialists are presented in alphabetical order. Some like Franz Carr, José Gonçalves, Andy Iro, Stefan Marinović, Steve Zakuani and others with only fleeting and transient links with Everton are included for completeness. The profiles commence with American trialist Mike Angelotti, an exciting prospect spotted playing for the ASL's New Jersey Americans ...*

# Mike Angelotti

**played for**

Hartwick Hawks,
Pittsburgh Miners,
New Jersey Americans,
Everton (trial),
Connecticut Yankees,
Sacramento Gold,
New Jersey Americans,
Mercer County Community
College Vikings

A graduate of Hartwick College, a prominent force in NCAA Division I, the versatile full-back was drafted seventh overall by the NASL's New York Cosmos in 1975 but preferred to spend a couple of seasons in the ASL. He accompanied Skip Roderick, his New Jersey Americans pal, for extended trials at Everton in late-1976. Given the abundance of younger, more experienced defenders in Billy Bingham's squad, the 23-year-old returned to the ASL to play for teams on both the Atlantic and Pacific coasts. When the New Jersey Americans relocated to South Florida in 1979, Angelotti disappeared from the pro scene to turn out for the Mercer County Community College Vikings based in his hometown of Trenton, New Jersey.

Everton trialist: 1976/77

# David Byrne

**played for**

Atlanta Chiefs,
Toronto Blizzard,
Estoril,
Belenenses (Portugal),
Minnesota Strikers,
Baltimore Blast,
Toronto Blizzard,
Wichita Wings,
Tampa Bay Rowdies,
Hellenic (South Africa),
Santos (South Africa)

**coached at**

Michau Warriors (South Africa),
Santos,
Black Leopards (South Africa),
Avendale Athletico (South Africa)

Born in Guildford and raised in Cape Town, the son of England star Johnny 'Budgie' Byrne played both outdoors and indoors for the Atlanta Chiefs and the Toronto Blizzard. After establishing a reputation as both a maker and taker of goals in the NASL, he had trials with Everton in October 1983. The striker appeared in Peter Dornan's testimonial in which Linfield fielded George Best as a guest and scored twice in a 5-0 win. Not offered a contract by manager Howard Kendall, who weeks later snapped up Andy Gray from Wolverhampton Wanderers, Byrne moved to the Portuguese second tier for a couple of years before returning to North America to star in the MISL with the Minnesota Strikers and Baltimore Blast among others before starting his coaching career in South Africa.

Everton trialist: 1983/84

# Camden Buescher

**played for**
Everton (trial),
Northwestern University Wildcats

**coached at**
Adrian College Bulldogs
(Michigan)

The Toledo, Ohio-born teenager was spotted at a soccer camp organised for the Premier League in the USA and invited for a 10-day trial at Finch Farm during the 2013 Thanksgiving holidays. At that time, the young central midfielder was playing for both St John's Jesuit High School and the Pacesetter Soccer Academy. Buescher trained with the Everton youth teams and impressed observers with his ball skills, movement and competitiveness. His hopes, however, were hampered after picking up a nasty ankle injury. After returning to the USA and playing with the Northwestern University Wildcats in the Big Ten Conference for four seasons, he decided not to pursue a professional playing career. In 2019, Buescher was appointed assistant-coach at Adrian College in Michigan.

Everton trialist: 2013/14

# Franz Carr

**played for**

Blackburn Rovers,
Nottingham Forest,
Sheffield Wednesday (loan),
West Ham United (loan),
Newcastle United,
Sheffield United,
Leicester City (loan),
Aston Villa,
Reggio Audace (Italy),
Everton (trial),
Bolton Wanderers (loan),
West Bromwich Albion,
Pittsburgh Riverhounds

The Preston-born right-winger was a spring-heeled sprinter of near Olympic standard who lost his cutting edge with age. By far his most rewarding spell was at Nottingham Forest where he helped Brian Clough's team claim the League Cup in both 1989 and 1990. In due course, Carr turned out for a plethora of clubs but played only 75 senior games in eight years. His contributions at Everton were more modest. At age 31, the one-time rocket-man shone alongside fellow trialist Dalian Atkinson in emphatic Pontins League victories over Manchester United and Sheffield Wednesday in late-1997. However, neither man was offered a contract by manager Howard Kendall. Carr retired from football in 2000 following a spell in the USL A-League with the Pittsburgh Riverhounds.

Everton trialist: 1997/98

# Terry Cochrane

**played for**

Derry City,
Linfield,
Everton (trial),
Coleraine,
Burnley,
Middlesbrough,
Eastern AA (loan),
Gillingham,
Dallas Sidekicks,
Coleraine,
Millwall,
Hartlepool United,
Billingham Synthonia,
Marske United,
Billingham Town,
South Bank,
Ferryhill Athletic

**coached at**

Saudi Arabian Army,
Glenavon,
South Bank,
Hartlepool Ladies

Following trials during which he played in the Central League against Sheffield United in 1973, the teenage right-winger was rejected by Everton. Manager Billy Bingham claimed that his fellow countryman did not have the build for First Division football. After spending more five years in the Irish League, he was transferred to Second Division Burnley and then Middlesbrough for £233,333 – a record for a Northern Ireland footballer. Feisty as well as quick and skilful, Cochrane was an Ayresome hero for many years. As a Northern Ireland international, the winger is best recalled for his goal at Wembley Stadium in 1980 which earned a draw with England and the British Championship for the first time in 66 years. After missing out on the 1986 World Cup squad, he spent the summer playing indoor soccer in Dallas where he forged links with the US Army which resulted in him training and coaching the Saudi Arabian Army team during the First Gulf War in 1991.

Everton trialist: 1973/74

# Omar Daley

**played for**

Hazard United (Jamaica),
Everton (trial),
Reading (loan),
Preston North End (loan),
Portmore United (Jamaica),
Charleston Battery,
Bradford City,
Rotherham United (loan),
Motherwell,
Minnesota United,
Oklahoma City Energy

Born in Kingston, the versatile winger took part in Everton's 2002 tour of Austria, playing alongside a young Wayne Rooney. He made three pre-season appearances mostly as a substitute, and scored one goal. The youngster was offered a professional deal subject to work permit approval. Regrettably, Daley had insufficient Jamaica caps and rejoined Hazard United. After two loan spells in the English second tier, he helped the club (now renamed Portmore United) win the 2005 Jamaican League title. After a stint at the USL's Charleston Battery, Daley continued his travels to clubs in League Two and the Scottish Premier League. In 2013, the now veteran joined Minnesota United of the new NASL. The move ended his Jamaican career during which, despite injuries and club commitments, he made 75 senior outings for his country.

Everton trialist: 2002/03

# Abe Donzo

**played for**
Ottawa Fury,
Everton (trial),
Mont Bruno (Ottawa),
Gloucester Celtic (Ottawa)

Not the typical North American trialist. Donzo and his 15 siblings were born near the Guinea-Liberia border. At age 12, he left a United Nations refugee camp for a new life in Canada where Phil Roberts, a gridiron football coach at Ottawa University, became his legal guardian. Two years on, the 14-year-old was playing for the Ottawa Fury Under-17 side when he won the 'Soccer Dreams' television competition to find the best young Canadian soccer player and was awarded a two-year placement at Everton's academy. The promising marksman shone during his first set of trials until he suffered a knee injury which required surgery and extensive rehabilitation. He returned to Finch Farm for more trials but was released in 2011.

Everton trialist: 2007/08 & 2010/11

# Ronnie Ekelund

**played for**
Brøndby,
Barcelona,
Southampton (loan),
Manchester City (loan),
Coventry City (loan),
Lyngby (Denmark),
Odense (Denmark),
Everton (trial),
Toulouse,
Walsall,
San Jose Earthquakes,
California Cougars

**coached at**
San Jose Earthquakes

Born in Glostrup, Denmark, the talented playmaker had featured in the Brøndby first team at age 15 and was part of that club's Danish title-winning sides in both 1990 and 1991. After joining Barcelona, he represented Denmark at the 1992 Olympics but played a total of 33 minutes of La Liga action before joining Southampton and drifting around Europe. Without a club at age 26, he had trials at Finch Farm to assess his fitness and enthusiasm. Ekelund netted at Tranmere in the testimonial organised for John Morrissey Jnr. Following Everton's rejection, he helped Toulouse gain promotion to Ligue 1 and the San Jose Earthquakes to secure the MLS Cup in both 2001 and 2003. He wound down his career in the Professional Arena Soccer League (PASL) with the Stockton-based California Cougars.

Everton trialist: 1999/00

# José Gonçalves

**played for**

La Sallaz (Switzerland),
Yverdon Sport (Switzerland),
Basel,
Winterthur (Switzerland),
Venezia,
Thun (Switzerland),
Everton (trial),
Kaunas (Lithuania),
Heart of Midlothian (loan),
Heart of Midlothian,
Nürnberg (loan),
St Gallen (Switzerland),
Sion (Switzerland),
New England Revolution (loan),
New England Revolution,
NorthEast United (India),
Zürich

Comfortable at both left-back and centre-half, the Lisbon-born defender began his career in the lower leagues of Switzerland and Italy. In late 2005, while at Thun of the Swiss Super League, the 20-year-old took part in trials at Everton but manager David Moyes chose not to pursue his interest. Eventually, he moved to Vladimir Romanov's Kaunas, his club in the Lithuanian League, and was loaned back to Heart of Midlothian, his other club in the Scottish Premier League. Gonçalves joined the New England Revolution in 2013, initially on loan. Four years later, after his contract had expired, the defender joined North East United in the Indian Super League. Eligible to represent Cape Verde, Portugal and Switzerland, he remained uncapped.

Everton trialist: 2005/06

# Stuart Holden

**played for**

Clemson University Tigers,
Everton (trial),
Sunderland,
Houston Dynamo,
Bolton Wanderers,
Sheffield Wednesday (loan)

**associated with**

Mallorca

Raised in Sugar Land, Texas, the exciting young prospect trained with David Moyes' squad during its visit to Houston and had trials at Bellefield in 2004. Months later, he signed for Sunderland. After his progress was plagued by injuries, including a fractured eye socket sustained outside a Newcastle bar, the gifted winger helped the Houston Dynamo to claim the MLS Cup in 2006 and 2007. Bad luck accompanied him to Bolton where he broke a femur during a challenge by Manchester United's Jonny Evans. Though Holden represented the USA in the 2010 World Cup finals in South Africa, more injuries followed, including a torn anterior cruciate ligament against Panama in the 2013 CONCACAF Gold Cup final. The one-time 'future face of US soccer' retired in 2016, aged 29, to embark upon a broadcasting career with ESPN, NBC and Fox Sports.

Everton trialist: 2004/05

# Greg Hurst

**played for**

Stirling Albion,

Everton (trial),

St Johnstone,

Berwick Rangers (loan),

East Fife (loan),

Forfar Athletic (loan),

Berwick Rangers (loan),

Stenhousemuir,

Chattanooga Red Wolves

The 18-year-old raw prospect was granted extended trials on Merseyside during which he played for David Unsworth's Under-21 side in six pre-season friendlies in 2015 against the likes of Burscough and Glentoran. Though not offered a pro contract, Hurst jumped from the recently-demoted Stirling Albion of the Scottish League Two to St Johnstone of the Scottish Premier League in September 2015. But after failing to find his feet in Perth, the young forward was loaned to Berwick Rangers, East Fife as well as Forfar Athletic before joining Stenhousemuir of the Scottish League One in 2019. Soon, he was on the move yet again – this time to the Chattanooga Red Wolves for the rest of that club's opening season in the United Soccer League.

Everton trialist: 2015/16

# Andy Iro

**played for**
Kingsley United,
Everton (trial),
University of California at
Santa Barbara Gauchos,
Columbus Crew,
Toronto,
Stevenage,
Barnet (loan)

After he failed to impress during trials at Bellefield, the 17-year-old became an entrepreneur. Iro owned and operated his own grocery shop in Toxteth until he was shot in the thigh during a robbery. His life changed when he accepted a soccer scholarship to attend the University of California at Santa Barbara and graduated with a degree in sociology. There, Iro helped the UCSB Gauchos win the NCAA Division 1 championship. The towering 6ft 5in behemoth was taken by the Columbus Crew with the sixth overall pick in the 2008 MLS Super Draft. In concert with 6ft 4in tall Chad Marshall, he formed possibly the biggest central defence in US soccer history. After spending four seasons in Major League Soccer, and lifting the MLS Cup in 2008, Iro returned to the United Kingdom to join Stevenage in League One and Barnet in League Two.

Everton trialist: 2001/02

# Sean Johnson

**played for**

University of Central Florida Knights,
Atlanta Blackhawks,
Chicago Fire,
Everton (trial),
Atlanta United,
New York City

Despite the club's highly embarrassing loss to the Chicago Fire during its 2008 North American tour, it agreed to allow their host's 22-year-old goalkeeper train alongside compatriot Tim Howard at Finch Farm in late-2011. The 6ft 3in tall USA starlet was one of several young MLS players to venture abroad that off-season in order to accelerate the development of their skills and strengthen ties with the leading European clubs. Born in Lilburn, Georgia, Johnson left university early in order to enter the 2010 MLS Super Draft and was selected 51st pick overall by the Chicago Fire. He was included in the USA squads for the CONCACAF Gold Cup tournament in 2013 and 2017. More recently, New York City acquired his services from the Chicago Fire via Atlanta United.

Everton trialist: 2011/12

# Eric Klenofsky

**played for**

TSF Academy,
Monmouth University Hawks,
Jersey Blues,
Ocean City Nor'easters,
New York Red Bulls,
Everton (trial),
Richmond Kickers,
Hapoel Marmorek (Israel),
Toronto,
Tacoma Defiance

While with the New York Red Bulls, where he was a regular for the Under-23 side, the New Milford, Connecticut-native had trials at Finch Farm in late-2016. Despite his massive 6ft 6in frame, Klenofsky failed to impress and returned to North America to enter the 2017 MLS Super Draft. The 22-year-old shot-stopper was taken in the third round by DC United, with the 34th overall pick. Promptly, he was loaned to the Richmond Kickers and then signed for the USL Championship club without making an MLS appearance. Again, he failed to turn out for his new club before moving to Hapoel Marmorek in the Israeli Second Division. In early 2019, he continued globe-trotting and signed with Toronto and, most recently, with the Tacoma Defiance in the USL Championship.

Everton trialist: 2016/17

# Josh Lambo

**played for**

IMG Soccer Academy,

Everton (trial),

Dallas,

Tampa Bay,

DC United (trial),

Sheffield United (trial)

After training with the club's squad during its 2006 North American tour and at Finch Farm, the 15-year-old goalkeeper was offered a pro contract. Despite his Greek heritage, Lambo failed to secure a work permit and was taken as the eighth overall pick in the 2008 MLS Super Draft by Dallas. The Lansing, Michigan youngster had represented the USA at Under-20 level but never graduated to Major League Soccer and retired from soccer at age 21. Next in 2012, having converted to gridiron, the now place-kicker was recruited to play in the Southeastern Conference at Texas A&M University. Three years on, Lambo joined the NFL – first at the San Diego Chargers and then the Jacksonville Jaguars. At the close of the 2020 season, he had converted 88.7% of his field-goal attempts – his longest success being from 57 yards.

Everton trialist: 2006/07

# Stefan Marinović

**played for**

Waitakere United (New Zealand),
Everton (trial),
Wehen Wiesbaden (Germany),
Ismaning (Germany),
1860 Munich,
Spielvereinigung Unterhaching
(Germany),
Vancouver Whitecaps,
Bristol City,
Wellington Phoenix
(New Zealand)

After Marinović's participation in the New Zealand Under-19 tour of Austria, the 17-year-old keeper was invited for a trial with David Moyes' Everton in 2008. After being rejected, the Auckland-born goalkeeper returned to Waitakere United in the New Zealand Football Championship. Upon graduation from the Wynton Rufer Soccer School of Excellence, Marinović played for a series of lower league clubs in Europe. Following stellar performances as New Zealand's No 1, he joined the Vancouver Whitecaps of Major League Soccer in 2017. The next year, he played one game in the League Championship for Bristol City before moving onto the Australian A-League and his fifth different country in 10 years.

Everton trialist: 2008/09

# Zac MacMath

**played for**

IMG Soccer Academy,
Clearwater Chargers,
University of Maryland Terrapins,
Everton (trial),
Philadelphia Union,
Colorado Rapids (loan),
Vancouver Whitecaps,
Real Salt Lake

Following the success of the USA Under-20 team in the prestigious 2011 Milk Cup tournament in Ballymena, the young goalkeeper was invited to spend short stints at Finch Farm in 2011 and 2012 and train with Tim Howard under the tutelage of USA coach Chris Woods. Considered an athletic and gung-ho keeper who on occasions threw himself about like someone on a bouncy castle, he was drafted by the Philadelphia Union as the fifth overall pick in the 2011 MLS Super Draft. By chance, injuries demanded that the raw two-time high school All-American from St Petersburg, Florida be thrust into the spotlight as the youngest net-minder in MLS history and also feature in the vast majority of his club's 2012 fixtures. Four years and over 100 games on, he joined the Colorado Rapids.

Everton trialist: 2011/12 & 2012/13

# Stefani Miglioranzi

**played for**
Westchester,
St John's University Red Storm,
Everton (trial),
Portsmouth,
Swindon Town,
Los Angeles Galaxy,
Columbus Crew,
Los Angeles Galaxy,
Philadelphia Union

Born in Poços de Caldas, a spa resort north of São Paolo in 1977, the skilful midfielder captured the NCAA crown in 1996 and earned All-American honours in 1998 at St John's University in New York City. Shortly afterwards, the 21-year-old Brazilian spent around six weeks training with Everton at Bellefield. Drafted by the Chicago Fire, he chose to remain in the United Kingdom and join Alan Ball's Portsmouth. After four injury-plagued years, Miglioranzi moved to Andy King's Swindon Town. In 2006, he signed for the Los Angeles Galaxy only to be traded almost instantly to the Columbus Crew, who he helped capture both the MLS Cup and the MLS Supporters' Shield in 2008. After he wound down his playing days in Los Angeles and Philadelphia, Miglioranzi became a licensed football agent at First Wave Sports International in California.

Everton trialist: 1998/99

# Miklós Molnár

**played for**
B1908 (Denmark),
Fremad Amager (Denmark),
Hvidovre (Denmark),
Frem København,
Standard Liège,
Servette Genève (loan),
Saint-Étienne,
Everton (trial),
Lyngby (Denmark),
Frankfurt,
Herfølge (Denmark),
Lyngby,
Sevilla,
Kansas City Wizards,
B1908

**coached at**
B1908

A semi-pro at Frem København, Molnár was the top marksman in the 1989 Danish First Division when he was transferred to Standard Liège in Belgium. After a loan spell at Servette Genève, 'The Danish Dynamite' joined Saint-Étienne for £650,000 and struggled. So with manager Howard Kendall seeking fresh firepower, the 22-year-old striker had trials at Everton which included two pre-season friendlies in 1993. Failing to make an impact, he returned to St Etienne only to be released. At Lyngby, Molnár regained his eye for goal and led the 1997 Danish Superliga with 26 goals in 33 games. After a spell at Sevilla in La Liga, the Denmark international moved to the USA to play for the Kansas City Wizards and score the winner in the 2000 MLS Cup final against the Chicago Fire.

Everton trialist: 1993/94

# Bradley Orr

**played for**
Everton (youth),
Newcastle United,
Burnley (loan),
Bristol City,
Queens Park Rangers,
Blackburn Rovers,
Ipswich Town (loan),
Blackpool (loan),
Toronto (loan)

The local boy spent two seasons in the club's junior ranks before departing to Newcastle United. In 2006 while at Bristol City, the 19-year-old defender hit the headlines for the wrong reasons. First, he was shown a red card for attempting to head-butt his teammate Louis Carey during a match at Northampton. Next, he was jailed for 28 days following a booze-fuelled brawl outside a Bristol nightclub. On the pitch, the uncompromising right-back helped Queens Park Rangers snatch the League Championship in 2010 before moving up to Blackburn Rovers. However within five months of his arrival Ewood Park, the club was relegated from the top-flight and he was loaned to Ipswich Town, then Blackpool and finally Toronto. At age 31, Orr retired at the conclusion of the 2014 MLS season.

Everton youth player: 2000/01-2001/02

# Troy Perkins

**played for**

University of South Florida Bulls,
University of Evansville Purple Aces,
Cape Cod Crusaders,
DC United,
Everton (trial),
Northern Virginia Royals (loan),
Vålerenga (Norway),
DC United,
Portland Timbers,
Montreal Impact,
Seattle Sounders

**coached at**

Seattle Sounders

Not drafted after graduating from the University of Evansville, the Springfield, Ohio-born youngster was signed as a back-up goalkeeper by DC United in 2004. Perkins matured quickly. So much so that two years later the now 24-year-old keeper was invited to train at Finch Farm alongside fellow countryman Tim Howard and subsequently promoted to the starting line-up at DC United. After a season of masterful displays, during which he was voted the 2006 MLS Goalkeeper of the Year, Perkins moved to Vålerenga and helped his new club win the Norwegian Cup in 2008. Unable to settle in Oslo, the USA international returned to DC United before joining the Portland Timbers and the Montreal Impact where he grabbed two Canada Soccer Championships.

Everton trialist: 2005/06

# John Robinson

**played for**
Everton (trial),
Connecticut Yankees,
Mercer County Community
College Vikings,
South Liverpool

Born into a diehard Everton family of seven children on Spellow Lane, a stone's throw from Goodison, and raised in Widnes, he is the brother of right-back Neil Robinson – the first vegan footballer – and the late Sir Ken Robinson – the distinguished educationalist and author. Their father, a one-time head barman at the Winslow Hotel opposite Goodison's Main Stand, suffered a broken neck in an industrial accident while working at Kodak and was a quadriplegic for the rest of his life. Along with his brother Neil, he played for Everton's junior teams under the tutelage of coach Tommy Jones but was released on two occasions. At age 22, the versatile midfielder joined the ASL's Connecticut Yankees and then played for the Mercer County Community College Vikings – the New Jersey cradle for several USA soccer internationals.

Everton trialist: 1973/74 & 1974/75

# Skip Roderick

**played for**

Elizabethtown College Blue Jays,
Philadelphia Atoms,
Pittsburgh Miners,
New Jersey Americans,
Everton (trial),
Sligo Rovers,
New Jersey Americans,
Philadelphia Fever,
New Jersey Americans,
Philadelphia Fever,
Philadelphia Ukrainians,
Elizabeth

**coached at**

Philadelphia Fever,
Elizabethtown College Blue Jays,
Ocean City Nor'easters

The Springfield, Pennsylvania-born midfielder had played in both the NASL and the ASL before crossing the Atlantic Ocean for extended trials at Bellefield in 1976. Though unsuccessful, the 20-year-old signed for Sligo Rovers later that year and contributed to them securing the League of Ireland title. Broderick returned to the New Jersey Americans where he won the ASL Championship in 1977 and also played for the Philadelphia Fever in the MISL before bringing to an end his playing days in the German-American Soccer League. After a couple of spells in the early-1980s as interim boss at the Philadelphia Fever, he was hired as the head-coach of the Elizabethtown College, his alma mater, in the NCAA Division III. Over the next 37 seasons, he oversaw an admirable record of 548 wins, 68 draws and 162 defeats.

Everton trialist: 1976/77

# Omar Salgado

**played for**
Guadalajara,
Everton (trial),
Vancouver Whitecaps,
Charleston Battery (loan),
New York City,
Tigres UANL (Mexico),
Tampa Bay Rowdies (loan),
Jaguares de Córdoba
(Colombia) (loan),
El Paso Locomotive,
Las Vegas Lights (loan)

At age 15, the 6ft 4in midfielder left El Paso, Texas to play for Guadalajara, better known as Chivas, in the fourth level of the Mexican league system. In 2010, he caused controversy by accepting a call-up for the USA Under-20 team, having already played for the Mexican equivalent. After helping the USA collar the 2010 Milk Cup, Salgado spent part of that September and October training at Finch Farm. Upon returning to the USA, he entered the 2011 MLS Super Draft and was chosen as the first overall pick by the Vancouver Whitecaps. Unfortunately, Salgado fractured his foot while on international duty, missed the entire 2013 MLS season and struggled to realise his full potential. More recently, he signed for Tigres UANL in Liga MX and then the El Paso Locomotive in the USL Championship.

Everton trialist: 2010/11

# Collin Samuel

**played for**

Doc's Khelwalaas (Trinidad),

San Juan Jabloteh (Trinidad),

Falkirk,

Everton (trial),

Dundee United,

Toronto,

St Johnstone,

Luton Town,

Arbroath,

East Fife,

Sauchie,

Guaya United (Trinidad),

Ma Pau Stars (Trinidad)

**coached at**

Guaya United,

North East Stars (Trinidad)

Born in Trinidad and Tobago, the 21-year-old striker was fast – having clocked 10.4 seconds for the 100 metres when the world record set by Mo Greene was 9.79 seconds. Plucked from Caribbean soccer, his goals propelled cash-strapped Falkirk to the 2002 Scottish First Division title. Along with teammate Lee Miller, Samuel was invited for trials at Everton in an arrangement that sent two Under-21 players on loan to Scotland. Manager David Moyes did not proceed with a deal and Samuel signed for Dundee United for £100,000. Four seasons later, he joined MLS's Toronto. Released to reduce the number of foreign imports in the Toronto squad, he returned to the Scottish First Division to help St Johnstone snatch the 2009 title.

Everton trialist: 2002/03

# Oliver Shannon

**played for**

Everton (youth),
Clemson University Tigers,
Atlanta United,
Bala Town

After 13 years at the Everton academy, where he had featured in the club's Under-18 and FA Youth Cup teams, the box-to-box midfield grafter accepted an athletic scholarship to study and play at Clemson University in South Carolina. There, he helped the Tigers win the 2014 Atlantic Coast Conference and finish runners-up in the 2015 NCAA Division I Soccer Tournament. Equipped with a bachelor's degree, he entered the 2018 MLS Super Draft and was selected in the second round by high-flying Atlanta United, then managed by ex-Barcelona and Argentina boss Tata Martino. But after just one season in the second-string, the 22-year-old was released and returned to the United Kingdom to join Bala Town in the Cymru Premier, the national football league of Wales.

Everton youth player: 2001/02-2013/14

# Chris Spendlove

**played for**

Everton (youth),

Preston North End,

St. Helens Town,

Oklahoma City University Stars,

Austin Aztex,

GPS Portland Phoenix,

Wilmington Hammerheads,

Oklahoma City Energy

**coached at**

Oklahoma State University

Cowgirls,

Oklahoma City Energy,

Hartford Athletic,

Miami

A promising youth player at Everton, the local-born defender accepted an athletic scholarship to study for undergraduate and postgraduate degrees in health and human performance and play soccer at Oklahoma City University after being released in 2003. During his college career, Spendlove also turned out for the Austin Aztex Under-23 side as well as the GPS Portland Phoenix in the USL Premier Development League. Something of a late developer, he penned his first pro contract with the Wilmington Hammerheads at age 26. Soon afterwards, he retired to focus on coaching only to land in serious hot water. In 2015, while an assistant coach at the Oklahoma City Energy, Spendlove was acquitted of the manslaughter of a Liverpool police officer. Since then, he was hired as an assistant coach at Miami in the USL Championship – the second-tier of the US soccer pyramid.

Everton youth player: 2001/02-2002/03

# Danny Szetela

**played for**
IMG Soccer Academy,
Everton (trial),
Columbus Crew,
Racing Santander,
Brescia Calcio (Italy) (loan),
DC United,
Icon,
New York Cosmos

The midfield ball-winner first hit the headlines during the 2003 Under-17 World Cup finals in Finland. Soon afterwards, the 16-year-old American had impressive trials at Bellefield but turned down the club as he did not want to leave his family in New Jersey. Instead, Szetela signed for the MLS's Columbus Crew. Though linked with a transfer to Everton in 2006, the USA international signed for Racing Santander in La Liga and then Brescia in Serie B before returning to the USA to join DC United in 2009. Sidelined for three years until his right knee was rebuilt via a meniscus transplant, Szetela recovered to turn out for Icon, an amateur side in the fifth-tier of US soccer pyramid, in 2013 before moving to the New York Cosmos, where he won NASL titles in 2013, 2015 and 2016

Everton trialist: 2003/04

# Kris Twardek

**played for**

Ottawa South United,

Everton (trial),

Millwall,

Braintree Town (loan),

Carlisle United (loan),

Sligo Rovers,

Bohemians,

Jagiellonia Białystok (Poland)

After Ottawa South United Academy had arranged a partnership with Everton, Twardek was invited to train at Finch Farm on several occasions. However, the teenager – who was born in Toronto, Ontario and raised in the nation's capital by his Canadian mother and Czech father – elected to sign his first professional contract with Millwall in 2015. During his time in London, the winger made three senior appearances and represented the Czech Republic at different age levels, before changing allegiance. Twardek earned his first senior international cap for Canada against El Salvador in 2017. After loan spells in the lower leagues, he was released to join Sligo Rovers and then Bohemians in the League of Ireland Premier Division and Jagiellonia Białystok in the Polish Ekstraklasa.

Everton trialist: 2012/13

# Ian Woan

**played for**

Everton (youth),
Heswall,
Caernarfon Town,
Newtown,
Runcorn,
Nottingham Forest,
Barnsley,
Swindon Town,
Columbus Crew,
Miami Fusion,
Shrewsbury Town,
Syracuse Salty Dogs

**coached at**

Swindon Town,
Rushden & Diamonds,
Portsmouth,
Watford,
Burnley

Woan was part of the club's youth set-up in the mid-1980s, playing in the Lancashire League and the FA Youth Cup. Failing to progress, the local teenager drifted into non-League football. Then in 1990 at age 22, he was transferred from Runcorn in the Northern Premier League to Brian Clough's Nottingham Forest in the First Division for £80,000. The highly-skilled winger possessed a mesmeric left-foot and enjoyed a decade at the City Ground. He almost returned to Goodison in 1996 when manager Joe Royle offered £3 million for his services. Later Woan had two spells in the USA – first in Major League Soccer, then in the USL A-League. Sandwiched in between, he starred for Third Division Shrewsbury Town when Kevin Ratcliffe's men eliminated Everton from the FA Cup in 2003.

Everton youth player: 1983/84-1984/85

# Steve Zakuani

**played for**
Arsenal (youth),
University of Akron Zips,
Cleveland Internationals,
Seattle Sounders,
Everton (trial),
Portland Timbers

**coached at**
Tacoma Stars,
Bellevue Wolverines

Born in Kinshasa, Zakuani grew up in London and attended the Arsenal academy before enrolling at the University of Akron on a soccer scholarship. The speedy winger was the first overall pick by Seattle in the 2009 MLS Super Draft. A crowd favourite, he helped the Sounders win the US Open Cup in 2009 and 2010. After trials at Everton during the MLS off-season, his progress was stalled by an appalling injury in 2011 when a reckless lunge by Brian Mullan of the Colorado Rapids broke his tibia and fibula so badly that doctors feared amputation. As expected, the Congo international struggled to recapture his pace and confidence at Portland and retired at age 26. Now he offers help to youngsters through his non-profit organization, which organises soccer camps in the Seattle area.

Everton trialist: 2010/11

Bev Priestman

# 3.6

# TOFFEEWOMEN

Women's soccer was something of a late developer in the USA. It did not gain momentum until the passing of the landmark legislation, known as Title IX, in 1972 which spurred the creation of women's college teams across the country and the availability of athletic scholarships to some of the best young players worldwide – including many from the United Kingdom. While the initiative changed cultural attitudes toward women playing sports, many claim that the popularity of woman's soccer is directly related to the dominance of the US women's national team.

As for Everton, the women's side was conceived as Hoylake Women's in 1983 and merged with Dolphins YC to become Leasowe who hit the headlines by winning the 1987/88 North West League title and finishing runners-up to Doncaster Belles in the 1988 Women's FA Cup final. Then the following season as Leasowe Pacific, it defeated the Friends of Fulham 3–2 to lift the trophy.

In 1998, three years after it was re-named Everton Ladies, the club was crowned champions of the National Premier League. A decade on, now boasting an array of England international stars such as Fara Williams (172 caps), Jill Scott (149 caps), Rachel Unitt (102 caps) and Rachel Brown-Finnis (82 caps), it outplayed and defeated the previously all-conquering Arsenal Ladies side, which had won 10 titles, 10 FA Cups and 10 League Cups in 16 years, in the 2008 Premier League Cup final at Leyton Orient's Brisbane Road. In the 2010 FA Women's Cup final Everton Ladies beat Arsenal after extra time at Nottingham Forest's City Ground.

Impacted by the losses of England stars Jill Scott and Toni Duggan (76 caps) to Manchester City, Everton were relegated in September 2014, after 21 seasons in the top-flight. However, when Notts County folded, it was invited to re-join the FA Women's Super League in 2017. Ahead of the 2019/20 season, the club dropped 'Ladies' from its name and, after playing at the Arriva Stadium (home of Marine), Halton Stadium (Widnes RLFC) and Haig Avenue (Southport), moved to its own purpose-built ground at Walton Hall Park in early-2020.

Everton's players have strong and deep links with North America. Over the decades, many have accepted offers of athletic scholarships to play college soccer in the USA. Also, a few have turned out for professional teams in the National Women's Soccer League and the recently defunct USL W-League.

Willie Kirk, the manager of the team that competes in the Barclays FA Women's Super League explained: 'Soccer is the most popular sport for females in the USA. The number of participants is massive. If you've got a million players, you are bound to get at least two or three that are decent! The US women's national side has always been ahead of everyone because they placed a big emphasis on the physical side of the game. Its players tend to be stronger, bigger and faster than their opponents.

'I say to anyone going into the US college system – "One thing is for sure, you'll come back stronger, fitter and more aggressive." In the past, some members of our squad have progressed to play professionally in the National Women's Soccer League (NWSL) – the top level of women's soccer in the USA – and gain international honours. That said, we are catching up. A few years ago, an American would be the stand-out player in our league, now they're more likely to be one quality player among many. We have several players in our 2020/21 squad who gained experience in North America. Sandy McIver played for the Clemson Tigers, Claire Emslie enjoyed her college soccer in Florida and is on loan to us from the Orlando Pride and Australian Hayley Raso spent five years with the Washington Spirit and the Portland Thorns.'

Others who have attended US universities include Lucie Bronze (North Carolina), Jo Fletcher (Kentucky and Oregon State), New Zealander Olivia Chance (South Florida) and Lizzie Durack (Harvard). Natasha Dowie and Amber Stobbs, by contrast, advanced to play professionally in the National Women's Soccer League. Bev Priestman is the most recent Toffeewoman to grace the North American stage. In late-2020, at the tender age of 34, she was appointed head coach of the Canada women's team.

Born in Consett, County Durham and a graduate of Liverpool's John Moores University, she coached under Mo Marley at Everton Ladies and worked at the Football Association before departing to New Zealand to serve as the head of women's football development. In 2013, Priestman moved to North America to spend five years as the director of Canada's EXCEL programme, director of its Under-15 through Under-23 teams and assistant coach in John Herdman's women's senior set-up, guiding them to the bronze medal at the 2016 Olympics in Rio de Janeiro. Considered one of the top young coaches in the women's game, she was appointed assistant to England head-coach Phil Neville as well as coach of the Under-18 side in 2018. In her current Canadian role, Bev Priestman works with Richie Kyle, another graduate of Liverpool's John Moores University, who sent five years at the Everton academy before serving as first team coach at Blackpool between 2015-2017.

Mo Marley knows a thing or two about women's soccer. The central-defender was a key member of the Everton side between 1987-2002. She helped capture the 1989 Women's FA Cup with Leasowe Pacific and the 1997/98 FA Women's Premier League title. Marley earned 41 England caps before serving as manager of Everton Ladies between 2002-2012 and guiding them to success in the 2008 FA Women's Premier League Cup and the 2010 FA Women's Cup. Between the dismissal of Mark Sampson and the appointment of Phil Neville, she served as caretaker England boss in 2017/18.

The Everton legend recalled: 'The only time that Everton Ladies did a pre-season tour was to Canada in 2007, it was just before we signed Jill Scott from Sunderland. We went there representing the "Everton Way" programme – they wanted us to promote it from a women's football perspective. I remember that we flew into Toronto and played a local team and did some coaching sessions with local kids, then went on to play against Ottawa Fury. They paid some of our costs – so we had lovely facilities and warm weather, which were appreciated!

'Back then Everton Ladies were completely amateur. Arsenal were kind of semi-pro – they had players working in the club's environment. Our achievements were unbelievable – we won the League Cup in 2008, the FA Cup in 2010 but lost out on goal difference for the League title in 2009. It was all down to the commitment of our players. For Jill Scott to travel from Sunderland, Fara Williams from London and Rachel Unitt from Birmingham for a two-hour training session was extraordinary. We had Bellefield at 9.00pm on a Friday night, or Netherton at 8.00pm, and then did extra work in a local park.

'In the USA at that time, soccer was more female friendly. Some players from the Everton development team went out there on college scholarships. For them, it was a choice of another year not making the first team or going to the USA. Some might not have been able to afford to go to university at home. I'm sure that the credibility of playing for Everton would have gone in their favour when applying for a scholarship. In addition to receiving a full-time education, they benefit from training every day with fantastic state-of-the-art facilities. It was unrivalled anywhere in the world. Back then attendances over here were thin, actually pretty much non-existent, whereas they played in massive college stadiums with big crowds in the USA.

'I remember Rachel Brown being at the University of Pittsburg, which she really enjoyed – then studying at John Moores University. Nicole Johnson, who was in our development team, qualified in coaching and came back to play in the lower leagues. Lucy Whipp, who now plays for Birmingham City, was in our first team before going to St John's University.

'Everton has had a tradition of giving young players the opportunity to play and learn their trade – but it is getting less and less the case across the league. The pressure on younger players to meet the criteria for first teams is phenomenal. So it's a big decision between wanting to get in the first team and desiring an education. That's why USA colleges remain attractive as they can train full time and get minutes playing regularly.'

# MEMORIES OF TOFFEEWOMEN

## Natasha Dowie – an FA Women's Cup winner

*The centre-forward scored the winner in the 2010 FA Women's Cup final before exiting to Liverpool and then Boston in the National Women's Soccer League …*

'I'd had a really enjoyable year at Charlton in 2007 but the women's team folded immediately after the men's team got relegated from the Premier League. It would have been an easy decision to join high-flying Arsenal, but I was in touch with Mo Marley, my England Under-19 coach, about coming to Everton. I thought it would be cool to join Everton and try to knock Arsenal off their pedestal.

'At Everton it was unpaid so I had to find the odd bit of coaching to earn some money. We trained two or three times a week – at first at Netherton then later at Finch Farm. It would be at 8:30pm after the academy and boys had finished. A lot of players did a full day of work, then train until 10:30pm – so it was a crazy level of commitment. I had five great years at Everton. We won the League Cup and the FA Cup against Arsenal but painfully forfeited the title when we lost on the final day of the season. Recently, I re-watched the 2010 FA Cup final highlights and was in tears. I didn't realise just how much it got to me – it remains one of the best days of my professional career to date.

'By 2012 I saw Everton slipping behind. Also Mo had left the club which was upsetting for me. Matt Beard, who I'd worked with at Charlton, had taken over at Liverpool. He told me of his plans – bringing in international players from USA, Germany, Sweden and Iceland and that the club was going full time. Although it was sad to leave Everton, I was proved right as Liverpool won the league in my first two seasons there. The internationals coming over, included Whitney Engen who went on to win the World Cup with the USA, improved the standard and I learned something from all of them. I'd always had a desire to move abroad and challenge myself. So, I followed Beardy to Boston Breakers. It was extremely exciting to play in the NWSL – the most competitive women's league in the world. Even though it was a tough two years, as the team was struggling, I was so grateful for the opportunity and proud to be awarded the golden boot by the club for two years on the run.

'Americans are known for their running and aerobic abilities, so the fitness and athleticism of the players was a lot stronger than in England. The games were very end-to-end, with lots of turnovers – whereas in England it was a slower, possession-based style. I found that the most challenging thing on the body was the travelling; it was really tough when we were playing twice a week. Then there was the heat – I remember one game in Houston when it was so hot that I could hardly breathe. Adapting to the heat helped me when I went on to play in Australia between USA seasons. While I was over in Melbourne, the Boston club folded. I was not picked up by another American club in the draft as none had the money to pick up my contract. So I was clubless until my agent put me in touch with Linköpings in Sweden. Although I think that the European style of football suits my game more, playing in USA was an incredible experience. It made me a better player. I didn't mind rolling up my sleeves and not have everything handed to me. Also it makes me really appreciate the privilege of playing for a top club like AC Milan.'

### Rachel Brown-Finnis – a member of the English Football Hall of Fame

*The Everton and England goalkeeping ace studied and played in the USA. To this day, she remains impressed by the standard of American facilities and the self-belief and winning mentality of American players …*

'I was just 15 when I joined Liverpool from Accrington Stanley in 1995. The following year, I went to the USA for the first time. Michael Payne, a coach I had met at a Bob Wilson soccer camp, asked if I wanted to be a coach at a summer soccer camp over there. So after my GCSE exams, I flew out for six weeks and stayed with a soccer-mad family. To keep my hand in, I played in a couple of games for Alabama Angels – that is how I got scouted. I received offers of athletic scholarships from the University of Alabama and a couple of other colleges. In that six-week window, I saw the profile of US women's soccer players and what a college scholarship meant – it was above and beyond what I could access in England. I have always believed that if you don't take opportunities, you don't know what you're missing.

'So off I went to the USA in 1998. I hadn't appreciated Alabama's rich history in American football – the Bryant-Denny Stadium holds 110,000 but is only the fourth-largest stadium in the Southeastern Conference. It showed what college sports meant in the local community – it's a massive business. Thanks to the Title IX legislation, universities with revenues from men's American football have to provide an equal number of scholarships to women. All the university scouts are looking at high schools for recruits – so I was a bit of a left-field pick. Everyone else on my team was from North America. Athletes were treated well by the university. This made soccer easier for me. In British universities you'd have a constant battle between lecturers wanting more from you and the football coaches wanting more from you.

'In the summer of 1999, my friend's parents flew us to California for the Women's World Cup final. So I was there in the Rose Bowl with that visceral feeling of 90,000 screaming for the USA women's football team, and seeing that iconic moment when Brandi Chastain whipped off her shirt after the penalty shoot-out win. By then, I was an England senior payer, but sat there I was like a fan-girl – it was so far removed from my international football experience. It was the catalyst for me. It was the marker for what I wanted women's football to achieve in the United Kingdom. So, at every opportunity I would demand better of myself – and also of the people at the Football Association who were a million miles off what the sport could become in this country.

'The football experience at Alabama was brilliant, but after two years I decided it was not where I wanted to continue. It felt behind the times culturally with racism and sexism and I transferred to the University of Pittsburgh to complete my degree in movement science and play soccer in the Big East Conference. It was completely different football-wise and socially.

I loved it. Pittsburg felt a bit like Manchester and Liverpool in that it had been through an industrial revolution and was working class with a determined mentality. After the manufacturing nosedive in the 1980s, people were finding alternatives with a lot of creativity and music. I'd fly back every month for to play for England – thankfully, I was one of the few players that the Football Association had a budget for. Once an FA admin person booked me on a first-class flight – which was my budget blown for the whole year! I never saw her name on booking forms again.

'When university studies were finished I could have gone into the draft for the National Women's Soccer League (NWSL) but came back to really push things on in England. After Liverpool had been relegated, Mo Marley got in touch and I joined Everton. I loved every minute of it – playing with top international players like Fara Williams, Jody Handley, Natasha Dowie and Becky Easton, winning the FA Cup and getting so close to the League title a couple of times.

'Mo was always very innovative and selfless. She made me aware of a partnership they had with John Moores University. So I applied for a postgraduate certificate in education (PGCE) scholarship and they offered me a part-time course over three years. When I qualified in 2006, Mo introduced me to the head of the community department at Everton and, for the next seven years, I worked there on various educational projects – which was brilliant. I could bang the drum for women's football to the students and was a link to the club. I am quite comfortable asking awkward questions and would ask the club's media department why they weren't coming down and reporting on our games. I want our sport to be better and progressive. The role came to an end in 2012. It was an Olympic year and, to give myself every chance of making the Great Britain squad in London, I had to concentrate on football. After topping Group E, winning our games against Brazil, Cameroon and New Zealand, we lost to Canada in the quarter-finals and finished fifth.

'Top US stars, like World Cup winners Alex Morgan, Tobin Heath and Christen Press, coming to play in England is nothing but brilliant. They have made the Women's Premier League a much better product and improved its commercial outlook. Hopefully, they can light the touch paper for our players with the standards that they set and the way they see themselves as athletes first and foremost – and not inferior to men. With luck, our players will soak up the self-belief and winning mentality that the Americans demonstrate day-in day-out. Even a 0.5% improvement as an individual or as a team can be huge.'

### Emma Wright-Cates and her blue blood

*Wright boasts a tremendous Everton lineage. Her uncle Tommy made 374 senior appearances for the club in the 1960s and her cousin Billy made 198 appearances in the 1970s. She played for Everton in the 1990s before moving to the USA to coach at different universities …*

'Being a girl in a male dominated sport drove me on. My Dad would tell me, "You can do anything you set your mind to." I played with lads at school until I was 14. They were super-supportive but when we played other schools it was, "Oh, here's this girl." I just keep quiet and let my feet do the talking. My Dad, who had 10 siblings, settled in Bolton and every weekend we visited his family. Going to Goodison was a regular thing. The fact that Uncle Tommy and my cousin Billy had played for the club was just a bonus. You don't appreciate or value it until you get older.

'At 15, I was playing for Bolton. In all honesty I didn't know Everton had a women's team until my Auntie Mary saw an article in the programme saying they were holding try-outs in the summer. I ended up playing for Everton for two and a half years. When I was in school it was a challenge to get to practice at Knowsley Park or Bellefield on week nights. Mary often took me – a lot of people made sacrifices for me. My first start was the day after my 16th birthday. It was a tremendous moment of pride. Generally, I got 50 or 60 minutes per match – which was practically unheard of. The Everton team was like family. We bounced off one another.

'Mo Marley told me about the National Women's Football Academy in Durham. It was for the best players in the country as clubs had no female academies. It turned out to be one of the best choices I have ever made. So I was working at McDonalds and going to school at the Academy. My Dad and Aunty Mary would take me to practice/games but when they couldn't I would crash at Mo's or Tina Mason's (another teammate). They would pick me up at Lime Street Station, feed me and entertain me. We played at Marine's ground and Goodison. When we played against Liverpool at Anfield, my family refused to enter as they are all Blues!

'When I was 19, I saw a video of the 1999 World Cup in the USA. The crowds looked incredible and I said to myself, "I want a piece of that." As a "bubble" player, I was not good enough to challenge for a place in the national team so I decided to go abroad to improve myself. I went to Central Connecticut in August 2000. College soccer was good – playing regularly and having access to resources like a nutritionist, a strength and conditioning coach, a vision clinic – as well getting an education. I couldn't have balanced all of those things at home. Next, I did a post-graduatte degree at Christian Brothers. I was an assistant coach there. In 2006, I went to spend the summer with Reykjavík in the Iceland pro-league. There, I tore my ACL and my LCL. It was a tough decision to stop playing but I had got the bug for coaching. Throughout my life people had encouraged and supported me, so I really liked giving that back to people coming through. I am now in my third-year coaching in San Antonio – an amazing city. The University of the Incarnate Word is a hidden gem and I am very excited about what the future holds for Cardinal soccer. I hope my former, current and future players are inspired to push boundaries, take risks and pursue their dreams.

'I took my son to the Chelsea game last Christmas (2019) and saw Big Dunc enjoy his moment in the limelight. The atmosphere in the Main Stand was amazing. Finn was only three but could not help but join in with "Come on you Blues". It's in the blood.'

*Again, profiles of the dozen Toffeewomen most closely associated with North America start with Lucy Bronze, the UEFA Women's Player of the Year in 2019 and FIFA's Best Women's Player of the Year in late-2020 ...*

# Lucy Bronze

**played for**

Sunderland Academy,
Blyth Town,
Sunderland Ladies,
University of North
Carolina Tar Heels,
Sunderland Ladies,
Everton Ladies,
Liverpool Ladies,
Manchester City Ladies,
Olympique Lyonnais,
Manchester City Ladies

Right-back Lucy Bronze has enjoyed one of English football's most illustrious football careers. Born in Berwick-upon-Tweed in 1991, at the age of 18 – and shortly after losing the 2009 FA Women's Cup final – she moved on to the University of North Carolina. There, she won All-American honours as well as the NCAA Women's Soccer Championship. In 2010 she signed for Everton and developed a reputation for her swashbuckling displays. In November 2012 she followed Natasha Dowie and Fara Williams to Liverpool, where she won the FA Women's Super League titles (FA WSL) in 2013 and 2014. Two years later, the top-class footballer helped Manchester City win the 2016 FA WSL title, in which they conceded only four goals all season. In addition she captured the 2017 FA Women's Cup and netted the winning goal in the 2017 FA WSL Cup final. Bronze enjoyed even more success at Olympique Lyonnais – including three UEFA Women's Champions League titles and three Division 1 Féminine League crowns. Also, she was voted the 2019 UEFA Women's Player of the Year and, to date, has been awarded 81 England caps.

Everton: 2010/11–2012/13

# Rachel Brown

**played for**

Accrington Ladies,
Liverpool Ladies,
University of Alabama
Crimson Tide,
University of Pittsburgh Panthers,
Liverpool Ladies,
Everton Ladies,
Íþróttabandalag Vestmannaeyja
(Iceland) (loan),
Arsenal Women (loan)

Although born in Burnley, Brown was a product of the US college system – the keeper having spent two years in Alabama and another three in Pennsylvania. Earlier, the 5ft 7in youngster had played for Liverpool in the 1996 FA Women's Cup final at age 15 years and 302 days when that club drew with Croydon (later known as Charlton Athletic Women) before ultimately losing on penalties. Upon her return from the USA, Brown found that her former club had been relegated and therefore joined its neighbours in early-2003. She went on to enjoy at 12-year stay at Everton – the highlight being when the club defeated Arsenal 3–2 after extra-time in the 2010 FA Women's Cup final. Initially capped in 1997, she made a total of 82 senior appearances for England. In addition, she was an important member of the Great Britain squad at the 2012 London Olympics. In 2016, Rachel Brown-Finnis was inducted into the English Football Hall of Fame.

Everton: 2003/04-2013/14

# Olivia Chance

**played for**

University of South Florida Bulls,
Claudelands Rovers
(New Zealand,
Breiðablik (Iceland),
Everton Ladies,
Bristol City Women,
Sheffield United Women,
Brisbane Roar

Born in Tauranga on New Zealand's North Island, the diminutive midfielder attended the University of South Florida, where she spent four years playing for the Bulls in the Big East Conference, and later the American Athletic Conference (ACC). In 2017, following spells in New Zealand and Iceland, she joined Everton then in the FA Women's Super League 2. After winning the 2017 FA WSL2 Spring Series, the club was invited to replace Notts County in the top flight. Subsequently, the 25-year-old joined Bristol City before dropping down to the FA Women's Championship with Sheffield United. Most recently, in late-2020, Chance moved to Brisbane Roar in Australia's W-League. To date. she has been awarded 24 senior caps by New Zealand.

Everton: 2017/18–2018/19

# Natasha Dowie

**played for**

Watford Ladies,
Fulham Ladies,
Charlton Athletic Women,
Everton Ladies,
Barnet (loan),
Liverpool Ladies,
Melbourne Victory (loan),
Doncaster Rovers Belles,
Boston Breakers,
Melbourne Victory (loan),
Melbourne Victory (loan),
Linköping (Sweden),
Melbourne Victory,
Vålerenga (Norway) (loan),
AC Milan Femminile

Born in Abu Dhabi, Dowie spent her early career in London. At age 19, she joined Everton after Charlton Athletic disbanded its women's team, and became a key member of the sides that captured the 2008 Premier League Cup and the 2010 FA Women's Cup. The 5ft 8in striker spent five years with Everton before tagging along with Fara Williams to Liverpool, where she netted 46 times in 67 league games to win FA WSL titles in 2013 and 2014. Later, Dowie had four separate spells with Melbourne Victory in the Australian W-League, where she captured the 2019 Premiership title, and one with the Boston Breakers in the National Women's Soccer League (NWSL). When the league folded, Dowie was not selected in the dispersal draft and signed for Linköpings in the Swedish Damallsvenskan, then Vålerenga of the Norwegian Toppserien and AC Milan Femminile in Serie A. Though continually on the fringes of the England set-up – missing the Women's World Cup finals in both 2011 and 2015 – Dowie was awarded 14 senior caps.

Everton: 2007/08–2011/12

# Lizzie Durack

**played for**

Western Sydney Wanderers,
Everton Ladies,
Harvard University Crimson,
Everton Ladies,
Chelsea Ladies

Born in Sydney, Australia, Durack kicked off her youth career with the North West Sydney Koalas and was selected to represent for the Australia Under-17 side in 2010. The goalkeeper joined the Western Sydney Wanderers for the 2012/13 W-League season. While training with the England Under-19 squad in early-2013, Durack secured a place at Everton as the understudy for veteran Rachel Brown. Subsequently, she moved to the USA to study human development regenerative biology at Harvard University and play for the Harvard Crimson and helped them capture Ivy League championships in 2013, 2014 and 2016. In Massachusetts, she was capped by England at Under-23 and senior levels. After graduating, Durack re-joined Everton only to sign for Chelsea in mid-2018. One year later, she retired from professional soccer at age 25.

Everton: 2013/14 and 2017/18

# Claire Emslie

**played for**

Hibernian,

Florida Atlantic University Owls,

Bristol City,

Manchester City,

Orlando Pride,

Melbourne City (loan),

Everton (loan)

Raised in Penicuik, the hometown of Alex Young – 'The Golden Vision' – Emslie kicked off her career at Hibernian, winning the Scottish Women's Premier League Cup in her first season. After studying the physiology of physical exercise at Florida Atlantic University in Boca Raton, the 22-year-old forward joined Bristol City – leading their promotion to the FA Women's Super League. Emslie picked up more silverware at Manchester City, where she captured the FA Women's League Cup and the FA Women's Cup in the 2018/19 season. Almost immediately, the enterprising striker moved to the USA to sign for the Orlando Pride of the National Women's Soccer League. She was loaned to Melbourne City in late-2019 and helped her new club defend its W-League Premiership title and claim the W-League Championship. In due course, Emslie was loaned to Everton for the 2020/21 campaign and played in the 2020 FA Women's Cup final. Following her international debut in 2013, she went on to score Scotland's first-ever World Cup goal and earn 30 international caps.

Everton: 2020/21-present

# Jo Fletcher

**played for**

Everton Ladies,
Liverpool Ladies,
University of Kentucky Wildcats,
Oregon State University Beavers,
Tranmere Rovers Ladies,
Doncaster Rovers Belles,
Birmingham City Ladies,
Charlton Athletic Ladies,
Lincoln Ladies,
Watford Ladies

The Malpas-born goalkeeper has the distinction of playing for all three senior Merseyside clubs as a teenager. After exiting Tranmere Rovers, she spent one season with Everton – leaving the reigning FA Women's Premier League champions for Liverpool. In 1999, Fletcher moved to the USA and spent two years studying biology and playing soccer at the University of Kentucky in the Southeastern Conference (SEC) and another two years at Oregon State University in the Pacific Coast Conference (Pac-10). On returning to England, she studied for a master's degree in exercise science and nutrition at the University of Chester and played for Tranmere Rovers, Doncaster Rovers Belles and Birmingham City before joining the British Army in 2005. Fletcher made nine appearances for England that year, but her international outings ended when she joined the Army.

Everton: 1997/98

# Jody Handley

**played for**

Shrewsbury Ladies,

Wolves Women,

Liverpool Ladies,

Detroit Mercy University Titans,

Liverpool Ladies,

Everton Ladies,

Doncaster Rovers Belles,

Everton Ladies,

Doncaster Rovers Belles

Born in Stafford, Handley kicked off her career as a midfielder with Shrewsbury Ladies, Wolves Women and Liverpool Ladies, who lost the 1996 FA Women's Cup final to Croydon, before attending the University of Detroit Mercy. After one year in the USA, she spent another three seasons at Liverpool before signing for Everton Ladies in 2000 and then Doncaster Rovers Belles, who lost the 2002 final to Fulham. Now an exciting winger, she rejoined Everton, who lost the 2005 final lost to Charlton Athletic. In due course, she captained Everton to successes against Arsenal in both the 2008 Premier League Cup final and the 2010 FA Women's Cup final. Months after the club's relegation in 2014, the 34-year-old star ended her 12-year association with Everton Ladies. Struggling to overcome injuries at Doncaster, she hung up her boots in mid-2015. Handley represented England on 38 occasions.

Everton: 2000/01 and 2004/05-2014/15

# Hayley Raso

**played for**

Canberra United,

Brisbane Roar,

Washington Spirit,

Melbourne Victory (loan),

Portland Thorns,

Canberra United (loan),

Brisbane Roar (loan),

Brisbane Roar,

Everton

The exciting 18-year-old winger first tasted success when she was part of the Canberra United side that won both the Australian W-League Championship and W-League Premiership in 2012. Two years later she joined Brisbane Roar, her hometown club. Next Raso moved onto the North America and signed for the Washington Spirit of the National Women's Soccer League (NWSL) and the Portland Thorns, who she helped win the 2016 NWSL Shield and 2017 NWSL title. Later, she lifted more silverware. Loaned to Canberra United and Brisbane Roar, the Australian ace captured the Australian W-League title with both clubs. In 2018, Raso fractured three vertebrae in her back in a collision at Portland and it was feared that she would not walk again. After being sidelined for six months, she signed another loan agreement with Brisbane Roar. In due course, the Australian Matilda joined Everton and was a member of the side defeated by Manchester City in the 2020 FA Women's Cup final.

Everton: 2020/21-present

# Amber Stobbs

**played for**

Arsenal Women,

Chelsea Ladies,

Hofstra University Pride,

Washington Spirit,

Reading Women,

Everton Ladies,

West Ham United Women,

Charlton Athletic Women,

Crystal Palace Women

Born in London, Stobbs played for Arsenal Women and Chelsea Ladies while in high school. In 2010, she travelled to the USA to study for a degree in psychology and master's degree in sports science at Hofstra University located in Hempstead on Long Island, New York, playing football for the Hofstra Pride in the Colonial Athletic Association. During her time in the USA, Stobbs helped the Washington Spirit Reserves capture the 2015 USL W-League crown. Months on, the attacking midfielder signed for Reading of the FA Women's Super League 1. In early-2017, she moved onto Everton – then in the FA Women's Super League 2 – and was a key member of the side that won the FA WSL2 Spring Series, which ran from February to May 2017 and allowed the league to convert to a winter schedule. Shortly afterwards, she moved south for spells with West Ham United, Charlton Athletic and, most recently, Crystal Palace in the FA Women's Championship.

Everton: 2017/18

# Rachel Unitt

**played for**

Wolves Women,

Everton Ladies,

Fulham Ladies,

Everton Ladies,

New Jersey Wildcats,

Leeds City Vixens,

Birmingham City Women,

Notts County Women,

Solihull Motors,

London Bees

One of the most accomplished British footballers of her generation, the powerful left-back earned 102 senior caps and picked up every meaningful honour in the English game. After two seasons with Wolves Women, the teenager began her long association with Everton. Her time on Merseyside was punctuated by a three-year spell at Fulham, where she won the FA Women's Premier League Cup and the FA Women's Cup, both in 2002 and 2003, as well as the FA Women's Premier League title in 2003. This was followed by a brief loan to the New Jersey Wildcats, where she played a handful of games with her England teammate Rachel Yankey and helped to capture the 2005 USL W-League championship, the second tier of women's soccer in North America. At Everton, Unitt celebrated victories in the 2008 FA Women's Premier League Cup final and the 2010 FA Women's Cup final. Then at age 30, the Walsall-born defender spent two years at Birmingham City where she lifted the FA Women's Cup again in 2012. Rachel Unitt was inducted into the English Football Hall of Fame in 2016.

Everton: 2000/01 & 2004/05-2010/11

# Emma Wright

**played for**

Bolton Ladies,

Everton Ladies,

Doncaster Belles,

Central Connecticut State
University Blue Devils,

Slippery Rock University
of Pennsylvania Rock,

Reykjavík

**coached at**

Christian Brothers University
Lady Buccaneers,

Southeastern Louisiana
University Lady Lions,

Fort Worth Panthers,

George Washington University
Colonials,

Pass and Move LLC,

University of the Incarnate Word
Cardinals

A lifelong Evertonian from a famous royal blue family, Wright joined Everton Ladies at age 15 in 1996 and helped the club capture the 1997/98 Premier League, losing one game that season. After spells at the National Women's Football Academy and Doncaster Belles, the determined central-midfielder moved to the USA in 2000 to study and play soccer at universities in Connecticut and Pennsylvania and Tennessee. She kicked-off her coaching career at Christian Brothers University in the Gulf South Conference, Southeastern Louisiana University in the Southland Conference and George Washington University in the Colonial Athletic Association. Later she coached the Fort Worth Panthers in the Women's Premier Soccer League and ran her own training company (Pass and Move). Wright is currently head-coach of the women's soccer team at the University of the Incarnate Word, a private Catholic university in San Antonio, Texas, competing in the Southland Conference.

Everton: 1996/97-1998/99

# PART FOUR

# NORTH AMERICAN FANS

# TOFFEE SOCCER SURVEY

In mid-2020, during the lockdown associated with the Covid-19 pandemic, the authors conducted a cursory and unscientific survey of Everton fans residing in the USA and Canada to ascertain why they supported the club.

A sample of some 100 fans were asked to list their two favourite reasons. Some responses were more predictable than others.

**The 10 most popular reasons are:**

1   My UK family connections
2   I wanted to be different and not a Top 6 bandwagon jumper
3   The club's illustrious history and traditions
4   Everton's association with USMNT players
5   Everton is a blue collar/working class club
6   Tim 'T-Ho' Howard in my soccer hero
7   Respect for the club's community values and projects
8   Evertonians do not exhibit a sense of entitlement
9   The passionate atmosphere at Goodison Park
10  Landon 'Captain America' Donovan

**Another 10 opinions:**

11  The long list of Everton firsts
12  My best friend is a Toffee
13  Everton has spent most seasons in the top-flight
14  Everton takes care of its old players and fans
15  The club's Christian roots
16  The deeds of Speedo Mick
17  Howard Kendall's success in the 1980s
18  The humour of Roger Bennett
19  Everton are plucky underdogs
20  Blue is my favourite colour

**And bringing up the rear:**

21  I'm a masochist

# 4.1
# WHY EVERTON?

Traditionally, the unswerving love for Everton Football Club was passed from one generation to the next generation throughout the blessed households in Merseyside, South Lancashire, North Cheshire and North Wales. By contrast football enthusiasts in North America without British connections have to decide which club to support. It is an important decision with lifelong consequences.

The authors surveyed a cross-section of supporters based in USA and Canada, and others who have travelled to North America to attend tour games, and asked a simple question, 'Why Everton?' Why support a club that currently lags behind the elite? For many it was not an instant attraction. Most conducted research before making their selections and found that Everton's pedigree, history and traditions are unrivalled. Many were drawn by their fellow countrymen who have worn the club's colours such as Landon Donovan and Tim Howard, known in the Obama White House as 'The Secretary of Defence', only to discover that these stars were simply a gateway to a club that has been in the top-flight for 118 seasons. For others, the club's giant heart is simply second to none.

Over the past decade, few Evertonians have interacted with as many American visitors as Richie Gillham, one of the driving forces behind the Everton FC Heritage Society. This group of diehard fans research, chronicle, preserve and promote the club's amazing and peerless 143-year history. The ongoing work of the Society is diverse and not limited to writing expert articles for websites, producing a library of 60 Everton books or restoring over a dozen graves of former players at locations across the country.

'We organise exhibitions on match-days at St Luke's church hall on Goodison Road,' says Gilham. 'It's a labour of love. Many of our 30-plus members spend hours arranging the exhibits highlighting the goals of Dixie Dean, the skills of Alex Young, the saves of Neville

Southall, the blood, sweat and tears of Alan Ball, and much more. The topics are endless – as are the displays of images which stretch for 100 ft and are tailored for both old experts and young novices. Perhaps more important than the exhibitions, book signings and visits by former-players, the venue provides a meeting place for – what's the buzz word – "engagement" and chatting about football, as well as for meeting old friends and making new ones.

'St Luke's provides a unique pre-match experience and every week I bump into enthusiastic fans that have crossed the Atlantic to watch Everton. They are fascinated by our history and appear to love the club just as much as homegrown Blues. They say that no US or Canadian sporting club has such rich traditions – things that many of us take for granted. Also, they can acquire souvenirs such as an authentic Everton programme from the week that they were born. There must be thousands of these framed old treasures on the walls of rooms in Illinois, Texas, California and even the Yukon. North Americans are fascinated by the club's slate of initiatives, especially those related to the tours, players and coaches who contributed to the development of professional soccer in their homeland.'

Unquestionably, Everton has committed fans in North America. Their support is as notoriously fervent and friendly as those on Merseyside. Here several of them explain in their own words what attracted them to the club, why they love Everton and how they follow its exploits.

### Lyndon Lloyd, San Raphael, California

'The year was 1986, my mother had dragged her three sons to England and I, having quickly been immersed in football, was in search of a team. Then one Saturday afternoon in Buckinghamshire, I was watching a Football Focus feature about Everton and its centre-forward Gary Lineker. Hand on heart, there are few things in life about which I have been as sure as that moment when I said to myself, "That's my team." Whether it was the name, the royal blue or simply that cosmic higher calling, I was an Evertonian from that moment forth.

'I loved that I was unique as a Blue at school. Within weeks, I experienced the first roller-coaster of highs and heartbreaks that have become the shared Evertonian experience when I watched the 1986 FA Cup final – jumping around the lounge with joy as Lineker put us ahead then being reduced to tears when Johnston and Rush had shattered my dreams. My 13th birthday treat was a first visit to Goodison, a frigid, windswept experience sat in the Top Balcony for one of the dreariest Merseyside derbies imaginable. But more away matches would follow that season, culminating in me listening rapt to BBC radio in the car in Bristol while my family toured the city as Everton beat Norwich to clinch the title in my first full season as a fan. I had caught the tail end of our golden era and it would be eight years before I got to celebrate the only other trophy that the club has lifted in my 34 years as an Evertonian. Although success has been rare, supporting this grand old team has enriched my life in ways that that skinny kid from South Africa could never have imagined.

'Thanks to my website (ToffeeWeb.com), I have come to know some fine people, forged friendships and developed an affection for a city that I might not otherwise have even visited.

When I travel to the United Kingdom, it's Liverpool that feels like home. I'm not a Scouser yet I feel grateful that I spent my adolescent and early adult years soaked in the culture of Merseyside football. I attended games regularly up and down England and experienced the incomparable magic of dancing around Goodison's centre circle in the pouring rain with a few thousand friends.

'It gladdens me to know that in the intervening years, my labour of love has served as a similar outlet for other expats and international fans, as well as a destination for Evertonians from across the United Kingdom. Not only is it blessed with an array of articles and submissions from its readers – from insightful analysis and expertly-researched historical pieces to heartfelt stories and humorous anecdotes – ToffeeWeb has been a thriving forum for discussion, debate and shared catharsis.

'Thankfully, the growth of the game in North America has been reflected in increasingly complete and authentic coverage of the Premier League. With all 380 games a season either broadcast or streamed live it somewhat paradoxically, means that I get to see Everton games in their entirety more now than I ever did. One of my greatest experiences was when my sporting worlds collided at the home of the San Francisco Giants in 2013 and Everton played Juventus at AT&T Park. It was surreal, to say the least, to see my beloved football team play in a stadium I had attended scores of times since to watch a completely different sport. Best of all were the social events that surrounded that fixture, the highlight being a Grand Old Evening that brought together a dozen Blues for a night of Everton chat over drinks and a slap-up dinner and in the heart of the city by the Bay.

'ToffeeWeb fulfils a need to give back, strengthen my bonds to the club and spread the gospel across the globe. There may be seemingly endless pain and frustration on the pitch but being an Evertonian continues to be the most rewarding and centering aspects of my existence no matter how far from Goodison I may physically be.'

### Nick Jones, Chicago, Illinois

'People in Chicago look confused when I tell them I'm from Liverpool and support a team they've never heard of, but it's easy to set them straight. Everton is the real Merseyside club. More recent success would be nice, but there's so much to be proud of when you are an Evertonian: all of the celebrated firsts, Everton in the Community, the history and names like Dixie Dean, being founder-members of the Football League, and one of the first ever professional clubs.

'My brother left Merseyside when I was a toddler. I saw him at Christmas but never really knew him. As fate would have it, he moved back in the early-1980s when I was a teenager. We decided to meet every other week at The Abbey Pub and go to the match together. During those three glorious years, Everton won two titles, the European Cup-Winners' Cup, and the FA Cup. My brother and I lived every fan's dream and went to Wembley half a dozen times. Nowadays, I watch almost every match at my local Everton pub, AJ Hudson's near

Wrigley Field. Owned by a Blue, it has become the headquarters of the Chicago Evertonians. I read any and every bit of Everton news I can get my hands on via the club website, BBC, the Liverpool Echo, lots of blogs and supporters' sites. People come and go. Life changes. I've changed countries. Got married and have three children. Lived in five different cities. But there's a blue thread throughout. It has established countless friendships, been fundamental to a lifelong bond with my brother and today is one of the strongest connections I have with my teenage son.'

### Shaun Weale, Kincardine, Ontario

'My family decamped to Canada in 1977. By then, I had caught the blue bug. For my seventh birthday, my father took me to the match against West Ham. It may have been 47 years ago, but I can remember the day vividly. The sights, the sounds, the smells and the celebrations – thanks to Mick Bernard and Jim Pearson. Back then, we lived in Great Sutton – a residential area popular with some of my heroes. About twice a week I would ring Bryan Hamilton's doorbell and ask him for autographs for my school-mates – that was until the afternoon his dog bit me. Dad concluded that I must have mentioned the incompetence of Clive Thomas once too often.

'Growing up as a Blue in Ontario, I kept in touch with football on Merseyside through my grandparents who would send copies of the Liverpool Echo and Everton programmes. We were blessed that the Sunday edition of the Toronto Star published the results and tables. As for television coverage, TSN started to show one English game per week around 1984. The show was hosted by a massive Blue named Dick Howard. Watching Howard Kendall's men in his company was pure joy. I taped the ones featuring Everton and have a collection of VHS tapes in the loft – but no VHS player.

'I couldn't make the games played in my own neck of the North American woods in1985 but attended those in Texas in 2004 and Ohio in 2006. Although I travelled alone, I was soon adopted by the fans who had travelled from Merseyside. They were as friendly, enthusiastic, loyal and funny – in an amusing way – as they were during my childhood. As for the Grand Old Lady, my last visit was on Boxing Day 2017 for the scoreless draw between Sam Allardyce's men and Chelsea. Looking around the stadium that frosty day, I realised that I love Goodison Park – its wonderful people and its wonderful memories. Some Blues take its charm for granted, but to me it is like entering into a time-machine – the sights and sounds of the tradition and heritage. As a youngster, it smelled of success and silver polish.'

### Brian Molina, Sandy, Utah

'I was chosen in 2013. I knew the so-called Top 6 clubs weren't for me and was impressed by everything I had learnt about Everton. The club just felt right. Since then, I have made friends all over the USA and the UK that I hope to have for life and have been invited to watch-parties in six other cities including Portland, San Diego and San Francisco. Travelling is more enjoyable when you have fellow Blues you can meet up with. So far, I have made four visits to Goodison. It took me until the third trip to see an Everton goal, much less a win, but it was so sweet when it happened – much better than I could have imagined. I'll never forget walking into Goodison for the first time and feeling the excitement and passion from my fellow Blues, but one of my best memories is my first trip over the pond with the EvertonUSA group. Our guide was talking to us in the Finch Farm cafeteria when there was an audible gasp from the group as Roberto Martinez came around the corner to greet us. He talked to us about the team and thanked us for crossing the Atlantic to watch Everton. What other top club would have arranged such a surprise?'

### Rich Ballezzi, Philadelphia, Pennsylvania

'I have followed soccer my entire life, but after the unrivalled excitement associated with the 2010 World Cup, I found myself wanting more. So, I turned to the most competitive league in the world – the English Premier League. I didn't pick a team right away, I just watched as a neutral, but it was tough to ignore USA's No 1 between the sticks for Everton. So, I did my research and discovered the rich history and ambition of Everton, with a fanbase as passionate as those of Philadelphia's teams.

'I rooted for Everton for the first time in the fourth round of the FA Cup against Chelsea. I knew then I was an Evertonian and went onto experience the thrilling replay which ended in a victory in a penalty shoot-out. Predictably, this was followed by my first Everton heartbreak as they were bounced from the competition by lowly Reading. I continued to follow them for the remainder of the season. Then in a dream scenario, it was announced that Everton would be coming to Philadelphia that summer. When I got to the stadium, I was stunned at the number of Everton supporters in attendance. I questioned if these people were from Liverpool or are there more Americans like me who support Everton. This led to my discovery of the Philadelphia Evertonians and that Everton games weren't something I had to experience alone on my couch 3,000 miles from the action. There was O'Neal's, a pub in Philadelphia, where other Evertonians watched the matches together. Since then, I have met new friends that have profoundly changed my life. The matchday trip to O'Neal's has become the focal point of my week. It has become as big of a part of my life as the Philadelphia sports teams I hold close to my heart.

'In January 2016, I made the trip across the pond. After the 2-1 success against Manchester City in the first-leg of the League Cup semi-final, I decided that if Everton made it to the final I would return to hopefully see the club win its first silverware since 1995. Unfortunately, City prevailed and Wembley would have to wait. Fortunately, it was only delayed a few months, as the victory over Chelsea booked both of us a trip to Wembley to take on Manchester United in the FA Cup semi-final. I set off for London alone, but met other Evertonians who made the experience unforgettable despite the result. My next trip across the pond in April 2018 was to Goodison, where I got to taste the atmosphere, took pictures of the Dixie statue, enjoyed pre-game drinks at the Winslow and heard Z-Cars. Sitting in the Gwladys Street End was truly a surreal experience, but the cherry on the top was Theo Walcott smashing home the winner over Newcastle in front of me. Everton is and always will be a huge part of my life.'

## Ed Bottomley, Milford, Michigan

'My father's standards were set by Kendall, Harvey and Ball. Therefore supporting Everton was never a choice. It is as much a part of me as the colour of my eyes or my middle name. My earliest memories were names rather than games. Hearing him say that he loved Gary Lineker like a son, and looking at a picture of the striker and thinking "Brother?" During our first visits to Goodison, I was astonished by the noise. One time against Blackburn, I was so excited my teeth chattered all game. My bond with Everton is different. My heroes weren't superstars, they weren't the best. I didn't witness titles like my father did. More often than not we were struggling at the other end of the table. The Old Lady, and the fans who have been filling that stadium for decades are what makes Everton truly special. Goodison brings hope. On our day, we can beat anyone. Everyone quakes in their boots at a full throated Goodison.

'Everton, through my kids' eyes must be a very odd thing. They watch me arrive back from work, open my mouth and excitedly belch 'Guess what happened today? They watch my wife, gently suppressing a sigh, ask, "Is this about work? Or Everton?" It's always about Everton. Always. I live in Michigan, 3,594 miles from Goodison with my American wife Karin and five kids. James Dylan, Margaret Rose, Grace Isabelle, Charles Edson and William Rhys. Fifteen years ago, no one seemed to care about my type of football. I remember my brother-in-law tying his shoelaces in front of the television as Wayne Rooney was getting sent off against Portugal and can still see his annoyed face when I asked him to move. I started blogging about Everton just to talk to someone else about my team. And I shared that writing on social media, which was in its infancy. Now social media is my career. It's always about Everton. Always.

'These days, I can wear my long warm hug of a coat adorned with a tasteful club badge, out and about in Michigan and people talk to me about Everton. At the check-out in the local grocery store, "How are Everton doing this season, sir?" At our local restaurant, "I hear Moise Kean isn't doing that well so far." At work, "The second-half was great, The Old Lady was roaring!" Last year, after Everton lost a horror show to Newcastle, and I was howling at my phlegm flecked television, Gracie (kid #3) asked me, "Dad, why do you like these people? They don't know you and you don't know them. They can't hear you shouting." I still haven't given her an adequate answer.

'The progression of proper football on this side of the Atlantic has been amazing. One game a week, and rarely Everton, was the meagre diet. Now, I can hold Everton in the palm of my hand. Stream it on any television I like. Pause it, record it, repeat it. Football has taken off. Twitter is where I keep in touch with Everton. There is a fantastic community on there and an immediacy to the format. Makes me feel close to Goodison – a place that I adore. I'll miss it when we leave. I have a good friend, Carlos, who is Brazilian. When his father came to visit him in Michigan, I spent three hours talking to him about football. He barely spoke a word of English. We just threw names of players at each other. When I mentioned Pelé, he grinned and replied "Yes! At Goodison! Great place!" He was right. It is. Whether it's your first visit or your one hundredth, Goodison is home to us all. That makes us family.'

### Gerry Quinn, Turriff, Aberdeenshire

'My father was an avid Blue, as were his 11 brothers and sisters. My early years supporting Everton were from the comfort of Crosby, where I would watch the BBC teleprinter on a black and white television with my Dad using me as his remote control. In the 1960s, I would accompany Uncle Dick and his son to Goodison, we would meet in the Supporters' Club before every match. After joining the Royal Navy most of my Everton-obsessed life was spent following the club from far away; via live radio somewhere off the Falklands for the 1985 First Division title victory, FA Cup final defeat and European Cup-Winners' Cup triumph, and somewhere in the Mediterranean panicking when Dion Dublin equalised in 1998 to send me and an Evertonian deep sea diver to the opposite bridge wing away from the radio for yet another cigarette. More recently in the comfort of my Houston abode, I preferred live television but have been guilty of hiding behind the couch most matchdays when following a very average Everton side.

'During our time living in the USA, my wife and I attended several pre-season games. I recall driving around Houston after we had beaten Pachuca in a well-flagged motor as proud as punch, sitting among Everton fans in Dallas chanting "Adios, Adios" and waving goodbye to the Club America fans before their team equalised in injury time. Of course, the Mexicans returned to their seats and, after they won the penalty shoot-out, chanted "Adios, Adios" towards us. There were similar adventures to Salt Lake City in 2007, Denver in 2008 and the nation's capital in 2011. And how can I forget, the "Grand Old Evening" celebrations at Grand Café in San Francisco's Union Square in 2013? This was a fabulous get-together organised by David and Elizabeth France. Most of the 15 had not met before but departed as lifelong friends.

'That evening, I asked if I could tell a true story about an item missing from his Everton Collection. It went … "1985 was a great year – but became a frustrating time in my life. That spring I was a Bridge Watchkeeping Officer on the HMS Danae on a 6-month deployment around the Falkland Islands. I had missed Everton winning the league and losing the FA Cup final but desperately awaited a video of the Rapid Vienna game. In those days we had no cell phones or satellite television, so my wife asked her Dad to tape the match and forward it to me. It took 17 days to reach my end of the world. Promptly, I went to insert the tape into the video player. It wouldn't fit. Only after I tried again did I realise that it was a Betamax tape and a VHS machine. My hurt was complete. I walked up to the Helideck to compose myself and then in sheer frustration hurled the tape as far out to sea as I could. Therefore Dr David, I want to apologise because that bloody tape is one historical item that you will never be able to add to your Everton Collection as it remains God knows how many thousands of metres down on the muddy seabed of the South Atlantic Ocean!"'

### Mike Gaines, Brookings, Oregon

'I had spent years searching for an English club. Then Kevin Sheedy converted his double free kick against Ipswich in 1985. I remember pointing at the television and saying, "That's my

player – that's my team!" I had no idea what a unique niche I had found. For most of the next three decades my support was via television, and through daily visits to ToffeeWeb, until I got the chance to see Everton play in person – 2013 in San Francisco against Juventus and the memorable John Stones penalty.

'A pilgrimage to Goodison was always something for next year or perhaps the one after. At age 60, a miraculous remission from a desperate illness gave me the opportunity in 2017 and the support of the friends I had made over the years on ToffeeWeb paved the way. I was received like family and squired about like a visiting dignitary. As for Goodison, I cried when I took my first look at the pitch and again when Tom Davies scored after 32 seconds. I saw two wins at Goodison - Everton beat Burnley 3-1 and Leicester 4-2, walked on the sacred turf and took an illicit pen at the Park End where Sheedy had netted 32 years earlier, had my picture posted on the half-time scoreboard, met Leighton Baines and Tom Davies, and most of all made deep friends who will be a part of my life forever. A 2018 trip to see the Merseyside derby at Anfield and revisit my friends felt almost like coming home.

'That's what Everton is to me – the supporters who inherited the blue mantle from their fathers and grandfathers and have generously shared that tradition with an American who knew little of it. Through the books of David France and James Corbett I've learned about the distinguished history of the club and many ToffeeWeb raconteurs have shared their recollections of games and players long past. So today when I stagger out of bed to switch on my computer to watch the game and join the Forum. I'm not cheering or cursing the Blues; I'm sitting down for a weekly family reunion.'

### Bridget Bryson, Cumming, Georgia

'As a girl in Puddington in the Wirral, my passion for Everton came from my mother making a throwaway comment that my grandpa was not happy that my red brothers didn't support his team – Everton. The die was cast, I would support the family team. I love that Everton was my grandfather's team and probably his father's too. I've always felt that it was a local club, not a tourist attraction. Between 1985-1988, I was studying architectural design at Liverpool Polytechnic and matchdays were a dream. My favourite was winning the league at Carrow Road. My car had been stolen, so my mother lent me her lovely Peugeot on the grounds that I wasn't to take it out of the city ... so I drove to Norwich. We sang all the way through the match. The drive back, waving to fellow supporters and savouring the moment, was glorious.

'At Goodison, I preferred the Street End and, as a short female, often started in one place and ended in another – but everyone looked after me! Z-Cars was always wonderous. I miss the throngs walking to the ground, the banter and excitement in the air. We always stopped to have my matchday sausage, gravy, and chips.

'After moving overseas in the 1990s, I stepped away from Everton for a period – it was hard to follow the club from the USA back then. My scrapbook travelled with me, as did the memories, but I didn't get to watch much football until the Premier League was on television.

Today, Everton is a huge part of my life. I long for matchdays at the Limerick Junction where my husband and I watch games with the Atlanta Evertonians.

'As a teacher, I visit Merseyside in the summer as there isn't long enough during other breaks. During my last visit, I found the EitC hub and went in for a coffee – what lovely people! I thoroughly enjoyed chatting with them and reliving the past. You never hear about Everton in the USA. It always annoyed me that a club that is so giving, wasn't lauded as it should be here. Anyway, a cab driver in Liverpool told me about the supporters' group in Atlanta. I had no clue! The next game was the derby! So, we joined the Atlanta Evertonians. We were in a different pub then – half red, half blue. Let's just say, things got a bit rowdy. We were definitely louder until the Pickford incident which resulted in Divock Origi's winner for Liverpool in late-2018. It was heart-breaking. It was raucous. Just as it should be. Through the upset and ire, I was home.

'Everton is there for me too. After I had donated to EitC, they sent me a letter about tax status with some government scheme. I explained that I paid US taxes. In passing, I mentioned that my mother was still at home and wouldn't want to confuse her with tax information. The next day, I received a letter, asking whether I wanted someone to check on her. That's family.'

### Darryl Ritchie, Victoria, British Columbia

'My love of Everton began with an insult in 2011. I regret that I used the term "Reds" to describe two local residents, namely Elizabeth and David France, when they brought in a magnificent commendation awarded by the City of Liverpool to be framed at our specialist shop on Douglas Street. You can image the reaction – it was like poking a hornet's nest.

'In what seems like a lifetime ago, I had never heard of Everton Football Club before, but after a little research into Everton and Dr Everton I became besotted - make that infected. And to date, I've been unable to find a cure. In the words of my fellow Canadian Leonard Cohen – there ain't no cure for love. In recent times, my condition has worsened. David Moyes was boring. Ronald Koeman was useless. Roberto Martinez was clueless. I won't tell you what I thought of Sam Allardyce. As for Carlo Ancelotti? Maybe, just maybe. Time will tell. Anyway, I now own a closet full of Everton swag and a maintain a dream to visit Goodson before the wrecking ball does its thing. And it all started with an insult.'

### Gerry Gibson, Winston-Salem, North Carolina

'Around 2012, I embarked on the highly personal decision of choosing where to place my Premier League allegiance. I was leaning towards Everton because the club's colours of blue and white have always felt right to me and its name felt timeless and without gimmick. But I needed more than that. So, I researched the club and found a psychological connection. Everton came from a working-class area. It wasn't a wealthy club. With transfers, they needed a lot of bang for their buck. I didn't know any Everton supporters at that time. It was a choice that I made by myself for myself.

'There was something else – the conditioning that my brain had formed with sports. I'm from North Carolina where everyone has a favourite college basketball team. At that time, my family supported the UNC Tar Heels but, for some reason, I chose the Demon Deacons of Wake Forest University, who weren't exactly setting the world afire. They were a smaller school that needed recruits to be hidden gems with a high work ethic to win games. Sound familiar?

'Back to 2012, when I was leaning toward Everton. That December I discovered that Everton were playing Tottenham on national television. I thought, "Okay, this will be the game that decides it." I recall that the contest had entered injury with the visitors leading through a Clint Dempsey goal when something happened. Steven Pienaar scored to tie it up and the stadium simply erupted. Then Nikica Jelavic banged in the winner and the Everton fans displayed a passion that I had never witnessed before. Instantly, I realised that Goodison was a sacred place for them. Their enthusiasm and pride were palpable, even though the television screen. Then and there, I knew that I would be an Evertonian for the rest of my life.

'The club is a way in which I connect with others and I'm a regular contributor to the Toffee Blues YouTube channel and podcast. The fans with whom I discuss all things Everton have embraced me, even though I'm American and haven't been supporting the club since birth. My family rarely misses a match. Whether by television, radio or Internet, there's always a way to be with Everton from afar. Though we've never been financially comfortable to have "gone the game", embarrassing as that is to say; I'm determined to experience the atmosphere at Goodison before the club moves to its new waterfront palace. Mark my words!'

### Tony Sampson, Chicago, Illinois

'From an early age I can remember my Dad's stories about games he had seen, victories celebrated, and the players he knew or had met. My favourite was the 1966 FA Cup final - his journey down to London, the Wembley crowd of over 100,000; and a game that people would never forget. Not only a Goodison regular, his job meant that he had personal links to some of his heroes. As a young man he owned a cobbler's shop in Walton where he would mend the shoes of one Everton's most famous sons – Brian Labone. Having my Dad looking after the footwear of a legend (therefore playing a small role in his success) was a story I loved.

'My father took me to Goodison at age six. He would park 15 minutes from the ground and carry me on his shoulders as I gripped his ears. The Paddock was our first home. I can remember walking up the stairs onto the terraces and being struck by the brilliant green of the pitch, the smell of the place, the noise and the closeness of the people. Then a number of years on, I was chosen as a mascot at the start of the 1983/84 season. Listening to *Z-Cars* pitch-side, walking onto the hallowed turf and meeting so many legends is an experience that will never leave me. For the record, I wasn't a lucky mascot. We lost 1-0 to West Ham.

'Everton has always brought me a sense of belonging. Part of a wider community where everyone has the same belief, passion and unswerving loyalty – in victory or defeat. As we went to more matches, we would stand next to familiar faces. Despite not knowing about their lives or backgrounds, we formed a special bond and shared the ups and downs of supporting Everton. Since moving to Chicago in 2019, one of our priorities was to find a place where we could watch Everton. We selected AJ Hudson's on the north side of the city, which we had heard was a "soccer pub". As we walked through the door the first thing we saw was a 20ft x 20ft banner bearing the words "Pride of Merseyside – Chicago Toffees". Since then, we make the weekly 40-mile pilgrimage at strange times of the morning to watch the televised games. With a core group coming together every week – a mix of exiled Scousers and locals who have decided that Everton is their team - the passion and devotion is unmistakable.'

### Roger Deborde, Columbus, Ohio

'I fell in love with Everton on Saturday, 5 February 2011, a 5-3 win over Blackpool. I was a freshman in college taking a class at 10.30am on weekends and discovered the game online while waiting for my class. I never went in. I fell in love and watched the whole match. I knew then and there I was destined to be an Evertonian.

'The club is special. They are family. There's no gatekeeping. There's no band-wagoning. Either you're an Evertonian, or you just don't get it. I've been welcomed and offered lodging, food, tickets, etc. from Evertonians on Twitter should I be able to make the trip just because I'm part of the family. No other club in any other sport has that. It's a group, make that a family, that I can be a part of. A place I can feel safe and feel like I belong.'

### Jamie Crowley, Ponte Vedra Beach, Florida

'Moving from Pennsylvania to the Peninsula State, and having played hockey growing up, and with no ice to see for miles, I decided to take up a long-lost fascination – footy. I studied all of the Premier League teams for two months before declaring allegiance. Everton was my team. A city similar to Boston. my place of birth, with a high Catholic percentage and strong Irish heritage, and a struggling team (at that point in time) but with a rich history. Who in the world wants to be a bandwagon-jumper? Only fools pick Manchester United, Manchester City, Liverpool and Chelsea. I was chosen. I just didn't know it at the time!

'After Jamie Carragher blatantly wrestled Joleon Lescott to the ground with impunity, referee Mark Clattenburg – advised by Steven Gerrard – dismissed Tony Hibbert and Dirk Kuyt almost dissected Phil Neville with a two-footed lunge yet stayed on the pitch to score two penalties including one in injury time during the 2007 Goodison derby, that was it for me. The rest is 'istory. Once Everton has touched you – say in 2007 just to pick a date randomly – nothing will be the same. I never miss a game. My five sons, namely Donovan, JC, Rendon, Colin and Quintin are Blues – to varying degrees, of course, as in any family you would find in Merseyside. Everton have weaved an indelible mark into the fabric of my being. It is, as a long-distance, television, American-based fan, inexplicable. What can I say? The club grabbed a hold of my soul and simply won't let go. Best to not fight it; it's such a wonderful ride.'

### Michael Setterberg, Brooklyn, New York

'After watching two or three matches on television, I hadn't felt connected to any Premier League club that I had seen and decided to look closer at a few more. I remember intuitively knowing that Everton was the one for me. I was intrigued by its history. As the son of a hometown jeweller and a church organist and the grandson of a milkman, Everton's connection to its fans and community stood out. I immersed myself in anything I could find about Everton. I spent many weekend mornings finding ways to watch matches, even on delay. Then in the summer of 2008, Everton had a pre-season match scheduled in Colorado. My wife and I hopped a plane to Denver and made it to the match. Being able to see the squad and shout them on from yards away made me feel part of something unique. It was then that my wife and I agreed that for my next birthday, we would travel to Goodison. We took in the match against Stoke from the Lower Gwladys Street. Although Leon Osman's equaliser was at the opposite end, it made it no less scintillating and invigorating. To experience a matchday at Goodison was all that I needed to make the trip a success.

'I made it back almost two years to the day for the Goodison derby. After an ominous opening during which we were reduced to 10 men, Liverpool were awarded a penalty and Dirk Kuyt stepped up to take the spot-kick. Tim Howard was up for the task and kept the match scoreless. In response, the Goodison faithful erupted with a "U-S-A! U-S-A!" chant. I will never forget that moment of excitement and pride. In the end, it was not our day but it is the pursuit of such moments that keeps me setting my alarm for early weekend wakeups, keeps me heading to the pub to watch alongside friends old and new, and keeps me travelling to Europe to cheer on the beloved boys in blue.'

### Brendan Holland Browne, San Francisco, California

'Needless to say, I started watching Everton matches so I could follow Tim Howard, Brian McBride, Landon Donovan and Joe Max-Moore. By 2008 I had formed a bond with the club. I liked the old-school club feel. I liked the long winning history. I liked the current underdog status. Also, I liked that it was a working-class club whose players gave their all on the pitch and would go toe-to-toe with the best in the world. Everton could line up against any other squad believing that they could win.

'But the thing that took me to the next level of fandom was the people. I have met so many amazing people because of the club. I'm blessed to live in San Francisco, a beautiful city that attracts a lot of tourists, so we have guests at McTeague's, the base for the San Francisco Evertonians, almost every week. I'm always taken aback as to how warm our supporters are. Today, Everton is a massive part of my life.'

### Terry White, Panama City Beach, Florida

'We lived in Crosgrove Road, off Queen's Drive. My earliest recollection is sitting on a bollard outside Anfield Cemetery waiting for my Dad to return from the match. I've been told that my

Nana was not happy when she had to stay in while the men went to Goodison. Nana and Mum would go shopping to County Road, pushing me in the pram. At three-quarter time, when the gates were opened to allow fans out, they would go in to watch the last 15 minutes, leaving me outside! My first game was an FA Cup tie against Nottingham Forest in 1954. At age seven, I was hooked.

'In 1977, Barclays Bank DCO sent me to Atlanta and then the US Virgin Islands. Football scores were sketchy. Even though my love for the Blues had not changed, I wasn't close enough to have the same depth of feeling about results. I relocated to northern California in 1982 where my prime source of football scores was the *San Francisco Chronicle*. Match details arrived in letters sent every two weeks by my Dad including cuttings from the *Liverpool Echo* and the *Daily Post*.

'The events of the mid-1980s were just scores with a few notable occurrences. The news of the 1984 FA Cup victory came from a delighted father to an anxious son who had waited all day by the telephone. I was working in San Francisco on the day of the European Cup-Winners' Cup final. There was a Reuters news machine located on the floor above and I was sufficiently senior to be able to wander in front of it from time to time. Whereas the 1995 FA Cup final was on the television at home. It was a lonely watch until my wife got up to check why I was shouting so loudly. Nowadays, she verifies the score on her mobile phone before checking on me.

'Televised games began in the 1990s but were primarily bootlegged showings in local Irish pubs. Which is where my father and I were one Saturday morning in April 1995. My parents had come to visit me in California, and my Dad was disappointed that he would have to miss the semi-final against Tottenham. That was until I discovered that the match was being shown live in a bar in Cupertino, about 20 miles away. In the exceedingly early hours, we arrived there to find a mass of blue and white inside. Of course everything is different now, thanks to NBC. But my match day attire is still a blue shirt, blue underpants, light shorts and my blue and white scarf which sits on top of the television set when we win. I am too old to change my ways; and why should I want to?'

### Matthew Durington, Baltimore, Maryland

'Why support a big money club when you could support one with a blue heart and soul? The history, the traditions, the songs, the celebrations make being an Everton supporter special. Matchdays at the local pub are family reunions with my fellow Toffees. And the chain of American players just adds to that connective tissue of fandom.

'My devotion to the club began in 2013 and has increased ever since. I saw Everton play Valencia during the International Champions Cup in Miami and finally travelled to Merseyside to watch a game in 2017. It was against Hull City, then managed by Marco Silva, and we won 4-0. I did a stadium tour the day before, was interviewed by Everton TV and met the helpful staff at Goodison.

'Right away, I sensed that I was part of a special family. Game-day was a religious experience from drinks at The Winslow Hotel, where I never paid for a beer once folks found out we had travelled from the United States, to squeezing through the historical turnstiles, buying a half-time pie, and feeling the old wooden grandstand sway with the crowd. The epic experience provided me with an unparalleled feeling of belonging.

'Nowadays, Everton Football Club is integral to my life and I'm even referred to as "Everton Matt" locally. You can glance in pretty much any direction in my house and see a replication of Rupert's Tower in some form or another.'

### Patrick Brian Smith, Montreal, Quebec

'I grew up in Hertfordshire and made many trips to see Everton play in London, the Midlands, the South and Merseyside. I come from three generations of Everton fanatics. My great-grandfather, Fred, saw Dixie Dean score his 60th goal against Arsenal in the 1920s. My grandfather, Brian, followed the Blues all over the world in the 1960s and 1970s, including the infamous European Cup tie at Panathinaikos. They were both farmers and came from a long line of agricultural workers in Lancashire. My Dad, Keith, experienced the highs of the mid-1980s being at Norwich when we clinched our second title in three seasons as well as enjoying that memorable night in Rotterdam. Sadly, I have not been quite so lucky.

'I have lived in Montreal since 2014 but my life continues to revolve around Everton Football Club, it's one of the ways I keep in touch with friends and family back in the United Kingdom. I always make it to a match or two when I'm back in the winter and the spring. Whereas in Canada, I have a subscription to the DAZN streaming service which shows all Premier League games and I rarely miss an Everton match. Podcasts are the main way I keep in touch with the goings-on at Goodison during the week: The Blue Room, All Together Now, The Unholy Trinity and Royal Blue. So, what makes Everton so very special to me? Hand on heart, you won't find a more loyal, community-focused fanbase on the planet.'

### Brendan Connolly, Frodsham, Cheshire

'I went to my first match at age 11 and received my first-season ticket at age 15. For the past 10 years, my wife Carolyn, two sons and I have been season-ticket holders in the Gwladys Street Stand. We have been fortunate to follow Everton overseas, as a family to Greece and Thailand and on my own to Kenya and the Ukraine. One of our most memorable trips was to attend the International Champions Cup games in 2013. First up was mighty Juventus at AT&T Park. In our house, the game is fondly remembered for John Stones' cheeky penalty kick, Tim Howard's inspirational penalty save and my son's appearance on EvertonTV.

'Away from the action, I was invited to one of David and Elizabeth France's get-togethers at a posh restaurant in San Francisco, along with some American Blues that neither they nor I had never met before. At the same time, my wife Carolyn and Mikey headed off to a meet and greet with the Everton team. After learning that they hadn't been allowed into the adults only

establishment, Elizabeth demanded that they join us to be fed and watered. We had a great evening. When you place 20 Evertonians around the dinner table, they became friends and within three hours become brothers and sisters for life. To hear about the research many of the American guests had undertaken to select a Premier League club with values that dovetail with their own was heart-warming.

'After chief executive Robert Elstone, who was a guest at the dinner, heard of their disappointment, he invited all three of us to meet the players at the team hotel the following day. To be honest, I was a tad envious of my son as he chatted and rubbed shoulders with Leighton Baines and Leon Osman. Then his wildest dream can true. Mikey was selected to be one of the club's mascots at the game against the even mightier Real Madrid at Dodger Stadium. Dressed in all blue, he was thrilled to be on the pitch with Kevin Mirallas, his favourite footballer, never mind Cristiano Ronaldo. Not surprisingly, the third game against Valencia in Miami was an anti-climax.

'Our 2013 trip was a wonderful adventure for the Connolly family and the Everton family. These are the moments in time that make your heart skip a beat and your adrenaline soar – like playing three of Europe's top teams in three fantastic stadiums in three great cities and, best of all, meeting so many wonderful American people.'

### Marshall Lamm, San Francisco, California

'For a decade. David Kurtz and I have organised pilgrimages to Goodison. Via EvertonUSA, we guided hundreds of like-minded Evertonians to the promised land and made many small dreams come true. Our guests ranged in age from 20 to 70-year-olds and come from across the mainland and Alaska. For some, it's not only their first visit to Merseyside but their first adventure outside of North America. While they know all about Everton Football Club, we must remind them that Brits drive extra fast usually on the left and that they should look both ways before crossing the narrow roads.

'Everyone is impressed by the intimacy and passion at Goodison. It is without equal. The people are so welcoming, knowledgeable and engaged in the action. Nonetheless, I remain amazed that some 40,000 people can down a beer, eat a pie and visit the bathroom during the half-time break. Then there is the history displayed by the Heritage Society at St Luke's Church and by the Everton Collection on the timeline around the stadium. When you scratch the surface of its rich history, you can't help but fall in love with the club.

'I was raised in Texas and played soccer in high school and college. It was in Dallas that the gods of football spoke to me via Preki. Yes, that Preki. Mr Radosavljević, who was a member of the Dallas Sidekicks indoor team that played at the Reunion Arena, often served as our guest coach. He talked glowingly about Everton. I was impressed. However, it was many years before I travelled to Goodison. My life changed on 28 February 2009 with a 2-0 victory over West Brom. I can close my eyes and picture the crowd's reaction to the goals by Tim Cahill and Louis Saha.

'At my local pub in San Francisco, our regulars are augmented by new California residents, travelling businessmen and British holiday-makers who need a Toffee fix. We have a routine. Before kick-off, everyone must introduce themselves and within two hours the like-minded fanatics have become lifelong friends or rather brothers and sisters. It's special to be a part of a football community in which the bonds are so strong. One of my favourite family reunions was in Miami in 2013 when we arranged for an Everton Tailgate, along with the kind folks from the Lion and Eagle Pub in Miami, in the parking area outside of what is now known as the Hard Rock Stadium. Over 300 Evertonians attended the tailgate party. They had come from all over the USA – all over the United Kingdom and all over the world to support Everton. That evening we had a whip-round and presented one of those giant cheques to Graeme Sharp, along with a big thanks to EitC's Carena Duffy. That's what Evertonians do. We don't merely support the club – we support one another.'

### George Hakopian, Los Angeles, California

'I was a big supporter of the US national team and was excited to see Tim Howard join Manchester United. When he was loaned out, I naturally followed him to Everton. It was still pretty tough to watch Everton matches at the time, but whenever I could, I would. Then after a person I knew from church was hired by Everton as a sport scientist, I took a personal interest in not only his success but the club's as well.

'By the time that Landon Donovan had gone to Everton on loan, I was obsessed with the club. Everything about its values, its fans, and its history just drew me in and I never looked back. I don't think I selected Everton at all. Everton sort of just came into my life and became a part of me. It's in my fabric. It's such a special family to me and I really feel that I am a part of something no other football club has. It is an unexplainable attachment that many others feel in the United States. My matchday routine involves waking up early in the morning and heading out to the Fox and Hounds pub in Studio City, a 20-minute drive away, to meet with other Southern California supporters before the 7.00am kick-off. During the week, I spend a lot of time connecting and interacting with other supporters on Twitter. It's allowed me to meet with so many fans to a point where I've created friendships of a lifetime.

'In 2016, I was able to visit Goodison. I was actually going through some difficult times mentally for a couple of years. My wife Annie, who was pregnant with our third child, told me that I should go to England and experience a match. She felt a change of scenery and such an experience would help. And it helped beyond measure. Aside from the match, my experience in Liverpool with the supporters and everyone who represented the club was unexplainable. Unbelievable, actually. The love and warmth I was shown from everyone is unlike anything I could have imagined. I always say God used Everton to bring me back to life. I don't say that lightly. Honestly, the match was secondary compared to just being able to spend time with Evertonians in the city and feel even more a part of this special family.

'One of the more interesting experiences I've had with Everton was meeting Michael Keane when he visited the Hollywood area over the summer. By chance, we were able to reach out to him and ask if he'd would like to meet with some Everton fans. He was more than willing, and while we were speaking, I mentioned that I'm a barber and if he wanted a cut for him to let me know. The next day, he asked if I could meet them at the house they were renting. He insisted that I brought my seven-year-old son along who ended up playing football with him as I gave his friends haircuts. It is something that Jakob will remember for the rest of his life.'

### Mike Murphy, Reston, Virginia

'Wayne Rooney may have made his name and fortune at Manchester United but, for American Blues like me, he always will be one of us. In his two seasons at my MLS team – DC United, he scored goals in about half of his games including a 68-yard cracker against Orlando in June 2019. I've never been a fan of goals from the halfway line scored by the likes of David Beckham. NFL kickers do it every week and get fired if they miss. But Rooney's effort was scored with his football brain – not his football boots. Even though it was so remarkable that I spilt my brewski celebrating, the goal pales in comparison with his sensational last-ditch tackle and 50-yard assist for the game-winning goal against Orlando in August 2018. The commitment that he showed typified his North American career. He wasn't here just for the money like Beckham, Gerrard, Lampard and too many others, Wayne Rooney was in Major League Soccer for his love of the game – a love that was nurtured at Everton.'

### Elizabeth France, Sedona, Arizona

'I've been happily married for 45 years, even though there has been another woman on our lives. I have never complained because Gwladys Street has introduced me to the type of friends that everyone deserves. The three of us have resided in North America since 1977 and have met Blues everywhere we have lived. When talking about the Everton, strangers become long lost brothers within minutes, mixing the present with the past as if the club's history was our personal history.

'Back in 2011, at the dinner celebrations held after the City of Liverpool had bestowed an honour on my husband, I asked attendees to reveal what Everton means to them. Mayor Joe Anderson nailed it when he declared, "Family." Expletive removed. At the Liverpool Anglican Cathedral five years later when we hosted another of our farewell dinners, I invited people to explain what makes Everton so special. The consensus was "My Fellow Blues." I've always been aware of the special bonds between family members and, irrespective of accents, that we are the type of community that people advocate but rarely experience. We are special. Expletive removed.

'Following Everton from across the Atlantic Ocean is neither easy emotionally nor physically. In the early days, when US television was no friend of soccer, we had to hunt for results. In Indiana, they came via the *Sunday Times* in the Purdue University Library on Tuesdays. In California, we received the pink *Football Echo* on Thursdays. Our lives changed in Texas when we bought a Sony short-wave radio. It looked like something from a military surplus store and came with a netting antenna, no doubt invented by John Brodie. So on Saturday mornings, if my other half was not making the 10-hour flight to the match, we would convert our living room into something from a Halloween haunted house to receive the faint signal from the BBC World Service containing the second-half commentary of a top-flight match followed by the full-time results. The latter would change the mood of the household. An Everton win guaranteed sunshine whereas a home draw or any defeat meant a weekend of mourning. In these days of mental health awareness, I have often wondered why Johns Hopkins University or some other prestigious US institution has not studied the negative impact of football.

'The Everton family has rekindled my senses of belonging and identity. It has never let me down. On the other hand, the club has been in decline for 31 of those years. Some American friends new to soccer question the age at which you should choose your club. Because the decision affects your whole life, they believe that an amnesty should be offered at age 18 and again at 60, allowing a change allegiance with impunity. Many see no point in supporting a club with no promise of glory. In response, I advise them that if they seek guaranteed success then Everton Football Club isn't for them, but if they want to be a part of something special and enjoy an uncommon camaraderie, then welcome to the family.

'I have lived in five US states and one Canadian province and have assured my friends, neighbours and anyone who will listen to me that supporting Everton has never been easy but will provide them with some of the best times of their lives. So what makes our bonds extra special? Well, we exhibit a fortitude that manifests as an independence of spirit and lack of deference. We are blood brothers and sisters, passionately loyal to one another rather than a commercial brand, who – as my other half says – radiate a collective warmth that puts more conventional families to shame.'

### Eva Corry, Toronto, Ontario

'I emigrated from Belfast in 1968 but never lost touch with Everton. Back then we made do with newspaper reports but are now blessed with coverage of the EPL on Canadian television. So, I'm up at 7:30am on Saturdays to watch the Toffees in action. The result – win, lose or draw – sets the mood for the weekend. I've been over to Goodison during visits back to the United Kingdom. Also, I attended both matches when the reigning league champions played in Toronto in mid-1985.

'Why Everton? I'm proud that my father was the late Jackie Coulter, the Everton left-winger who – in tandem with his Ireland teammate Alex Stevenson – tormented opponents. He joined Everton from Belfast Celtic in 1934 and would have enjoyed many more years at Goodison were it not for a broken leg suffered on international duty.'

### Ruth Katz, Morristown, New Jersey

'I was introduced to Everton by a friend who had been a glory hunter in the 1980s. When he abandoned me for a job in Austin, I was left with his old Honda to cover his rent arears and my addiction to all things blue. Over time, I've become debt-free but unable to kick the blue habit. For many years, Everton was my personal secret. I rarely talked to strangers or even friends about it. While I went cold-turkey during the Walker/Kendall III period, I needed my regular fix to deal with the pressure of raising two energetic kids after I got married. Since then I have been able to admit my dependency, watch televised games and attend live games in Philadelphia and Liverpool. But nothing compares with the Old Lady of Goodison Road. Our family travelled to Chester in 2013 and visited Bath, Stonehenge, Lacock, Oxford, Stratford-upon-Avon and that other historic treasure – Goodison Park. There the cab driver suggested we walk the final 100 yards and savour the pre-match experience. Most of all, I remember the mood of the fans. They looked so intense – as if going into battle.

'Lately, Everton has behaved like a Powerball winner without clear direction. It has wasted possibly $500 million on decent players, most of whom turned out to be duds, and terrible coaches. I do not expect an Everton team to top the EPL, but I do expect it to contain grafters rather than grifters. As for the club's relationship with US fans, it can no longer rely on our love affair with Tim, Landon and Joe-Max. In the eyes of young fans, they are yesterday's men. To attract new fans, it must capture trophies and invest some of its lottery winnings developing the Everton brand over here.'

### Kouroush Toumadje, San Diego, California

'In the mid-1980s, a relative of mine would send copies of *Shoot!* magazine from England and it didn't take me long to feel the magnetism of Everton. As time passed, I would watch footage provided by relatives and my soccer coach. Back then, the few fans who followed English soccer supported Manchester United or Liverpool, so I took pride in the fact that nobody had heard of Everton. Of course, our standing declined in the 1990s, but I remember getting Setanta Sports and being able to watch some live matches. I was amazed by the passion at Goodison.

'I visited the Grand Old Lady for the first time for the Merseyside derby in early-2015. I was thrilled to have a ticket the Lower Gwladys Street Stand. But when I sat down, I could see only half of the pitch – which crowns by about 6ft. Therefore, every time the ball was on the opposite side, the folks around me would stand up. I'll never forget the sound of the seats clattering - the noise that would pass through Goodison like a perfectly synchronised wave. It was a sound and feeling of unity that I feel in the Grand Old Lady. As for the game, it was one of few clear-cut chances. Seamus Coleman nearly won it at the last minute when he took a pass from Ross Barkley. In acres of space, he unleashed a shot from the edge of the box towards the top left corner only for the Liverpool keeper to save - it was Everton's first shot on target.

'Often my kids say that I love Everton more than them, to which I respond, "Everton has been part of my life longer and before you were born." Most of the folks I've met during my travels to Merseyside have become lifelong friends – more like family. Everton supporters are just as amazing at the club itself.'

## Clayton Hill, Toronto, Ontario

'After an unfortunate spinal injury, I was laid up and started watching soccer matches. I fell in love with the game. It was not about individual accomplishment or individual skill as much as the coordination and collaboration of the team. Plus, it was not as aggressive as a lot of North American sports and not as boring as baseball. So how did I become an Evertonian? I did a bit of research into the history of a few clubs. Everton were supporting the Ontario Soccer Association and I really liked its working-class roots. I did not want to be a Top 6 fan; it takes all the fun out of winning if you win all the time. In due course, I learned that one of my good friends had been following the Toffees for many years as he played soccer at school with a certain Tom Radzinski.

'The Toronto Toffees were founded in 2004. There are about 50 of us who range in age from 25-year-olds to retirees. We meet at Scallywags, a pub in downtown near the junction of Yonge and St Clair. You can get up to 18 of us watching a match – depending on the time of day. By comparison, Liverpool's support is crazy. They also go to Scallywags, so when it is the Merseyside derby we prefer to sit upstairs to keep far away from them. I have not yet got over to see Everton at Goodison, but my partner and I hope to as part of our honeymoon. Serendipitously it just so happened that she, too, is an Evertonian. She was in the United Kingdom for a time and lived in Aigburth.

'There are similar groups in Montreal, Nova Scotia, Calgary and Vancouver. The fans on the ground can only do so much and the only way to grow support further is through outreach by the club. Because Canada has one-tenth of the population of the USA, we are often just included with Everton's endeavours there. Everyone wants to see Everton play here in North America – somewhere we could fly or drive to without great expense. It would grow support for the club. It would be great to see Evertonians getting together at official events. Say, one on the West Coast, one in Dallas or Chicago and one perhaps one in New York or Miami. Of course, it would be great to host something in Toronto but perhaps our group isn't large enough yet.'

## Bryan Yurcan, Morristown, New Jersey

'Like many Americans, I played soccer growing up. By the time I was old enough to fully appreciate the game, the US newspapers and magazines did not cover soccer, the NASL had gone belly up and European games were rarely televised. Therefore, I did not have a favourite team until 2008. Initially, I was attracted to Everton because Tim Howard played for them. After doing some research about the club's working-class ethos and remarkable history, I knew that it was the one for me.

'I suppose I have always been drawn to underdogs. But what makes Everton Football Club so special is the camaraderie among the fans. Every time I meet another Evertonian in North America it feels like we are family. The one time I visited Goodison in 2014, the local supporters treated me like a long-lost cousin.'

## Ian Lowe, Toronto, Ontario

'I'm originally from Belfast. The first game that I ever saw on television was the 1963 Charity Shield match against Manchester United. Everton won 4-0. In a flash, I decided to be an Everton fan and, as a result, would go over on the boat to watch matches throughout the late-1960s. But when I came to Canada in 1974 there was not much I could do to follow the boys in blue and white. You could telephone somebody in the United Kingdom to get the scores – which was ridiculously expensive. So in the mid-1980s I bought a short-wave radio and caught the second-half of games on the BBC World Service. Because Everton were doing well, they were often featured.

'I watched the FA Cup finals on Canadian television, but there was not much more coverage until Setanta Sports started to feature one Premier League game on Saturdays. Therefore, I would pay about $5 to get in the pub where they would serve breakfast and I would watch the match. After the English Premier League started to be shown on regular television, the interest has exploded. I have seen every Everton game in the past decade.

'In 1985 I was at Varsity Stadium for Gary Lineker's first outing. There was a game on the Wednesday and one on the Saturday. There was a good crowd on both occasions, especially since soccer was not doing that well at that time. These days, I'm a member of the Toronto Toffees and go to Scallywags in the city centre to watch games. The bar is quite well known so if someone is over on holiday or business they will show up for the match.

'Whenever I visit Ireland, I try to get to a couple of games. I would love to live in Liverpool for a year and have a season ticket, just to see what it would be like. It's a bucket list item, even though it probably won't happen.'

## Rob Vera, Oklahoma City, Oklahoma

'My name is Rob. I'm 40. And I am a Blue. If those sound like the almost semi-ominous words of an addict, there's a reason for that. As I've written countless times across a variety of channels, there is no hard drug like the one called Everton. That fact at times has caused me great pain as all things that you love inevitably do, but the overriding joy that the affiliation to such an incredible club and it is even more incredible people have brought to my life have made any strife worth it.'

'I could never have known when on a whim I decided to investigate soccer as a placeholder for my beloved NHL, when it lost a season to a lockout in 2004/05, that I would begin a journey which has seen me travel to Merseyside and make numerous friends who have changed my life and the way I see the world. In 2004, I was working at Oklahoma City University when a Nigerian friend recommended I look into the Premier League. I began to research clubs and decided that I wanted one that was special, but not necessarily a frontrunner. I came upon Everton and began to follow their exploits in what would ultimately be the magical Champions League run of 2004/05.

'What I didn't know at the time was that our long-time soccer coach was a guy named Brian Harvey, who is an OCU legend with the college soccer stadium named for him in appreciation of his decades of service. We had spoken countless times before the subject of Everton Football Club was brought up – only for me to find out that he was the brother of the great Colin Harvey. It was as if the football gods themselves were confirming that Everton had touched me.

'Well, the rest is history. I've been over to see Everton on three separate trips. My most recent match was the opener of 2019/20 against Watford where I sat on the front row of the Lower Gwladys. I've never had a better view of any professional sport in my life. My fondest memory is the first Everton win I saw live - at home against Crystal Palace in October 2018. I feared it was headed for a 0-0 draw before a headed-winner by Dominic Calvert-Lewin brought genuine tears of joy to my eyes. I celebrated madly with the rest of the Lower Gwladys end. I've never felt anything like it. Years of waking up early on weekends to watch every match available had led to that moment and nothing will ever top it. The club is beyond sport. It is a family that I can never lose. My name is Rob. I'm 40. And I am a Blue.'

### John Flynn, Peterborough, Ontario

'I grew up in Wallasey but, after visiting relatives in Canada, left for Ontario in 1975. As a 20-year-old Evertonian, I had been a Goodison regular. I adored Alan Ball and had attended 37 games during the magical 1969/70 title-season. In Canada, I discovered that there wasn't much soccer coverage and I used to phone the *Toronto Star's* 800 number for the scores. Now and then, there would be a soccer write-up in the *Sunday Star* but no guarantee that Everton would be mentioned. Initially, my grandads came to my rescue. One would post me the *Pink Echo* and the other would send me the matchday programme. Then in the early-1980s, after buying myself a shortwave radio, I was able to listen to games on Saturday mornings. Thankfully when the Sports Network arrived on cable television, it had a weekly show called The *Soccer News* and Everton were featured quite often.

'I attended Everton's game against Inex in the summer of 1985. A carload of friends, all Canadians who had only heard of Everton Football Club through me, travelled from Timmins, Ontario – a 9-hour/450-mile drive – to watch the reigning Football League champions in Toronto. There were quite a few other noisy Evertonians in the crowd. The game finished 1-1. The highlights of the day included seeing Sir Stanley Matthews, who lived locally, outside the stadium and having a Toronto cop take a picture of me sat on the Everton bench with Peter Reid and Alan Harper. Unfortunately, something went wrong with the film in my camera and you'll have to take my word for it.'

### Eric Howell, Overland Park, Kansas

'When the MLS started in 1996, I followed the Kansas City Wiz, which became the Wizards and then Sporting Kansas City, but was looking to support an English team. The fact that Preki, Mo Johnston and Paul Rideout had played in Kansas piqued my interest in Everton.

And then Tim Howard was signed from Manchester United. I wasn't looking for a club that was constantly winning trophies or had been bought for a lot of cash. Everton just kind of made sense and, after meeting the fanbase online, felt right.

'In 2010, I was the Kansas City correspondent for the *Around the League* MLS podcast and was looking to do one on Everton. Via Twitter, I asked for someone local to Everton to provide some insight and Peter McPartland reached out to me. We struck up a friendship and worked hard to build up "Followtonians". Our tagline was "Same club – different accent", so it had an all-inclusive vibe. The podcast was geared towards the international listener. It was a way to talk about Everton every week. We averaged 10,000 – 20,000 downloads for each episode and had over 100,000 for the one featuring Landon Donovan. With a career change in 2017, I couldn't dedicate as much time towards the podcast and Peter moved onto establish ToffeeTV.'

### Andrew Lambert, New York City, New York

'My grandfather once told me that he was at Goodison when Dixie scored his famous 60th goal in 1928. Everyone threw their cap into the air in celebration; my grandfather never did get his back. I imagine he didn't care too much. In 1966 my father was at Wembley to see us win the FA Cup. I would like to say that I completed the treble by being at Wembley in 1995. Sadly, I had left Merseyside and my season ticket behind, and started a journey that eventually brought me to the USA in 2003.

'In between, I worked at Kyoto University. There, I followed Everton's final-day escape against Coventry in 1998 in the dead of night by watching Bolton versus Chelsea, the only game available on a friend's satellite network. Everton needed to equal Bolton's result to stay up and live updates were provided; but what I remember most clearly from that day was the chances Bolton missed to equalise. The bike ride home across the city was sombre. Perhaps they were good years to be incommunicado.

'After Japan, I moved to Hawaii to attend graduate school, stopping for about eight years before moving to the mainland to teach. As a US-based fan back in 2003, before the days of fast internet or multiple soccer channels, following the Blues involved a delay. It was a tough time to be so distant. Wayne Rooney was emerging and there was genuine excitement about the potential of the team. I used to sneak into the department's computer room between seminars to claim my share of the excitement. It was a personal vigil, with no one around to share in the feelings. Even a Liverpool fan would have been welcome. Fortunately, not long after I arrived, I met an ex-pat who was an Arsenal fan. She would keep an eye out for Everton games broadcast on cable television. So, I'd often forgo knowing the result on Saturday in the hope that, come Monday, a video tape would be waiting for me. And about once a month, there was.

'For those few hours there was the timeless and placeless pleasure of something so familiar – the buzz and excitement of a live game. Vividly, I remember watching Everton falling 3-0 behind to Manchester United in February 2004 and fighting back to equalise, only to lose to a late goal by Ruud Van Nistelrooy. Things are much easier now, with communities of Everton fans around the country and all Premier League matches readily available. One of these days, I will complete that treble, and be there in person when we win finally silverware.'

### Habib Erkan, San Antonio, Texas

'In the fall of 1985, I was in the Houston Public Library researching my then three favourite European soccer clubs (Ajax, Barcelona and Inter Milan) when I came across an article about the Heysel Stadium disaster. The writer's emphasis was not the human tragedy; rather he explained how Liverpool's bitter rivals were enjoying one of the best periods in their history and had got totally screwed by what happened. As a lawyer, something about the injustice of the incident made me immediately attracted to the Toffees and loath the Reds. The more I learned about Everton's history, the deeper the attraction became. For my 60th birthday I travelled to Goodison to watch the Toffees destroy Hull 4-0 and meet some members of the 1985 team.'

### James Boyman, Portland, Maine

'Following Everton Football Club was a gradual journey for me. I first got an understanding of soccer through the FIFA video game and discovered the Toffees while watching the Fox Soccer channel on cable television – then something drew me in. I live in Maine where not a lot of people around me are aware of the English Premier League, much less Everton Football Club. So, I didn't have an outlet for my fandom. Alex Johnson, who lives in Virginia was doing the American Toffee Podcast, so I offered to participate as a guest in September 2018. We kept at it and the show has kicked into another gear.

'In February 2020, Alex and I made our first pilgrimage to Goodison Park for the Premier League clash with mighty Manchester United. Prior to heading over to the United Kingdom, we reached out to the Everton Fan Engagement team located in the Royal Liver building. They were extremely helpful and arranged for us to go on the Goodison Legends tour on the day before the match – during which we met Neville Southall, Ian Snodin and Mark Higgins. It was amazing.

'We had heard that Tim Howard would be in Liverpool that weekend and asked if there was any way we could scoot down to the Everton Two shop in the city centre to see him but were told that the timings would not work out. Anyway, the following day, in a ruse by the wonderful Fan Engagement team, we were lured to Goodison for a pitch-side interview about our trip. As we were talking to the cameraman we felt gentle taps on our shoulders. Before we knew what was happening, we were shaking hands with our Everton and USA hero. Alex and I were absolutely shellshocked, to say the least. We talked for a minute or two and he offered to take part in the American Toffee Podcast. A few months later, Tim appeared on the show and could not have been more generous with his time. He is a true Evertonian and a great guy.'

**Ian Macdonald, Crosby. Merseyside**

'Neil Diamond's "Coming to America" was playing as we touched down in Houston in 2004. Many Blues had checked into the same hotel and I was welcomed by Jimmy from Huyton holding a blow-up doll wearing an Everton top and shorts. A sure-fire hit with the locals, he proclaimed: "They know who Everton are now!"

'The match against Pachuca at the magnificent Reliant Stadium was an eye-opener as to the ways in which North America treat its sports fans. Footballs and shirts were thrown into the stands. Vendors ran up and down the aisles distributing hotdogs, ice cream and popcorn. At the bar I was asked for my ID, I was 40 at the time and flattered by the challenge. Unhappily, there was a bit of a problem at full-time. Some Everton fans were seething that the team hadn't acknowledged them. Back at the hotel, Mark decided to ring the Everton manager – disrupting his sleep.

'The late-night call worked, and David Moyes and Alan Irvine met with us the following morning. We expressed our displeasure at how the club's employees had snubbed its supporters who had made the 5,000-mile trip. Though a little heated, the discussions were productive. Anyway, at the end of the next game against Club America, the manager and his players came over to the section containing a few thousand Blues and waved enormous Kenny Everett hands to say thanks.

'When following Everton overseas, our fans know how to behave as well as enjoy themselves. There are so many new friendships to make and old friends to meet. For example, in their former hometown, David and Elizabeth France arranged a fantastic get-together for all Blues travelling from the old country at a downtown sports bar with free beer and a free Texas-sized buffet. Even though we were surrounded by gigantic skyscrapers, it felt like we were home from home.

'Of course, many fans double as tourists. From Houston, we went to NASA, Austin and New Orleans, where a storm had devastated the area. While we were there, a local politician arrived with his entourage and was asking people where they were from. A guy near me said "Texas - The Lone Star State," another next to me said "Florida - The Sunshine State." After he noticed our Everton tracksuits, I proclaimed that I was from Merseyside. Amusingly, he asked what state that was in. Instantly, I countered: "A worse state than here!"

'On to Utah in 2007, where many of us decided to take a pre-match excursion to Las Vegas. There were so many Everton shirts on the famous Las Vegas Strip that the locals must have thought we were part of some massive Toffee Convention. On the flight to Salt Lake City far away from craziness of Sin City, I sat next to two well-dressed young men from the Church of Jesus Christ of Latter-day Saints returning home after their two-year stint as missionaries in Asia. Politely they asked me, "Sir, why are you coming to our beautiful city?" Without any hesitation, I countered: "To get back at you and knock on your doors!" They laughed and invited me to their Mormon temple. In response, I politely advised them we had our own

Golden Vision and our own Temple named Derek. My mate proudly showed them his old tattoo of Duncan McKenzie. To Barry's embarrassment, they were convinced it was their local heart-throb Donny Osmond.

'After the defeat at the Rice-Eccles Stadium, we suspected that another game would be held somewhere – most likely in California. After we got my mate Colombo on the case, Marti, Mick, Mark and I flew to San Francisco. Our stay was eventful. We visited some great pubs where the locals were really friendly, and men kissed each other like we do when Everton score. Going to Alcatraz, we had a KEIOC flag draped over the front of the boat. Our protest created so much fuss that we made the local radio and newspapers. Best of all, we helped to keep Everton in our city.

'Then while watching the seals at Fisherman's Wharf, we heard that Everton were to play David Beckham's Galaxy. This news quickened our pace. So much so that we were pulled over by the police on our way down the coast to Los Angeles. I told the officers that we were members of a cult following our idols from the home of the Beatles. I don't think they believed or understood a word that I said. Scratching their heads, they let us go on our way. I thanked them, "May the Holy Trinity be with you – Kendall, Harvey and Ball."

'Along with other Blues who had received news of the unadvertised fixture, we arrived at the Herbal Life Stadium to discover that the box office was closed, and that Everton would be playing a college team on a public pitch. Before you could say Budweiser, Kenny, Andy, Dave and their many friends arrived from Los Angeles with vehicles full of beer and other vital supplies for the mandatory tailgate party. David Moyes was evidently unhappy with our noisy congregation and the police were called. Thankfully, the officers were amused and let us stay.

'Now to Chicago and Denver in 2008. Along with Washy and Dominic, I opted for some sightseeing before moving onto our match destinations. We stayed in Brooklyn with Mark and Stephen, members of the New York supporters' group that meets at Mr Dennehy's Irish Pub in Greenwich Village on match-days. They took us to the East Side where Ziggy Stardust had lived. I've adopted Bowie as an honorary Evertonian because of the amount of times he included the word "blue" in his songs just like Elton John. Finally, we flew to the Windy City where Chang, then Everton's shirt sponsors, had arranged for the fans to meet the team at the Globe Pub. It was another great night during which I met Chris, a disabled supporter from Crosby who was restricted to a wheelchair, and his carer Percy. Now that's royal blue devotion.

'Embarrassingly, the Chicago Fire played their reserve side and beat us. Licking our wounds, we visited the Sears Tower where we bumped into a few of our players. They thought we were mad travelling so far to see them play in a friendly. I explained that some of us had not missed a match anywhere for over 15 years. Next, we visited Wrigley Field. Part way through the stadium tour our guide invited questions so, I asked, "Why don't the Cubs tear down this place and move out of town?" There was deafening silence. I may as well have said that all Americans were fat and war mongers. I clarified that my soccer club back home proposes to do just that. The tour group responded unanimously that we would regret it. Many proclaimed, "You will lose your identity and destroy your soul." I used this story at the Destination Kirkby public enquiry.

'Our next stop was Denver and the Colorado Rapids. My best memory of the narrow victory was some divvy in a Liverpool shirt – who had a young child with him – gave us grief throughout the game. I thought he must have a death wish. Especially at the end when he invaded the pitch and was arrested. Of course, he could have been running away from Kenny who, let's just say, can handle himself.

'In 2011, it was another family gathering – this time in Philadelphia and Washington DC. I was so desperate to go that I volunteered to decorate the house and landscape the garden. Accompanied by Eddy and Lee, we stopped off in New York to take in a Bruce Springsteen gig before driving to the home of the Liberty Bell. I recall that Tim Howard was rested – much to the dismay of the local soccer fans. After losing to the Philadelphia Union, we felt compelled to visit the Museum of Art and run up the Rocky Bilboa steps to scream "Adrian (Heath)." Thankfully, we won in Washington DC where lots of Americans spotted our shirts and asked where we were from. This time I replied, "The home of The Beatles." I never use the L word.

'Looking back, I'm grateful to Everton for providing me with such great opportunities to visit North America and for my ensuing divorce after going there too often.'

# EPILOGUE
# LAND OF OPPORTUNITY

Soccer may be the most popular sport on the planet, but it is required to battle with two codes of gridiron football, baseball, basketball and ice hockey for the hearts, minds and dollars of North America sports fans. While the beautiful game cannot declare victory, it seems to have made inroads during the past three decades.

In that short period, the standard of professional soccer has improved greatly. The US men's national team is no longer a pushover, as discovered by Graham Taylor's England in 1993 at Foxborough and Fabio Capello's super-stars during the 2010 World Cup at Rustenburg, and is listed in the top 25 in the FIFA rankings. Similarly, Canada is no easy mark and was ranked 73rd in early 2021. As for women's soccer, the USA leads the world – having won four World Cups and four Olympic golds. Canada is not too far behind. It was ranked eighth alongside Brazil in early 2021. Equally as important, the health of both Major League Soccer and the National Women's Soccer League have never been more robust.

Today, professional soccer is omnipresent thanks to the television broadcasts of games in the MLS and the top European leagues – of which the English Premier League is the most favoured at present. However, public interest is likely to explode when the USA, Canada, and Mexico co-host the 2026 World Cup finals. Given that this buoyant audience represents a tremendous opportunity for strengthening the international fanbases of Premier League and other leading European clubs, two burning questions exist: a) how is Everton currently perceived in the North American market and b) how should the club differentiate itself from its competitors?

Despite the club's pedigree – 118 seasons in the top-flight, nine titles – and unrivalled links with the USA and Canada including romantic hook-ups with Tim Howard and Landon Donovan, Everton Football Club has yet to become a household name. Whereas Manchester United have found American fans willing to queue for hours to snap up tickets, the empty seats at Everton games tell a different tale.

To address the burning questions, the authors sought objective feedback from experts with their fingers on the pulse of the professional game in North America. Arguably, no one is better position to confirm the club's current standing than one of the USA's most popular soccer broadcasters. Roger Bennett is a die-hard Evertonian and a co-host, along with Michael Davies, of the *Men in Blazers* television show on NBCSN: 'Back in the 1990s, soccer had been cast as "America's Next Big Thing", its past little more than a collection of false dawns and hyperbolic predictions. Since then, I have marvelled from World Cup to World Cup as the game's profile has inexorably risen nationwide. It has been steady growth rather than instant success. Today soccer is a part of American life and no longer a fad such as the pogo stick, the hula hoop or a pet rock named "Hibbo".

'With its history of boom and bust, the question is often asked as to why more and more Americans have fallen under football's poetic sway. Many theories have been advanced. The most likely is the advent of the worldwide web and streaming. Just as baseball thrived on radio and American football was the perfect television sport, the beautiful game's rise has been driven by the Internet which has enabled fans in North America to follow their teams as closely as supporters in the old country. Today, soccer is omnipotent.

'In 1995, I remember being in Chicago searching for the FA Cup semi-final on the available 500-plus cable channels. Sadly, without success. There was Cuban baseball, Aussie Rules football and even competitive hot-dog eating but no hint of Everton versus Tottenham Hotspur. In desperation, I called my father and for the next 90 minutes he held his phone against the radio so I could listen to the Radio Merseyside commentary. Nowadays, there must be more televised soccer in the USA than in any other country. In addition to MLS, there are live broadcasts of games in the EPL, La Liga, Bundesliga, Liga MX, Serie A, Ligue 1, and the UEFA Champions League. Of course, the sport's profile will mushroom in advance of the 2026 World Cup.

'As for Everton, despite the club's lack of success on the pitch during the Internet era, I detect that it has over-performed in attracting transatlantic fans. Partly because our American DNA is unrivalled. With Joe-Max and Preki and fleetingly Landon Donovan and Brian McBride, no European club has enjoyed such a rich seam of American talent. Plus, there is Tim, who in my eyes is as great an Everton ambassador as he was a great Everton goalkeeper. And partly because many Americans do not want to jump on the latest bandwagon, but seek a force of good and something to believe in – tradition, heritage, community and core values. They want an emotional connection with something special. But as our beloved club invests in North American expansion it must not ignore its local supporters. Traditionally, club allegiance was passed from fathers to sons and retained for life. Nowadays, this is no longer the case. To retain loyalty, it must work extra hard tending and cultivating its fans old and new. As for the route to maximise its North American profile, popularity and fanbase, the best option is winning – success in the Premier League and participation in the Champions League. America loves a winner. Always has done, always will do.'

These observations are endorsed by Clive Toye who knows more than a thing or two about North American soccer. The ex-president of the Chicago Sting (1978-1979), chairman of the Toronto Blizzard (1980-1984), general manager of the New York Cosmos (1971-1977), where he was instrumental in signing Pelé and Franz Beckenbauer, and member of the US Soccer Hall of Fame noted: 'The sport is light years from what it was five decades ago. All North Americans know what soccer is.

'Nowadays, soccer pitches are everywhere and there are zillions of young people playing the game. The 24/7 media coverage of Major League Soccer, the different European leagues and the USA national teams is staggering.

'As for the blue half of Merseyside, when North Americans think of the city of Liverpool, they focus on The Beatles and Liverpool Football Club. Even with the planned office in Florida, the Everton staff will have to work hard to create an image and cultivate a presence. In New York, manager Gordon Bradley and I spent most of our time promoting the Cosmos. Our mantra was "We don't expect you to see us until after we have seen you." Everton will have to do something similar.'

Kevin Baxter of the *Los Angeles Times* offered an equally honest perspective: 'When it comes to making inroads into the North American market, Everton are late-comers to the party. At present, the Merseyside club is not mentioned in the same breath as the English and European elite who participate in the International Champions Cup and promote aggressive marketing campaigns from their US bases. Barcelona and Bayern have offices in New York, and Paris St Germain have them in New York and Los Angeles, to enhance brand visibility, develop new partnerships and nurture its fanbase, which has flourished in recent years following tours to North America.

'Soccer exploded seven years ago when NBC Sports obtained the broadcast rights. At that time, viewers were encouraged to pick their EPL team. Unfortunately, Everton were struggling in mid-table at that time and weren't too popular. To date, they have not made much of an impact and failed to take full advantage of former players such as Tim Howard and Landon Donovan and prominent fans known to the American public, such as Roger Bennett, Tony Bellew and even Sir Paul McCartney.

'In my eyes, Everton is so different from the glossy money clubs. It is the type that many Americans can relate to. But it needs to tell its story and educate US soccer fans about its remarkable history and its community values reflected in the Blue Mile – in reference to the neighbourhood which surrounds Goodison and encompasses Walton, Everton, Kirkdale and Anfield, the Everton Free School, the People's Hub and the Blue Base, the dozens of community out-reach initiatives designed to change the lives of less fortunate local people and, of course, Speedo Mick. Everton need to remind people that success on the field is fleeting but history and values last forever.'

North of the border, no one is better equipped to assess Everton's standing in Canada than Dick Howard, the television analyst on ESPN, CBC, CBC, CTV, TSN, Fox and columnist for the *Toronto Sun*. The lifelong Evertonian, who in played the NASL, earned five Canada caps and was inducted into the Canada Soccer Hall of Fame in 2002, reported: 'Soccer has never been more popular in Canada. Coaching academies are proliferating so much that millions of boys and girls of all ages, shapes and sizes participate weekly. When I was Chair of the Ontario Soccer Association Technical Committee, Everton's Tosh Farrell came over to conduct clinics and our Under-16 team played their Everton counterparts at Finch Farm in 2007.

'The 4-4 result made me appreciate how far the Canadian game had come. A few years earlier, we would have lost by a cricket score. Professionally, there is a national league with teams from coast to coast, so there is a path to follow for young players. I am quite confident that Canada will qualify for the World Cup in Qatar and, of course, we'll be in the tournament as co-hosts in 2026.

'The coverage of English soccer is second-to-none. Everton fans around Toronto are mainly expats and their numbers pale into comparison with their counterparts supporting Liverpool. I am afraid that Everton is way down the totem pole behind Manchester United, Manchester City, Arsenal and Chelsea. Sadly, we have been reduced to the "other team in Liverpool." Therefore, the key to our growth in Canada is to get back into European football.'

Although the Toffees are not the most popular in terms of numbers, they possess some of the most loyal, whole-hearted and passionate followers of soccer in North America. who are just as committed to the royal blue cause as their brothers and sisters on Merseyside. While their numbers are unknown, existing North American fans can be separated into expats or others with Merseyside roots and younger fans who selected the club for one reason or another – some quite bizarre. After surveying hundreds of Evertonians in the USA, it is evident that most young Americans first heard about Everton through the Howard-Donovan portal. After these stars grabbed their attention, they fell headed over heels in love with other players, the club's unparalleled heritage, community values and everything royal blue and, of course, not being Liverpool Football Club or another member of the modern-day elite.

Clearly, there is the need to better understand the existing North American fanbase. Professor Andrew Lambert, another lifelong Evertonian at the City University of New York, explained: 'The experience of being a fan in North America is different. There are fewer Evertonians around, and more distance between us. Social media has made a big difference, connecting fans and would-be fans. But social media can be shunned entirely, turned off, or treated with disdain in a way that relations with real people and daily life cannot. So, beyond the realm of social media, how should we understand the experiences of North American fans?

'One thing different is the relationship to Goodison. For those living on Merseyside, going to the match is a ritualised and heady event, which anchors the experience of being an Evertonian: the walk to the ground, the pre-match routines of chip shops and pub, the street sounds and smells, and perhaps a post-match routine too (depending on result and mood); and during the week, there is the school or workplace banter with other Blues and Reds. These habits are at the heart of everyday Everton life. Over here, experiencing Everton in that way regularly is not possible, except for those willing to travel and immune to jetlag. Goodison becomes an idealised destination, a pilgrimage to be spoken of with reverence. Without those anchoring experiences, the relationship is different. In day-to-day life, supporting the club is inevitably a more solitary experience. There are bars for watching games but the constant reinforcement from others is lacking. This includes the motivation provided by Reds, who do us the service of provoking a deeper commitment to our own club. Over here there isn't the same kind of local response.

'Something else that is different is the path to becoming an Evertonian. Fans typically emerge by osmosis – family and friends induct them into the tribe before a considered choice is possible; but most folks in the USA lack connections like family and proximity. Also, while a lot of Merseyside Blues were forged by Howard Kendall's teams in the 1980s, most North American fans have never known such good times. They have had to think about which team to support and have chosen Everton for a reason. For some, it can be our North American players. But many fans choose Everton because the club appeals to something they value.

'Picking Manchester United feels a little fraudulent, and perhaps a little boring. Choosing Everton seems to represent its own set of values. Solidarity, increasingly unfashionable in modern life, is one such value (the Everton family), loyalty another – how do you know you are really loyal if your team is always winning? Integrity is yet another. My research in New York examines how being a football fan is about developing a personal narrative, in which one's own history is bound up with the club's history. If we can tell ourselves a wondrous story, which interweaves our own lives and personal milestones with the life of the club, then we have found a "home place", regardless of geography. Everton Football Club seems well-positioned to nurture such values and the bonds they create.

'Even though North Americans love plucky underdogs, it adores winners. Hopefully, while the manager and his charges strive to overcome the chronic underachievement on the pitch that has spanned the past 30 years, the club will seek to communicate, engage and visit its North American fans in order to strengthen old bonds and establish new ones. It must enhance its presence with tours, fan events and other longer-term initiatives.'

The general consensus is that no single English club will conquer the land of opportunity. Despite its pedigree, Everton can expect competition – especially Premier League clubs with more experience of North American sports fans. Arsenal's Stan Kroenke owns the Colorado Rapids (MLS), Los Angeles Rams (NFL), Colorado Avalanche (NHL), Denver Nuggets (NBA). Also Liverpool's John Henry, Tom Werner and their Fenway Sports Group oversee the Boston Red Sox (MLB), Manchester United's Glazer Family control the Tampa Bay Buccaneers (NFL) and Fulham's Pakistani-American tycoon Shahid Khan leads the Jacksonville Jaguars (NFL). The club has made a meaningful start to strengthening its presence with the formation of a plethora of supporters' groups and the introduction of youth-oriented initiatives. But to reinforce and expand its ties with North America, it is clear that the club must further nourish its existing supporters by organising events, festivals, pre-season tours and more.

As for attracting new supporters based in the New World, it is anticipated that under the leadership of Farhad Moshiri, Denise Barrett-Baxendale and Carlo Ancelotti, Everton Football Club will become a more respected and enduring force in the Premier League. Such overdue success in England, followed by regular participation in European competitions, will lead to a bigger slice of the North America pie.

Graham Smith, the businessman who was a Chelsea director, a football agent and a tour organiser extraordinaire says: 'It is unfortunate that the club has yet to take advantage of its special place in North American soccer. I think that it should have provided more support to the USA-based youth development initiatives of Tosh Farrell, formed special bonds with a couple of MLS clubs and continued to invite the promising American players to Finch Farm during the MLS off-season. The latter is something that the Bundesliga clubs have done so successfully for the past decade. Off the pitch, Everton have fallen behind the likes of Rangers and Celtic in organising annual celebrations for their loyal and passionate fans in the USA and Canada.'

David Kurtz at EvertonUSA regrets his failure to organise such an event in early-2016: 'For a decade, Marshall Lamm and I coordinated the network of 100 supporters' clubs, where Blues of all ages can meet, vent, cry, and celebrate with friends. For many years, we helped Everton become the first European club to cater to the transatlantic market by providing access to matchday tickets, travel packages and US-specific merchandise. Four years ago, we planned an "Everton Weekend" at the Planet Hollywood Hotel and Casino (owned by ex-director Robert Earl) in Las Vegas to honour the eternal bond between Everton and North America. Sadly, it didn't happen for one reason or another.'

Expat Tony Sampson is another who sees opportunities for enhancing Everton's presence in the USA: 'It was clear that more could be done to bolster the connection between the established supporters' groups and our Merseyside-based club in order to give US-based fans a voice on key issues related to expansion plans.' Elected as the first North American representative of the EFC Fans' Forum, the official link between the club and its fans, his first step was to conduct a survey of Evertonians worldwide – nearly 45% of respondents were from the USA. Through a newly established network of the leaders of the supporters' clubs, his focus has been on better connecting the fanbase, giving it a platform for direct input into the club's engagement and growth strategy. In late-2020, he noted: 'Success on the pitch is a key factor, but the recruitment of people with the global reach of Rodriguez and Ancelotti provides a tremendous opportunity to accelerate the club's growth plans.'

Indeed, one of the club's greatest assets is its current manager. Carlo Ancelotti is revered by football people worldwide – having claimed the Champions League on three occasions and domestic titles in England, France, Germany and Italy. His presence adds a certain cachet that over time will make North Americans acknowledge, approve and admire Everton. As an added bonus, his wife is Canadian and they have a home in Vancouver, BC. It is evident that Everton must follow its manager example and establish a well-resourced base in North America and use it to oversee the promotion of its brand through a combination of youth academies, regional offices, digital content, commercial partnerships, fan events and friendly matches in the USA and Canada.

Under the watchful eyes of David Moyes and later Roberto Martinez, Everton toured North America in 2004, 2006, 2007, 2008, 2009, 2011 and 2013. That said, the first team has not been there for eight years. Though these pre-season getaways are important in promoting the club, their impact is temporary. Once the tourists have departed, the local fans re-focus on the NBA, NFL, MLB, NHL and MLS.

If the club is to raise its profile in North America, it must treat future tours as more than exercises for pre-season conditioning. Lyndon Lloyd of ToffeeWeb noted, 'To enhance its reputation and status, Everton must compete vigorously against its European and South American opponents and defeat all MLS foes. Since the victory over Pachuca in 2004, our performances have been disappointing. We have recorded one outright win, five draws and seven defeats. For North American Blues, there is nothing worse than to travel vast distances across the continent only for Everton to not show up.'

In summary, Everton is a special club for real soccer fans. It is one of trail-blazing initiatives, rich traditions, uncommon values, venerated ambassadors, good people and more on both sides of the Atlantic Ocean. As for North America? Professional sports will remain a critical component of its contemporary society. While professional soccer is unlikely to dethrone American football, basketball or baseball, the beautiful game will continue to prosper. With unswerving commitment, investment and desire, the USA and Canada offers tremendous opportunities for Everton Football Club to create its own healthy and distinct niche in the soccer market.

Of course, the fertility of the North American soccer market has been recognized by the club. Richard Kenyon, director of marketing, communications and community, outlined Everton's ambitious plans: 'The links with the USA are long, distinguished and unique. And, as well as being a huge source of pride in the modern era when the Premier League has become a truly global product, they give Everton a great opportunity. Over recent years we have been actively building a presence in the USA. We have invested in the growth of our supporters' clubs – and now have one in nearly every state, we have been linking with youth football clubs across the country to establish formal partnerships with our academy and, hopefully, we will roll out an extensive soccer camps programme in the summer of 2021.

'We also have a formal arrangement with the legendary Tim Howard which sees him acting as an ambassador for us stateside and have plans to open an office in Florida in the very near future to provide a year-round presence. This physical base will enable the club to further capitalise on the opportunities presented by our rich and diverse links with North America. Our US-based team will be charged with further growing our fanbase and securing strategic and commercial partnerships, using all the assets at our disposal – not least James Rodriguez whose image, on signing with us from Real Madrid, fittingly adorned the giant screens in New York City's Times Square and Miami Beach on Labor Day 2020.'

**David France, Rob Sawyer and Darren Griffiths**
January 2021

# ACKNOWLEDGEMENTS

Social contract dictates that authors give credit where credit is due.

This publication could not have been possible without the help and cooperation of many people on both sides of the Atlantic Ocean. Above all, the authors would like to start by expressing their sincere gratitude to Elizabeth France, Paula Sawyer and Michelle Griffiths for their indefatigable patience. Also they are beholden to Prof Denise Barrett-Baxendale for her introduction, Tim Howard for providing his insightful foreword and Landon Donovan for his quote highlighted on the back cover.

As for the contents of this weighty book, they are indebted to Richie Gillham, secretary of the Everton FC Heritage Society, the trail-blazing organization which documents and celebrates the history of the club, for sharing the findings of his own research, Billy Smith and James Smith for supplying the match reports via their Blue Chronicles website (bluecorrespondent. co.uk), Steve Johnson for the utilisation of the in-depth statistics detailed on his Everton Results website (evertonresults.com), Bradley Cates for furnishing the transfer data detailed on his website (efcstatto.com), Phil Martin, the renowned football historian and collector – born on the same day as the senior author – and his daughter Helen Martin for providing access to his unrivaled library of football publications, and the folks at the English National Football Archive for sharing their incomparable databases (www.enfa.co.uk).

They would like to thank Peter King for producing the colourful caricatures which are part of the mind-blowing Dr Everton's Toffeemen project (containing caricatures and profiles of over 2,100 men associated with the club since the days of St Domingo and including professional and amateur players, trialists, wartime guests, coaches, managers and directors) and also Lord John Grantchester at the Everton Collection Charitable Trust for the use of programme images from the peerless archives.

Also they would like to express their sincere appreciation to Richard Kenyon, Scott McLeod, Mo Maghazachi and other friends at Everton Football Club for the continued support, Brendan Connolly and their many colleagues at the Heritage Society for their encouragement and Tony Sampson, the North American-based member of the club's Fans' Forum, for his counsel.

Then there are the 70 or so footballers who provided contributions. These include Victor Anichebe, Jay Armstrong, Cody Arnoux, Earl Barrett, Jim Barron, Jose Baxter, Roger Bennett,

Gregg Berhalter, Billy Bingham, Rachel Brown-Finnis, Leigh Cowlishaw, Terry Darracott, Natasha Dowie, Tosh Farrell, Jimmy Gabriel, Ray Hall, Jimmy Harris, Paul Harris, Wayne Harrison, Asa Hartford, Brian Harvey, Adrian Heath, Jimmy Husband, Tommy Jackson, Gary Jones, Roger Kenyon, Joleon Lescott, Willie Kirk, Anders Limpar, Mike Lyons, Mo Marley, Cliff Marshall, Jimmy Martin, Brian McBride, Duncan McKenzie, Mick Meagan, Brian Monaghan, Joe-Max Moore, Derek Mountfield, David Moyes, Carlo Nash, Leon Osman, Anton Peterlin, Bev Priestman, Paul Rideout, Tomasz, Radzinski, Bruce Rioch, Antonee Robinson, John Robinson, Skip Roderick, Wayne Rooney, Steve Seargeant, Oliver Shannon, Graeme Sharp, Adam Smith, Graham Smith, Brad Stewart, John Stones, Steve Tashjian, George Telfer, Derek Temple, Colin Todd, Clive Toye, James Vaughan, Ray Veall, Robert Warzycha, David Weir, Tommy Wheeldon, Bruce Wilson and Emma Wright-Cates.

Some 40 other contributions were provided by Rich Ballezzi, Dmitry Barano, Kevin Baxter, Ed Bottomley, Bridget Bryson, Brian Bunk, Brendan Connolly, Eva Corry, Jamie Crowley, Roger Deborde, Matthew Durington, John Flynn, Mike Gaines, Gerry Gibson, George Hakopian, Clayton Hill, Brendan Holland Browne, Eric Howell, Nick Jones, Ruth Katz, David Kurtz, Andrew Lambert, Marshall Lamm, Lyndon Lloyd, Ian Lowe, Ian Macdonald, Martha Mae, Brian Molina, Mike Murphy, Greg O'Keeffe, Tony Onslow, David Prentice, Gerry Quinn, Darryl Ritchie, Michael Setterberg, Patrick Brian Smith, Kouroush Toumadje, Bob Vera, Shaun Weale, Terry White and Brian Yurcan.

Photographs were kindly furnished by Rich Ballezzi, James Boyman, John Duchak, Matt Durington, George Haokopian, Alex Johnson, Marshall Lamm, Steve Landy, Tony Sampson, Michael Setterberg, Kourosh Toumadje and Clay Tranium.

The three co-authors would like to acknowledge the professional support of Leslie Priestley for his design and layout of the book and, finally, the expertise of James Corbett at deCoubertin Books for his advice and professional knowhow in publishing the limited edition of this tome.

# IN MEMORIAM

Martha (AKC Ranzfel Jacobean Lady) – a canine Evertonian – passed away in late-2020. She made a significant contribution to the production of this book. Always a hurricane of unconditional love, Martha kept me company 24 hours a day, seven days a week as the manuscript evolved. She eavesdropped on hundreds of transatlantic telephone calls and slept by my feet despite the clickety-clack of my keyboard.

Since her death, our home has been empty – no demands for tummy rubs, no chasing of tennis balls, no unearthing of golf balls (she amassed over 2,000), no growling at the Reds on the television or the Kopite coyotes in the garden, and no exuberant barking when the good guys score. Martha watched some 300 Everton games during her life, often between the gap in her paws. Unlike her older brother Walter (AKC Ranzfel Blue Boy) who died in late-2017, she witnessed her favourites top the Premier League – albeit for a short time.

Martha met some great Evertonians. She escorted author Becky Tallentire to the southern rim of the Grand Canyon, guided webmaster Lyndon Lloyd around the red rocks of Sedona and spent many hours dazzling Alex Young – The Golden Vision with her stamina, if not her football skills, on the village green at Roche Harbor, San Juan Island.

I am convinced that English Cocker Spaniels are put on this earth to make Evertonians happy. So much so that at night I wave at their bright stars in the black Arizona sky and promise to be the person that they thought that I was.

**David France**

# BIBLIOGRAPHY

## NEWSPAPERS AND PERIODICALS

*Athletic News* (1891)

*Birmingham Daily Post* (1891)

*Calgary Herald* (2003)

*Chicago Daily Tribune* (1956)

*Daily Record* (2020)

*Edmonton Journal* (1956)

*Globe and Mail* (1956 and 1985)

*Liverpool Daily Post* (1891 and 1961)

*Liverpool Echo* (1928-2013)

*Liverpool Mercury* (1891)

*Ludlow Advertiser* (1956)

*Montreal Gazette* (1961)

*New Jersey Advocate* (1956)

*New York Herald Tribune* (1956)

*New York Times* (1907)

*Philadelphia Inquirer* (2011)

*Soccer Observer* (1967)

*St Louis Globe* (1956)

*St Louis Post-Dispatch* (1956)

*The Sun* (1893)

*Vancouver Sun* (1934 and 1956)

*Washington Post* (2011)

## BOOKS

Allaway, Roger, Jose, Colin and Litterer, David; *The Encyclopaedia of American Soccer History*; Scarecrow Press, 2001

Ball, Alan; *It's All About A Ball*; W H Allen, 1978

Ball, Alan; *Playing Extra Time*; Sidgwick & Jackson, 2004

Bennett, Roger and Davies, Michael; *Men in Blazers Present Encyclopaedia Blazertannica*; Knopf, 2018

Buckland, Gavin; *Money Can't Buy Us Love: Everton in the 1960s*; deCoubertin Books, 2019

Corbett, James; *Everton Encyclopedia*; deCoubertin Books, 2012

Corbett, James; *Everton: School of Science*; Macmillan, 2003

France, David and Prentice, David; *Dr Everton's Magnificent Obsession*; Trinity Mirror Sport Media, 2008

France, David; *Alex Young – The Golden Vision*; Skript Publishing, 2008

France, David: *Everton Crazy*; GSHOF, 2016

France, David; *Gwladys Street's Blue Book*; Skript Publishing, 2002

France, David; *Gwladys Street's Hall of Fame (Edition III)*; Skript Publishing, 1999

Hollander, Zander; *The American Encyclopaedia of Soccer*; Everest House Publishers, 1980

Howard, Tim; *The Keeper: A Life of Saving Goals and Achieving Them*; Harper, 2014

Johnson, Steve; *Everton: The Official Complete Record (Second Edition)*; deCoubertin Books, 2016

Jose, Colin; *NASL: A Complete Record of the North American Soccer League*; Breedon Books Sport, 1989

Jose, Colin; *North American Soccer League Encyclopaedia*; Saint Johann Press, 2003

Kendall, Howard and Ross, Ian; *Only the Best is Good Enough: The Howard Kendall Story*; Mainstream Publishing, 1991

Kendall, Howard; *Love Affairs and Marriage: My Life in Football*; deCoubertin Books, 2013

Kennedy, David; *A Social and Political History of Everton and Liverpool Football Clubs: The Split*; Routledge, 2016

Kennedy, David; *The Man Who Created Merseyside Football: John Houlding*; Rowman & Littlefield, 2020

Kilbane, Kevin and Merriman, Andy; *Killa: The Autobiography of Kevin Kilbane*; Aurum Press, 2013

Matthews, Tony; *Who's Who of Everton*; Mainstream Publishing, 2004

McKenzie, Duncan with Saffer, David; *The Last Fancy Dan: The Duncan McKenzie Story*; Vertical Editions, 2009

O'Bryhim, Tim and Romalis, Michael; *Make This Town Big – The Story of Roy Turner and the Wichita Wings*; Create Space Independent Publishing, 2016

Orr, George; *Everton in the Sixties - A Golden Era*; Blueblood, 1997

Osman, Leon; *Ossie: My Autobiography*; Reach, 2014

Ponting, Ivan; *Everton: Player by Player*; Guinness Publishing, 1992

Reid, Peter and Ball, Peter; *An Everton Diary*; Futura Publications, 1988

Reid, Peter; *Cheer Up: My Autobiography*; Trinity Mirror Sport Media, 2017

Richards, Ted (editor); *Soccer and Philosophy: Beautiful Thoughts on the Beautiful Game*; Open Court Publishing, 2010

Sawyer, Rob and France, David; *Blue Dragon: The Roy Vernon Story*; deCoubertin Books, 2019

Sawyer, Rob; *Harry Catterick: The Untold Story of a Football Great*; deCoubertin Books, 2014

Sharp, Graeme and Griffiths, Darren; *Sharpy: My Story*; Mainstream Publishing, 2007

Tossell, David; *Alan Ball: The Man in White Boots*; Hodder & Stoughton, 2017

Toye, Clive; *A Kick in the Grass*; St Johann Press, 2006

Westcott, Chris; *Brian Harris - The Authorised Biography*; Tempus Publishing, 2003

Westcott, Chris; *Joker in the Pack: The Ernie Hunt Story*; Tempus Publishing, 2004

# ABOUT THE AUTHORS

### David France

During his early life on Merseyside and the past 44 years in North America, David has been besotted with Everton Football Club. So much so that he has travelled over two million miles to support the club and introduce his trail-blazing initiatives. In addition to writing a small library of Everton books, he created the Hall of Fame, established the Heritage Society, registered the Former-Players' Foundation, and combed the globe to assemble football's finest archives, now celebrated as The Everton Collection. Universally lauded as 'Doctor Everton', David is the Life President of the Everton FC Shareholders' Association. In 2011, Liverpool's Freedom of the City panel conferred him the prestigious title of Citizen of Honour for services to football in Liverpool, the first to receive the award since Bill Shankly. The next year, he was awarded an OBE for his services to football in the United Kingdom and Europe.

### Rob Sawyer

A fourth generation Toffee, Rob's great-grandfather, William J Sawyer, was the club's secretary between December 1918 – November 1919 as well as a highly respected Everton director between August 1920 – October 1930 who was active in the recruitment of Dixie Dean. Admired as a diligent researcher and football historian, Rob is a popular columnist for ToffeeWeb – the first independent Everton website, and an enthusiastic member of the Everton FC Heritage Society. He has authored three other Everton books, *Harry Catterick: The Untold Story of a Football Great* released in 2014, *The Prince of Centre-Halves – The Life of Tommy 'TG' Jones* in 2017 and most recently *Blue Dragon – The Roy Vernon Story* in 2019.

### Darren Griffiths

A lifelong and diehard Blue, Darren has been a key member of the club's media department for more than two decades. In his current role of Broadcast and Liaison Manager, he is involved in editing the matchday programme and scripting, voicing and producing club videos and podcasts. Celebrated worldwide as 'The Voice of Everton Football Club', Darren has hosted hundreds of royal blue events, including the annual shareholders' meetings at the Liverpool Philharmonic Hall, and provided regular interviews with players and managers as well as live match commentaries for EvertonTV. Also, he has co-authored a dozen editions of *The Official Everton FC Annual* and Graeme Sharp's biography *Sharpy: My Story*, published in 2006.

# ABOUT EVERTON IN THE COMMUNITY

Everton in the Community is one of the UK's top sporting charities and is considered one of the Premier League's leading community schemes due to the quality and reach of its programmes. Established in 1988, it has been at the forefront of social intervention and has never been afraid to tackle the serious issues affecting the people of Merseyside. The Club's official charity received Freedom of the City, Liverpool's highest civic honour, in 2008 in recognition for its impact to the local community and in 2020 was visited by The Duke of Cambridge to find out more about its work and how it uses its influence to assist both its supporters and the local community.

Everton Football Club resides in the Kirkdale ward, which is one of the most deprived 5% of neighbourhoods nationally. Over half of the children live in poverty, while the area faces challenges related to unemployment, crime, health, housing and education. In response, Everton in the Community delivers more than 40 programmes a year, designed to combat mental health, employability, dementia, education, disability, poverty and homelessness. These programmes aid people of all ages, cultures and backgrounds from 130 venues across the city region. Everton in the Community is open and inclusive to all.

In the wake of the ongoing coronavirus pandemic, Everton in the Community and Everton Football Club launched 'Blue Family', a coordinated outreach and engagement campaign to provide vital assistance to the most vulnerable, socially isolated and at-risk members of the community and has helped more than 30,000 families and individuals with emergency food parcels, assistance with utilities, mental health support and welfare calls.

The charity is soon to commence work on a purpose-built mental health facility close to Goodison Park that will promote positive mental health and deliver support relating to suicide awareness and prevention. The building will be a part of the Goodison Campus which has already seen £10 million invested in the regeneration of the area surrounding the stadium including Everton Free School, The Blue Base and The People's Hub. The Club recently received approval for its community-led legacy development at Goodison Park which will see its current home redeveloped to provide a range of community assets after it has moved to Bramley-Moore Dock. The Goodison Park Legacy Project will ensure that Everton remains in the heart of the Liverpool 4 community once the Club's stadium has moved to the waterfront.

For more information on Everton in the Community visit www.evertoninthecommunity.org.

# ABOUT DECOUBERTIN BOOKS

deCoubertin Books is a leading independent publisher, which publishes outstanding non-fiction titles predicated on high editorial and production values. We work with some of the biggest names in sport and sportswriting and our books have been nominated for numerous awards.

The principles underlying the project on its 2009 foundation were simple: to have meticulous editorial standards; to pursue excellence in design and to bridge the worlds of physical and digital. Furthermore, we felt it important to only take on projects we passionately believed in.

That mantra has served us well. Today our authors represent a distinguished slice of international sport and media. The footballers we have on our books share a combined 431 international caps, 20 English league titles, 11 FA Cups, 5 European Cups, 2 World Cups as well as Serie A, Bundesliga, Scottish Premier League and Footballer of the Year medals. They have played for or managed clubs including Manchester United, Real Madrid, Arsenal, Liverpool, Everton, Manchester City, AC Milan, Borussia Dortmund, AS Roma, Rangers and Fiorentina. They also include journalists, contributors and broadcasters from virtually every significant news organisation in the United Kingdom and beyond.

deCoubertin has also published a number of Everton related titles. These include autobiographies of four of the club's Millenium Giants – Howard Kendall, Bob Latchford, Neville Southall and Dave Hickson – as well as biographies of TG Jones, Roy Vernon and Harry Catterick. Everton's history has been told in acclaimed titles, such as *Here We Go: Everton in the 1980s; Money Can't Buy Us Love: Everton In The 1960s; The Everton Encyclopedia; and Faith of our Famillies: Everton an Oral History*, which was longlisted in the 2018 Sports Book of the Year awards.

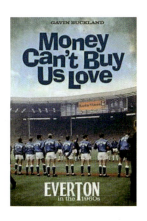

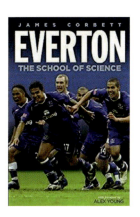

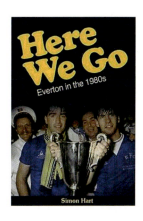

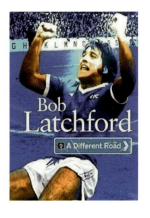

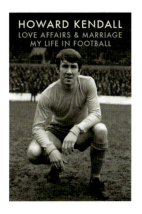

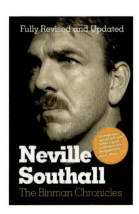

# TOFFEE SOCCER

## ROLL OF HONOUR

Ian Kidd

John Myers

Jeffrey J Cronin

Paul Killie Kilroy

Paul Cullinane

Rob Pattison

Jonathan Haley

John Beamish

Denis Deary

Anthony Bird

Richard Humphrey

Michael Murphy

Patrick Thomas Rooney

Ray Redfern

Christopher W Capper

John Peel

John Lewin

Jamie Riley

Jimmy Walker

David Weston

John Shearon

Ian Pilkington

Robert Lucas

Paul Cullinane

Michael Andrew McGiveron

Andrew Cornmell

Preston Miller

Joey King

John V Ievolo

Brian Molina

The Fafoutis Family

Mark Hollins

Lester Durkan

Dermot McCaughan

Roy Condon

Brian Garside

The Henrys

Joseph Miller

Jim Percival

Matt Percival

Sam Percival

Han Duijvendak

Anthony Gavin

Stephen M Lepore

Roy Condon

Michael Polley

Sam France

Zoe Beales

Phillip Wright

Garrett Post

Brennan Schwab

Jamie Yates

Tom Moore

John Bridson

The Sumner Family

Dave Guile

Eva and Arthur Corry

John Burness

Alan Burness

Simon Fletcher

William Hughes

Shawn Donaghue

Josh Rants

Carlos Maury

Geoff Harrison

Emily Anzicek

The Yoxall Family

Kevin Robert Smith

Victor Poole

Andrew Jones

James Yoxall

David Vivyan

James Birrell

Keith Patrick Moran

John Raftery

David Howard

Tony Sampson

Charlie Sampson

Joe Sampson

Todd Miller

David Barnes

Jan Grace

Jimmy Milner

Ruletero Toffee

Clay Trainum

John Lyon

Stephen Lyon

David Lyon

Evie Lyon

Theo Lyon

Marc Seritella Jr

Guy Rigby

Lyndon Lloyd

Phil Parker

Tony Walsh

Jonathon Edwards

# TOFFEE SOCCER

## ROLL OF HONOUR

Alex Fumagali

Jason Murray

David Kurtz

Jeff Stollenwerck

Ian Murray

Paul McParlan

Joe Clitherow

Nigel Houghton

Neil Jones

John Waddington

Paul Brown

Andrew John Hughes

Paul Owens

Katie Owens

Christopher Powell

Thomas Wheeldon

Roger Wilson

Lennon McNee

Lee Harrison

Martin Bainbridge

Michael Abrams

Rob Preece

Matthew Durington

Phil Martin

Brian Harvey

Nicole Harvey

George Orr

Ryan Borrett

Jenni Hyyppa

Kaisa Hyyppa

Tony Wainwright

Chris Ireson

Barry Hewitt

Robert W Rushton

Dave Loweth

John Robinson

Martin Vijay Kulkarni

Graham John Price

Jeremy Breakfield

Derek Golden

Les Horgan

William Kilmurray

Robert Morrissey Jr

Damian Carville

Keith Parsons

David Doran

Colin Lord

Phil Orme

Kourosh Toumadje

Austin Rathe

Bridget Bryson

Martyn Halliwell

Craig McDonald

Dave Yadron

Sandeep Sahi

Martin McShane

Gerry Gavagan

Bernadette Gavagan

Paul McMenamin

Steve Mahon

Andy Clarke

Jayney Jones

Frank Keegan

Andy Weir

Robert Ken Mathias

Darryl Ritchie

Alex Maher

Paul Jones

Mark Cadley

John Williams

Paul Fowler

Paul Simpson

Marshall Lamm

Andrew Roberts

Stephen Sutton

Ryan Jones

Daniel Burdsey

KP Jones

Dennis Stevens

Wade Scheffner

George Hakopian

Pat Brewer

Kathi Brewer

Bryn Griffith

Turk Behlmann

Kevin Keating

John Blain

Paul Richardson

Mark Cartman

Bill Cooper

Mason Butler

Mark De Haan

Jeff Wallner

Patrick Phyle

M Pierce

Joan Sawyer

www.decoubertin.co.uk